The SAT 1 For Dummies, 6th Ed

The Essay: What You Must Do

- Always focus your answer on the provided topic.
- Jot down some ideas and organize them before writing the essay.
- Allow a couple of minutes for revision.
- Be sure your handwriting is readable.

Writing Multiple Choice: What to Look for

- **Verbs:** Check tense and number (singular or plural).
- **Pronouns:** Check number (singular or plural), case (*I* or *me, who* or *whom,* and so on), and clarity.
- **Word choice:** Look for words used improperly (*affect* instead of *effect,* and so forth).
- **Punctuation:** Check apostrophes, commas, and end marks.
- **Descriptions:** Check location (descriptions should be near what they're describing) and clarity.

Critical Reading: Hints for Sentence Completions

- Insert your own word into the sentence and then check the choices to see which one matches your chosen word.
- Apply real-world knowledge.
- Look for words that change the sentence from positive to negative or vice versa, such as *therefore, however,* and *but.*

Critical Reading: Comprehension Techniques

- Read the introduction to each passage carefully so you know what the passage is about and, perhaps, something of the author's viewpoint.
- Glance at the questions before reading the passage so you know what you're looking for.
- Never skip a vocabulary-in-context question.
- Remember that the SAT looks for positive, not negative, comments about groups of people.
- Titles or main ideas must cover everything in the passage, without being too general.
- In the margins, jot down the key ideas that each paragraph covers.

* Even though this is a Cheat Sheet, don't ever cheat on the SAT. Digest the information on this sheet, but leave the actual piece of paper at home when you take the test!

For Dummies: Bestselling Book Series for Beginners

The SAT 1 For Dummies, 6th Edition

Quick Reference Card

What to Bring to the SAT

- Admission ticket
- Calculator you're familiar with
- High protein snack (such as nuts, trail mix, cheese, or protein bar)
- Photo ID
- Several sharpened No. 2 pencils and a good eraser
- A watch
- Your mind

General Tips for the SAT

- Get a good night's sleep.
- To keep your nerves in check, don't discuss the test with friends before the test or during breaks.
- Guess only when you can eliminate two out of five choices.
- Never skip a grid-in.
- Concentrate on the easy questions (often, but not always, the first questions in each section) if time is an issue.

Math: Facts to Remember

- Some phrases — *less than, fewer than, shorter than, subtracted from* — reverse the order of subtraction (four less than x is $x - 4$).
- In a triangle, the largest angle is opposite the largest side, and the smallest angle is opposite the smallest side.
- The sum of two sides of any triangle must be larger than the length of the third side.
- In a circle, inscribed angles are half as large as their arcs.
- A tangent line and a radius always make a right angle.
- To solve a linear equation, isolate the variable on one side of the equal sign.
- A base to the zero power equals one.
- Anything quadratic on the SAT can usually be factored.

Math: Formulas You Need to Know

- If the mean of n numbers is m, the sum of the numbers is the product of mn.
- To find the number of ways for a sequence of events to occur, multiply the number of ways to do each event (rolling two dice: $6 \times 6 = 36$ possibilities).
- In percent problems, $\dfrac{is}{of} = \dfrac{\%}{100}$
- FOIL $(x + a)(x + b) = x^2 + bx + ax + ab$ (FOIL tells you the order in which you should approach an algebra problem: First, Outer, Inner, Last. See Chapter 16 for a full explanation.)
- Slope Formula: $\dfrac{y_2 - y_1}{x_2 - x_1}$
- Distance = square root of $(x_2 - x_1)^2 + (y_2 - y_1)^2$

For Dummies: Bestselling Book Series for Beginners

The *SAT I
FOR
DUMMIES®
6TH EDITION

by Geraldine Woods

WILEY

Wiley Publishing, Inc.

The *SAT I For Dummies, 6th Edition

Published by
Wiley Publishing, Inc.
111 River St.
Hoboken, NJ 07030-5774
www.wiley.com

Copyright © 2005 by Wiley Publishing, Inc., Indianapolis, Indiana

Published by Wiley Publishing, Inc., Indianapolis, Indiana

Published simultaneously in Canada

For general information on our other products and services, please contact our Customer Care Department within the U.S. at 800-762-2974, outside the U.S. at 317-572-3993, or fax 317-572-4002.

For technical support, please visit www.wiley.com/techsupport.

Wiley also publishes its books in a variety of electronic formats. Some content that appears in print may not be available in electronic books.

Library of Congress Control Number: 2004112344

ISBN: 0-7645-7193-1

Manufactured in the United States of America

10 9 8 7 6 5 4 3

1B/RQ/RR/QU/IN

About the Author

Geraldine Woods has prepared students for the SAT, both academically and emotionally, for the past three decades. She also teaches English and directs the independent study program at the Horace Mann School in New York City. She has written more than 40 books, including *English Grammar For Dummies, Research Papers For Dummies,* and *College Admission Essays For Dummies,* all published by Wiley. She lives in New York City with her husband and two parakeets.

Dedication

For Harry, who is more than ever in my heart; for Linda, my friend of 40 years; and for Gillian, an honorary New Yorker who will have to take this test one day soon.

Author's Acknowledgments

Peter Bonfanti, a great "math guy," created the math explanations and examples in this book. Always courteous, even when told to provide five more problems *now, if not sooner,* Peter is a fine teacher and a valued member of "The Supper Club." I also acknowledge my debt to the late Suzee Vlk, who wrote the earlier editions of the *For Dummies* SAT prep books. I thank Albert Wu, my former student and accomplished comedy writer who came up with the idea for mock SAT questions and graciously allowed me to use it. I appreciate the courteous attention and help of my agent, Lisa Queen, and Wiley editors Kathy Cox and Alissa Schwipps. Finally, I thank my students — SAT prep, English, and independent study seminar participants — who make teaching the finest job in the world.

Publisher's Acknowledgments

We're proud of this book; please send us your comments through our Dummies online registration form located at www.dummies.com/register/.

Some of the people who helped bring this book to market include the following:

Acquisitions, Editorial, and Media Development

Senior Project Editor: Alissa Schwipps

Acquisitions Editor: Kathy Cox

Copy Editor: Chad Sievers

Technical Editor: Susie Watts

Senior Editorial Manager: Jennifer Ehrlich

Editorial Assistants: Courtney Allen, Nadine Bell

Cartoons: Rich Tennant, www.the5thwave.com

Composition

Project Coordinators: Adrienne Martinez, Erin Smith

Layout and Graphics: Karl Brandt, Lauren Goddard, Denny Hager, Mary Gillot Virgin

Proofreaders: Laura Albert, John Greenough, Betty Kish, Dwight Ramsey

Indexer: Lynnzee Elze

Publishing and Editorial for Consumer Dummies

Diane Graves Steele, Vice President and Publisher, Consumer Dummies

Joyce Pepple, Acquisitions Director, Consumer Dummies

Kristin A. Cocks, Product Development Director, Consumer Dummies

Michael Spring, Vice President and Publisher, Travel

Brice Gosnell, Associate Publisher, Travel

Kelly Regan, Editorial Director, Travel

Publishing for Technology Dummies

Andy Cummings, Vice President and Publisher, Dummies Technology/General User

Composition Services

Gerry Fahey, Vice President of Production Services

Debbie Stailey, Director of Composition Services

Contents at a Glance

Table of Contents

Introduction

irst, lower your shoulders. Now unclench your knees and take a deep breath. No, I'm not a yoga instructor. I'm giving you these directions because if you're like most people, the very thought of the SAT makes you huddle into a basic turtle shape. To add even more grief to your life, you've probably heard that the SAT is changing. Beginning in the spring of 2005, the dreaded test has grammar on it! And writing! Are you really surprised that your head tends to tuck protectively close to your chest whenever you contemplate the SAT?

But you don't have to turn into a candidate for physical therapy just because a standardized test looms in your future. I have a little secret: The SAT isn't as bad as you think, especially now that you've shown wisdom and foresight in buying this book. (Yes, I count modesty as one of my many virtues.) The SAT *is* horrible in some ways. For one thing, the test kills a perfectly good weekend morning, when you could be sleeping or doing something noble such as discovering a cure for nail fungus. Plus, the new test gobbles up an extra 35 minutes of your life. Yet the SAT, although challenging, isn't any harder than everyday school tests, and in a lot of ways, it's easier.

But you can't go cold to the SAT and expect to give it your best shot. A little preparation goes a long way (all upward), and your score will climb nicely if you invest just a small portion of your life getting acquainted with the ultra-annoying exam. Don't you at least want to be prepared so the directions and format aren't a surprise on SAT-day? Furthermore, a little practice can help you avoid the SAT's tricks and traps after you discover how to spot them. Working with *The SAT I For Dummies,* 6th Edition, ensures that when everyone else's shoulders rise with tension, you'll be poised and relaxed, ready to show the world (well, the part of the world that most concerns you at this stage in your life — the colleges) how brilliant you are.

About This Book

The SAT is one of the standardized tests that fall like mudslides on almost everyone applying to a college or university in the United States and to a couple of English-speaking institutions abroad. A few schools don't require any standardized tests, preferring instead that their applicants concentrate on answering questions such as "Why breathe?" and "Peanut butter — inevitable or technological?" If you're planning to attend one of those schools, I offer my congratulations. You can put this book down now and go bowling. But if your college — or at least the one that you hope will be your college someday — requires a standardized test, you're probably facing either the SAT or the ACT. I'm assuming the SAT, because you plunked down the cash for this book. (What? You charged it to Grandma's trust fund? No matter. The point remains the same. You're reading this book because you have to take the SAT.) If you just love tests and want to take both (in which case you should seriously consider getting a life), check out Wiley's *The ACT For Dummies,* 3rd Edition, by Suzee Vlk.

Ideally the SAT gives colleges a way to measure your ability to succeed in their hallowed halls. It doesn't, really, but it does give the admit guys an actual number (a set of numbers, really) to compare you to all the other applicants. If you have a high SAT score, you have a better chance of getting into Really-Wanna-Go-There University.

The SAT I For Dummies, 6th Edition, takes you through each section of the test, explaining what the little test-devils are looking for and how you can find it. In this book, you can pick up a few ways to increase your vocabulary painlessly, because, as Yogi Berra (famous Yankee shortstop and language-wrecker) *didn't* say, "Nine tenths of the SAT game is half vocabulary." As a bonus, I scatter SAT words and definitions throughout the book, including in paragraphs having nothing to do with vocabulary *per se.* (By the way, *per se* means "as such" or "for itself.") In addition, *The SAT I For Dummies,* 6th Edition, includes a quick review of the math and grammar essentials that tend to pop up on the exam.

Just to make your life a little more confusing, two SATs are out there, waiting to torture you. The biggest and the one most colleges require, the SAT Reasoning Test, formerly known officially (and still affectionately) as the SAT I, is the one I'm preparing you for in this book. The other SAT, cleverly named the SAT Subject Test, or formerly known as the SAT II, is a set of exams geared to subjects in school — languages, sciences, math, history, and so on. *The SAT I For Dummies,* 6th Edition, doesn't deal with those tests, though you may want to check out some other *For Dummies* titles (such as Wiley's *Algebra For Dummies,* by Mary Jane Sterling, *Biology For Dummies,* by Donna Rae Siegfried, and so forth) to get a good review without a lot of hassle.

In *The SAT I For Dummies,* 6th Edition, you also find in-depth analysis and sample sets of each type of question that the SAT dumps on you — Sentence Completions, math grid-ins, and so forth. Just to kill still more of your free time, I include a detailed explanation with each answer, so you know what you answered right and wrong and why. Lastly, I give you two practice tests that you can take under true-test conditions. (No, they're not real SATs, because the company that produces the test is sitting on those rights and making a ton of cash doing so. Your test may not have exactly the same number of questions in exactly the same order. But the tests in this book are as close as anyone can come without invoking lawyerly attention, and they'll do the job.) Also, check out `www.dummies.com/go/sat1fd6e` for updates on this evolving exam.

Just like every *For Dummies* book, you don't have to read everything from cover to cover. No, I don't mean that you should skip the entire book. (Pause for a shudder of horror at the very thought.) Instead pick and choose just what you need from the wide range of topics included in *The SAT I For Dummies,* 6th Edition. For example, if you're a whiz at Reading Comprehension but math sends you screaming into the night, don't bother focusing much on Part II. Instead, concentrate on Part IV. Check out the Table of Contents to see what areas you want to focus on and then start chugging away. You can also check out the intro bullets at the beginning of each chapter under "In This Chapter" to specifically see what you can accomplish by spending your precious time going through that text. Be selective, and you'll be prepared for the exam *and* caught up on your sleep — and homework — when you face the SAT.

Conventions Used in This Book

To help you navigate through this book, I've set up a few conventions:

- ✔ *Italic* is used in three different ways:
  - For introducing new terms, particularly in the math chapters
  - For referring to words in multiple-choice answers
  - For emphasizing a word or point
- ✔ **Cascade font** is used to highlight vocabulary words that are defined.
- ✔ **Boldfaced** text is used to indicate the action part of numbered steps and the main items in bulleted lists.
- ✔ Monofont is used for Web addresses.

What You're Not to Read

Like many teachers, I love trivia, but I understand that useless facts are an acquired taste, and you may have something better to do than read about the development and use of the SAT. Nevertheless, I couldn't resist throwing in some information about the exam, which you can find in some of the gray boxes called sidebars, which I cleverly disguise as SAT questions. Skip them, unless you're trying to take your mind off your next dental appointment or your last big breakup. You don't need to know anything about the exam except how to ace it. And if you memorized the dictionary when you were 12, feel free to skip the vocabulary sidebars too!

Foolish Assumptions

I recently met a graduate of a university famous for the ivy climbing over its brick wall who told me that he had taken the SAT an extra time — *after* he had already been accepted — just to see whether he could achieve an even higher score. As I gave him a discreet once-over, checking for other signs of mental illness, he added, "I like taking tests."

In writing this book, I assume several things about you, including that you have nothing at all in common with my friend, who is actually quite sane, despite his love for sharpened No. 2 pencils.

My other assumptions include

- ✔ That you hate standardized tests but want to achieve a high score.

- ✔ That you have plenty of better things to do with your time than to plow through a ton of useless information. For you, then, I put in what you need to know and what you need to practice, and nothing else except for a few lame jokes, but hey, humor me. (No pun intended.)

- ✔ That you've taken the usual math and language arts courses in elementary and early high school — through, say, algebra and trigonometry and sophomore English. So even though I review the basics of those subjects, I'm not actually trying to teach you something that you've never seen before.

If you know that English grammar is a pitfall for you, feel free to increase my profit margin by purchasing *English Grammar For Dummies,* which provides a complete tour through the wonderful world of nouns, commas, and all that stuff. Ditto (but without increasing my royalties, because someone else wrote them) for the math challenged: *Algebra For Dummies* by Mary Jane Sterling and *Geometry For Dummies* by Wendy Arnone are the books you want. Wiley publishes all these titles.

I hope (but don't count on the fact) that the SAT you've signed up to take *isn't* less than 12 hours or more than two years away. This book is useful to would-be SAT-takers who think planning ahead involves putting your foot on the floor a nanosecond before standing up and those who are sitting around watching their teeth just in case they get a cavity someday. In Chapter 2, I provide a schedule for the obsessively late, the obsessively early, and the normal crowd in between.

Finally, though a lot of the silly jokes in this book arise from interactions with my teenage students, I don't base everything on that age group. If you're hitting college after living a little, good for you. This book can help you find your groove. (You have to handle the all-nighters yourself.)

How This Book Is Organized

You don't need any extra chores if you're in the last year or two of high school. You're at maximum warp in sports or extracurriculars, and you've finally figured out how to impress the freshmen. Now's the time to enjoy life. Nor do you need a million-hour prep course if you're holding down a job or burping a baby (or both). Happily, this book doesn't take a thousand hours of your time. In fact, this book should claim only about 25 or 30 hours or perhaps even less of your valuable time, depending upon how fast you read and how often you stop to check your instant messaging. (Chapter 2 gives you a couple of possible schedules, depending upon when you're starting your SAT prep and how harried your life is.) The following sections outline what's where.

Part I: Surveying the Field

This part provides an overview so you know what's facing you. It includes a bowl of alphabet soup (ACT, SAT Reasoning, SAT Subject, PSAT/NMSQT) and information on what colleges expect and how they interpret your scores. This part also helps students with special needs (foreign students, learning disabled, and so on) navigate the exam and tells everyone how and when to study for it.

Part II: Reading Critically

Part II takes you through the wonderful world of Reading Comprehension, explaining the three types of questions (Sentence Completions, the new short reading passages, and long passages) and the best strategies for each. Tons of practice questions get your reading muscles in shape.

Part III: Writing for Fun and Profit

Fun indeed. Part III opens the grammar toolbox so you can tackle this new topic on the SAT. Part III explains how to apply grammar rules to Error Recognition questions as well as to Sentence and Paragraph Revisions. In this part, you also discover the best approach to the essay, also new to the exam, and how to beat the clock when you write one.

Part IV: Take a Number: The Math Section

Time to fire up the calculator — either the one in your head or the little plastic job with batteries. This part takes you on a whirlwind tour of the concepts most likely to help you on the SAT math questions. It includes a ton of sample problems (no, not the "I wouldn't date you if you were the last person on earth" type but the "what-is-the-value-of-x" sort) and shows you the most efficient way to solve them, with or without a calculator, a handy little gadget you're allowed to bring to the test.

Part V: Where the Rubber Meets the Road: Practice Tests

This part contains two practice tests that prepare you well in terms of style and content for the new SAT. However, the number of questions and the placement of sections (whether you have Math or Critical Reading as section two, for example) may vary on the real SAT. No matter. If you practice with the sample tests in Part V, you'll be prepared.

So sharpen your pencil, lock the door, turn off the DVD, and prepare for take-off!

Part VI: The Part of Tens

The famous *For Dummies* Part of Tens. I include two quick, light-hearted chapters about how to de-stress and what to double-check when you're taking the SAT.

Icons Used in This Book

Icons are those cute little pictures in the margins of this book. They each indicate why you should pay special attention to the accompanying text. Here's how to decode them:

A hint about strategy — what the all-star test-takers know and the rookies want to find out.

This icon identifies the sand traps that the little SAT-demon test-writers are hoping you fall into.

Short of throwing chocolate sauce on a dictionary and eating it for dessert, these vocabulary builders are the best tactics for increasing your personal word count. They're also a lot easier to digest.

This icon identifies questions resembling those on the actual SAT.

Where to Go From Here

Okay, now that you know what's what and where to find it, you have a choice. You can read every single word I've written (I love you! Will you let me shake your hand?) or you can check out only the parts of *The SAT I For Dummies,* 6th Edition, that address your "issues," as they say on afternoon talk shows. In other words, if you feel confident with your math skills but panicky about the reading questions, hit Part II first and give Part IV a pass for now, at least. Or, if vocabulary is your personal monster, read the long-range vocabulary-building tips in Chapter 2 and flip through the whole book, scanning all the Vocabulary Builder icons you encounter. Another good path is to take one of the sample tests in Part V, score it, and focus in on your weak spots. And be sure to log on to www.dummies.com/go/sat1fd6e for breaking news about the new exam.

No matter what you do next, start with one thing: Lower your shoulders. Calm down, stay loose, and score big on the SAT.

Part I
Surveying the Field

The 5th Wave   By Rich Tennant

©RICHTENNANT

2005 SATI TESTING CENTER

"I'm sure you've all heard about the changes in the SATI with the emphasis being on math and writing."

In this part . . .

As an SAT candidate, you should follow one cardinal rule: Know your adversary. In this case your adversary is a little paper booklet with a deceptively innocent appearance. Don't be fooled; the SAT holds one key to your future. To make your fight with the SAT fair, you must tour the SAT's native habitat and figure out how to speak its language.

Part I is a field guide to the SAT: What it tests, when to take it, where to find it, and how it helps your chances for admission to college. Part I also explains when to guess and what to do to stay calm on SAT-day.

Chapter 1

Pouring Your Brain into Little Ovals — the SAT

- -

In This Chapter

▶ Determining which test to take

▶ Signing up for the SAT

▶ Allowing for special needs

▶ Previewing the SAT reading, writing, and math sections

▶ Understanding SAT scoring

- -

You may be wondering why you're stuck with the SAT. Unbelievable as it may seem, the test was established to help, not *annihilate* (wipe out completely) students. Right about now you're probably thinking that I'm giving you the old "it's for your own good" line that authority figures always use when they're about to drop you off a cliff. But the SAT was created to level the playing field — to predict the likelihood of academic success of students, regardless of family background, connections, and other privileges. The SAT has never actually succeeded in this lofty goal, and the college admissions playing field still resembles the Alps more than the Great Plains. However, the SAT does give colleges a *number* for each student that, theoretically at least, measures the ability of everyone who takes it without regard for the dollar value of trust funds sitting in the vault.

In this chapter — whether you have a trust fund or not — you can find the ABCs of the SATs. . . .why you need to take the exam; when, where, and how often to take it; where to send your scores; and how to deal with special needs. Chapter 1 also provides a peek into the structure of the exam itself.

Sitting for the SAT Instead of ACTing Up

Most college applicants pass through one of two giant gates on their way into U.S. colleges and some foreign schools. One is the ACT, and the other the SAT. Most colleges accept scores from either test; check with the admissions office of the colleges on your list to be sure you're taking the tests they prescribe. (Good general rule for college admissions: Give them what they want, when they want it.) The SAT and the ACT tests are roughly the same in terms of difficulty. Unless you're really obsessed, don't bother to take both.

The ACT, for reasons lost in the mists of time, has always had grammar questions. (If you're taking the ACT, don't forget to check out *ACT For Dummies*, 3rd Edition by Suzee Vlk [Wiley].) The SAT is the new kid on the grammar block. Because you're reading *The SAT I For Dummies*, 6th Edition, instead of downloading the latest rap song, presumably you're taking the SAT.

What exactly is an SAT?

What does SAT stand for?

(A) Stressed Awed Teens

(B) Stupendously Awful Test

(C) Selectively Advantaged Totalitarians

(D) Scholastic Aptitude Test

(E) Nothing

Answer: (E). Okay, (D) used to be correct, but the test company changed the name in response to critics' charge that the SAT didn't really measure aptitude. Now the letters SAT are just letters. After the reconfiguration of the test, the dreaded exam became the SAT I/Reasoning Test. Why the change? To torture you more. Okay, seriously, the SAT-ists (no, not sadists, but pretty close; the people behind the SAT) changed the test to preserve their market share by including more writing, a skill that colleges prize.

Don't confuse the SAT I with the SAT IIs. Both terms, by the way, are now officially *obsolete* (out-dated, so yesterday) because the company that makes them has renamed them the SAT Reasoning Test and SAT Subject Tests though the name SAT I remains in popular use. Whatever you call them, be sure you know the difference. The SAT Reasoning Test does the proverbial 3 R's — reading, 'riting, and 'rithmetic (but clearly not spelling). The SAT Subject Tests cover biology, history, math, and a ton of other stuff. They're either not required or required in various combinations by many schools.

Many libraries and nearly all bookstores have college guides — 20-pound paperbacks describing each and every institution of higher learning you may apply to. Check out the colleges on your list to see which tests they accept or require. You may also visit individual college Web sites for the most up-to-date requirements. Because the SAT Reasoning Test has gone through major changes recently, older printed materials probably aren't accurate.

Should you take the PSAT/NMSQT?

The PSAT/NMSQT is

(A) what you see on the bottom of the bowl when you don't eat all the alphabet soup

(B) the noise you make slurping the aforementioned soup

(C) a test that prepares you for the SAT and screens scholarship applicants

(D) the average tile selection when I play word games

(E) a secret government agency that investigates music downloads from the Internet

Answer: (C). The PSAT used to be short for the "Preliminary Scholastic Aptitude Test," back when the initials SAT actually meant something. Now PSAT just means "Pre-SAT." The NMSQT still stands for something — the

"National Merit Scholarship Qualifying Test." Though it has a two-part name, the PSAT/NMSQT is just one test, but it performs both the functions described in (C). If you're a super brain, the PSAT/NMSQT may move you into the ranks of semifinalists for a National Merit Scholarship, a *prestigious* (high status) scholarship program. You don't have to do anything extra to apply for a National Merit Scholarship. Just take the test, and if you make the semifinals, the National Merit Scholarship Program will send you an application. Even if you think your chances of winning a scholarship are the same as Bart Simpson's passing the fourth grade, you should still take the PSAT/NMSQT. The PSAT changed along with the SAT and mirrors the new SAT, though the PSAT is slightly shorter and doesn't include an essay. Taking the PSAT gives you a feel for the SAT itself — the test conditions, the format, and (I hate to admit) the pressure.

If college isn't in your immediate future, you may want to take the SAT just to see how you do. If your plans include a stint in the armed forces or hitchhiking through Borneo before hitting higher education, you can keep your options open by taking the SAT before you go. Also, if you take the SAT while formal "book-learning" is still fresh in your mind, you may do better. Then when you retire your thumb or trigger finger, you have some scores to send to the college of your choice, though if a long period of time has passed, the colleges may ask for an updated score. (How long is "a long period of time"? It depends on the college you're applying to. Some may ask for an updated SAT after only a couple of years; others are more lenient. Obviously, whether you took three years off to work on the world's deepest tan or ten years to decipher the meaning of an obscure archaeological site also influences the admissions office decision on SAT scores. Check with the college(s) you're interested in and explain your situation.)

Getting Set for the SAT: Registering for the Right Test at the Right Time

The SAT is given at select high schools throughout the United States and in English-speaking schools in many other countries. Even home-schoolers can take the SAT, though not in their own living rooms. To find the test center nearest you or to request a registration form, ask the college or guidance counselor at your high school. If you're home-schooled, call the nearest public or private high school. Or, you may register through the SAT Web site (www.collegeboard.com). If you have special needs, paper is your route. Get the forms at your school. You can also request a form via the plain, old-fashioned telephone; try 609-771-7600 for the general customer service center. (Also check out the "Meeting Special Needs" section later in this chapter.) If you're stranded on a desert island without phone, Internet, or school office (in which case the SAT is the least of your problems), try writing to the College Board SAT Program, Princeton, New Jersey 08541 for the forms you need. The SAT Reasoning Test costs about $41.50, though fee waivers are available for those in financial difficulties. (See "Meeting Special Needs" in this chapter for more information.)

Where the SAT helps the most

The SAT counts the most in

(A) small, private colleges where people say hello even if they hate you because they're going to run into you five times a day for four years

(B) public universities with an enrollment larger than the population of Tokyo

(C) keeping a job with Donald Trump

(D) deciding whether Howard "Tall as a Himalaya" Jones should play center or forward on the basketball team

(E) the yearbook popularity contest

Answer: (B). Small private colleges can take the time to pour over your essays and talk to every applicant. They certainly check your SAT scores, but they can more easily see those numbers as part of a total picture. Large public universities, on the other hand, are underfunded and severely understaffed, as in "Put those 20,000 applications over there with the other 150,000 that came in yesterday." With a huge freshman class and rooms full of applications, they need quick and easy determinants. Thus they're more likely to give extra weight to things that can be quantified, such as SAT scores.

In high-stress situations — Martian invasions, nuclear meltdowns, the cancellation of your favorite TV show — rumors *abound* (grow and thrive). So too with the SAT. You've probably heard that certain versions of the SAT — the ones given in October or November or the ones given in a particular state — are easier than others. Not so. The SAT contains one section that you *must* answer that counts for absolutely nothing. . . for you. It's called the *equating* section. The test-makers use this section as a statistical tool to ensure that all the SAT tests, regardless of when or where they're given, are equal in difficulty. No matter how well you do on the equating section, or (in case you're having a bad day) how badly you blow it, the equating section won't affect your score.

The SAT pops up on the calendar seven times a year. You can take the exam as often as you want. If you're a *masochist* — you enjoy pain — you can take all seven tests, but most people stick to this schedule:

Autumn of junior year (about 1¾ years before college entrance): Time to take the PSAT/NMSQT.

Spring of junior year (about 1¼ years before college entrance): Take the SAT strictly for practice, though you can send your scores in if you're pleased with them.

Autumn of senior year (a bit less than a year before entrance): The SAT strikes again. Early-decision candidates prefer taking the test in October or November; regular applicants may choose from any of the three autumn dates, including December.

Winter of senior year (half-year before entrance): Some SAT-lovers take the exam in autumn and again in the winter, hoping that practice will make perfect, at least in the eyes of the colleges. The high scores won't hurt (and you probably will improve, just because the whole routine will be familiar), but don't put a lot of energy into repeated bouts of SAT fever. Your grades and extracurriculars may suffer if you're too fixated on the SAT, and you may end up hurting your overall application.

If you're transferring or starting your college career mid-year, you may sit for the SAT in January, March, May, or June. Check with your counselor or with the college of your choice and go with that recommendation.

Everyone takes the SAT on Saturday except for those students who can't for religious reasons. If you fall into that category, your SAT-day will be Sunday. Get a letter from your *cleric* (religious leader) on letterhead and mail it in with your registration form.

In terms of test sites, the early bird gets the worm. (Did you ever wonder why no one ever deals with the worm's fate? He got up early too, and look what happened to him.) When you register, you may request a test site, but if it's filled, you'll get an alternate. So don't delay; send in the form or register online as soon as you know when and where you want to take the exam.

Meeting Special Needs

If you have a learning disability, you may be allowed to take the SAT under special conditions. The first step is to get an Eligibility Form from your school counselor. (Home-schoolers, call the local high school.) You may also want to ask your college counseling office for a copy of the *College Board Services for Students with Disabilities Brochure* (pamphlet). If your school doesn't have one, contact the College Board directly. Send in the form well in advance of the time you expect to take the test. Generally, if you're entitled to extra test time in your high school, you'll be eligible for extra time on the SAT.

Atención! What every foreign student needs to know about the SAT

First, welcome to the U.S.'s worst invention, the Seriously Annoying Test (SAT), which you're taking so that you can attend an American institution. Getting ready for this exam may make you consider another American institution, one with padded rooms and bars on the windows. But a high SAT score is certainly within reach for individuals who have studied English as a second language. Here's one secret: The SAT's formal vocabulary is actually easier than American conversational English and slang. So if even if you look at the sky in puzzlement when someone asks, "What's up?", you should be able to decode an SAT question. (By the way, "What's up?" is a general inquiry into your state of mind, current occupation, and plans for the immediate future.) As a foreign student, pay special attention to the vocabulary builder icons in this book. You may want to keep a notebook or a computer file of new words you encounter as you work the sample questions.

Also turn your concentration up to "totally intense" in the math section of this prep book because arithmetic doesn't change from language to language. Neither does geometry or algebra. If you can crack the basic language used to put forth the problem, you should be able to rack up a ton of points.

What does extra time really mean? Extra time equals 1½ the usual amount for each section. In the past, the SAT simply added 50 percent more time to the entire test and allowed the student to work on any section for as long as he or she wanted, with the whole thing done in the "time and a half" allotted. The new SAT requires extended-time test-takers to stay on one section at a time, with time and a half allowed for each section. So if regular test-takers have 20 minutes for a section, extended-timers get 30 minutes.

The SAT also provides wheelchair accessibility, large-print tests, and other accommodations for students who need them. The key is to submit the Eligibility Form early so that the SAT-maker — the College Board — can ask for any extra documentation and set up appropriate test conditions for you.

If your special need resides in your wallet, you can apply for a fee waiver, which is available to low-income high school juniors and seniors who live in the United States, Puerto Rico, and other American territories. Ask your school counselor for an application. (As in everything to do with the SAT, if you're a home-schooler, call the local high school for a form.)

The SAT charges extra for more than four score reports to colleges, for late or changed registrations, and for "extras" like extra-quick reporting. It *doesn't* charge extra for special needs accommodations, such as large print or wheelchair accessible testing.

Measuring Your Mind: What the SAT Tests

Statistically, the SAT tests whether or not you'll be successful in your first year of college. Admissions officers keep track of their students' SAT scores and have a pretty good idea which scores signal trouble and which scores indicate clear sailing. Many college guides list the average SAT scores of entering freshmen.

That said, the picture gets complicated whenever the wide-angle lens narrows to focus on an individual, such as you, and admissions offices are well aware of this fact. How rigorous your high school is, whether you deal well with multiple-choice questions, and how you feel physically and mentally on SAT-day (Fight with Mom? Bad romance? Week-old sushi?) all influence your score. Bottom line: Stop obsessing about the SAT's unfairness (and it *is* unfair) and prepare.

The college admission essay is a great place to put your scores in perspective. If you face some special circumstances, such as a learning disability, a school that doesn't value academics, a family tragedy, and so on, you may want to explain your situation in an essay. No essay wipes out the bad impression created by an extremely low SAT score, but a good essay gives the college a way to interpret your achievement and to see you, the applicant, in more detail. For help with the college admission essay, take a look at *College Admission Essays For Dummies,* published by Wiley and written by yours truly.

The SAT doesn't test facts you studied in school; you don't need to know when Columbus sailed across the Atlantic or how to calculate the molecular weight of magnesium in order to answer an SAT Reasoning question. Instead, the SAT takes aim at your ability to follow a logical sequence, to comprehend what you've read, and to write clearly in standard English. The math portion checks whether you were paying attention or snoring when little details like algebra were taught. Check out the next sections for a bird's eye view of the three SAT topics.

Critical Reading

This topic pops up three times per SAT, in terms of what counts toward your score. (All SATs include an extra section either in reading or math that the SAT-makers use for research only.) You face two 25-minute sections and one 20-minute section of Critical Reading, a fancy term for reading comprehension. Each section may contain Sentence Completions and/or Reading Comprehension passages that are either short (about 100 words) or long (700 to 800 words). You also see a set of paired passages — a double take on one topic from two different points of view.

Sentence Completions

The Sentence Completions are just fill-ins. You may encounter one or two sets of nine or ten questions. Sentence Completions test vocabulary and your ability to decode the sentence structure, as in the following:

The SAT Sentence Completion section is guaranteed to give you a headache, so the test-makers thoughtfully provide _____ with each exam.

  (A) aspirin

  (B) dictionaries

  (C) answer keys

  (D) tutoring

  (E) scalp massage

Answer: (A). Given that the sentence specifies "headache," your best choice is "aspirin," at least in SAT world. In real life you may prefer a day at the spa, but the test-makers haven't included that option. (E) is a possibility too, but the SAT goes with the best answer, not the only answer.

Reading Comprehension

Reading Comprehension questions are a mixture of literal (just-the-facts-ma'am) and interpretive/analytical. You may be asked to choose the meaning of a word in context or to assess the author's tone or point of view. Passages may be drawn from the natural and social sciences, humanities, or fiction, as in the following:

Thanhowser was frantic to learn that the first GC-MP8 handheld was already in circulation. And here he was wasting his time in college! The degree that he had pursued so doggedly for the past three years now seemed nothing more than a gigantic waste of time. The business world, that's where he belonged, marketing someone else's technology with just enough of a twist to allow him to patent "his" idea.

In line 5 the word *his* is in quotation marks

(A) because it's a pronoun

(B) because the reader is supposed to hiss at Thanhowser, whom everyone hates

(C) to show that the idea really came from someone else

(D) to demonstrate that the idea really came from a female masquerading as a male

(E) because the typesetter had some extra quotation marks

Answer: (C). These quotation marks refer to Thanhowser's claim to "someone else's technology." Although he isn't quoted directly, the quotation marks around "his" imply that Thanhowser says that a particular invention is his, when in fact it isn't.

Writing

To the *chagrin* (disappointment or embarrassment) of English teachers everywhere, the SAT Writing test contains only a sliver of actual writing: one 25-minute essay on a topic that you've never seen before, plus 25 minutes' worth of short answers. Why so little writing? As those of us who sit with four-foot high piles of essays on our laps know, it takes a long time to read student prose. The SAT test-makers must pay people to read and score essays — a much more expensive and time-consuming proposition than running a bubble sheet through a scanner. The multiple-choice questions check your ability to recognize errors in grammar, punctuation, and word use and to make sentence revisions. You also see a couple of *pseudo* (fake) first drafts of student essays and answer some questions about the writer's intentions. In these longer passages, you again have to select the best revisions.

Error Recognition

Error Recognition questions are long sentences (they have to be long to allow enough room for four possible errors) with underlined portions. You choose the portion with a mistake or select (E) for "no error."

Flabbergill <u>denounced his lover</u> for her <u>work with</u> the Revolutionary <u>Band, he</u> had a new
        (A)   (B)   (C)

bass guitarist lined up whose musical talents <u>were, he</u> said, "awesome." <u>No error.</u>
                               (D)   (E)

Answer: (C). Each half of the sentence can stand alone, so a comma may not join them. You need a semicolon or a word such as *and* or *so* to glue the two parts together.

Sentence Revision

In these questions the test-gurus underline one portion of a sentence and then provide four alternatives. (A) always repeats the original wording.

Having been turned down by fifteen major league baseball teams, Gilberdub changed to basketball, and he succeeded <u>in his goal where he was aiming to be a professional athlete</u>.

(A) in his goal where he was aiming to be a professional athlete.

(B) in that he reached his goal of aiming to be a professional athlete.

(C) where he became a professional athlete.

(D) in his goal of becoming a professional athlete.

(E) because he wanted million-dollar sneaker ads.

Answer: (D). Just kidding about (E), though an endorsement contract actually was Gilberdub's motivation.

Paragraph Revision

These questions throw you into the mind of a fairly competent student writer who has had only enough time to complete a first draft of an essay on a general topic. Some of the questions ask you to combine sentences effectively; others resemble the Sentence Revision section — an underlined portion with possible improvements or alternate versions of entire sentences.

Essay

This section is the only spot in the Writing section that you actually get to write something. And I do mean *write*. For those of you who have keyboards permanently implanted under your fingernails, this section may be a handwriting challenge. And, thanks to ever-evolving technology, an image of your essay — inkblots, saliva drools, and all — will be available on the Web to the college admission offices that are reviewing your applications. Start practicing your penmanship.

In terms of what you write, the essay is a standard, short discussion of a general topic that the SAT-makers provide. You have to take a stand and defend it with evidence (literature, history, and your own experience or observation). The main challenge is time: You have only 25 minutes to think, write, and revise.

Mathematics

In the new SAT, gone are the dreaded quantitative comparisons, which asked you to figure out which of two items was larger. Added are questions that rely on Algebra II and some advanced topics in geometry, statistics, and probability. Your SAT contains two 25-minute math sections that count (and perhaps one equating section that the SAT uses for its own statistical analysis only). Almost all the questions are multiple choice, in which you choose the answer from among five possibilities. Ten are *grid-ins* in which you supply an answer and bubble in the actual number, not a multiple-choice letter. Look at the following sample math problem:

If $xy - 12 = z$, and the value of x is 2, which of the following must be true?

(A) z = the number of days since you've had no homework

(B) $y = 12 + z$

(C) $z = 2y - 12$

(D) $2y - z = 100$

(E) y > the number of hours you have to spend studying SAT math

Answer: (A). Just kidding. It's actually (E). Oops, kidding again. The correct choice is (C).

For a peek at a grid-in, check out Chapter 13.

Scoring at the SAT

No, I'm not talking about *that* kind of scoring. I'm talking academics here, or at least the SAT's version of academics. Each half of the SAT used to be scored from 200 to 800, giving you a combined maximum score of 1,600. Now that the new SAT is in place, 1,600 is just a high-rent address on Pennsylvania Avenue (the White House), and the maximum score is 2,400 (top score of 800 on each of three main sections: Critical Reading, Writing, and Math).

You get one point for each correct answer you supply on the SAT, and for everything but the essay and math grid-ins, you lose ¼ point for each incorrect answer. (If you make a mistake on a grid-in, you receive no points but nothing is deducted.) Two (severely underpaid) English teachers who have undergone special training in SAT scoring read the essay. Each reader awards it 1 to 6 points. If the readers disagree by more than one point, which happens in about 6 percent of the essays, a third super-expert reader weighs in. When you get your writing score, you see a 20 to 80 score for the multiple-choice questions and an essay subscore of 2 to 12.

Meeting market demand, or, why the SAT is changing

The SAT has changed because

(A) the company that makes the test needed a new product line

(B) the test-making gremlins were getting bored and sought a new challenge

(C) the students taking the old exam were having too much fun

(D) admissions offices demanded higher test scores

(E) a study of Americans' grammar knowledge showed gaps the size of Jupiter

Answer: (A). That's right, (A). The Educational Testing Service (ETS), a mega-exam company based in Princeton, New Jersey, produces the SAT. ETS wants to stay in business and make money. So when the University of California — one of its largest customers — announced a couple of years ago that it may drop its SAT requirement, ETS trembled. When more colleges followed suit, ETS had the institutional equivalent of a nervous breakdown. It scrambled to address the universities' concerns that the SAT didn't truly measure the skills and abilities needed for college-level work. Specifically, the colleges wanted higher-level math and some evidence that their applicants could read and write. So the new SAT includes a writing sample and grammar questions (two areas formerly taken care of by the SATIIW, the achievement test in writing, which is now dead as a day-old fish fillet) and math typically taught in Algebra II courses.

The SAT isn't curved, but raw scores are converted to the 200 to 800 format. Surprisingly, you can get a couple of answers wrong and still receive a perfect 800.

To guess or not to guess, that is the question. The answer is a definite *maybe*. On the grid-ins, always guess because there is no penalty for a wrong answer. If you have no clue on the grid-ins, bubble in your birthday or the number of cavities you had during your last checkup. For the other five-answer, multiple-choice questions, try to eliminate obviously wrong answers. If you can dump one, you have a one in four chance of guessing correctly. Go for it. If you can't eliminate anything, leave the question blank. Always guess if you can eliminate two of the five choices because the odds favor you. Students who make this sort of educated guess usually score higher on the SAT than they would have if they'd left more blanks.

The SAT company (the College Board) sends your scores to up to eight colleges. The basic fee for the test is $41.50, with the first four score reports free, but you pay $7 extra for additional score reports. (Prices, of course, are always subject to change, and don't expect any to go down. Check the College Board Web site for pricing changes.) If you're applying to more than eight colleges, you can request additional score reports on the (How do they think of these names?) Additional Score Report Request Form.

For a higher fee ($8), you can get a detailed analysis of your test performance — how many of each sort of question you answered right and wrong. Then you can tailor your prep hours to the stuff that's hard for you. Ask for *Student Answer Service* when you register. For even more money ($16), the SAT sends you a copy of the questions and your answers, but only for certain test dates. Look for *Question and Answer Service* when you register.

If you're planning to take another SAT, spring for the Answer Service. Seeing what you got wrong gives you a blueprint for review.

Chapter 2

Getting Ready, Set, and Going: Preparing for the SAT

*W*hat? You've discovered how to tie your shoelaces and you still haven't started to prepare for the SAT? Tsk. Tsk. You're in trouble. You should have begun to study *in utero* (before birth) by having your mother play vocabulary tapes next to her stomach. And all that time you wasted in kindergarten playing with blocks when you could have been studying square roots! You'll have to give up sleeping to make up for lost time. And don't even think about that party.

Does the preceding paragraph sound like the voice inside your head? If so, you need to take a deep breath and release that anxiety. SAT prep can start at many different points in your life and still be effective. In this chapter, you find long-term and short-term strategies for SAT prep, as well as medium-length prep for the Average Joe and Josephine. And for those of you who suddenly realized that The Test is next week, I provide a panic-button scenario. Lastly, I explain what to do on the night before the test (speaking of panic) as well as the morning of SAT-day, to maximize your score.

Flying with the Early Bird: A Long-Range Plan

Okay, so you're the type of person who buys summer clothes in December. (By the way, thanks a lot. Because of you, all the department stores feature bikinis when I'm trying to buy a sweater.) To put it another way, you're not in diapers, but the test isn't coming up within the next year. Congratulations. Check out the following long-range SAT prep plan:

✔ **Sign up for challenging courses in school.** If you're in high school, *eschew* (reject) courses like "The Poetry of Greeting Cards" and "Arithmetic Is Your Friend." Go for subjects that stretch your mind. Specifically, stick it out with math at least through Algebra II. If high school is in your rearview mirror, check out extension or enrichment adult-ed courses.

✔ **If possible, take a vocabulary-rich course.** When I say that a good vocabulary is key to SAT success, I'm not indulging in *hyperbole* (exaggeration). If your school offers classes with a lot of reading, go for them. Some schools even have whole courses devoted to vocabulary (mine has a course in Greek and Latin roots). These classes may not be as exciting as "Cultural Interpretations of MTV," but they pay off.

✔ **Get into the habit of reading.** Cereal boxes, Internet pop-up balloons, and 1,000-page novels — they're all good, though they're not all equal. The more you read, and the more difficult the material you read, the more your reading comprehension improves.

✔ **Do a daily crossword puzzle in your newspaper or check out *Crossword Puzzle Challenges For Dummies* by Patrick Berry (Wiley).** I know. Crossword puzzles seem like a good way to become a candidate for Nerds Anonymous. But you can discover a lot by *pondering* (thinking deeply about) language on a daily basis. Plus, some people (me, for example) actually enjoy crossword puzzles. But then I never claimed to be anything other than a nerd.

✔ **Write letters to the editor.** The editor of anything. Find a point of view and start sending off your prose — to the school or local paper, to national magazines, to radio or television stations. The SAT essay calls upon you to make a case for your point of view. The more you get used to creating a written argument, the easier the essay will be. As a side benefit, you may have a civic impact.

✔ **Keep your math notebooks.** Resist the urge to burn your geometry text the minute the last class is over. Keep your math notebooks and folders of homework papers. From time to time, go over the important concepts. The notebook may *evoke* (call to mind) the context in which you studied right triangles or square roots. For example, if you see a stain next to an explanation of factoring, it may take you back to that immortal day when Herbie threw a spitball at you while the teacher was working out a factoring problem on the board. If you're mentally back in the class, you may find that you remember more of the mathematical explanation the teacher gave. (Of course, if you spent the rest of the class lobbing spitballs back at Herbie instead of paying attention, you're out of luck. Turn to Chapter 14 for a general math review.)

✔ **Look through the chapters in this book that explain the structure of each type of SAT question.** When SAT-day dawns, you shouldn't be facing any surprises. Be sure that you're familiar with the directions for each section so that you don't have to waste time reading them during the actual exam.

✔ **Take both practice exams in Part V of this book.** After you identify your weak spots (not that you actually *have* any — just areas where you could be even more excellent), hit the practice chapters for the type of questions that bother you.

✔ **Take the PSAT/NMSQT.** This "mini-SAT" gives you a chance to experience test conditions. It may also open the door to a pretty snazzy scholarship, the National Merit.

TIP

The best vocabulary builder

The most efficient way to increase your vocabulary is to

(A) eat five pages of a dictionary every day

(B) wallpaper your room with an old thesaurus

(C) create your own personal dictionary

(D) date an English teacher

(E) watch 5,000 hours of television a week

Answer: (C). If you're a good reader, chances are you skip over unfamiliar words and just figure out the meaning of the sentence or paragraph without them. That's a fine technique for reading, but not for vocabulary building. To implant those new words in your mind, take a moment to jot them down. You can use an index card or a computer file. Write the sentence you found the word in, and then the definition. A dictionary is fine for definition-finding, but a handy adult or teacher works just as well. Don't ask for every possible meaning of the word, just the definition that fits the original sentence. From time to time, read over your personal dictionary. Because you discovered the words in context, you have a better chance of remembering them. As a bonus, you can totally impress your parents when you yell something like "What does *ubiquitous* mean?" (*ubiquitous* = found everywhere, like Jennifer Lopez's love interests.)

As the SAT approaches, you long-range planners can relax. You're in a fine position to *condescend* (act superior) to all the goof-offs who didn't even begin to think about the exam until junior year in high school. (What? You're one of those goof-offs? Never fear. I offer some hope, which you can find in the next section.)

Hitting the Golden Mean: A Medium-Range Plan

In this category you're conscientious but not obsessive. You have a bit less than a year before SAT-day (in high school terms, you're a junior), and you have a reasonable amount of time to devote to SAT prep. You're in fine shape, though you may have to take some ribbing from the "I've got a career plan even though I'm not old enough for working papers" types. Here's your strategy:

- **Do all you can to extract maximum vocabulary growth from your last school year before the SAT.** Make friends with words. Listen to talk radio (the stations with on-air fundraisers, not the drive-by call-in shows that feature a hot discussion of the Yankees chances for a three-peat) or watch sophisticated talk shows on television (not the shows that feature oatmeal addicts and the men and women who love them). Take some thick books out of the library and use them for more than a missile to hurl at your annoying little sister. *Peruse* (read thoroughly, scrutinize) the newspaper every day, preferably one that stays away from extensive coverage of celebrity botox.

- **Work on your writing.** If your school offers an elective in nonfiction writing, go for it. Or, volunteer to write for the school newspaper. Write letters to the editor (see a fuller explanation in "Flying with the Early Bird: A Long-Range Plan," earlier in this chapter). Become comfortable with the sort of writing that makes a case for a particular point of view, because that's what you have to do on the SAT.

- **Get a math study-buddy.** I'm not talking about a tutor. Yes, you can find out a lot from someone who dreams quadratic equations. But you can also profit from studying with someone who is on your own level of ability. As the two of you work together, solving problems and doping out formulas, you can pound the knowledge firmly into your brain. All teachers know that you learn best what you have to explain to someone else. Plus, a study-buddy probably can explain what he or she knows in a different way. If the teacher's explanation didn't do it for you, your friend's may.

- **Resurrect your Algebra II book or borrow one from a friendly math teacher.** Look through the chapters that made you tear your hair out the first time you went through the book. Refresh your memory with a sample problem or two.

- **Look through *The SAT I For Dummies*, 6th Edition.** Read the explanations of each type of question. Be sure that you know the directions and format cold.

- **Take one of the practice exams in Part V of this book.** After you know which sort of question is likely to stump you, do all the relevant practice questions.

- **Take the PSAT/NMSQT.** You can't pass up a chance to experience the exam in its native habitat (a testing center), even if the test is shorter than the real SAT.

If you follow this plan, you Golden Meaners should be in fine shape for the SAT. (I refer to the ancient Greek ideal, the Golden Mean, also known as the perfect middle. If this expression makes you say, "It's all Greek to me," you may want to read some Greek mythology. References to those stories show up all the time in the SAT.)

Controlling the Panic: A Short-Range Plan

The SAT is next month or (gulp!) next week. Not ideal, but not hopeless either. Use the following plan to get you through alive:

- **Read Chapter 1 of this book carefully.** Find out what sort of questions are on the exam and when guessing is a good idea. Take a quick look at the chapters that explain each type of question.

- **Do one practice exam from Part V.** Devote a whole 3½ hours to this task, even if you have to let something else slide.

- **Work on at least some of the practice questions for all your trouble spots.** Obviously, the more practice the better, but even a little can go a long way in SAT prep.

- **Clear the deck of all unnecessary activity so you can study as much as possible.** I don't recommend that you skip your sister's wedding (or your physics homework), but if you can put something off, do so. Use the extra time to hit a few more practice questions.

I teach seniors, and every year I see at least a couple of students put themselves in danger of failing English 12 because they're spending all their homework time on SAT prep. Bad idea. Yes, you want to send good scores to the colleges of your choice, but you also want to send a decent high school transcript. Prepare for the test, but do your homework too.

Should you take an SAT prep course?

SAT prep courses

(A) don't make a huge difference in your score

(B) employ Ivy League graduates who are paying off college loans until their film deals come through

(C) provide jobs for unemployed doctoral candidates finishing dissertations on the sex life of bacteria

(D) keep underpaid high school teachers from total *penury* (poverty)

(E) are great places to pick up prom dates

Answer: All of the above. I won't explain (B) through (E), because unless you're desperate for a prom partner,

you're probably interested only in (A). The company that makes the SAT has studied the effects of SAT prep courses and found that in general they have a minimal effect on your score — about 10 points for verbal and 15 to 20 points for math. A few long-term courses do make a slightly bigger difference (25–40 points combined verbal and math), but because you have to devote 40+ hours to them, you get approximately one extra point per hour of study. Not a very efficient use of your time! You've already proved your brilliance by purchasing *The SAT I For Dummies*, 6th Edition. If you work your way through the book with some care, you've done enough.

Snoozing through the Night Before

No matter what, don't study on SAT-day minus one. The only thing that last-minute studying does is make you more nervous. What happens is simple: The closer you get to test day, the more you take notice of the stuff you don't know. On the eve of the test, every unfamiliar vocabulary word is outlined in neon, as is every *obscure* (not well known, hidden) math formula. And every time you find something that you didn't know — or forget something that you did know at one time — your heart beats a little faster. Panic doesn't equal a good night's sleep, and eight solid hours of snoozing is the best possible prep for three plus hours of multiple-choice questions.

Also, resist the urge to call your friends who are also taking the test. Chances are they're nervous. The old saying, "Misery loves company," definitely applies to the SAT. Instead, place everything you need on The Morning in one spot, ready and waiting for use. Lay out some comfortable clothes, preferably layers. If the test room is too cold, you want to be able to add a sweater. If it's too hot, you may find removing a jacket or sweater helpful without getting arrested for indecent exposure.

After you set up everything for SAT-day, do something that's fun . . . but not too much fun. Don't hit the clubs or party down with your friends. Find an activity that eases you through the last couple of pre-SAT waking hours. Go to sleep at a reasonable hour (alarm clock set) and dream of little, penciled ovals patting you gently on the shoulder.

Getting there is half the fun

On the morning of the SAT, what should you avoid more than anything?

(A) a relaxing session of your favorite cartoons

(B) a two-hour detour on the road to the test center

(C) a kiss from Grandma

(D) a slurp from your dog

(E) a swim with your pet goldfish

Answer: (B). Did you ever watch an old sitcom on television, one with a pregnancy plot line? Inevitably the mad dash to the hospital is lengthened by a detour, a traffic jam, or a wrong turn. On SAT-day, you *don't* want to be in that old sitcom. Make sure that your journey to the test center is event-free. Try the route there at least once before test day, preferably at the same time and on the same day of the week (that is, Saturday morning, unless you're taking the test on Sunday because of religious observances) so you know what sort of traffic to expect. Leave the house with plenty of time to spare. The idea is to arrive rested and as relaxed as someone who is facing 200+ minutes of test can be.

Sailing through SAT-Day Morning

SAT-day isn't a good time to oversleep. Set the alarm clock and ask a reliable parent/guardian/ friend to verify that you've awakened on time. If you're not a morning person, you may need a few additional minutes. Then, no matter how nutritionally challenged your usual breakfast is, break out of the box and eat something healthful. Unless it upsets your stomach, go for protein (eggs, cheese, meat, tofu, and so on). Stay away from sugary items (cereals made primarily from Red Dye No. 23, corn syrup, and the like) because sugar gives you a surge of energy and then a large chunk of fatigue. If you think you'll be hungry during the morning, throw some trail mix, fruit, or other non-candy snacks into your backpack. Then hit the road for the test center.

If disaster strikes — fever, car trouble, little brother's arrest — and you can't take the SAT on the appointed day, call the College Board and request that they transfer your fee to the next available date.

Bringing the right stuff

Be sure to have these items with you:

- ✔ **Admission ticket for the SAT:** Don't leave home without it! You can't get in just by swearing that you "have one, at home, on top of the TV."

- ✔ **Photo identification:** The SAT accepts drivers' licenses, school IDs, passports, or other official documents that include your picture. The SAT doesn't accept Social Security cards or library cards. If you're not sure, ask your school counselor or call the SAT directly.

- ✔ **No. 2 pencils:** Don't guess. Look for the No. 2 on the side of the pencil. Take at least three or four sharpened pencils with you. Be sure the pencils have usable erasers or bring one of those cute pink rubber erasers you used in elementary school.

- ✔ **Calculator:** Bringing a calculator is optional. You don't absolutely *need* a calculator to take the SAT, but it does help on some questions. A four-function, scientific, or graph- ing calculator is acceptable. Anything with a keyboard (a mini-computer, in other words) or a handheld PDA (personal digital assistant) is barred. So is any device that needs to be plugged in or that makes noise. If you're the type of person who wears both sus- penders *and* a belt, just in case one fails, bring a back-up calculator and extra batteries.

- ✔ **Handkerchief or tissue:** I add this one because as an experienced proctor, I know that absolutely nothing is more annoying that a continuous drip or sniffle. Blow your nose and do the rest of the room — and yourself — a favor!

- ✔ **Watch:** In case the wall clock is missing, broken, or out of your line of vision, a watch is crucial. Don't bring one that beeps, because the proctor may take it away if it disturbs other test-takers.

After you arrive at the test center, take out what you need and stow the rest of the stuff in a backpack under your seat. Don't forget to turn off your cell phone or beeper, if you have one.

The test proctor doesn't allow scrap paper, books, and other school supplies (rulers, com- passes, highlighters, and so on) in the test room, so be sure to leave these items behind. Also, no iPods or other musical devices. You have to swing along to the tune inside your head.

Handling test tension

Unless you resemble Data, the emotionless android from the *StarTrek* television series (the one with the bald captain), you're probably nervous when you arrive at the test center. Try a couple of stretches and head shakes to *dispel* (chase away) tension. During the exam, wriggle your feet and move your shoulders up and down whenever you feel yourself tightening up. Some people like neck rolls (pretend that your neck is made of spaghetti and let your head droop in a big circle). If you roll your neck or move your head to either side, however, be sure to close your eyes. Don't risk a charge of cheating. Just like an Olympic diver preparing to go off of the board, take a few deep breaths before you begin the test and anytime during the test when you feel nervous or out-of-control.

You get one break per hour, which you probably want to spend in the bathroom or out in the hallway near the test room. During breaks, *stay away* from your fellow test victims, including your best friend. You don't want to hear someone else's version of the right answer. ("Everything in section two was a (B)! I got negative twelve for that one! You didn't? Uh oh.") If you like pain, allow yourself to talk over the test with your friends *after* the whole thing's over — great SAT-day night date talk, if you never want to see your partner again. After you finish the exam, you can obsess about wrong answers until the cows come home. (Where do cows go? To the mall? To the office? I'm from New York City, so the only cows I see are pictures on milk cartons.)

Starting off

The test proctor distributes the booklets with, I always think, a *vindictive* thump. (*Vindictive* means "seeking revenge," the sort of attitude that says, "Ha, ha! You're taking this awful test and I'm not! Serves you right!") Before you get to the actual questions, the proctor instructs you how to fill in the top of the answer sheet with your name, date of birth, Social Security number, registration number, and so forth. Your admission ticket has the necessary information. You also have to copy some numbers from your test booklet onto the answer sheet. You must grid in all those numbers and letters. Filling the bubbles with pencil is such a fun way to spend a weekend morning, don't you think?

Don't open the test booklet early. Big no-no! You'll be sent home with a large "C" (for Cheater) engraved on your forehead. Just kidding about the forehead, but *not* kidding about the sent home part. The proctor can can (no, not can-can) you for starting early, working after time is called, or looking at the wrong section.

The proctor announces each section and tells you when to start and stop. The proctor probably uses the wall clock or his/her own wristwatch to time you. When the proctor says that you're starting at 9:08 and finishing at 9:33, take a moment to glance at the watch you brought. If you have a different time, reset your watch. Marching to a different drummer may be fun, but not during the SAT. You want to be on the same page and in the same time warp as the proctor.

Focusing during the test

Keep your eyes on your own paper, except for quick glimpses of your watch. No, I'm not just saying so because cheating is bad and you'll get busted. Keeping your eyes where they belong is a way to concentrate on the task at hand. If you glance around the room, I guarantee you'll see someone who has already finished, even if only three nanoseconds have elapsed since the section began. You'll panic: *Why is he finished and I'm only on question two? He'll get into Harvard and I won't!* You don't need this kind of idea rattling around in your head when you should be analyzing the author's tone in passage three.

If your eye wants to run around sending signals to your brain like "I glimpsed number fifteen and it looks hard," create a window of concentration. Place your hand over the questions you've already done and your answer sheet over the questions you haven't gotten to yet. Keep only one or two questions in eye-range. As you work, move your hand and the answer sheet, exposing only one or two questions at a time.

You aren't allowed to use scrap paper, but you *are* allowed to write all over the test booklet. If you eliminate a choice, put an X through it. If you think you've got two possible answers but aren't sure which is best, circle the ones you're considering. Then you can return to the question and take a guess. (See Chapter 1 for a full explanation of when to guess and when to skip.)

I had an uncle who always buttoned his sweater so that he had two extra buttonholes left at the bottom. As you grid in your answers, avoid ending up like my uncle. When you choose an answer, say (to yourself), "The answer to number 12 is (B)." Look at the answer sheet and be sure you're on line 12, coloring in the little (B). Some people like to answer three questions at a time, writing the answers in the test booklet and *then* transferring them to the answer sheet. Not a bad idea! The answer sheet has alternating stripes of shaded and nonshaded ovals, three questions per stripe. The color helps you ensure that you're putting your answers in the correct spot. Take care not to run out of time, however. Nothing from your test booklet counts; only the answers you grid in add to your score.

Pacing yourself

The SAT-makers do all kinds of fancy statistical calculations to see which questions fool most of the people, most of the time, and which are the equivalent of "How many points are awarded for a three-point field goal?" (That was an actual question on an athlete's final exam in one college, no kidding. Needless to say the athlete was considered a top prospect for the school's basketball team.) After the test-makers know which questions are easy, medium, and hard, they place them more or less in that order on the exam (except on the reading comprehension passages). What this means is that as you move through a particular section, you may find yourself feeling more and more challenged. What this also means is that you should be sure to answer (and grid in) everything from the beginning of a section. As you approach the end, don't worry so much about skipping questions. You get the same amount of credit (one point) for each right answer from the "easy" portion of the test as you do for a correct response in the "hard" section.

When you talk about easy and hard, one size doesn't fit all. A question that stumps 98 percent of the test-takers may be a no-brainer for you. So look at everything carefully. Don't assume that you can't answer a question at the end of a section; nor should you assume that you know everything in the beginning.

Part II
Reading Critically

The 5th Wave
By Rich Tennant

Brad felt foolish letting a fly on the wall distract him from his SAT.

In this part . . .

The SAT Critical Reading section isn't the place for you to comment, "Paragraph two is a bit boring. A little dialogue would spice it up." Instead, it's a spot for you to show that you have the ability to comprehend college-level prose. Not that the exam actually fulfills its goal, mind you, but it does measure your ability to register facts, make inferences, and pick up *nuances* (subtleties) of tone and style.

Part II helps you sail through the SAT sea of *verbiage* (a mess of words with only a little content). Chapter 3 describes each type of question you have to answer and provides some helpful hints for passages from each area the SAT addresses — social and natural sciences, humanities, and literary fiction. Chapter 4 analyzes the types of questions that follow long and short passages so you know instantly how to identify the best answer. Chapters 5 and 6 give you practice passages, while Chapters 7 and 8 address Sentence Completions.

Chapter 3

Reading Between (and on) the Lines: Preparing for the Critical Reading Section

In This Chapter

▶ Knowing what to look for in natural and social science, humanities, and literary fiction passages

▶ Prioritizing the questions

▶ Passing over the questions you don't know

▶ Increasing your reading speed

▶ Scoping out the basis of Sentence Completion questions

Two seconds after Ugh the Cave Dweller first carved some words on a rock wall, a prehistoric teacher-type asked, "What does 'Mastodon eat you' imply?" and the critical reading exam was born. Okay, maybe it wasn't Ugh, and maybe the prehistoric teacher-type went for vocabulary ("What is a 'mastodon'?") instead. But guaranteed, somebody asked something, because teacher-types have been around forever and they can't resist comprehension tests.

And comprehension is the name of the game, or at least the version of the reading game that the SAT plays. Critical Reading, which replaced Verbal on the old SAT I, now includes Sentence Completions and short and long passages. In this chapter, I help you polish some reading skills that can help you get through all the questions with flying colors. I also show you how to read faster and how to zero in on the questions you're more likely to answer correctly.

Getting Acquainted with Critical Reading Passages

In their definitely-not-infinite wisdom, the SAT test-devils have determined that 70 minutes of highly artificial reading tells colleges how equipped you are to plow through 50 or 60 pounds of textbooks each semester. They throw three sorts of questions at you, generally in three sections, though you may have four if you've been chosen for a reading *equating* section. (An equating section is the SAT-makers' chance to try out new questions. In other words, you're working for them when you do an equating section, even though you pay a test fee instead of receiving a paycheck. How unfair.) Here are the big three types of questions:

✔ Long passages (700–800 words)

✔ Short passages (100 words or so)

✔ Sentence Completions

The long and short passages are followed by questions about the passage's main idea, the author's tone and attitude, the passage's facts, the meaning of certain words, and the implications of various statements. In the Sentence Completions, you take the best word and shove it . . . into the sentence.

The SAT attempts to mimic reading that you'll actually face in college, though I personally have never had a course that required me to read random bits of information on a topic I've never seen before, don't care about, and will never see again. (Oh wait. I *have* had courses like that.) Because students of all majors take the SAT, the passages come from all areas of learning, with the exception of mathematics, which gets its very own section on the SAT.

Regardless of length, the SAT Critical Reading questions that are based on passages tend to fall into only a few categories, each with its special traps (and trapdoors). In this section I take (okay, drag) you through each one.

Investigating science passages

Don't expect a page torn from a physics textbook. (Though having taken physics, I can certainly understand the impulse to tear up the textbook. On the other hand, one of the best science students I ever taught took great delight in shredding a Jane Austen novel, page by page, as he read it. There's no accounting for taste, as the saying goes.) The science passages on the SAT Reasoning Test aren't imparting facts. True, they contain facts, but instead of simply explaining a biological process or an era of geological activity, the Critical Reading science passages frequently present an argument or theory about some aspect of science. Or, the passages discuss the implications of scientific phenomena.

This design originates from the SAT's goal, which is supposed to measure reasoning, not fact acquisition. So the test-devils have to give you something to reason *about*. Instead of textbooks, the passages resemble the sort of book you may read when you're writing a term paper on global warming, cloning, or another issue that draws controversy or discussion. (But not too much controversy. The SAT-makers get yelled at for so many things that they are reluctant to add ammunition to their critics' arsenal. In terms of political correctness, the SAT plays it safe.)

When you're attacking a science passage, try these tactics:

- ✔ **Look carefully for the author's stance.** If the passage is about space travel, figure out what the author is *advocating* (making a case for). Science passage questions often ask about the author's point of view.

- ✔ **Don't worry about technical vocabulary.** If the SAT uses a tough word, the definition probably is tucked into the sentence, as in *The rise of flibbertigistics, the study of uncontrollable nose movement, is attributed to an increase in the use of chili sauce.* You don't have to know what *flibbertigistics* means because the sentence tells you that it has to do with twitchy noses.

- ✔ **Identify the argument.** Many science passages present a dispute between two viewpoints. The passage may make a case for the theory that dinosaurs died out because a meteor crashed into the earth and then give an alternative explanation, such as the idea that the giant, pea-brained animals chose to become extinct rather than face the SAT. The SAT questions may zero in on the evidence for each theory or make you decide which one the author likes best.

- ✔ **Notice the examples.** The SAT science passages are chock-full of examples. The questions may require you to figure out what the examples prove.

The best thing about science passages is that they're accessible even to the kind of student who plans to take *Biology for Poets.* If you're a science fan, of course, you're in even better shape.

Poring over social science passages

In 1589 some group did something that no one cares about and that has no importance whatsoever and that is now the subject of an unbelievably boring article. Is that your view of social science? If so, the SAT is unlikely to change your mind. The SAT may permanently *derange* (disturb the workings of) your mind, but you'll still think that social science is boring, if that's your starting point. If you like the social sciences (anthropology, sociology, education, cultural studies, and so on), you may find the SAT passages interesting. As you plow through the history/social science SAT Critical Reading passages, take heed of these points:

✔ **Tune your mind to 21st century ideas and sensibilities.** In the past, critics have hit the SAT for orienting too much material toward white males, and wealthy ones at that. Questions like *The commandant's yacht moored at the country club's private pier because . . .* have disappeared from the SAT, if in fact they ever did appear. (Big argument going on over that one, but you don't have to worry about it. You just have to take the test.) Now the SAT has bent over backward to include material about people of color, women, and the economically disadvantaged (though I haven't seen much about teachers, who certainly fall into that category). Expect to see some social science passages about these groups. Also expect to see a point of view that *debunks* (disproves) an old, white-male centered theory, such as the one that names Columbus as the discoverer of America. (It turns out there was a *veritable* [for real] traffic jam on the Atlantic and Pacific oceans way before Columbus set sail. All sorts of people — Vikings, ancient Chinese, and others — got to America before old Chris.)

✔ **Go for the positive.** In addition to an increased sensitivity to gender, race, economic level, and the like, the test-makers play safe in other ways. The SAT doesn't criticize anyone with the power to (1) sue or (2) contact the media. So if you see a question about the author's tone or viewpoint, look for a positive answer unless the passage is about war criminals or another crew unlikely to be met with public sympathy.

✔ **Take note of the structure.** The social science passages frequently present a theory and support it with sets of facts or quotations from experts. Look for this structure and keep it in mind when you're asked the significance of a detail. The detail is probably evidence in the case that the author is making.

✔ **Look for opposing ideas.** Experts like to argue, and human nature — the ultimate subject of social science passages — provides plenty of arguable material. Many SAT passages present two viewpoints, in the paired passages and elsewhere. Look for the opposing sides, or identify the main theory and the objections to it.

This short tour through the wonderful world of social science passages gives you just a taste. Take a peek at the sample questions in Chapter 5 for a full meal.

Hovering over humanities passages

The term *humanities* always makes me laugh. Where do they think science and math come from — artichokes? Human beings are the subject of humanities passages, specifically art history, history, literature and the arts, culture, and language. (No, not the dreaded irregular verbs that you poured over in Spanish class, but the theory of language.) If you face a humanities passage on the SAT, think about these points:

✔ **Think positive.** For reasons described in the section "Poring over social science passages," the SAT has an interest in highlighting groups that have traditionally been ignored by the school curriculum (to say nothing of politicians handing out tax breaks). If you see a passage about a woman artist, a Native American language, or the like, search for a positive answer to questions about their significance.

✔ **Notice the details.** Humanities passages often contain a great deal of description, as in *the sculpture is carved from solid maple and displayed on a base of pancakes.* No detail is unimportant. The questions attached to the passage may not ask you about the pancakes directly, but you may be queried about the artist's attitude toward digestion or organic flour. Don't let your attention wander; take note of the small stuff.

✔ **Stay attuned to word choice.** You may encounter a *memoir* (someone's memories, written from a personal point of view). Memoirs are perfectly suited to questions about the author's tone (bitter, nostalgic, fond, critical, and so forth). Pay attention to *connotation* — not the definition but the feeling of a word. For example, *slender* isn't the same as *skinny*. Connotation clues matter a lot in memoir passages.

✔ **Keep the big picture in mind.** Humanities questions frequently single out one example and ask you to explain the context or significance. Think about the big picture when you get one of these questions. How does the detail fit in? That's what you're really trying to determine. (For more information on this type of question, check out Chapter 4.)

Of course I'm an English teacher and thus prejudiced in favor of the humanities, but I find these passages easier to get through than the science selections. But even if you're not a fan of the humanities, you can handle these passages if you keep these points in mind.

Reading literary fiction

Literary fiction is defined as anything an English teacher says is worth the trouble to read and discuss. To put it another way, with very few exceptions literary fiction sells far fewer copies than the books on the bestseller list. SAT literary fiction is rare (you're more likely to encounter memoirs), but it does show up occasionally. Follow these points to a higher score:

✔ **Forget about plot.** Plot isn't important in fiction passages because in 750 words, not much can happen. Concentrate on identifying scene, character traits, tone, point of view, and symbols.

✔ **Think metaphorically.** Everything is in the passage for a reason, and never more so than in literary fiction. If line 5 says that the banana was rotten, you can bet that's a metaphor for society or that the author will use the rotten banana to show a character's unreasonable fear of cylindrical fruit.

✔ **Listen to a literary passage.** Of course, you can't make any noise while taking the SAT, but you can let the little voice in your head read expressively, as if you were acting it out. Chances are you can pick up some information from your mental reenactment that you can use when answering the questions.

✔ **Cut your losses if you're lost.** Literary passages are the *mavericks* (the loners) of the SAT world. They can be about anything and in any style. If you start to read one and feel totally lost, skip it and go back later, time permitting.

Literary passages are sometimes one of a pair of readings on the same topic. To find out more about these terrible twins, read the following section "Doubling your trouble."

Doubling your trouble

Every SAT contains at least one set of paired passages. You may find a firsthand account of an immigrant's life and one by a historian who has studied immigration and its effect on the economy. Or a slice of a scientist's biography may be matched with an explanation of the significance of her discovery. Each passage is rather short; the two together may reach 850 words. When you're facing double trouble, keep these ideas in mind:

- ✔ **Watch for differences.** Remember that changing authors means changing — slightly or greatly — the point of view, bias, and tone.

- ✔ **Take it easy.** Some of the questions refer to the first passage and some to the second. A handful asks you to compare passages or to find common aspects of both. Do the easy questions for each passage and then go back to the harder questions.

Chapter 4 goes into more detail on the specific reading comprehension skills needed for all the SAT passages, including the pairs.

Following the Order of Difficulty

Unlike the Sentence Completion questions, which the SAT test-making demons place in order of difficulty (from easy for the first couple questions to more difficult), the long and short reading passage questions don't move from easy to hard. The order of the questions attached to the passages relates to the passage itself. Question 1 may ask about lines 12–14, question 2 about lines 24–28, and so forth. Questions about the entire passage (the author's attitude or tone, main idea, and so forth) may be anywhere but are often at the beginning or at the end of the set.

This characteristic of the SAT means that the SAT *isn't* the most annoying reading test ever constructed. That honor belongs to the kind of reading test that measures memory. Need a little extra explanation? Some reading tests throw around a thousand facts about, say, antelopes and then come up with a question like this one:

Antelopes have

(A) long ears

(B) short ears

(C) hearing aids

(D) good sign language

(E) bandanas

Faced with this question, you have to first reread the whole thing, or second try to remember which paragraph discussed antelope ears. Instead of measuring comprehension, this question checks your ability to keep an outline in your head. Now *that's* annoying. The SAT, on the other hand, asks this sort of question:

In lines 25–30, the author indicates that antelope ears are

(A) long

(B) short

(C) assisted by hearing aids

(D) irrelevant because the antelopes have developed good sign language

(E) wearing stylish bandanas

Notice how the memory factor is absent? You're directed to lines 25–30 (and the lines in SAT passages are conveniently numbered by fives) for the answer. All you have to do is retrieve it.

Skipping When You're at the End of Your Rope

Because the questions referring to the SAT Critical Reading passages aren't in order of difficulty, you need to make some quick decisions about what to do and what to skip, particularly as you get to the end of the time allotted. In general, follow these steps:

1. **Answer the factual questions.**

2. **Go to vocabulary in context, the *in line 18 "flubbermub" means* type of question.**

3. **Start with the questions that ask you to interpret the author's tone or purpose. If anything is unclear, skip it.**

4. **If the test-making demons ask main idea, relation between paragraphs, and inference questions, do those that seem obvious to you and skip the rest. Go back if you have time for the tough ones.**

5. **In paired passages, answer all the passage one questions that you know immediately and then all the passage two questions that you can ace with no trouble. Then hit the shared passage queries.**

No matter which questions you answer first, remember one important rule: You get as many points for a correct answer to an easy question as you do for a correct answer to a hard question. I know, it's not fair. But then again this is the SAT. Fairness *isn't* part of the deal. Also, remember that you get no points for a skipped question, but you *lose* a quarter point for a wrong answer. Don't guess wildly. (For a detailed explanation of scoring, see Chapter 1.)

Making a Long Story Short: Reading Quickly

When I was in high school, my health teacher — just out of college and not much older than the students she was teaching — was afraid to assign the sex-education chapter of the text-book. Maybe she feared angry calls from the PTA or maybe she just didn't want to face the two-dozen sets of teenage giggles. So she dropped the birds and the bees and instead taught us how to speed-read. I was annoyed at the time (After all, who's not interested in sex?), but reading fast does come in handy, especially in pressured situations like the SAT.

You don't have to set your sights on becoming a Kentucky Derby winner, but if you plow through paragraphs at a turtle's pace, a few simple tricks may make a big difference in how many questions you have a chance to answer and thus how high you score.

A few SAT prep courses advise you to save time by reading only bits of the Reading Compre-hension passages. Bad idea, in my humble opinion. At least some of the questions on the SAT Critical Reading ask you to assess the entire piece, pinpointing the author's tone or overall point of view. If time is a problem, work on reading faster, not on reading less.

To increase your reading speed, try these techniques:

✔ **Wind sprint.** If you're a track star, you run a lot at a steady pace, but occasionally you let out all the stops and go as fast as possible for a short period of time. When you're reading, imitate the runners. Read at a steady pace, but from time to time push yourself through a paragraph as fast as you possibly can. After a couple of minutes, go back to your normal reading speed. Soon your "normal" speed will increase.

✔ **Read newspaper columns.** When you read, your eye moves from side to side. But you have *peripheral* (on the edge) vision that makes some of those eye movements unneces-sary. To practice moving your eyes less (and thus speeding up your progress), read a narrow newspaper column. Try to see the entire column-width without moving your eyes sideways. If you practice a couple of times, you can train your eye to grasp the edges as well as the center. Bingo! Your speed will increase.

✔ **Finger focus.** If you're reading something wider than a newspaper column, you can still reap gains from the peripheral-vision training described in the preceding bullet point. Just place your finger underneath the line you're reading, about a third of the way in. Read the first half of the line in one, stationary glance. Then move your finger to about two thirds of the way across. Take in the second half of the line in just one more glance. There you go! Your eyes are moving less, you're staying focused, and you're reading faster.

✔ **Hit the high spots.** People who make a living analyzing such things (and can you imagine a more boring career?) have determined that nearly all paragraphs start with a topic sen-tence. If you want to get a quick overview of a passage, read the topic sentence of each paragraph *slowly*. Then go back and zoom through the details quickly. Chances are you can get everything you need.

Understanding Sentencing Guidelines

The Sentence Completions don't add a whole lot of enjoyment to your SAT-day, but they don't break your head open either. The Sentence Completion questions rely on the human ability to construct a bridge when faced with a smallish gap between two ideas. If the gap is the size of the Grand Canyon, no bridge will *suffice* (that's "meet the requirements" to normal people who haven't memorized the dictionary). Here's what I mean:

GRAND CANYON GAP: Ms. Slurb _____ when her ice cream fell.

WHY IT'S A GRAND CANYON GAP: She may have *cheered* because she was on a diet and morbidly afraid of the calories in the ice cream, even as she *succumbed* (gave in) to temp-tation. Or, she may have *groaned* when her ice cream fell because she had spent the last three hours ignoring her boyfriend as she searched for a scoop of butter pecan. You really can't tell, given the information in the sentence.

SMALLISH GAP: Desperate for a sugar fix, Ms. Slurb _____ when her ice cream fell.

WHY IT'S A SMALLISH GAP: Given the *sugar fix* statement, you can easily figure out that *groaned* is the answer.

Some SAT Sentence Completions contain two blanks instead of one, but regardless of number, they all require you to make a logical leap over a smallish gap, with the help of word clues in the sentence and common sense. In Chapter 8 I go into detail about how to ace the Sentence Completion section.

The *mis*-ing link

Adding the "mis" family to your vocabulary is a sure-fire way to score higher on the SAT. Do you sometimes make a *mis*take and *mis*behave in front of the *mis*anthropic teacher who has a long, thick ruler and isn't afraid to use it because she totally hates people? Don't *mis*construe (misunderstand) my meaning: I'm not that sort of teacher. I do, however, *mis*manage my time, especially when I've been out partying when I should be home marking essays.

Welcome to the *mis* family, known for its *bad* manners and *wrong* ways. When you *mis*take, you take something wrong. When you *mis*behave, you behave badly. Here are a few more relatives in the *mis* family:

✔ *Misalign:* To deviate from the straight, or aligned course. A walk down a bumpy path illustrates what happens when the construction crew runs late and misaligns the paving stones.

✔ *Misanthropes:* People who think people are basically bad. Picture a hermit on top of an alp, hiding in a cave. (*Misanthropic* is the adjective.)

✔ *Misconstrue:* A twin of misapprehend, as in *Hard-of-hearing Horatio misapprehended the command to blow his horn and instead saluted the captain by sewing a thorn.*

✔ *Misnomer:* A wrong term, or wrong name, as in *Calling him "Honest Abe" is a misnomer, given that he has been arrested 569 times.*

✔ *Misogynist:* Rounds out the I-hate-you category. A misogynist is someone who thinks women are bad and (in my experience) does everything possible to show it.

Chapter 4

The Long and the Short of It: Answering Critical Reading Passage Questions

In This Chapter

▶ Decoding Critical Reading passage questions

▶ Honing techniques for each type of Critical Reading question

▶ Creating a strategy that suits your reading style

*W*hether your agony lasts a minute (100-word passages), a little longer (750-word passages), or a lot longer (the paired passages), you *can* crack the SAT Critical Reading section. Half the battle is figuring out what the SAT-writers actually want to know, so in this chapter I translate some common jargon from SAT-speak to regular English. I also show you the best way to attack each type of SAT Critical Reading question. Finally, I show you how to rely on your strengths and how to minimize your shortcomings as you work your way through the passages.

Hiding in Plain Sight: SAT Question Jargon

SAT-style questions tend to repeat a few basic patterns, and if you make friends with those patterns now, you can do better on SAT-day. The following list is a sampler of the SAT's most common jargon, decoded:

> ✔ **According to the passage, all of these statements about the mushrooms are true except . . . :** You have to determine which one is false.

> ✔ **In line 14, *graberoo* means . . . :** Not in the universe you live in, but the definition in line 14.

> ✔ **The passage implies that . . . :** The passage has no statement giving this idea, but the passage leads you to believe that the idea is true.

> ✔ **Which statement is supported by the examples in paragraph two (lines 15–22)?:** If you're a trial attorney, what case are you making with the evidence in paragraph two?

> ✔ **The anecdote about the bubblegum (lines 45–48) suggests that . . . :** Why is the author talking about bubblegum? Probably not because he or she is desperate to chew. Think analogy or symbol.

> ✔ **Which statement best describes the relationship between Glog's Theory of Cocktail Stirring and Beldok's Olive Intensity Scale?** Compare these two crackpots and find an answer that expresses their similarity or difference.

> ✔ **The author's tone can best be described as . . . :** Does the author bellyache, praise, sigh, weep, or shout? What mood do the words reflect?

> ✔ **The main idea of the passage is . . . :** What title would you give this thing?
>
> ✔ **Lines 8–15 chiefly concern . . . :** What title would you give to lines 8–15? Or, what's the most important idea in lines 8–15?
>
> ✔ **Lines 8–15 chiefly support the idea that . . . :** Why did the author put those lines in, other than to insure a royalty check? What purpose do they serve?
>
> ✔ **The primary purpose of this passage is . . . :** No, not to take up space and torment you. Why is the author writing this passage — to convince you of a point of view, to warn you, to explain something, to defend something, to debunk or criticize something? You choose.

I know SAT jargon sometimes seems like a foreign language. When normal people want to know, say, what fly eyes are like, they ask, "What are fly eyes like?" The SAT-makers aren't normal. They say something like the following:

According to the passage, all of these statements about fly eyes are true EXCEPT:

(A) Fly eyes are exceptionally well suited to flirting.

(B) Fly eyes go nicely with sky blue sweaters.

(C) There are too many eyes on the average fly head.

(D) Mascara is *not* a good idea.

(E) Most flies are very vain about their eyes and consult a plastic surgeon at the first sign of drooping.

No, I'm not going to try to answer the question, for fairly obvious reasons. I'm just pointing out that before you can decide the fly-eye issue, you have to decode some SAT jargon. The SAT-makers are telling you that four statements are true and one is false, and you have to select the false one. Needless to say, regular human interactions seldom ask you to identify lies, unless you're in a singles bar or checking late passes at school detention.

Now that you know a little about Critical Reading passages, continue reading to discover some tactics to give the little SAT-demons exactly what they want.

Taming the Wild Reading-Passage Question

When you enter Critical Reading Passage World, take weapons. Not whips and machine guns, but logic and comprehension skills. This section shows you how to tame the wild SAT reading question, whether it's attached to long or short passages.

Factually speaking

Real-world knowledge never hurts, but the SAT Critical Reading questions never require you to know anything beyond what is in the passage. So even though you once blew up the chemistry lab, don't panic if you're facing a passage about toxic waste. Everything you need to know is right there; you don't need any extra chemistry (unless you're bonding with a really cute proctor).

Never skip a fact-based question because they're almost impossible to get wrong. The test-demons even refer you politely to the proper line in the passage so you can go directly to the answer you desire.

SAT fact questions *do* have a couple of traps built in. Sometimes the test-writers word the passage in a confusing way. Decoding the meaning successfully depends upon picking up the word clues embedded in the passage. You may want to memorize these words so that they're in neon lights in your brain. Here are a few of the SAT's favorite little words:

- ✔ **Except, but, not, in contrast to, otherwise, although, even though, despite, in spite of:** These words indicate contrast, identifying something that doesn't fit the pattern.

- ✔ **And, also, in addition to, as well as, moreover, furthermore, not only . . . but also, likewise, not the only:** When you see these clue words, you're probably looking for something that *does* fit the pattern.

- ✔ **Therefore, because, consequently, hence, thus, accordingly, as a result:** Now you're in cause-and-effect land.

- ✔ **Than, like, equally, similarly:** Time to compare two ideas, two quantities, two people, two actions . . . you get the idea.

- ✔ **Until, after, later, then, once, before, since, while, during, still, yet, earlier, finally, when:** You're watching the clock (or calendar). Think about the order of events when you see these clue words.

Time to pull out your secret decoder ring so you can attack this sample question, based on a nonexistent passage that I would actually love to read.

According to the passage, the distinction between "Mustard Yellow" (line 11) and "Hot Dog Pink" (line 55) is

(A) Picasso was extremely fond of hot dogs laced with mustard.

(B) Both colors are created with the same artificial chemicals.

(C) Mustard Yellow is found in nature, but Hot Dog Pink is found only in baseball stadiums.

(D) Neither color will ever reach the wall of the author's living room.

(E) Mustard Yellow belongs to the blue family.

Answer: (C).

Okay, I'm kidding in this question (What else is new?), but I actually tuck in a few real points about SAT fact questions. Notice that the question asks you to find a *distinction,* or difference. Right away you can rule out (B) and (D), because they state common characteristics. The sneaky SAT-demons play tricks on people who read the question too quickly. You can also rule out (A) because it doesn't mention either color. That choice represents another SAT habit; the test-writers throw in an answer that may be true according to the passage (which contained a whole section on Picasso's eating habits as they related to his color choices) but irrelevant in terms of the question. The test-demons are hoping you choose (A) because you remember the bit about Picasso's favorite snack, ignoring the fact that (A) doesn't address the color issue. (By the way, I made this up. For all I know Picasso was a vegetarian.) (E) may be okay if the passage emphasizes the color families and tells you that while Mustard Yellow can party down with the Blues, but Hot Dog Pink can't. The passage doesn't, so (C) is your best bet. This choice clearly states a *distinction,* which is what the question calls for.

Identifying word clues is especially crucial in the 100-word passages. Because they can't rely on lengthy discussions of boring ideas to trick you — or to put you to sleep, which amounts to the same thing — the test-writers choose little words to trip you up. If you see one of the words or phrases from the previous bulleted list, underline it and take it into account when you're choosing an answer.

Clue words show up in the questions too. Be *vigilant* (on your guard) when reading the questions, not just while perusing the reading passage itself.

Defining moments

Many SAT questions ask you to define a word as it's used in the sentence. Teacher-types like me call this exercise "vocabulary in context."

Never skip a vocabulary-in-context question because chances are the answer is right there in the sentence. And if it isn't right there, figuring it out is easy. Here's an example:

In line 12, "snoggled" means . . .

Perhaps you've never heard of "snoggled." Not surprising, because I made it up. But doesn't it sound like something the school nurse would warn you about? *Snoggling leads to uncontrolled movements of the eyebrows* . . . Even without a dictionary definition, you can figure out the meaning of the word because of its context. For example, look at the rest of the paragraph on the test:

> Overcome by passion the moment he snoggled her perfume, Oxford trailed Lympia pathetically around the house.

Okay, now you can clearly see that *snoggled* has something to do with sniffing, scenting, or otherwise catching a whiff of. If one of your choices is "smelled" or a synonym of "smelled," you're home free.

Vocabulary-in-context questions do contain one big sand trap. Many of these questions ask you for the definition of a word you probably know. But — and this is a big but — the passage may use the word in an odd or unusual way. And of course, one of the choices is usually the word's definition that you know, just sitting there waiting for the unwary test-taker to grab it. For example:

In line 55, the word *deck* means

(A) to hit so hard that the receiver of the blow falls over

(B) a floor of a ship

(C) the compartment at the rear of an automobile

(D) a wooden structure built onto the side of a house

(E) to adorn with decorations

If you selected (E), go to the head of the class, because line 55 was a lyric to a famous Christmas carol, "*Deck* the halls."

Bottom line: Always answer a vocabulary-in-context question, but never answer one without actually checking the context.

Decoding symbols and metaphors

Appearances often deceive on the SAT. The passage may contain one or more anecdotes or details that have a deeper meaning. The questions may resemble these:

✔ **In the second paragraph, the author compares his trip to Shea Stadium to a treasure hunt because . . . :**

✔ **The fly ball mentioned in line 8 symbolizes . . . :**

✔ **The long wait for hot dogs (line 12) primarily serves to illustrate . . . :**

The SAT-writers are checking whether or not you can grasp the Big Picture. For example, once when I was in high school (When? A brontosaurus lived down the block), the teacher compared voting rights to a set of milk bottles. If everyone's rights were respected, the milk bottle was full. If some people were *disenfranchised* (not allowed to vote), the milk bottle was only half full. In a dictatorship, the milk bottle was empty. As he blathered on about democracy and full milk bottles, one student's hand waved in the air. "Milk doesn't come in bottles anymore," she remarked. "It's all cartons now."

Clearly this student was missing the Big Picture. She was focusing on the detail, but she wasn't grasping what the teacher was trying to convey.

The best strategy for symbol/metaphor questions is to form a picture in your brain. Refer to the list of questions at the opening of this section and pretend that you're playing a videotape of the trip to Shea Stadium featuring the fly ball or the wait for a hot dog. Then ask yourself *why* the author wanted to place that picture in your brain. Perhaps the trip to Shea (on your internal videotape) is bathed in golden light and accompanied by mellow violins. The comparison to a treasure hunt may show you that the author was searching for his lost youth, which he found unexpectedly at a baseball game. Or, when you run the tape of the fly ball smacking into the author's forehead, complete with blood and cries of anguish, you may realize that the incident embodies the shock of his realization that baseball is no longer the idyllic sport he once played.

When faced with a symbol/metaphor question, try to experience the moment (but only for a moment, because time is short on the SAT) and feel its purpose.

Taking an attitude

An *attitude* in a reading passage goes way beyond the "don't take that attitude with me" mood that parents drop into with depressing regularity. In SAT jargon, an attitude is critical, objective, indifferent, and so forth. These clue words may pop up in the choices:

- ✔ **For:** pro, positive, in favor of, leaning toward, *laudatory* (that's "praising," to normal people), agreeable, *amenable* (willing to go along with), sympathetic

- ✔ **Against:** doubtful, offended, anti, resistant to, contrary to, counter to, *adversarial* (acting like an enemy), opposed, critical of, disgusted with

- ✔ **Neutral:** objective, indifferent, noncommittal, impartial, *apathetic* (not interested), unbiased, *ambivalent* (can't decide either way or has mixed feeling)

To answer an attitude question, first decide where the author lands — for, against, or neutral — in relation to the topic. Check for clue words or for other words expressing approval or disapproval.

Even in a dry-as-dust passage about the low water table in some country you've never heard of, the author has an attitude, and the SAT may ask you to identify it. Check out these questions:

- ✔ **The author's attitude toward the Water Minister's statement in line 88 can best be described as . . . :**

- ✔ **In response to the proposed law on Water Table Placemats, the author's comments are . . . :**

If you're looking for a positive answer in an attitude question, start by crossing out all the negative or neutral choices. In the preceding Water Table law question, for example, you can instantly dump *argumentative, condemning,* and similar words if you know that the author favors the law.

A variation of the attitude question asks you to identify the author's "tone." Some of the same clues mentioned in the preceding lists of "for," "against," and "neutral" words also help you out with this type of question. Tone questions include emotions. Check for irony, amusement, nostalgia, regret, and sarcasm.

For example

Quite a few SAT Critical Reading questions ask you to figure out why an author used a particular example:

- ✔ **The example of the fish scaler demonstrates that . . . :**
- ✔ **The author's statement that the fish smelled "putrid" (line 2) serves to . . . :**
- ✔ **The quotation from the hotel clerk about the choice of movies rented exemplifies . . . :**

The key to this sort of question is to get inside the writer's mind. "Why is that particular example in that particular place?" The example may be a small detail in a paragraph full of details. If so, decide what title you would give to the paragraph. Suppose that the fish scaler is in a paragraph describing kitchen tools. Depending upon the paragraph's contents, you may choose "Stuff in my kitchen that I never use" or "Stuff in my kitchen I can't do without" as a good title for the list. After you get the title, the answer choice should be obvious. The fish scaler example may lead you to a statement like "Many people buy kitchen utensils they never use" or "The proper tool makes any job easier."

Alternatively, the example may be one complete paragraph out of many in the passage. In that case, what title would you give this passage? Chances are the title can lead you to the correct response.

Covering all bases: The main idea

In reading terms, you probably find that the *main idea* questions on the SAT give you choices that fall into the too-broad, too-narrow, off-base, and just-right categories. A just-right choice includes all the supporting points and details in the passage, but isn't so broad as to be meaningless.

You frequently get at least one main idea question that applies to the entire passage. Think of the main idea as an umbrella protecting you from a driving rain as you walk down a street. If the umbrella is too large, the wind will blow you away. If it's too small, you'll get wet. You need one that fits perfectly. Imagine for a moment that you're trying to find a main idea for a list like the following: jelly, milk, waxed paper, light bulbs, and peaches. A main idea that fits is "things you can buy at the supermarket." One that is too broad is "stuff." A too-narrow choice is "food," because very few people like the taste of light bulbs, and everyone who does is locked up in a padded room somewhere. A completely off-base main idea might be "canned goods."

A variation on the main idea asks about a paragraph, not the passage as a whole. Use the same guidelines to choose the correct answer.

Making inferences

You make inferences every day. (An *inference* is a conclusion you reach based on evidence.) Perhaps you come home and your mother is chewing on the phone bill and throwing your bowling trophies out the window. Even though she hasn't stated the problem, you can guess that the call you made to the bowling team in Helsinki wasn't included in your basic monthly calling plan.

The SAT Critical Reading section has tons of that sort of inference. You get a certain amount of information and then have to stretch it a little. The questions may resemble these:

- What may be inferred from the author's statement that she is "allergic to homework" (line 66)?
- The author implies in line 12 that small stuffed animals . . .
- The author would probably agree with which of the following statements?

To crack an inference question, act like a Sherlock Holmes clone. You have a few clues. Perhaps, you have a set of statements about small stuffed animals: Very young kids tend to eat these little stuffed animals; unmarred stuffed animals fetch high prices on eBay; children seldom appreciate presents for more than a few moments after receiving them. You get the picture? Then ask yourself what sort of conclusion you may come to, given the evidence. Stretching the stuffed animal example, you may think that buying and selling stuffed animals for a profit is better than ignoring your little nephew's birthday. After you reach a conclusion, check the choices to see what matches.

If you're asked to infer, don't look for a statement that is actually in the passage. Inferences reside, by definition, between the lines. If the statement is in the passage, it's the wrong answer.

Deciding Which Comes First — the Question or the Answer: An SAT Dilemma

Every time I tutor for the SAT (and I tutor a lot), my students ask me whether they should read the passage first or the questions first. A variation of this query is whether to read the passages at all. (For the record: I don't recommend skipping the passage. Ever.) As to the other question, the decision should arise from your personal style. Are you good at keeping details in your head? If so, go for the read-the-question-first option. Don't read all the choices; just glance at the *tag line* (the beginning of the question) so you have a rough idea what the test-demons are focusing on.

If you feel that your head is filled with too many facts already, settle in with the passage before you look at the questions. Keep your pencil handy and circle anything that looks particularly important. Write a word next to each paragraph, summing up its main idea ("hot dog line," "argument for the designated hitter" and so on) Then hit the questions and locate the answers. Many students who have scored high on the SAT took marginal notes, so give it a try!

It's all Greek to me

The Greek myths have provided the English language with tons of words, some of which may show up on the SAT, often in Critical Reading passages. Check out the following examples:

🖌 ***Achilles heel:*** A weak or vulnerable spot, as in *Darth's Achilles heel is his affection for long, dark cloaks. He can resist any purchase but that.*

🖌 ***Herculean:*** Extraordinarily powerful, as in *With a herculean effort, Agnes picked up her SAT word list and began to memorize.*

🖌 ***Jovial:*** Jolly, as in *his jovial mood was not spoiled by the arrival of a bill for dues to the Optimists' Club.*

🖌 ***Mercurial:*** Having rapid mood changes, as in *Agnes' mercurial personality keeps her friends on their toes*

because they never know whether she will hug them or dump hog entrails on their heads.

🖌 ***Narcissistic:*** Referring to the kind of person who wears mirrored sunglasses inside out, the better to admire his or her own face, as in *Polly's narcissistic insistence on including every little incident of her life was responsible for her biography's 1000-page length.*

🖌 ***Odyssey:*** A long, eventful journey, derived from Odysseus' 20-year trip home from the Trojan War, as in *Peter's vacation, with a side trip through the Bermuda Triangle, was a real odyssey.*

But no matter whether you read the passage or question first, never skip the italicized introduction to a passage. Many SAT passages are preceded by a short italicized description along the lines of *This passage comes from the diary of a 16th century maniac* or *The author of this passage was locked in an SAT test site for fourteen days before being rescued.* The description orients you to the passage and may help you to decide the author's tone. For example, after being locked in an SAT exam room, the author probably isn't going to write a hymn of praise to your favorite test. The maniac reference alerts you to the fact that the narrator may be unreliable. You don't get a factual question based on the italicized introduction, but you may be sure that the SAT doesn't waste words, and whatever the test-writers say in italics is useful in some fashion.

Chapter 5

Reading for Points: Practicing Full-Length Critical Reading Passages

. . . .

In This Chapter

▶ Focusing on answering questions in single passages

▶ Taking a stab at paired passages

. . . .

My seventh grade teacher used to thump around the classroom yelling, "Read! Read! Read!" as she slapped a metal ruler on the desk and occasionally on the head of any inattentive student. Whenever I remember her, I think (a) these days she'd probably get sued for the ruler hits, and (b) she was right about the reading. The only way to become a better reader is to practice. And the only way to become a better SAT critical reader is to practice (Guess what!) Critical Reading passages.

In this chapter, I provide the raw material. You stir in the brainpower for a higher score.

When the reading is critical: A roadmap to a higher score

Just to hammer home the message, keep these points in mind when you're stuck in the Critical Reading section:

✔ Read the question carefully. Circle the clue words so you're sure that you know what they're asking.

✔ Be wary of answers that are true statements (actually *in* the passage) but irrelevant in terms of the question.

✔ Don't skip vocabulary-in-context questions, but take care to reread the sentence in which the word appears before answering.

✔ Don't answer inference questions with a statement that appears in the passage.

✔ Main idea questions and author attitude queries require you to think about the entire passage.

Hitting the Singles Scene

SAT single passages exist in their own little universe. Even if you see two passages placed one after the other on your exam, don't apply information from one passage to questions from another. In this section I provide two single, stand-alone, practice Critical Reading passages.

The paired passages, on the other hand, do relate to each other. The paired passages are easy to find because they include a joint introduction along the lines of "These two passages address the issue of eyebrows that run amok . . ."

Passage 1

In this passage from The Secret Life of Dust *(Wiley, 2001), author Hannah Holmes discusses some airborne particles, diatoms.*

Line Flying diatoms don't add significantly to the airborne vegetable matter, in terms of simple tonnage. But when these glass-shelled algae do take a spin through the atmosphere, they raise interesting questions. They seem to defy the size limit for far-flying dust, for one thing. And they may sometimes fly with a purpose.

(05) Michael Ram, a professor of physics at the University of Buffalo, has become an expert at teasing these tiny organisms out of ice cores from Antarctica and Greenland. Deep glaciers preserve thousands upon thousands of fine layers, each representing a year. And trapped in each layer is a sprinkling of fallen desert dust, stardust, volcanic ash, pollen, insect parts — and diatoms. Ram melts a bit of ice, then puts the remaining sediment under a microscope.

(10) The diatoms, he says, stand out due to their geometric perfection. Desert dust, under the microscope, resembles shattered rock. But diatoms often resemble delicately etched pill-boxes or broken shards of the same.

Most diatoms spend their brief lives adrift in rivers, ponds, lakes, and oceans. And when they die, their little shells sink. Ram says the ideal source of diatom dust is a shallow lake

(15) that shrinks in the dry season, exposing the sediment at its edges to the wind. Africa and the western United States are both pocked with excellent candidates.

Ram originally intended to use the diatoms he found to trace the source of the dust and diatoms in each sample: if the ice of one century was rich in North American diatoms, and the next century's ice held African diatoms, he could conclude that the prevailing wind had

(20) shifted. This might reveal something about the dynamics of climate change. But Ram's diatoms proved coy about their place of origin. Many of them look alike. Scientists with more diatom expertise are pursuing this line of inquiry.

And Ram's diatoms have caused additional head scratching. Generally, scientists don't expect things much larger than a few hundredths of a hair's width to fly long distances. But

(25) Ram has seen disks as wide as a hundred, or even two hundred, microns — that's a whopping two hairs in diameter. "These diatoms are large, but they have a large surface area, and they're light," Ram speculates in the accent that remains from his European upbringing. "They're like Frisbees. They're very aerodynamic."

The size of the diatoms may also relate to the strength of the wind that lifted them. An

(30) uncommonly strong wind can lift uncommonly large dust, as a survey of hailstone cores has suggested. Carried up into a storm cloud and then coated in ice until they fell again have been such "dusts" as small insects, birds, and at least one gopher tortoise. Perhaps a large diatom is not such a challenge.

But a third source of puzzlement is what appears to be a complete colony of diatoms

(35) that evidently dwelled smack atop the Greenland glacier about four hundred years ago. It is common for living diatoms to blow into melt pools at the *edges* of glaciers and there start a family. But the founder of the little clan Ram discovered apparently flew all the way to the center of the immense island before dropping into a puddle. And that pioneer was still in good enough shape to launch a modest dynasty.

1. The phrase that most nearly describes "flying diatoms" (line 1) is

   (A) living or dead algae that may be transported through the air

   (B) single-celled animals that can fly

   (C) glass-shelled, winged animals

   (D) living algae imprisoned in glass

   (E) dead algae borne through the air by wind

The tough part about this question is that most of the choices have some element of truth in them. But in SAT Land, some isn't enough. Paragraph one makes it clear that diatoms may be living or dead, so (D) and (E) are nonstarters. Because they "fly" with the aid of wind, (B) and (C) drop away, given that these choices imply or directly specify wings. All that's left is (A).

2. The word *teasing* (line 6) in this context may best be defined as

   (A) mocking

   (B) coaxing

   (C) annoying

   (D) disentangling

   (E) shredding

Surprisingly, all the other choices are in fact definitions of *teasing,* but the one that fits here is *disentangling.* The correct answer is (D).

3. Diatoms puzzle researchers because

   (A) they sometimes appear in unexpected places

   (B) they have glass shells

   (C) their surface is extremely small, given their weight

   (D) they may be carried by wind after death

   (E) none of the above

Two choices (B) and (D) are true, but not puzzling, and (C) is untrue. (A) makes the cut because lines 34–39 discuss the "puzzlement" of the colony in the Greenland glacier.

4. A title that best expresses the contents of this passage is

   (A) Characteristics of Algae

   (B) The Lives of Diatoms

   (C) A Scientific Study of Diatoms

   (D) Michael Ram's Life and Work

   (E) Windborne Diatoms

Titles, like the swimsuits you tried on last summer, may be too big, too small, or just right. In this set of answers, (A) and (B) are too big, which in reading terms means too general. (C) and (D) are too small, or too specific. They focus on one part of the passage, instead of on the whole. (E) is the best because it takes into account all the contents except paragraph three, which is clearly inserted as background information, creating a context for the rest of the information about diatoms.

5. Which statement may be inferred from lines 17–22?

    (A) Winds from North America and from Africa blow in the same direction.

    (B) Ram's analysis showed that all diatoms from Antarctica and Greenland ice originate in the same shallow lakes.

    (C) Ram does not know enough about diatoms to differentiate one type from another.

    (D) Diatoms change over the course of a century.

    (E) Diatoms originating in Greenland differ from diatoms originating in Antarctica.

Ram was hoping to find a wind shift, so wind from North America and wind from Africa must blow from different directions. Hence (A) isn't the prizewinner here. (B) and (D) are wrong, based on the passage, which also says that Ram couldn't tell the diatoms apart. Someone with "more diatom expertise" was needed for this task, so (C) is the best answer.

6. The example of hailstone cores (line 30) primarily

    (A) shows how dust is examined

    (B) illustrates wind direction

    (C) explains what weather conditions diatoms face

    (D) reinforces the idea that wind can carry heavy particles

    (E) contrasts with the methods used to study diatoms

The preceding paragraph says that the distances diatoms travel solely via wind power puzzle scientists. Line 30 says that "uncommonly strong wind can lift uncommonly large dust," and the *hailstone core* example reinforces this point. (D) is the correct answer.

After you finish the first practice passage, profile your strengths and weaknesses by checking which type of question stumped you. Here's the key: Questions 1 and 3 were a fact-finding mission, question 2 tackled vocabulary, 4 hit the main idea, while 5 required you to make an inference or to interpret a metaphor. Question 6 concerned the significance of an example. For help with any of these question types, check out the corresponding section in Chapter 4.

Passage 11

In this excerpt from Dickens' 19th-century novel Great Expectations, *the narrator recalls a Christmas dinner. Note: "bobbish" means "hungry," and "Sixpennorth of halfpence" is a nickname referring to a very small quantity of British money of the period. "N.B." means "note well."*

Line   I opened the door to the company — making believe that it was a habit of ours to open that door — and I opened it first to Mr. Wopsle, next to Mr. and Mrs. Hubble, and last of all to Uncle Pumblechook. N.B., I was not allowed to call him uncle, under the severest penalties.

(05)   "Mrs. Joe," said Uncle Pumblechook: a large hard-breathing middle-aged slow man, with a mouth like a fish, dull staring eyes, and sandy hair standing upright on his head, so that he looked as if he had just been all but choked, and had that moment come to; "I have brought you, as the compliments of the season — I have brought you, Mum, a bottle of sherry wine — and I have brought you, Mum, a bottle of port wine."

(10)   Every Christmas Day he presented himself, as a profound novelty, with exactly the same words, and carrying the two bottles like dumb-bells. Every Christmas Day, Mrs. Joe replied, as she now replied, "Oh, Un-cle Pum-ble-chook! This IS kind!" Every Christmas Day, he retorted, as he now retorted, "It's no more than your merits. And now are you all bobbish, and how's Sixpennorth of halfpence?" meaning me.

(15) We dined on these occasions in the kitchen, and adjourned, for the nuts and oranges and apples, to the parlour; which was a change very like Joe's change from his working clothes to his Sunday dress. My sister was uncommonly lively on the present occasion, and indeed was generally more gracious in the society of Mrs. Hubble than in other company. I remember Mrs. Hubble as a little curly sharp-edged person in sky-blue, who held a conventionally juve-nile position, because she had married Mr. Hubble — I don't know at what remote period —
(20) when she was much younger than he. I remember Mr. Hubble as a tough high-shouldered stooping old man, of a sawdusty fragrance, with his legs extraordinarily wide apart: so that in my short days I always saw some miles of open country between them when I met him coming up the lane.

Among this good company I should have felt myself, even if I hadn't robbed the pantry,
(25) in a false position. Not because I was squeezed in at an acute angle of the table-cloth, with the table in my chest, and the Pumblechookian elbow in my eye, nor because I was not allowed to speak (I didn't want to speak), nor because I was regaled with the scaly tips of the drumsticks of the fowls, and with those obscure corners of pork of which the pig, when living, had had the least reason to be vain. No; I should not have minded that, if they would
(30) only have left me alone. But they wouldn't leave me alone. They seemed to think the oppor-tunity lost, if they failed to point the conversation at me, every now and then, and stick the point into me. I might have been an unfortunate little bull in a Spanish arena, I got so smart-ingly touched up by these moral goads.

7. Which statement may be inferred from lines 1–2?

   (A) The door that the narrator opens is normally locked.

   (B) The door that the narrator opens is never used for company.

   (C) The narrator is not normally allowed to open the door for visitors.

   (D) Different doors are used on special occasions and for everyday entries.

   (E) The doors in the narrator's house are always kept open.

Lines 1–2 contain the statement that the narrator was "making believe that it was a habit of ours to open that door." *That door* implies a contrast with another door, so you can rule out (A), (C), and (E). The two remaining choices present no real puzzle. Because company is arriving, (B) can't be correct. Bingo — (D) is your answer.

8. The author's attitude toward Uncle Pumblechook and Mrs. Joe in paragraphs two and three (lines 4–13) may best be characterized as

   (A) mildly critical

   (B) approving

   (C) admiring

   (D) ambivalent

   (E) sharply disapproving

The description of Uncle Pumblechook (Isn't that one of the all-time great names?) clearly shows that (B) and (C) won't do, because "a mouth like a fish" isn't an approving or admiring comment. (D) is a possible, because clearly the author isn't "sharply disapproving," given that the negative comments are quite tame (*ambivalent* means "of two opinions"). But (A) is the best. If the two characters are pretending to do something that they've never done before and do so every year, the author is critical of them, but only mildly so.

9. The move from the kitchen to the parlour is compared to Joe's change of clothes because

    (A) Mrs. Joe is uncomfortable with both

    (B) both take place only on special occasions

    (C) the narrator is confused by each of these actions

    (D) Mrs. Hubble is always present for both of these actions

    (E) Joe insists upon both of these changes

Mrs. Joe is "uncommonly lively," so (A) is out. The passage gives no indication that Joe insists on anything, so you can rule out (E). Mrs. Hubble isn't really a factor, and the narrator's general confusion isn't specifically connected to clothes or location. The best is (B), because Joe's change is referred to as "Sunday dress" and (B) refers to "special occasions."

10. The details in paragraph 5 (lines 24–33) serve to

    (A) show how the author enjoys Christmas dinner

    (B) explain the behavior of the dinner guests

    (C) describe a 19th-century Christmas celebration

    (D) make the case that the narrator is not treated well

    (E) illustrate 19th-century child-rearing practices

The author is certainly *not* enjoying dinner, so (A) is out. The dinner guests' behavior (B) is possible, but the details tell you more about how the narrator is treated than about the guests' general behavior. (C) and (E) are too general. (D) is the only one to make the cut.

11. The metaphor of "an unfortunate little bull in a Spanish arena" (line 32) means that

    (A) the narrator, like a bull in a bullfight, is a target of teasing attacks

    (B) the narrator's table manners are more like those of an animal than a polite child

    (C) the narrator did not participate actively in the conversation

    (D) the dinner guests were the targets of the narrator's mocking comments

    (E) the dinner resembled a festive sporting event

The guests are described as unwilling to leave the narrator alone, so you can rule out (D) and (E), because the narrator isn't the attacker (there goes D) and the dinner isn't a fun occasion ([E] calls it "festive"). (C) is true but has no relationship to the bullfighting image, and neither does the statement about table manners. The narrator is, however, described as the target of attacks by the guests' statements, just as the bull faces attacks in a bullfight. (A) is the correct answer.

12. The author of this passage would most likely agree with which statement?

    (A) Children should be seen and not heard.

    (B) The narrator has a happy life.

    (C) Holiday gatherings may be joyous occasions.

    (D) People often show off during holiday gatherings.

    (E) Holiday celebrations should be abolished.

The change from one room to another, the use of a special door, the ceremonial exchange of gifts — all these details prove that the characters in this passage are showing off, putting on airs, pretending to be better than they really are, and in general acting like contestants on a reality show. (D) fills the bill.

Speaking of reality, time for a reality check. Look at everything you got wrong and figure out your weak spots — facts, inference, main idea, and so on. Here's the key: Questions 7, 10, and 12 are about inference; 8 is about attitude; 9 is about symbol, and 11 is about metaphor. After you know what to work on, turn to Chapter 4 for some tips.

Trying Out Paired Passages

Paired passages double your trouble, but if you approach them properly, they also double your score. Twice as many chances to get the answer right! Expect some questions on passage I, some on passage II, and a couple that address the similarities or differences between both passages.

The first passage is an excerpt from The Dawn of Human Culture *by Richard G. Klein and Blake Edgar (Wiley, 2002). The authors discuss the shift in behavior that took place about 50,000 years ago when human beings began to paint, create music, fabricate bows and arrows, and bury their dead with elaborate rituals. The "Younger Dryas" period referred to in line 1 was a sudden, sharp change to colder and drier weather that took place near the Mediterranean Sea about 11,000 years ago. The second passage comes from* The Secret Life of Dust *by Hannah Holmes (Wiley, 2001). The author also addresses climate change.* **Note:** *An* oviraptor *is a type of dinosaur.* Mount Pinatubo *was a volcano that erupted in 1991.*

Paired passage 1

Line   Conceivably, the trigger was a climatic event like the Younger Dryas of 11,000 years ago, but the "dawn" occurred during a long interval of fluctuating climate that on present evidence did not include a comparably dramatic episode. Even if one is eventually detected, it will be difficult to explain why it prompted such a far-reaching behavioral response, when yet
(05) earlier, equally or even more radical climatic spikes did not. The most notable preceding spike was a millennium-long bout of intense cold that followed the Mt. Toba volcanic supereruption in Sumatra, Indonesia, about 73,500 years ago. The Mt. Toba eruption was the most massive in the last 2 million years and perhaps in the last 450 million years. To provide perspective, Toba ejected roughly four thousand times as much material as Mt. St. Helens
(10) (Washington State) in 1981 and about forty times more than Mt. Tambora (Sumbawa Island, Indonesia) in 1815. The Tambora eruption was the largest in historic times, and the aerosols from it reduced sunlight and global temperatures so much that 1816 became known as "the year without a summer" when New England experienced snow in July and August. The far more extensive aerosols from Toba produced a "volcanic winter" akin to the "nuclear winter"
(15) that some have hypothesized would follow a new world war, and the effect was accentuated and prolonged by feedback from a global trend toward colder climate in the early part of the last glacial period. Plant and animal populations must have declined sharply almost everywhere, and the impact on human populations was probably catastrophic. Yet, the aftermath of Mt. Toba is notable precisely because it did not provoke a revolutionary cultural response.
(20) This lack of a response supports artifactual evidence that people possessed limited ability to innovate before 50,000 years ago.

Paired passage 11

Line   One very clear message in the ice is that the Earth's climate is naturally erratic. According to the dust and gases trapped in the ice, the climate is always — always — in flux. If it's not getting warmer, it's getting colder. Year to year the shifts may be masked by an El Niño, a La Niña, a Mount Pinatubo, or some other temporary drama. But decade to decade, century to
(05) century, the world's temperature is in constant motion.

    On a grand scale our moderate, modern climate is abnormal. Through most of the dinosaur era the planet's normal state was decidedly steamier. When the oviraptor perished in the Gobi Desert, the world may have been eleven to fourteen degrees hotter, on average.

    Then, just 2.5 million years ago, the planet entered a pattern of periodic ice ages, punc-
(10) tuated by brief warm spells. The ice caps, as a result, have taken to advancing and retreating intermittently. The glaciers have ruled for the lion's share of time, with the warm "interglacials" lasting roughly ten thousand years each. We inhabit an interglacial known as the Holocene, which ought to be coming to an end any day now. The thermometer, however, does not seem poised for a plunge.

(15)   All things being equal, no climatologist would be surprised if the Holocene persisted for another few thousand years — climate change is that erratic. But all things are *not* equal. Human industry has wrought profound changes in the Earth's atmosphere since the last warm period.

1. In Passage I, which position do the authors take on the relationship between climate and human culture?

   (A) Human beings are capable of ignoring climate.

   (B) Some extreme shifts in climate have not been accompanied by dramatic changes in human behavior.

   (C) Climate and human behavior are completely unrelated.

   (D) Dramatic climate changes lead to important changes in human culture.

   (E) As climate changes, so does human behavior.

Most of the choices are as extreme as the weather shift described in the passage, but the authors take a more moderate approach. Lines 3–4 make clear that some climate changes haven't radically altered human behavior, thus (B) is correct.

2. The example of Mt. Toba in Passage I primarily

   (A) illustrates a radical climate change that did not greatly influence human culture

   (B) reinforces the theory that climate changes always involve colder weather

   (C) shows that no part of the earth is immune to climate change

   (D) explains how volcanoes influence climate

   (E) relates the decline in plant and animal population to volcanic eruptions

Mt. Toba's eruption is described as much greater than the eruption of Mt. Tambora, which the passage calls "the largest in historic times." (Apparently the authors have never seen an SAT-related tantrum.) Toba's effect on climate is given indirectly, through the explanation of the unusually cold weather that followed the relatively minor eruption of Mt. Tambora. (D) and (E) may have tempted you because the passage *does* relate volcanoes and climate and plant and animal populations *did* decrease after Tambora blew its top. But the passage is about climate and human behavior, so (A) is the best answer.

3. The word "historic" in line 11 of Passage I may best be defined as

    (A) having great importance

    (B) during the era of recorded history

    (C) taught in history classes

    (D) past

    (E) of a given era

Did choice (A) tempt you? *Historic* often means "having great importance." But in this passage, the authors are comparing the eruption of Tambora, which is detailed in the record books, to that of Mt. Toba, which took place before history was even a glimmer in your favorite teacher's eye. (B) is the correct answer.

4. In Passage I, how are "the year without a summer" (line 13), "volcanic winter" (line 14), and "nuclear winter" (line 14) related?

    (A) All were caused by volcanic eruptions.

    (B) All affected weather in New England.

    (C) None could have been prevented.

    (D) All show the radical effects of climate change on human culture.

    (E) All three involve shifts to colder weather brought about by particles in the air.

(A), (B), and (C) are out of the picture because the last of the trio, *nuclear winter,* hasn't happened (fortunately for the entire Earth). The point of the passage is that climate changes don't necessarily bring about radical alterations in human culture, so (D) stands for dead-in-the-water. (E) fits the bill because the passage implies that volcanoes and nuclear weapons eject particles into the air, and those particles turn the temperature downward.

5. In Passage I, what most nearly defines "artifactual" as it is used in line 20?

    (A) historical

    (B) climatic

    (C) geological

    (D) archaeological

    (E) controversial

If you're checking on human behavior of 50,000 years ago, archaeological evidence is the way to go, so (D) is the correct answer.

6. In Passage II, the author mentions the *oviraptor* (line 7) to illustrate

    (A) the difference between human and animal responses to climate

    (B) how living creatures adapt to many climates

    (C) a creature that became extinct because of climate shifts

    (D) how the dinosaurs were affected by climate

    (E) a dinosaur that lived during a warm period

The author doesn't develop the *oviraptor* example. Choices (A)–(D) are out because they call for a more extensive discussion of the dinosaur in question. (E) is the correct answer.

7. In Passage II, which phrase most nearly defines "any day now" (line 13)?

   (A) within a week

   (B) within a month

   (C) within a year

   (D) during our lifetime

   (E) within a thousand years

The author of Passage II certainly takes the long view. Paragraph 4 specifically says that even a few thousand years would be possible, but that amount of time is labeled as *erratic,* or without a consistent pattern. So the best answer is (E).

8. Compared to the authors of Passage I, the author of Passage II

   (A) describes volcanic eruptions as only one factor in climate change

   (B) believes that climate change has much greater effect on human behavior

   (C) takes a more scientific view of climate

   (D) sees climate as having greater historical importance

   (E) thinks that the Earth's climate will change more rapidly

The emphasis in Passage II is "what else is new," at least in terms of climate. The author does mention Mt. Pinatubo, but Passage I has a lot more on volcanoes and climate. (A) is correct.

9. Evidence from both passages supports the idea that

   (A) Climate change is not a natural process.

   (B) Human beings cannot withstand radical climate changes.

   (C) Human activity affects climate.

   (D) Climate changes constantly.

   (E) Climatologists must study human behavior to understand temperature patterns.

Passage I makes a big deal about "spikes" in climate, and Passage II flat out tells you that climate changes constantly. (C) may have lured you because the author of Passage II does state that human activity is a factor; Passage I, however, ignores the human effect on the weather. If you selected (D), pat yourself on the back and breathe deeply. Only one more question to go!

10. The title that best fits both passages is

   (A) Global Warming

   (B) Climate Change

   (C) Volcanoes and Climate

   (D) Human Effects on Climate

   (E) Climate's Effects on Humans

(A) is out because Passage I talks about spikes of cold temperature, and Passage II doesn't really deal with volcanoes (C). Passage I ignores human effects (D), and Passage II mentions the climate's effects on human beings only in passing (E). As a result, (B) is the correct answer.

Chapter 6

Abbreviating the Agony: Practice Questions for Short Reading Passages

In This Chapter

▶ Practicing for the 100-word Critical Reading passages

▶ Applying good reading techniques to short passages

The 100-word (give or take a sentence) Critical Reading passages are the newest kids on the block, the block being the *Scintillating Astute Trumpery,* fondly known as the SAT. (By the way, *scintillating* = dazzling, *astute* = clever, and *trumpery* = rubbish or thing without value, and Donald Trump has nothing to do with it). The little SAT-devils analyze all SAT questions, new or not, to the max before placing them on an actual exam. However, the SAT-makers may still tinker with this section a bit after a few hundred thousand people have had a shot at answering these Critical Reading questions during the first year of the new SAT. So don't be surprised if the test you take has a couple more or fewer short Critical Reading passages.

For advice on Critical Reading passage strategy, check out Chapter 4. In this chapter, get ready to rumble through two practice sets.

Practice Set One

Don't peek at the answers until you have answered the question. After you're done, add up your score. If you answered more than four right, you're doing great. Take the night off. If only one or two made it into your correct column, hit the next set.

Passage 1

This excerpt from a 19th-century novel describes a female tavern owner's dilemma.

Line   To maintain the discipline of the tavern, nevertheless, the presence of a man was desirable; she understood this. Besides, the condition of an old maid did not seem to her at all inviting, and she did not care to wait the epoch of a third youth, before making a choice. But what would the unsuccessful candidates say? Would not this decision be at the risk of kin-
(05)   dling a civil war, of provoking perhaps a general desertion? Then, too, accustomed as she was to command, the idea of giving herself a master alarmed her.

1. According to the passage, the narrator

    (A) wants to hire three youths to help in the tavern

    (B) is deciding whether to hire a youth or an old maid

    (C) is confused about running a tavern

    (D) understands that a man will help keep order in the tavern

    (E) does not like giving orders

(D) is correct. The clue is in sentence one. The narrator "understood" that the "presence of a man" was "desirable" in order to "maintain the discipline of the tavern." You can dump choice (A) because she "did not care to wait for a third youth," so she's not hiring three people. (B) bites the dust because she's worried about becoming an old maid herself, not thinking about hiring one. The passage directly contradicts (C) and (E).

Passage 11

This passage is an excerpt from The Hidden Universe *by Roger J. Tayler (Wiley), a science text.*

Line   Astronomy is very different from other sciences in that it is observational rather than experimental. Almost all of the information that an astronomer gathers about the Universe is in the form of electromagnetic waves, such as light and radio waves, which travel to the Earth from distant objects. From the properties of these waves an attempt is made to under-
(05) stand the structure and evolution of the Universe. At the outset there is one major problem. The observations can only be interpreted by use of the laws of physics, but these laws of physics have only been established through experiments on the Earth and in its immediate neighborhood at the present time.

2. The passage implies that the laws of physics

    (A) may not be the same away from the Earth

    (B) can never change

    (C) are a problem for scientists because they cannot be the subject of any experiments

    (D) apply only to waves

    (E) have been verified in environments away from the Earth

---

Battling short passages: The plan of attack

As you approach the short Critical Reading passages, follow this plan:

✔ Pay close attention to any information in italics describing the passage.

✔ Circle any clue words in the questions so that you understand what the test-writers are looking for (the false answer, the one statement that's true, an assumption, the tone or attitude of the author, and so on).

✔ Concentrate on the information in the passage. What you know from real life has no place in an SAT Critical Reading question.

✔ Triple-check the context, particularly with a vocabulary question. At least one alternate meaning of the word is listed among the choices, so context matters.

✔ Pay attention to word choice when answering questions about the author's tone or attitude.

The passage contains a couple of clue words — "different" (line 1) alerts you to a contrast, and "only . . . on the Earth . . . at the present time" (lines 7–8) puts you on notice that anything away from the Earth is doubtful. The enticing-but-wrong answer here is (C), because the passage does describe the problem of not being able to verify the laws of physics — away from the Earth. The laws of physics may certainly be verified "on Earth," including the law that whenever I drop a sandwich it will land jelly side down. (A) is correct.

Passage III

This excerpt from The House of Science *by Philip R. Holzinger (Wiley, 1990) discusses world population growth in relation to food supply.*

Line   Given the present growth rate of 1.6 percent, the world's population will more than double in your lifetime. But is this rate of growth likely to remain the same? With a significant portion of the world's population currently malnourished or undernourished, can the earth sustain a population more than twice the size it has now? Some scientists think it can, but a
(05)   great many think it is unlikely, given our present resources and technology. We *have* made strides in feeding the world's population. For example, scientists have come up with new strains of wheat, rice, and other crops that produce a good deal more per plant than the old strains did. These new strains are part of what is known as the *Green Revolution*.

3. What assumption does the author make about the rate of population growth?

(A) Scientists should work to increase the rate of population growth.

(B) The Green Revolution will lower the growth rate of population.

(C) The present growth rate of population must change as the number of people on earth increases.

(D) Without adequate food, the rate of population growth will slow.

(E) A growth rate of 1.6 percent is ideal.

The clue is the question pair in lines 2–4. Placing them together implies a cause-and-effect relationship. Another clue is the description of agricultural improvements. Plopping them in a paragraph about population links the two. (D) is correct.

4. In this passage, the "Green Revolution" (line 8) refers to

(A) changes in the way plants are harvested

(B) new types of plants

(C) plants that yield more food, in addition to other advancements in agriculture

(D) an increased concern for ecology

(E) population control through food rationing

The passage talks about new crops and then throws you the label "Green Revolution," so the revolution has to have something to do with food and/or plants. That eliminates (D) and (E). (C) wins the race because the last sentence in the passage says *part* of the Revolution, so other factors must exist. (C) is right.

Passage IV

This paragraph about food safety comes from Basic Statistics *by Olive Jean Dunn (Wiley, 1964, 1977).*

Line   [A] newspaper article several years ago stated that it is safer to eat in restaurants than in homes or at private affairs. The statistical basis for this conclusion was that health departments receive fewer reports of food poisoning from restaurants than from picnics, private parties, and private homes. The conclusion that restaurant meals are safer than home meals
(05) does not follow from the fact that more reports of food poisonings come from picnics, private parties, and private homes than come from public eating places. First, we would have to know the number of meals served in each type of eating place in order to compare them. Second, food poisoning from a restaurant meal is often difficult to trace to the restaurant, so that restaurants *may* be less safe than private homes even though fewer cases of food poisoning
(10) are reported per meal served.

5. The author believes that statistics

   (A) should be used to evaluate the safety of restaurants

   (B) prove that restaurant meals are safer on the whole than most people think

   (C) accurately measure the safety of picnic food

   (D) can easily be misinterpreted by the media

   (E) are the media's most valuable source of information

The SAT-demons tucked a bunch of false clues in these choices, hoping to distract you. The passage criticizes the newspaper article that evaluated the safety of restaurant meals. (D) and (E) deal with media, so they're both in the running. (E) loses the race, however, because of its vagueness. (A) and (C) are contradicted by the passage, and (B) falls away because of the word *prove*. (D) is right.

6. In line 9 the word "may" is italicized because the author

   (A) thinks that restaurants are more dangerous than most people believe

   (B) wants to emphasize that no valid conclusion about the safety of restaurants may be drawn without more information

   (C) is confused about the safety of various food sources

   (D) believes that many cases of food poisoning are not reported

   (E) is emphasizing how little is known about restaurant meals

An italicized word nearly always creates emphasis, as in "The SAT is an *awful* test." So (B) and (E) are the best bets, with (E) voted off the island because it says nothing about safety. If you selected (B), pat yourself on the back.

Practice Set Two

Now that you have a couple passages under your belt, try a second set.

Passage 1

This passage about leadership comes from The Transformational Leader, *by Noel M. Tichy and Mary Anne Devanna (Wiley, 1986, 1990).*

Line   In the United States there is a continuing shift in the demographics of the workforce. In 1985 white males became a minority in the workforce, yet they continue to hold virtually all the positions of power in large organizations. Similar pressures are emerging in Japan as women look for a more meaningful role in society. No society is immune to this growing
(05) hunger for opportunity and equity. Laws and sanctions to correct inequity are formulated by the government but they are implemented by organizations. And it is in the implementation that the debate about equity begins. The core challenge is to mobilize an increasingly pluralistic workforce where many groups have no significant decision-making role. This tends to set up the dynamic for confrontation rather than collaboration.

1. The authors imply that

    (A) women have too many decision-making roles in international organizations

    (B) Japanese women are discontent with traditional roles

    (C) white males in the United States hold too little power in the workplace

    (D) laws to change the ethnic or gender balance of power are easy to put into effect

    (E) white males are now a minority in the American workforce

The false positive in this question is (E), because the passage states that white males *are* a minority in the American workforce. So anyone who zoomed through the question got this one wrong. Why? Because the question asks what the authors *imply,* not what they actually say. The statement in lines 3–4 about Japanese women's search for "a more meaningful role" is the clue that nails down (B). No one searches if he or she is already content. (B) is correct.

2. What is the meaning of *sanction* in line 5?

    (A) blessings

    (B) praise

    (C) approval

    (D) penalties

    (E) actions

A vocabulary-in-context question is usually a cinch, so long as you take the time to read the context. The passage says, "Laws and sanctions to correct inequity are formulated by the government." The law doesn't give *blessings* (A) or *praise* (B), and *approval* (C) is rare. Besides, you can't correct a mistake with approval. *Actions* (E) is vague. Two cheers for (D).

Passage 11

This selection from Physical Science in the Middle Ages *by Edward Gran (Wiley, 1971) describes the origins of universities in Western Europe.*

Line   [T]he spontaneous emergence of universities was intimately associated with the new learning that had been translated into Latin throughout the course of the twelfth century. Indeed the university was the institutional means by which Western Europe would organize, absorb, and expand the great volume of new knowledge; the instrument by which it would
(05) mold and disseminate a common intellectual heritage for generations to come. While the universities of Paris and Oxford became renowned as centers of philosophy and science and Bologna for its schools of law and medicine, all three . . . shaped the university into a form that has persisted to this day.

3 According to the passage, once many works had been translated into Latin,

   (A) Latin could more easily be taught in universities

   (B) universities were formed to translate more books

   (C) knowledge could be shared among scholars

   (D) the language was not understood by university students

   (E) scholars could no longer appreciate the knowledge gained by past generations

The clue in sentence one "intimately associates" "learning" and Latin. (If you saw "intimately" and your mind ran away from the passage, slow down. You're taking a test here, not planning a romantic evening.) Because the universities are sharing "learning," you need take only one tiny step from Latin to learning to universities, where you find — in addition to keg parties and tailgate parties — "scholars." (C) is correct.

4. The author implies that

   (A) all true universities teach philosophy, science, law, and medicine

   (B) the establishment of universities was the result of a carefully planned effort

   (C) law and medicine were not appreciated in Paris and Oxford

   (D) today's universities should have an international student body

   (E) today's universities owe much to an intellectual effort in the 12th century

Zero in on line 5, where you find "generations to come," and line 8, which mentions a form that "has persisted to this day . . ." which by the way is Tuesday. (Just kidding.) Now you can check out (D) and (E), which talk about "today's universities." (E) relates to the rest of the passage, the 12th-century part. (E) is correct.

Passage III

In this passage from a 19th-century novel the narrator reminisces about a childhood friend.

Line   Ratsey was always kind to me, and had lent me a chisel many a time to make boats, so I stepped in and held the lantern watching him chink out the bits of Portland stone with a graver, and blinking the while when they came too near my eyes. The inscription stood complete, but he was putting the finishing touches to a little sea-piece carved at the top of the
(05) stone, which showed a schooner boarding a cutter. I thought it fine work at the time, but know now that it was rough enough; indeed, you may see it for yourself in Moonfleet churchyard to this day, and read the inscription too, though it is yellow with lichen, and not so plain as it was that night.

5. The carving referred to in the passage

   (A) was probably a tombstone

   (B) was primarily created by the author

   (C) contained only words

   (D) has hardly aged at all

   (E) was intended to protect eyesight

You're in a churchyard, carving, and the carving stays around long enough to gather *lichen* (little plants) and blur its words. Think "tombstone" or monument, and only tombstone is an option. Bingo! (A) is right.

6. A *schooner* and a *cutter* (line 5) are

    (A) carving tools

    (B) names carved on the stone

    (C) types of stone

    (D) associated with the sea

    (E) mineral formations

Even if you were unfamiliar with the words (which name types of boats), line 4 tells you that the carving is a "sea piece." (D) is the only one that deals with the sea.

Passage IV

This passage from Rogue Asteroids and Doomsday Comets *by Duncan Steel (Wiley, 1995) describes the damage that may be caused by the impact of an asteroid (chunk of space rock) on our planet.*

Line   A 500-meter asteroid crashing into a desert — for example, the Outback of Australia or the Sahara — would devastate an area of about 160,000 square kilometers and cause substantial damage over a far greater region. For example, if the asteroid fell in the Outback, all of the cities in Australia would almost surely be shaken flat. This would not, however, be the
(05) worst-case scenario. The consequences of the same asteroid arriving a few hours earlier and perhaps landing in the Pacific Ocean between New Zealand and Tahiti would be far worse. This is because the impact would generate an enormous tsunami (a huge ocean wave), often caused by earthquakes.

7. According to the passage, which of the following is true of both earthquakes and collision with an asteroid?

    (A) Neither shakes cities so strongly that buildings are flattened.

    (B) Both may generate tsunamis.

    (C) Both have the power to devastate deserts and oceans.

    (D) Both originate in the Southern Hemisphere.

    (E) Australia is less affected by earthquakes and asteroid collisions than New Zealand and Tahiti are.

The appealing-but-wrong choice is (C), because both are described in the passage as devastating. However, giant waves don't hit the desert, which is referred to in (C). Thus (B) is a better bet.

8. The passage mentions the Outback of Australia because

    (A) it is most likely to be hit by an asteroid

    (B) it has been hit by asteroids in the past

    (C) the Outback is a source of tsunamis

    (D) it serves as an example of a desert area

    (E) Australia has felt the effects of tsunamis but not asteroids

This question is a rule-out, as in rule out the wrong answers and what's left is correct. You can't justify (A) because the odds of an asteroid hitting the desert are never discussed. Ditto for (B) and (E) — the passage doesn't tell you whether an asteroid or a giant wave once hit the Outback. (C) is just plain wrong. (D) is correct.

Analyzing Your Scores

If you got approximately 50 percent correct, you're doing fine on these passages. Higher than that, all the better. If you chose the right answer for fewer than half, time to examine your reading habits. Scan Table 6-1 and 6-2, which label each question in this chapter by type:

Table 6-1	Set One Questions
Question	Question Type
1	Fact
2	Inference
3	Inference
4	Vocabulary-in-context
5	Inference
6	Attitude

Table 6-2	Set Two Questions
Question	Question Type
1	Inference
2	Vocabulary-in-context
3	Inference
4	Inference
5	Inference
6	Vocabulary-in-context
7	Fact
8	Example

When you look at the wrong ones, what tripped you up? Vocabulary? Zooming too quickly past clue words? Main idea? Inference? After you identify the weak spot, turn to Chapter 4 and review the appropriate strategy.

Chapter 7

Filling In the Blanks: Sentence Completions

In This Chapter
▶ Acquainting yourself with Sentence Completions
▶ Relying on familiar words
▶ Following easy steps to solve Sentence Completions

New York City subways used to be filled with signs advertising a school for shorthand. "If u cn rd ths, u cn gt a gd job," they declared. I never did try for the "good job" they were dangling in front of me, even though I "could read this" easily. But I did have fun watching people puzzle out the missing letters. (Hey, subway rides are boring. You have to do *something* to pass the time.)

A holdover from the old SAT I, Sentence Completions are only a little more complicated than the missing-letter ads on the subway. The words you see have all their letters — always a plus in reading! Also, the test-makers tuck some clues into the sentence so you can figure out what's missing. The hardest questions include words known only by people who eat dictionaries for breakfast. (Low carb, but not very tasty.)

On the new SAT Reasoning Test, you find sets of nine or ten Sentence Completions plopped into the Critical Reading sections. The usual SAT scoring applies: One point for each correct answer, no points for a skipped question, and a quarter point deduction for errors.

In this chapter, I explain how to approach the easy and mid-level Sentence Completions. I also provide strategies for the tough questions, including when to guess and when to skip.

Sampling the Sentence Completion Menu

If you're having a small anxiety attack right now worrying about Sentence Completions, take a deep breath and relax. In this section, you can discover how to identify the types of Sentence Completions, a task that is the first step in solving them.

Sentence Completions come in three main forms:

✔ Simple vocabulary, one blank
✔ Simple vocabulary, two blanks
✔ Tough vocabulary, one or two blanks

Each Sentence Completion section on the SAT has some single-blank questions and some double-blanks. Don't assume that the doubles are harder. Some are actually easier than the singles because more words equals more clues. Continue reading to see what the different types look like and then check out the "Reading Around the Blanks" section later in this chapter for some general tips on solving these little buggers.

In the following sections, I provide some Sentence Completion questions, which are similar to those on the real SAT though mine (she said modestly) are marginally funny and the SAT has no sense of humor whatsoever. I also provide solutions and some reasoning that I used to determine the answers. (Look up the "Completing the Sentence: Steps that Work" section later in this chapter for different strategies to help you ace the Sentence Completion section on your SAT.)

Simple vocabulary, one blank

Several Sentence Completion questions throw you the vocabulary equivalent of a softball, though you may not know every single word in them. However, the easy vocabulary doesn't mean that the sentence is a cinch. Some of these are really hard. Never fear: Your own experiences and observations may help. Also, the SAT-gremlins do play fair to the extent that they scatter word clues for the observant reader. Check this one out:

Because she was upset by the security guard's close attention, Winona stormed out of the lingerie store and remained _____ for the rest of the day.

(A) braless

(B) serene

(C) annoyed

(D) joyful

(E) hungry

Answer: (C). Here's the deal. Upon reading the sentence you immediately think of an innocent shopper tailed too closely by a security guard. You picture little Winona abandoning the piles of luxury underwear and heading home. Real-world experience tells you that Winona is probably annoyed or even indignant. As you check for clues, you notice *because* and *stormed*. The *because* tells you to focus on consequences. The *stormed* tells you about Winona's mood. Several words pop into your head when you think about the blank — *grouchy, mad, angry,* and so forth. When you check the choices, you see (C), *annoyed*. Bingo.

Sometimes clue words are omitted, but you can figure out the logic of the sentence anyway. (The sentence in the preceding question, for example, makes sense even if *because* is left out.)

> Upset by the security guard's attention, Winona stormed out of the lingerie store and remained _____ for the rest of the day.

To answer these questions, be aware of what the sentence implies as well as what it states.

Here's the same sentence with a twist:

Although she was upset by the security guard's close attention and stormed out of the lingerie store, Winona remained _____ for the rest of the day.

(A) braless

(B) serene

(C) annoyed

(D) joyful

(E) hungry

Answer: (B). The *although* sets up a contrast. Because she *stormed,* you know Winona was annoyed upon leaving the store. The *although* tells you that her mood changed and that (C) is the opposite of what you want. Choosing your own fill-in, you may opt for *peaceful.* (When you create your own fill-in, don't worry about grammar or proper English. Just concentrate on the meaning.) *Serene,* or peaceful, is the choice that fits best.

Suppose you create your own fill-in but nothing matches it. For instance, in the preceding question you may have said *alone* or *secluded.* Not bad, but not on the answer list. Time to try again. Either create a new fill-in or check out the choices and see what appeals.

Remember: More than one choice may work. In the preceding example, *joyful* contrasts with *stormed.* However, *stormed* has an element of anger in it, so *serene* is better.

Simple vocabulary, two blanks

Two for the price of one. What could be bad about that deal? Plenty. However, not as much as you think. The two-blank question is often easier than its single cousin because you get extra hints about the right choice. Take a look at this example:

Despite her _____ mood, Winona put on a _____ face when she faced the tabloid reporter.

   (A) positive . . . cheerful

   (B) unpleasant . . . friendly

   (C) thoughtful . . . interested

   (D) grouchy . . . irritable

   (E) depressed . . . sad

Answer: (B). Even if you've never been a celebrity, life in the 21st century has probably given you the impression that tabloid reporters can grasp the tiniest thread and turn it into a rope strong enough to hang a naïve interview subject. So (A), (B), and (C) are all possibilities, unless Winona is going for the sympathy vote, in which case (E) makes the cut. But the word clue *despite* tell you to search for opposites. You can rule out (A), (D), and (E) because they're closer to synonyms. (B) quickly emerges as the best choice — an opposite that also matches real-world clues.

If you're fairly sure that they know the correct word for either one of the blanks, zero in on the choices that fit and ignore the rest. But don't jump on an answer simply because it fits just one of the blanks. Go for something that fits both, because a short cut may easily lead you astray. As a matter of fact, the SAT-writers are crossing their fingers and hoping that you select the quick — but wrong — answer.

Tough vocabulary

If your caregiver had the foresight to shout vocabulary words at the sandbox you once played in, you may find these questions easy. Sadly, not many of the SAT-takers out there fall into this category. For normal people with average vocabulary, the "tough vocabulary" Sentence Completions are a challenge — but not always an impossibility. (For tips on improving your vocabulary, see Chapter 2.)

The best method of attack is to eliminate the choices that contain words you have never seen before. Then concentrate on the remaining answers. Follow the same strategy in reading the sentence that you followed for simple-vocabulary questions: Check for real-world links and look for word clues. Then examine your possible answers. If one fits, go for it. If nothing that you recognize makes sense, turn your attention to the *I-have-no-idea-what-these-words-mean* choices. Use the usual guessing rule. If you have eliminated one or more of the five choices, take a stab and move on to another question. If not, leave it blank and forget about it.

Many tough vocabulary questions have the definition right there in the sentence. Look for the definition and see if it jars anything loose in your brain. For instance, suppose the sentence reads as follows:

In her _____ mood, Winona sat frowning and took pleasure in nothing.

(A) affable

(B) jocund

(C) jovial

(D) morose

(E) narcissistic

Okay, the test-makers have given you one break. The entire second half of the sentence is a definition; you just have to find the word that fits. *Frowning* and *taking pleasure in nothing* = depressed. Fine. Now you just have to find a word that means "depressed." Reread the five choices. Anything register? If so, go for it. Or, if you know that some of the words *don't* mean "depressed," rule them out. Then apply the guessing rules. In the preceding example, by the way, *morose* = depressed, so the answer is (D). The other words are as follows: *affable* = friendly, *jocund* = joking, *jovial* = joyous, and *narcissistic* = egotistical, thinks he's/she's the center of the universe.

Reading Around the Blanks

If you're a reasonably competent reader, you probably know how to do Sentence Completions already. When you stare at a computer screen or pick up some printed material, chances are you occasionally run across an unfamiliar word.

What do you do when one of those new words pops up? No, you don't drop everything and head *virtuously* (righteously, on the side of the angels) for the dictionary. You probably don't have a lot of time for dictionary chores, and even if you did, you'd have to uncurl from the couch, move the snack plate, dislodge the cat, *find* the dictionary, and . . . well, you get the point. By the time you have your *Webster's* open to the right spot, you're out of reading time and in no mood for definitions.

Instead, when faced with a new word, you probably do what everybody else does: You read *around* the unfamiliar spot and figure out what the sentence is trying to say. You can usually figure out the main idea even when one of the words is a mystery. That's what able readers do: They crack the sentence using logic and common sense, guided by the clues tucked into the sentence.

Pause for a sigh of relief. What I'm telling you is that you don't have to create new and complicated strategies for Sentence Completions. You already know the strategies that work for you. You just have to fine-tune those strategies a bit to suit the SAT. Piece of cake.

Getting the lowdown on Sentence Completions

SAT Sentence Completions

(A) are best when buttered lightly and eaten with globs of strawberry jelly

(B) should be sent for a very long walk on a short pier jutting into any convenient ocean

(C) are tough even for those with good vocabulary and reading skills

(D) make up a bit less than a third of the Critical Reading portion of the SAT

(E) may be answered only if you're in touch with your inner thesaurus

Answer: (A). Just kidding. Though I do like strawberry jelly and I wouldn't mind dunking these questions in the Atlantic (B). The real clinkers here are (C) and (E). True, if you've been working on your vocabulary (see Chapter 2 for hints), you already have a leg up on SAT Sentence Completions. But even if you haven't been buttering pages of the dictionary and eating them with a dab of strawberry, you can still do well on this section if you stay alert to reading clues.

Uncovering word clues

Sentences fall into a small number of recognizable patterns. Sentences may follow chronological order, relate cause and effect, explain similarities, or add examples. They also contrast ideas or things and name exceptions to the rule. Certain words clue you in to the sentence structure. After you identify those words, you've solved the riddle. Take a look at the most prevalent clue words you may encounter on the SAT and example sentences:

- ✔ **After.** *Barney ate three dried fish after he went to the movies.* (The sentence doubles back in time from the fish to the movies.)

- ✔ **And, also.** *Brunhilda added three new ants to her all-bug baseball team, and she also acquired a terrific centipede pitcher that had recently cleared waivers.* (The sentence adds examples.)

- ✔ **But.** *Barbarosa bellowed for help for seven straight hours, but Bellicosa barely whimpered her distress.* (The sentence contrasts two Viking warriors.)

- ✔ **So.** *Bettina's aardvark wouldn't stop eating her pet ants, so she slapped him.* (The sentence moves logically from cause to effect.)

- ✔ **Then.** *Brini went to the movies and then ate two bags of popcorn.* (The sentence proceeds in a straight line chronologically from the movies to the oh-so-appetizing snack.)

In addition to the five preceding bulleted common SAT clue words, check out the following list for other clue words you may encounter:

- ✔ **Cause and effect:** Because, for, therefore, consequently, hence, thus, accordingly, as a result, ergo (only in truly boring academic writing, the type that should be banned from the planet, if not the solar system)

- ✔ **Comparison:** Than, equally, like . . . as, similarly, similar to, like

- ✔ **The exception to the rule (contrasting idea):** On the other hand, in contrast to, however, despite, in spite of, nevertheless, nonetheless, otherwise, although, though, even though

- ✔ **More of the same:** And, also, as well, in addition, not only . . . but also, furthermore, moreover, besides, likewise, not the only, such as, for example, for instance, showing, illustrating

- ✔ **Time marches on (or back):** Then, once, before, after, since, while, during, still, yet, until, up until, later, earlier, finally, in the end, when, originally

No! No! A thousand times *no!* Not to mention *never, but, nor, neither,* and other *negative* words. These word-gremlins pop up frequently in the Sentence Completions portion, a trap for the unwary. When you see a negative word, give yourself an extra moment to be sure you understand the sentence's meaning. A Grand Canyon-size difference separates *Fiona wanted to polish Nick's teeth more than anything else in the world* and *Fiona didn't want to polish Nick's teeth more than anything else in the world.* Also, be careful of double negatives. The SAT has good grammar, so you won't find a sentence completion saying something like *He didn't want no vegetables.* However, you may find this sentence: *Because Mattie didn't understand Martian, she had no interest in that newspaper.* Okay, maybe not that exact sentence, but one with a similar structure. Be sure to decode both parts of the sentence before choosing a completion answer.

Applying real-life experience

Want to increase your vocabulary, fast? Keep a notepad or a stack of index cards near you when you're reading. When you come across an unfamiliar word, take a moment to jot down the sentence. Later, check the word's meaning. You can use the dictionary or a handy teacher, even a parent. Note the meaning. Don't write *all* the possible definitions, just the one that fits the sentence. From time to time, review your word/sentence list — your personal dictionary. The words will stick in your mind because you didn't memorize a random list; you got them from something you were actually reading. The context helps keep the new words in your memory bank. (For more long-term vocabulary-building tips, check out Chapter 2.)

You can decode a few of the SAT Sentence Completions with a fast reference to your own, normal, happens-to-every-human experience. For example, suppose you're reading this passage:

> Alfonse, weary and depressed by the idea of still another meaningless date with Alfrieda instead of an evening with the love of his life, Altoonia, begged off by feigning a headache.

Okay, imagine that the word *feigning* is new to you. No big deal. Everyone's been in Alfonse's shoes, signed up to have dinner with a loser because the person he or she really wants to date has basically said, "Not in this universe" to all requests for romantic attention. So what do you do when you really can't take it anymore? You pretend to have a headache. Bingo. *Feigning* = pretending. Of course, if you're just reading, you probably don't take the time to say explicitly, "*Feign* is a fancy way of saying pretend." You just go on your gut instinct and keep reading, hoping to find out how Alfrieda reacts to her twentieth straight rejection. By the way, you probably didn't stop to look up *explicitly* in the dictionary. You decoded the sentence without that word, which means "openly or clearly, stated upfront" as in *My mother never explicitly told me to take out the garbage so she can't nail me just because half of the kitchen looks like a toxic waste dump.*

After you uncover the word clues and apply real-life logic, you probably have a pretty good idea what the sentence is trying to say. Now you're ready to complete it and on your way to a high score in the Sentence Completion section.

Completing the Sentence: Steps That Work

If you see a Sentence Completion with relatively simple words, read extra carefully. Be sure that you understand the meaning of the sentence before choosing an answer. To make your life even more miserable than usual, the SAT-writers usually place one very appealing wrong answer among the five choices in this sort of Sentence Completion. If you space out for even a second or if you overlook one picky little detail, you may fall headfirst into an SAT trap.

Introducing the *mal* family

Sentence Completions give your vocabulary a workout. To pump up those word muscles, get to know the "mal" family. As treacherous as Tony Soprano and his mother on a good day, the *mal* family of words are bad. Really bad. And not the kind of street slang where "bad" actually means "good." *Mal* words are bad through and through. Meet the family:

✔ *Maladapted:* Badly adapted, as in *A fish is maladapted for life in a birdcage.*

✔ *Maladroit:* *Adroit* means skillful, nimble, good with your hands, so maladroit means clumsy or bad with your hands, as in *The juggler was so maladroit that he broke all the eggs he was attempting to catch.*

✔ *Malady:* An illness or disorder, as in *Frontwax's malady was so embarrassing that he hid his left leg in a large paper bag whenever he went out.*

✔ *Malaise:* Depression, bad spirits, as in *Filled with malaise, Flautia frowned continuously.*

✔ *Malcontent:* A complainer, one who is "badly" content. *Oscar the Grouch is a malcontent.*

✔ *Malevolent:* Wicked, evil, spiteful. The basic movie villain is malevolent. Related word: *malevolence*

✔ *Malice:* Bad or ill will, as in *Lucretia's malice was so well known in her family that not one relative would agree to eat lunch with her without a food taster.* Related words: *malicious, maliciously*

✔ *Malign:* Speak badly of, as in *Elvira maligned her ex in front of the judge in a vain attempt to extract more alimony.*

✔ *Malignant:* Evil, also used for cancerous tumors. Related words: *malignancy*

✔ *Malodorous:* Bad or foul smelling, as in *Elvis's socks are so malodorous that no one will let him take off his blue suede shoes.*

For both types of questions — simply worded and vocabulary-laden — follow these steps:

1. **Read the entire sentence.**

   This step sounds too obvious to state, but some people actually try to choose an answer after reading only a couple of words. The SAT test-makers are ready for these "partial readers." They take care to provide a choice that looks fine but is the verbal equivalent of the halfway point in a dive into a waterless swimming pool.

2. **Check for clue words.**

   If you find any, underline them. (Not sure what a clue word is? Check out "Uncovering Word Clues" earlier in this chapter.)

3. **Decide what the sentence is trying to say.**

   You may not be able to get the whole meaning yet, but you should have some idea what target the sentence is aiming at. Don't look at the answer choices yet.

4. **If possible, make up a word or phrase that fits the blank(s).**

   You can't always do so, but if you can, you're nearly home free. Check the answers to see whether any choice matches your idea. If so, take that option and move on. If not, think about whether the answer is likely to be a positive or a negative word. Put a little plus or minus sign in the blank to remind you of the type of answer you're searching for.

5. **Eliminate the nonstarters.**

   You may be able to rule out some choices right away. For example, if you know that the blank indicates a change in direction for the sentence — a contrast, perhaps — you can dump all the choices that seem similar to the idea expressed in the rest of the sentence. If you've placed a plus sign in the blank, dump the negative words.

6. Check the remaining answers for the best match.

Even if you weren't able to come up with a possible fill-in, the answer choices may give you some ideas. Plug each remaining choice into the sentence until one fits snugly. If more than one answer is possible, go for the one that matches a clue in the sentence. In the SAT Sentence Completions you're always looking for the best answer, not just any old answer that may be okay.

If you have absolutely no idea what some of the words mean, follow the general rule on guessing. If you can eliminate one choice, take a guess. If you can't eliminate any choices, skip the question. No matter what, don't waste brain cells on a question that relies on a bunch of words that have never crossed your path. Move on to the questions that you have a better shot at getting right. (See Chapter 1 for the complete lowdown on guessing.)

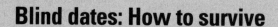

Blind dates: How to survive

So your friend set you up with The One. The date begins, and you're wondering how to behave. Here's a guide:

- If the date is *flippant* (takes nothing seriously, including your new sports car), practice *forbearance* (tolerance, patience).

- If he or she is a *zealot* (nuts for a cause), try not to *wince* (to move involuntarily as a result of pain).

- Don't give in to *wanderlust* (passion to explore other places — geographic places, that is) if the date's *vociferous* (loud and noisy).

- Control your *vituperation* (abusive language) despite your date's *vacuous* (lacking intelligence, empty of meaning) conversation.

- Don't become *truculent* (inclined to anger) if the date's *tremulous* (fearful, shaking).

Most of all, realize when you sign up for a blind date that it'll probably be a complete *fiasco* (failure).

Chapter 8

Practicing Sentence Completions

· ·

In This Chapter

▶ Getting comfortable with Sentence Completions

▶ Analyzing your strengths and weaknesses in solving Sentence Completions

· ·

Practice may not make perfect, but in Sentence Completions, practice definitely leads to higher scores. As you get comfortable with this type of question, you'll quickly zero in on the clue words and maneuver around the SAT's favorite tricks.

In this chapter, you find two sets of SAT-style Sentence Completions, arranged in increasing level of difficulty. After you finish a question, check the explanation directly underneath. No peeking! If you're too tempted, place a sheet of paper over the answer. Even if you get the correct answer, read the whole explanation. You may discover some new vocabulary and tricks of the trade.

Level of difficulty is always an individual decision, so you may find some of the earlier sentences more difficult and some of the latter sentences a walk in the park. But in general, look especially hard for traps in the last three Sentence Completions, including the ones in this chapter. Follow the "guessing rules" outlined in Chapter 1.

Tackling Sample Set One

1. Audrey Vazquez, who acknowledges Cervantes as a _____, takes inspiration from his famous windmill episode but raises the comedy to a new level.

   (A) model

   (B) descendent

   (C) obstacle

   (D) tragedian

   (E) contradiction

The key word here is *inspiration*. If Audrey Vazquez (author of *Fried Tonsils and Other Culinary Delights*) takes *inspiration* from Cervantes, Cervantes has to be something positive, and he has to come before Audrey's time. Boom! You can eliminate *descendent* and *obstacle*. Because the "famous windmill episode" is comedy, you can dump *tragedian*. *Contradiction* doesn't make much sense, so *model* is best. (A) is correct.

2. The labor leader's foray into astrology has been ignored by all but the most inclusive biographers, and even they tend to _____ this period in his life.

    (A) investigate

    (B) explain

    (C) fabricate

    (D) emphasize

    (E) minimize

The clue that cracks the sentence is *even*. You know you're going to continue the same idea from the beginning of the sentence, which tells you that the period is *ignored*. What fits with *ignored*? **Minimize** = to pay as little attention to as possible. (E) is correct.

3. The central achievement of *Macbeth* is Shakespeare's ability to _____ the politics of his day and _____ the interplay of ambition and conscience.

    (A) uncover . . . synthesize

    (B) dissect . . . reveal

    (C) penetrate . . . rearrange

    (D) analyze . . . confuse

    (E) idealize . . . downgrade

Think about the relationship between the two blanks. The first does something to "politics" and the second relates to "ambition" and "conscience." If you fill in the blanks with the first thing that comes into your head, you may say "dig into" the politics and "show" the ambition/ conscience connection. So you can immediately knock out (D) and (E), because *confuse* and *downgrade* aren't achievements. (A), (B), and (C) are all possible until you get to the second blank because *uncover, dissect,* and *penetrate* all tell you that Shakespeare is getting into politics. But only (B) fits when you hit the second blank. **Synthesize** means "to pull lots of loose ideas into a whole" or "to manufacture." *Rearrange* doesn't make sense. (B) has it all: If Shakespeare **dissects** politics, he slices into it and examines the pieces in detail, as generations of biology students have done to frogs, thus *revealing* the way ambition and conscience relate to each other. Three cheers for (B).

4. _____ that intentions have some _____ in a discussion of poetry, let us refer to the journal of Alex Plug, which clearly states that his sonnet "On Homework" was written to express disgust with the last biology assignment.

    (A) Denying . . . importance

    (B) Acknowledging . . . ambiguity

    (C) Granting . . . validity

    (D) Reiterating . . . irrelevance

    (E) Disproving . . . interest

You can rule out (A) because if you *deny* that intentions have *importance*, why bother listening to the author's explanation of how he wrote "On Homework"? You can drop (D) and (E) for the same reason. (B) leaves the playing field because Plug's journals *clearly* make a point, and **ambiguity** implies that more than one interpretation is possible. (C) is correct.

5. The failure of the parent to control his child's behavior meant that the entire streetcar had to endure a flow of meaningless _____ from a youngster barely old enough to talk.

 (A) prattle

 (B) joviality

 (C) criticism

 (D) maledictions

 (E) maladies

You know the sentence refers to a problem because the streetcar riders must "endure," or put up with something, so we can rule out *joviality* (fun, jolliness). "Barely old enough to talk" tells us that the problem concerns words; time to dump *maladies* (ills) and *maledictions* (curses). Criticism could be verbal trouble, but tiny little kids seldom lecture on the flaws in Spielberg's latest movie. *Prattle* — meaningless chatter — fits best. Pat yourself on the back if you said (A).

6. Although _____ images of the region persist, the area in fact has witnessed a _____ of economic and social activity.

 (A) photographic . . . mutation

 (B) sordid . . . devastation

 (C) illusory . . . decline

 (D) geographic . . . predominance

 (E) negative . . . resurgence

(E) is correct. The clue word *although* tips you off: The sentence contrasts two ideas. (E) gives you opposite directions — *negative* is on the way down, and *resurgence* (resurrection or rebirth) on the way up. No other pair contains this contrast.

7. The most controversial section is Ms. Haldock's frank _____ on patriotism.

 (A) platitude

 (B) metamorphosis

 (C) consensus

 (D) treatise

 (E) neologism

The clues are "controversial" and "frank" — concepts usually applied to ideas in written or oral form. (A), (D), and (E) may refer to words (*platitude* = soothing proverb or saying, *treatise* = a written discussion of ideas, and *neologism* = newly coined word). Of the three, only *treatise* fits with "controversial," an adjective applied to things that people argue about, such as Janet Jackson's choice of wardrobe at the Super Bowl. (D) is correct.

Now that you've completed a set, time to analyze yourself. No, get off the couch. We're talking sentence-completion strengths and weaknesses, not Freud's view of your obsession with empty milk cartons. (You're not interested in empty milk cartons? Hmm . . . m. *Very* interesting. But you don't have time for *that* now.) Look at the questions you answered incorrectly. Decide why you made a mistake. Was it an issue of vocabulary? Missing a word clue? Eliminating clearly wrong answers and then making a bad guess? After you examine your pattern of errors, you know what you need to work on. If it's vocabulary, check out Chapter 2 for some tips. Also look at the vocabulary builders icons tucked into this and all chapters. If word clues trip you up, reread Chapter 7.

Sampling Sentence Completions, Set Two

Now that you've figured out where your weak spots lie, try a second set. Remember that the earlier questions tend to be easier and the later ones for word-fiends only.

1. His expression was _____ at every game; I don't think I saw him smile even when his team scored a hundred points.

   (A) downcast

   (B) affable

   (C) joyful

   (D) pert

   (E) mirthful

You're looking for a downer, and the only word that doesn't apply to the can't-stop-grinning types is *downcast*. *Affable* = friendly, your basic chat-over-the-back-fence neighbor. *Pert* (also known as a shampoo) = chirpy, your basic kid-sister-on-a-good-day attitude. *Mirth* = laughter, so you can figure out *mirthful* yourself. (A) is correct.

2. The king's _____ was evident when he declined to increase the tax rebate for his loyal but _____ subjects.

   (A) benevolence . . . poverty-stricken

   (B) greed . . . undertaxed

   (C) laziness . . . stubborn

   (D) popularity . . . aged

   (E) miserliness . . . needy

The clues in the sentence concern the *tax rebate*. If the king "declined" (refused) to increase the *rebate,* he didn't lower taxes. So (A), the trap in this question, is out because if the king displayed **benevolence**, he'd take less money from his poor subjects. On the other hand, if he was showing **miserliness,** he was counting every penny and not returning any more than he absolutely had to, even though his subjects were *needy*. (E) is right.

3. The judges who select the recipients of Woodron Fellowships _____ the purpose of the foundation when they financed Elton Ebert's research on the origin of mathematics, a project that is sure to _____ that topic successfully.

   (A) violated . . . describe

   (B) exonerated . . . delineate

   (C) contravened . . . explicate

   (D) honored . . . illuminate

   (E) supported . . . obfuscate

Use real-world knowledge to get a foothold here. Fellowships are fancy scholarships and are designed to add to the body of knowledge. So any positive word in the first blank must be matched by a positive word in the second blank. Or, both blanks can be negative. The word "successfully" implies that you're aiming for positive, so you can rule out (A) and (C) (first choice negative) and (E) (second choice negative). (B) falls away because you don't **exonerate** a purpose (prove that the purpose is guiltless), though you can exonerate the officers of the Woodron Fellowship if you can prove that they didn't spend a month in the Bahamas snorkeling away the scholarship money. (D) is correct.

4. The comedian's _____ body made his emergence from the narrow chimney appear ridiculous and nearly impossible.

    (A) wizened

    (B) lithe

    (C) rotund

    (D) sooty

    (E) emaciated

What makes an entry through a "narrow" chimney "nearly impossible"? A fat body. Hence *rotund,* a word for the round guys who shop for pants with 60-inch waists. The other choices don't fit: *wizened* = shriveled up, *lithe* = graceful (think ballerina), and *emaciated* = thin to the point of starving. (D) was meant to distract you, because *soot* does come from chimneys. However, because *soot* comes from chimneys, a *sooty* body is the opposite of *nearly impossible* for anyone who has slithered down one. (C) is correct.

5. Agnell's submission is in stark contrast to her growing awareness of the value of _____ speech.

    (A) impromptu

    (B) controversial

    (C) rebellious

    (D) protective

    (E) timorous

You need a contrast to "submission," so you can rule out *impromptu* (off the cuff, unplanned), *protective,* (serving to shield or defend) and *timorous* (fearful, shy). *Controversial* is a possibility, but *to rebel* is the opposite of *to submit,* so *rebellious* is a better choice. (C) is your best bet here.

6. The beauty queen received her award primarily for her _____.

    (A) protocol

    (B) pulchritude

    (C) luminescence

    (D) integrity

    (E) chicanery

Okay, *pulchritude* sounds like something you'd get arrested for, but it actually means "beauty." The next closest is *luminescence,* because beautiful people tend to shine, but this word is better for things that really light up, like 40-watt bulbs. *Protocol* (the rules of diplomacy) and *integrity* (honesty) don't win beauty crowns, though *chicanery* (trickery) might. Still, (B) is best.

7. The _____ spectator did not hesitate to offer his opinion on every aspect of the game, even though he knew very little about sporting events.

    (A) inhibited

    (B) vociferous

    (C) credulous

    (D) brusque

    (E) judicious

Vociferous people talk a lot and loudly — just the sort of spectators who think they know everything. *Inhibited* people are restrained and quiet. *Credulous* (believing too easily, as in "You'll sell me the Brooklyn Bridge? Great!") and *judicious* (wise) don't fit; neither does *brusque* (rude, abrupt). (B) is right.

8. The approaching rain gave us a(n) _____ excuse to escape the _____ party.

   (A) ubiquitous . . . jovial

   (B) unsolicited . . . riotous

   (C) plausible . . . boring

   (D) multifarious . . . elegant

   (E) intrinsic . . . obligatory

This relatively easy sentence becomes a killer when you look at the word choices, which are strictly for the "I read the whole thesaurus last night" set. But you can take an educated guess on the second blank. If you're talking about an *excuse* and an *escape,* the party is probably *boring* (choice C). Then real-world clues help. You want to get out of a boring party? Plead weather, and you'll be believed because your excuse is *plausible,* or believable. The other choices don't come close, though (B) may have caught your eye because rain is *unsolicited* (not asked for) and parties may be *riotous* (the neighbors may call the cops). (C) is correct.

After you finish the second set of Sentence Completions, review the ones you answered incorrectly. Do you see a pattern to your mistakes? Analyzing both sets, can you identify a problem area? Make a New Year's resolution, even if it isn't January. Work on vocabulary or go after word clues. And when you try the sample full-length SAT practice tests in Part V, hit the Sentence Completion sections with an awareness of your strengths and weaknesses.

Here's how to play to your strengths.

- ✔ If you have an *uncanny* (weird, unexplained, *X-Files* territory) ability to decode sentences but have trouble with vocabulary, always take a guess on questions in which you know most of the words.

- ✔ If vocabulary is your strong point, trust your instincts, even if a word is only vaguely familiar to you.

- ✔ If decoding is an issue, spend a moment circling the key words in the sentence before you look at the clues. Read sentences with negative words extra carefully.

Meeting the *bene* clan

The *bene* family has a shortcut to heaven, and if you get to know them, Sentence Completions (and everything on the SAT Critical Reading) will be easier. Everything the bene family touches turns out well, because *bene* signals goodness. Check out these branches of the family tree:

- ✔ *Benediction:* Blessing, as in *Though Scylla sought her father's benediction, she knew in her heart that he would never approve of her career as a mime.*

- ✔ *Benefactor:* One who has done a good or charitable work, as in *Blaljik is the charity's chief benefactor.*

- ✔ *Beneficent:* Good-natured, charitable, as in *Benji the Beneficent refused to impose taxes until he had*

pawned all the royal jewels to meet his kingdom's expenses.

- ✔ *Beneficial:* Good for you, as in *This dose of horrible-tasting medicine is beneficial.*

- ✔ *Beneficiary:* The one you're doing good for, as in *Your insurance policy's beneficiary gets the dough when you die.*

- ✔ *Benefit:* Advantage, good (as in for your own . . .).

- ✔ *Benevolence:* Good will, as in Santa's basic attitude.

- ✔ *Benign:* Good, also used for a noncancerous tumor.

Part III
Writing for Fun and Profit

The 5th Wave   By Rich Tennant

"So, on that analytical writing test, how'd you do with that 'existence of God' question?"

In this part . . .

The Sumerians scratched on wax and clay, the Egyptians penned on papyrus or carved on stone, and medieval monks bent over parchment. You get a bunch of green ovals and a sheet of lined paper. Welcome to the SAT Writing Sample.

This new instrument of torture (the old SAT didn't test writing) provides you with four ways to display your authorial prowess. One is an essay, written quickly under conditions that would send the best writer screaming into the night. Another is Error Recognition, in which you recognize, but don't correct, grammar faults. Next up, Sentence Revision. The SAT-writers underline a section of a sentence and give you a selection of ways to change it, for better or worse. Finally, the testers throw a couple of student compositions at you and ask how to improve the writing.

In this part, I take you through each of these tasks, steering you away from common pitfalls and toward winning techniques.

Chapter 9

Speed Writing without Shorthand: The Essay

• •

In This Chapter

▶ Responding to the essay prompt

▶ Collecting your thoughts and material quickly

▶ Taking the plunge: Writing away

▶ Revising the essay for maximum points

• •

The SAT now includes an essay that the test-makers give you a whole 25 minutes (count 'em!) to write. Why the change? Because college professors complained that their students didn't write well and high school teachers (me included) replied that the SAT didn't evaluate writing.

Pressured by teachers, especially college profs who convinced their admissions offices to consider pulling out of the SAT, the company that makes the test agreed to add some actual writing to the exam. Not too much writing, mind you. Keep in mind that the SAT-writers have to pay people to read student work, not just plug in a scanning machine, which has the advantage of working 24/7 without bathroom breaks. They added just enough writing to be able to say that the SAT encourages student literacy.

Enter the essay. And, if you're a typical SAT candidate, exit confidence, self-esteem, and leisurely lunches, because you're spending all your time worrying about how to write the thing. Not to worry. In this chapter, I explain how to start, how to finish, and what to do in the middle, when you're actually writing.

Answering Promptly

The SAT essay portion starts off with an essay *prompt* — a couple of tiny paragraphs that act as the starting gun for the essay race. The SAT prompts consist of one or two short quotations or paraphrased statements from writers, politicians, philosophers, and the like. Next comes the question, which directs you to reflect on the topic and to write an essay based on your own experience, observation, or knowledge you piled up during all those years in school. Check out the following sample, drawn from my own feverish brain and not from anything written by the (fictitious) Minola Oxblood:

To admit responsibility is to enter the world of adulthood, for true maturity comes from facing the consequences of one's actions. On the other hand, Bart Simpson's famous comment, "I didn't do it; nobody saw me do it; you can't prove anything," resembles the defense of most modern politicians when faced with justifiable accusations of improper behavior.

Minola Oxblood, "I'm Innocent"

Assignment: How should people respond when they are justly accused of wrongdoing? To support your ideas, give one or more examples from literature, the arts, science, history, current events, or your own experience and observation.

The essay prompt is meant to mimic the sort of question a college professor might give on an exam. However, the SAT conveniently ignores two facts:

- ✔ No college test is 25 minutes long.
- ✔ College profs tend to ask questions based on their coursework, not on general observation and knowledge.

Also, the SAT has to be accessible to every student who takes the exam. Because students arrive at the test with a diverse array of courses and life experiences, the essay prompt has to be extremely general in order to cover everyone. So although a college professor of history may ask you to discuss the causes of the Peloponnesian War, knowing that you're supposed to have read three pounds of books on the subject, the SAT sticks to vague, abstract prompts. Look for essays on secrecy, loyalty, the future, the value of controversy, the impact of one's childhood, and other general concepts.

Because the SAT prompts are broad, you can probably adapt any number of life experiences to the question. Plus, tons of different literary works or current events can provide suitable evidence. Before the exam, look through your high school English and history textbooks and spend some time with the daily newspaper or news broadcast. You'll have some "evidence" fresh in your mind when you face the test.

Some students write and memorize an entire, general essay before the exam. Then when they're actually in the exam room, they write as much as they can remember of the prepared work and adapt it to the prompt by tacking on a new topic sentence. Bad idea. True, many different subjects and literary works can be twisted to fit a given prompt. However, the fastest way to fail the essay (yes, you *can* fail) is not to answer the question. In fact, the principal *criterion* (standard, plural = *criteria*) a scorer is told to consider is whether or not the essay addresses the assigned topic. So if SAT-writers are asking you about a response to wrongdoing (see the sample question earlier in this chapter), don't write about the value of democracy. Write about responses to wrongdoing in a democratic system, if you wish, but tailor your essay to the question.

Dickens counts more than your birthday, right?

When the SAT essay question is scored,

(A) graders throw spitballs at the screen if they find an essay particularly obnoxious

(B) examples from the students' personal lives count as much as examples from scholarly sources

(C) the really good essays are stolen and published under fictitious names

(D) the nation's supply of red ink drops to dangerous levels

(E) graders drink five or more double-caf soy lattes per paper

Answer: (B). SAT scorers are specifically told not to favor essays that cite "book" knowledge over essays that relate to a student's personal experience. So if the essay prompt concerns friendship, feel free to write about your best bud, the US-Britain alliance, or Huck Finn and Tom Sawyer. All are equal in the eyes of the SAT.

Organizing Your Thoughts — Timing Is Everything

Not even a half hour. All you get is 25 minutes. So when you turn to the essay, you should pick up your pen and begin to scribble furiously, right? Wrong. I know that my advice goes against your *innate* (inborn) urge to string words together for the entire time allotted. But you'll do better — you really will — if you spend 2 or 3 minutes gathering your thoughts. To shock you even more, I have to tell you that you should stop early and spend the last 2 or 3 minutes revising your work. That's right, folks. Given 25 minutes, write for no more than 20 and blow the extra 5 on sound writing process.

Follow this approach for the best results when writing your 25-minute essay:

First 2 or 3 minutes: Read the question, gather your thoughts, jot down a couple of ideas, and then number them (first idea, second idea, third, and so on).

Next 18 to 20 minutes: Create an introductory paragraph with a strong *thesis statement* (the main idea you're putting forth), write the body paragraph(s), and come to a conclusion. (For more information, read the "Writing" section, later in this chapter.)

Last 2 or 3 minutes: Reread your prose, correcting spelling and grammar.

Up from your faint yet? Good, because I want you take a few moments to check out the following reasons why process is crucial when you're producing a writing product under time and SAT pressure:

✔ You have only one answer sheet and must write on it by hand, unless you're entitled to use a keyboard because of a documented learning disability such as *dysgraphia,* the fancy term for difficulty in producing readable penmanship. If you plunge in immediately and begin to write, you may end up crossing out so much that the essay becomes illegible.

✔ You can't possibly produce a good, organized essay unless you take a moment to envision the logical structure.

✔ Even though you may remember the main idea of your example(s), some details will elude you unless you gather your thoughts before writing. While you're actually placing words on the page, you have to think about grammar, spelling, and all those other things that English teachers care about so much. You don't have time to recall the smaller, specific facts that bring your essay to life.

✔ In the heat of battle — and writing a fast essay *is* a little like walking through a war zone — you may make simple errors in mechanics (spelling "aren't" without the apostrophe, for example, or omitting a period from a sentence). When you reread, you have a chance to fix the mistakes.

Mastering the Writing Process

Tons of famous writers have written (What else?) about their approach to stringing words together. Though the individual details vary, just about everyone agrees that good writing comes from a sound process, one that allows you to gather ideas, order and express them, and revise your work. You'll be successful as an SAT writer if you follow this pattern.

Now for a few more details on each stage of the writing process.

Prewriting

Prewriting is everything you do before your pen hits the answer sheet. To illustrate the prewriting process, here's a sample prompt:

> An ancient proverb claims that a journey of a thousand miles begins with a single step, but that step is difficult to take in scuba flippers. Nevertheless, the traveler must not be discouraged by whatever obstacles fate places in the path to glory.
>
> —Allobald McCloud, *How I Swam the Pacific Ocean and Made a Lot of Money Talking About It*

Assignment: Many human journeys, both literal and metaphorical, nearly fail because the first step is too hard or too frightening for the traveler, but much may be gained by overcoming obstacles and continuing anyway. Comment on this statement based upon your own experience or from literary, scientific, or historical knowledge.

You start, of course, by zooming through the prompt and deciding what the SAT-devils are asking about. This prompt concerns journeys and the idea that some almost don't happen because beginnings are so hard. (Perhaps the test-makers were thinking of essay writing itself when they chose this prompt.) After you crack the prompt, run through your mental index for journeys you or someone else almost didn't take. Don't forget to consider journeys of the spirit (Sounds like a greeting card, doesn't it?) in which people take a hesitant step toward friendship, journeys of the mind in which a scientist, perhaps, takes the first step toward a discovery, and other nonliteral trips.

The SAT provides a quotation or two in the writing prompt, such as Allobald McCloud's immortal words in the preceding example. You don't need to refer specifically to the quotation in your essay, nor should you bother rewriting it. Just be sure that you address the issue the quotation presents.

Don't even think about touching the answer sheet until you have all your thoughts in order. The SAT test booklet is a fine spot for prewriting. Remember, however, that nothing you write on the test booklet counts toward your essay. Only the answer sheet is graded.

Imagine now that you have your idea: A "journey" you took toward the thumb-wrestling team two years ago. You almost didn't show up for tryouts because you were afraid that your friends would laugh at you. (They were all on the chess team.) But you went, you demonstrated good thumb technique, you made the team, and now your thumb is champion of the Northern Hemisphere. Idea selected, you concentrate on jotting down a few details of that first, eventful day:

Tryouts during lunch

Wrestled five thumbs in all

Pizza day

Thumb a little sore from piano practice the day before

Didn't know the coach

Couldn't believe the thrill of victory

Asked to join the team

Herbie helped me find the room

Won the second and third matches

When you're brainstorming ideas, don't worry about putting them in the appropriate order. Just write down whatever comes to mind about your chosen topic.

After you get these basic facts on paper, number them so you know which one to use first, second, third, and so forth. In the preceding list, I'd number the items this way: 1, 6, 2, 5, 4, 8, 9, 3, and 7. Other sequences are possible, but this one begins with thinking about the tryouts (they're during lunch and you'll miss the pizza), moves to the arrival at the tryouts (finding the room, worrying about an unknown coach, and a sore thumb), settles in at the tryouts (five matches, which ones you won, how you felt), and ends up with the result — making the team.

Setting the order is similar to outlining, the chore that your grade-school teachers probably assigned while insisting on a complicated system of margins and numbering. You don't have time for that sort of outline when you're taking the SAT. Just think about the order, throw numbers on the scrap paper, and get ready to write.

Writing

In the 25 minutes you have, you probably won't be able to create a fully formed, exquisitely detailed essay (unless, of course, your name is Shakespeare). The best you can hope for is an organized, reasonably specific piece. For that you need an introduction and a conclusion, with the meat of the essay — the evidence — in the middle.

As you can probably tell from the sample introduction, body, and conclusion that follow, I'm having some fun. You, however, probably shouldn't have any fun when you write the SAT essay (unless writing under pressure is your idea of fun). Yes, avoid boring the essay graders to death if you can, but don't inflict your humor on them. They're looking for clear, fluent writing for *college,* not for comedy clubs.

If you're referring to your own ideas and experiences, you may use *I* and *me* in your essay — what English teachers call "first person." However, if you're writing about science, literature, history, or current events, you may be more comfortable with "third person" — no references to yourself, just statements about other people, events, or things. The choice is yours.

Introductory paragraph

Just a couple sentences long, the introductory paragraph lets the reader know what you're writing about. For SAT purposes, make clear how your topic connects to the essay prompt. Something to draw the reader's interest would be nice, if you have time, because SAT-graders read for hours at a time and look kindly upon a student who takes the writing even a millimeter away from snoozeworthiness. Here's a possible thumb-wrestling introduction:

> The most difficult step in a journey may be the very first, as I found out the day I tried out for the thumb-wrestling team. Beset by hunger pangs and tempted by the tangy scent of pizza wafting from the cafeteria, I almost didn't attend. But something drove me to the door of room 221 that day, a desire to prove myself and to give my thumb a chance at excellence. I am very glad I did.

The preceding introductory paragraph accomplishes the basic tasks. Notice the tie-in to the question in sentence one: *the most difficult step in a journey may be the very first.* Sentence two also nails the essay to the question: *I almost didn't attend.* The introduction also makes the writer's position clear: *I'm very glad I did.* The paragraph isn't as thrilling as a Hollywood movie trailer, but it does engage the reader with a couple of mildly intriguing details — the pizza and the desire to prove the thumb's excellence.

A good introduction lets the reader know what the essay is about and what position the writer takes on the issue at hand. If the reader is puzzled at the end of paragraph one, you're in trouble.

Body

In the measly slice of morning the SAT gives you to write the essay, you won't be able to come up with more than one or two body paragraphs. Make the most of them! Present the specifics of your argument (in the example I've been using, the details of the thumb-wrestling tryouts) clearly and concisely. Here's a possible body for the thumb essay:

> The tryouts were held during lunch hour, and because I had missed school the previous day because of my piano recital, I wasn't even sure where the event was taking place. I had actually walked into the cafeteria, convinced that thumb wrestling wasn't in my future, when I spied my friend Herbie. Herbie urged me to attend and offered to escort me to room 221. Outside the door I nearly turned back. I didn't know the coach, and my thumb was throbbing as a result of four hours of piano practice for the recital.

> The first match against a thumb at least twice as big as mine was a washout. Fortunately, the next two matches went to me. As I savored the thrill of victory, I saw the coach eyeing me thoughtfully. Next he sent over his best wrestler. I played him twice, and twice I went down in defeat. I was sure my thumb-wrestling career was over. To my surprise and delight, the coach welcomed me to the team anyway!

Okay, so it's not *A Tale of Two Cities*. No matter. It includes enough detail to bring the reader into the writer's experience. To bring it back to the question, however, you need a conclusion.

Concluding paragraph

Conclusions are a real pain. When you get all the way to the end of your evidence, you just want to put the pen down and relax a little, at least until the next section of the SAT begins. Instead, you have to come up with still another paragraph. How annoying.

Annoying, but necessary. Without the conclusion your essay doesn't do its job, which is (apart from getting you into college, its *real* job) to show the reader the significance of everything you've written thus far. Think of the conclusion as the final nail in the poster advertising your point of view. Absent that nail, the poster will fall off the wall. Here's a conclusion for the thumb-wrestling essay:

> Now I'm the North American Thumb Wrestling Champ (high school division, under four-inch division). My sport has taken me to China, Japan, Uruguay, and downtown Peoria. None of the wonderful experiences I've had at thumb-wrestling tournaments would have happened had I not walked, sore thumb and all, to the tryout room two years ago. I can only imagine the number of human accomplishments that the world would be without if people allowed themselves to be frightened by the first step in their journeys.

Take a close look at what this conclusion accomplishes. It refers to the question *(first step)* and the author's point of view (*None of the wonderful experiences . . . would have happened*). In the last sentence the conclusion also takes the essay's ideas one, tiny, millimeter forward by referring to what the world would lack if others were deterred by the difficulty of the first step.

Also notice what the conclusion does *not* include: repetition of the material in the essay, a label *(in this essay I have proved that)*, or a completely new, unrelated idea (*I love pizza days*).

Polishing

Put the dust cloth away, but take out your best grammar and spelling knowledge. After the whole essay is on the page, reread it at least once. Neatly cross out any errors (the grammar review in Chapter 11 helps with this task) and write the corrections *legibly* in the space above the line. If you take a minute to check, the essay will score more points than an unedited, mistake-filled draft. Remember, anyone can make a ~~mitak~~ mistake, but the smartest test-takers correct their errors.

Scoring the Essay: Rubrics without the Cube

The SAT recruits desperate-for-cash or have-no-life English teachers (some fall into both categories) to score the essays. The readers used to sit in a windowless room, scoring essays until their eyeballs went on strike. Now modern technology allows the essay graders to sit in their very own living rooms, where their eyeballs still fry. The essays are sent electronically to each reader's computer.

An image of each essay is also posted on the Web, where colleges that you're applying to may view it, warts and all. Be sure to write neatly. I doubt that any institution will turn you down because you're a slob, but an illegible essay doesn't help your case for admission either.

The essay graders award from 1 to 6 points for each essay that answers the question. An essay that is off-topic receives no points at all. The scores from the two readers are added, so you'll get between 2 and 12 points for your masterpiece. If the scores are more than one point apart (one reader gave you a 6 and another a 3, perhaps), the essay goes to a super-reader, who decides your score. The score is *holistic* (seen as one in its entirety, not broken into parts). In other words, the graders don't award a tenth of a point for grammar, a half-point for organization, and so on. They just read it and plop a number on the whole thing.

However, the number isn't random. The SAT-graders follow a *rubric* — a set of standards — in awarding points. The graders consider several factors, including the following:

- ✔ Does the essay answer the question?
- ✔ Does it make a case for a point of view by providing appropriate evidence?
- ✔ Is the essay organized? Does it move logically from one idea to the next?
- ✔ Is the vocabulary appropriate?
- ✔ Is the writing fluent, with varied sentence structure and good use of language?
- ✔ Is the writing grammatical, with good spelling and punctuation?

After considering each of these factors, the SAT-grader rates your essay on a scale from 1 to 6 with (6) meaning outstanding, (5) effective, (4) competent, (3) inadequate, (2) seriously limited, or (1) fundamentally lacking. Even the "outstanding" essays may have a couple of errors, and the "fundamentally lacking" pieces may have a few good points.

Traveling through time

Your essay may be in chronological, or time order. After all, the human instinct is to put things in order, especially when it comes to time. Vocabulary follows instinct, and English is chock-full of word parts that indicate whether something happened *before* or *after* a given event. Meet the *ante* and *pre* (before) and *post* (after) families:

- ✔ *Antebellum, prewar,* and *postwar:* Before and after hostilities. Antebellum refers to the period in the United States prior to the Civil War. Prewar is more general.

- ✔ *Antedate* and *postdate:* If Lucinda's interest in Lou antedates her interest in Lex, she was interested in

Lou first. Postdate is what you do to a check when you're hoping the recipient won't cash it until you earn enough money to cover the check.

- ✔ *Antenatal, prenatal,* and *postnatal:* Before and after birth.

- ✔ *Anterior* and *posterior:* Not time words, but still derived from before and after. The front and back. *You sit on your posterior and present the anterior view to the world.*

Chapter 10

Practice Essays

● ●

In This Chapter
▶ Approaching the SAT essays with an open mind
▶ Working through some sample essays

● ●

Lock the dog in the rumpus room. Gag your little brother. Turn the phone off. Set a kitchen timer for 25 minutes, and tear out the answer sheet at the end of this chapter. It's time to practice essay writing so you aren't bowled over on SAT-day. This chapter contains eight SAT-style essay prompts, but I include only one answer sheet. I suggest you work through three essays. (Make as many photocopies as you need.) If you have the energy and drive to write all eight essays (good for you, but you really ought to get a life), don't write them all at one sitting. I can't guarantee that you won't become comatose by the time you're done.

Practicing What 1 Preach: How to Approach These Sample Questions

Unfortunately the SAT-writers don't give you a choice of essay topics on SAT-day, so don't read all eight and go for the one that immediately appeals to you. Pick a number from one to eight at random — your birthday month (unless you were born in or after September), how often you had ice cream yesterday, your favorite television channel — and settle in with that question. When the 25 minutes are up, put your pen down, shake the cramp out of your hand, and put the essay away. Later, when your brain has retreated a bit from its fried state, look at the essay objectively. Score it according to the grading criteria in Chapter 9.

Some of the quotations in the sample questions come from real literary works, and some from my own semi-sane mind. (I place asterisks by the semi-sane ones. Don't expect your local bookstore to stock the asterisked works.)

If your essay refers to literature, remember this rule: Underline the titles of full-length works (books or plays). Place the titles of shorter works (articles, poems) inside quotation marks.

Essay Prompt One

"It is a truth universally acknowledged, that a single man in possession of a good fortune, must be in want of a wife," wrote Jane Austen in her masterful work, *Pride and Prejudice*. Austen's characters act on assumptions about human behavior, and frequently these assumptions are proved wrong.

—Ray Bann, "Mr. Darcy's Error"*

"Assume that their goals are the same as ours; they want peace, security, and reasonable happiness." That's the advice the president offered to his negotiating team just hours before the cease-fire talks. With his statement in mind, we approached the enemy.

—Dolvin Eddlesworth, *Negotiating for Fun and Profit**

Assignment: What effect do assumptions have on human behavior? Draw upon your own experience or upon your knowledge of literature or world affairs in discussing whether assumptions are a positive, negative, or mixed factor.

Essay Prompt Two

Nineteenth-century author Sydney Smith wrote that truth is justice's handmaid. The Freedom of Information Act has opened the workings of the American government to public scrutiny, and justice has been served accordingly.

—Predieu Orant, *American Democracy in the Age of Instant Messaging**

Justice is truth in action.

—Benjamin Disraeli, 19th century British Prime Minister

Assignment: Comment on the relationship between truth and justice, supporting your ideas with evidence from literary works, current affairs, history, or your own experience.

Essay Prompt Three

American poet Henry Wadsworth Longfellow wrote of "the divine Insanity of noble minds" that creates "what it cannot find." Three centuries earlier, William Shakespeare related "the lunatic" to the poet because both create new realities.

—Gerbel Hamstar, "The Relation Between Craziness and Creativity"*

Assignment: Is realism the enemy of creativity? Must an artist or scientist ignore what is already known in order to move beyond established boundaries? Refer to your knowledge of art, literature, science, or personal experience to discuss the relationship between reality and creativity.

Essay Prompt Four

Where silence once reigned, the cellphone now interrupts. "Computer error" is blamed for almost every glitch in modern life, from erroneous weather forecasts to ridiculous tax bills. Modern life has become enslaved to technology.

—Lobelia Closper, *Free Yourself from Machines**

Assignment: Technology has not made our lives easier. Agree or disagree with this statement, supporting your position with references to your life or your reading.

Essay Prompt Five

Dionysius the Elder, being asked whether he was at leisure, replied, "God forbid that it should ever befall me!"

—Plutarch, Roman historian

Cultivated leisure is the aim of man.

—Oscar Wilde, British writer

Assignment: Is leisure time a blessing or a curse? Take a position on this issue and support your view with evidence from literature, history, current events, or your own observations and experiences.

Essay Prompt Six

Ignorance, the root and stem of all evil.

Attributed to Plato, Greek philosopher

Ignorance is bliss.

—Thomas Gray, British poet

Assignment: Should ignorance ever be preferred to knowledge? Discuss your views, supporting your ideas with reference to your life or reading.

Essay Prompt Seven

As a young man, Lyndon B. Johnson wrote about how uncomfortable it is to have ambition. The ambitious person, said Johnson, is discontented and restless. However, according to Johnson, ambition is what makes us strive for "better things in the future."

—Woefield Cowbus, *Life with LBJ**

Assignment: How much ambition is too much? Discuss your answer to this question with evidence from your observation, your life experience, or your reading.

Essay Prompt Eight

Science is fast outrunning ethics. Almost as soon as society decides whether a new medical technique may be justified, the procedure is outmoded. Cloning, the artificial prolongation of life, the ability to alter one's appearance or design one's offspring — what used to be the stuff of science fiction is fast becoming science fact. And science has implemented its discoveries without undergoing the necessary examination of its rights and obligations.

—Crewly Kind, "The Scientists' Dilemma"*

Assignment: Who should decide how and when, if ever, a scientific discovery should be implemented? Support your position with evidence from your knowledge of science, literature, history, current events, or from your firsthand experience of life.

Chapter 11

Joining the Grammar Police

In This Chapter

▶ Surveying the three types of grammar questions

▶ Creating strategies for each type of grammar question

▶ Reviewing the most frequently tested errors

---

*W*ho invented grammar anyway?" a student once asked me in a tone that strongly suggested she wanted to murder the perpetrator of dependent clauses and subject-verb agreement. Unfortunately, prosecuting the inventor of grammar isn't possible, given the current theory that grammar is hardwired into your head.

If you too have the urge to tear a grammar book into tiny little pieces, take heart. The SAT Reasoning Test now covers grammar, but the concepts the exam tackles aren't horribly difficult. Furthermore, I doubt the questions will bowl you over with tricky wording or clever surprises. In this chapter, I explain the three types that appear on the SAT Writing test, show sample questions from each, and explain the best approach to solve them. I then review some basic rules, and I promise you that I rein in the academic terminology as I do so. You have enough vocabulary stuffed into your head for the Critical Reading questions; you don't need useless technical words to name pronouns! However, if you're dying to fill your brain with tons of grammar rules, check out my book, *English Grammar For Dummies* (Wiley).

Write away, Dear

The SAT Writing section

(A) used to be a SAT II Subject test

(B) takes an hour of your life

(C) is a cheap solution to an expensive problem

(D) is slightly less annoying than a visit to the dentist

(E) all of the above

Answer: (E). Faced with growing discontent from their market (the colleges that require the test, not the test-takers themselves), the SAT-makers added writing to the SAT Reasoning Test. Because it costs a bundle to develop new tests, the SAT-makers grafted and reconfigured old tests to make the new SAT Reasoning Test. What you're taking now is a combo platter — one portion of reading, one of math, and one (leftovers, but nicely reheated) of writing. The writing gobbles up 60 minutes of your morning — 25 minutes for an actual, place-words-on-a-page-by-hand essay (see Chapters 9 and 10) and 35 minutes for multiple-choice grammar questions.

Surveying the Three Grammar Sections

Before you jump into the Writing section's multiple-choice questions, you need to know a little bit about what you're getting yourself into. (Don't worry. With a little patience and a once-over of the grammar rules in this chapter, you can handle them with no problem.) The Writing section contains three parts:

✔ Error Recognition

✔ Sentence Revision

✔ Passage Revision

These three types of questions check word choice, verb tense, pronouns, and all the other devilish details that English teachers love. You'll also find questions that check your style — whether you can write concisely (without extra words) and smoothly.

Bubbling the wrong answer: Error Recognition questions

Surprise! This section contains the only SAT questions that call for you to find the wrong answer. And if you're wrong, you're right. No, I haven't overdosed on super-caffeinated lattes. I'm talking about Error Recognition questions, a bunch of which show up in the SAT Writing section. Here's an example:

<u>Miseria, broke and</u> bewildered, wandered away from her <u>keepers, however,</u> she soon
      A

<u>found a campaign manager</u> and <u>successfully ran</u> for governor. <u>No error.</u>
     C   D   E

Answer: (B) is correct. *However* can't legally join two sentences, according to the grammar cops (see "Nailing Nouns and Capturing Colons: The SAT Grammar Review" later in this chapter for more on specific grammar rules). The comma in front of *however* should be a semicolon.

The key to Error Recognition questions is to pretend for a moment that the underlines don't exist. Just look at the sentence and see what sounds wrong, and then look for the letter. If nothing sounds wrong on first reading, check each underlined portion carefully. Still no mistake? Go for (E), which is always "no error." The following helpful do's and don'ts can make answering Error Recognition questions that much easier:

✔ **Do keep an eye open for incorrect punctuation.** Always check apostrophes and commas.

✔ **Do look for vocabulary mistakes.** Error Recognition sentences sometimes contain mistakes in vocabulary. Words that are commonly confused (*affect* and *effect,* for example) or nonexistent but still popular (*irregardless,* perhaps) may show up.

✔ **Do watch for inconsistent verb tenses.** Verb tense is a big deal. Don't neglect the singular/plural issue for verbs and pronouns.

✔ **Don't worry about the parts of the sentence that aren't underlined.** They're always correct.

✔ **Don't waste time figuring out how to correct the error.** Just find it and bubble it in.

✔ **Do skip the sentence if the answer is a complete mystery.** The SAT deducts a quarter point for a wrong answer and no points for a blank. If you can't eliminate two choices, cut your losses and move on to the next question.

✔ **Don't worry about spelling and capitalization mistakes.** They never appear in the Error Recognition sentences. Assume that the words are spelled correctly and that the capital letters are in the right spots.

Don't be afraid to choose "no error" if you can't find anything wrong. Everybody makes a mistake sometimes, but everybody gets it right sometimes too.

Improving sentences: Sentence Revision questions

One set of Writing questions — Sentence Revisions — presents you with sentences that have a portion underlined. Choice (A) is the equivalent of "no error" — the underlined portion as it appears in the sentence. The other four choices, (B) through (E), change the original a little or a lot. Take a look at this sample question:

Mothrup spent his free time <u>tearing up SAT prep books, setting fire to grammar texts, and diligent study.</u>

(A) tearing up SAT prep books, setting fire to grammar texts, and diligent study.

(B) tearing up SAT prep books and setting fire to grammar texts and diligent study.

(C) in SAT prep book tearing, grammar test firing, and diligent study.

(D) tearing up SAT prep books, setting fire to grammar texts, and studying diligently.

(E) tearing up SAT prep books, setting fire to grammar texts, and he studied diligently.

Answer: (D) is correct. All items in a list should be in the same form. *Diligent study* doesn't match *tearing* and *setting*.

Notice that each choice varies only a little from the original. You may find a question or two that needs a lot of changes to reach perfection, but in general, this part is the pickiest on the exam. Focus on details, and keep the following in mind:

✔ **Check for *homonyms*.** These are words that sound the same but are spelled differently (*who's* and *whose, here* and *hear,* for example).

✔ **Don't overlook punctuation.** Check all the commas, semicolons, and other punctuation marks.

✔ **Focus only on the underlined text.** You can't change anything in the sentence that isn't underlined.

✔ **Keep verb tense in mind.** Verb tense is a big deal in this type of question. See "Tensing up" later in this section for the lowdown on verb tenses.

✔ **Look for the best answer.** The SAT asks for the best answer, not the right answer. The distinction between these two is subtle. On this sort of question, you may find two choices that are grammatically correct, but one is more concise than the other. Go for the elegant choice.

Some test-takers find it helpful to read the original sentence, reword it mentally, and then look for a choice that matches.

Revising for fun and profit: Passage Revision questions

Do you have any old compositions lying on a shelf? Perhaps something that you wrote a few years ago? If so, you have some ready-made SAT practice material. Take out those sheets of paper and see how you could have improved the writing. Now you're ready for SAT Passage Revision questions.

The SAT Passage Revision presents you with what the SAT-writers call "a typical student's first draft" of an essay. The sentences in the passage are numbered, and followed by a batch of questions. You may be asked to fix one sentence or to consider the transition between two paragraphs. Other questions deal with organization (Is everything in the best place?), repetition, and sentence combining. Other questions address the author's purpose. The idea is to find out how you'd create a second draft without the hassle of actually writing a second draft. (Remember, hand-scored writing costs a lot.)

Here's a sample with a couple of questions:

⌐1⌐ When parents and teens argue, it tends to get ugly. ⌐2⌐ Teens are sometimes not trustful of their parents, and parents wish that their sons and daughters are more respectful.

⌐3⌐ This does not have to be the case.

⌐4⌐ Just the other day I asked my mother to withdraw me from the SAT prep course.

⌐5⌐ With all that I have to do, you don't need any extra work. ⌐6⌐ She immediately got on my case and asked me if I wanted a smack in the mouth. ⌐7⌐ I said, No, I'm not disrespectful.

⌐8⌐ Then we argued. ⌐9⌐ We argued for two hours. ⌐10⌐ Finally we came to an agreement.

⌐11⌐ She would not smack me in the mouth and I would attend the SAT prep course one more time. ⌐12⌐ Then she would allow me to be withdrawn if I promised to work on the *The SAT I For Dummies,* 6th Edition which is better anyway.

⌐13⌐ You may find yourself in this situation one day. ⌐14⌐ If you do, remember that smacking someone in the mouth is not a good alternative. ⌐15⌐ Ask yourself who's at fault before you strike. ⌐16⌐ Also, don't assume that you know everything.

1. What is the best revision of sentence one?

    (A) Parents and teens arguing can be ugly.

    (B) Parents and teens are ugly when they argue.

    (C) Arguments between parents and teens tend to veer out of control.

    (D) Parents arguing with teens are ugly.

    (E) Parents and teens argue, and it isn't pretty.

Answer: (C) is correct. Choices (A) and (E) have grammar mistakes; you need an apostrophe after "teens" in (A) and you should eliminate the vague "it" in (E). (B) and (D) change the meaning.

2. Which of the following statements best describes the purpose of paragraph two?

   (A) to alert child protection agencies about a bad home situation

   (B) to give an example of a parent/teen conflict that was worked out successfully

   (C) to show how annoying teens can be

   (D) to show how unreasonable adults can be

   (E) to advertise my book

Answer: If you selected (B), you're right on target, though I admit that (E) has some truth in it. (C) and (D) are easy to eliminate: The SAT avoids criticizing groups. (A) is from another universe, as "child protection agencies" aren't in the passage.

3. What is the best way to combine sentences 8–10 in paragraph two?

   (A) We argued for two hours before finally coming to an agreement.

   (B) We argued for two hours, finally we came to an agreement.

   (C) Arguing for two hours, an agreement was finally reached.

   (D) We argued and agreed for two hours.

   (E) For two hours we argued and then agreed.

Answer: (A) is correct. The others, apart from sounding clunky (Don't you love those technical terms?) have errors in grammar or meaning.

Don't expect to be thrilled by the subject matter or the writing in Passage Revision questions. The material is boring, but the questions are reasonably easy. Keep these strategies in mind, and the experience may not be as agonizing:

- ✔ **Read the whole passage before you hit the questions.** Don't skip over any text because you may miss something essential.

- ✔ **Generally ignore everything the SAT-writers don't ask you about.** Even if you're itching to make a particular sentence better, don't. But when you choose the best revision for something they *do* ask you about, be sure that your new sentence fits well with the sentences before and after it.

- ✔ **Don't forget to check for wordiness.** Go for the more concise revision, so long as the meaning of the original is maintained.

- ✔ **Remember that SAT passages have very simple organization.** Check for an introduction that tells the reader the topic and the writer's stance, a body that gives examples or that presents the situation's complexity, and a conclusion that sums up and extends the main idea slightly. If any of these parts are missing or out of order, take note. You may find a question addressing these issues.

- ✔ **Start with the easier questions.** Questions that refer to one sentence are easier, in general, than questions that refer to the entire passage. If you're pressed for time, go for the one-sentence questions first. You can always go back later to the whole-passage or whole-paragraph questions.

Nailing Nouns and Capturing Colons: The SAT Grammar Review

Okay, don't worry. I make sure this grammar review is quick and painless, and if you're pretty good in grammar, you can ignore this section entirely. Otherwise, zero in on your problem area, run your eyeballs over the WRONG and RIGHT examples, and then go bowling, satisfied that you've done your best to ready yourself for SAT grammar.

Agreeing with the grammar cops

In the wonderful world of grammar, *agreement* is crucial. Stop nodding your head! I'm not talking about comments like "yes, I also think we should defrost Antarctica." I'm talking about matching singular to singular, plural to plural. In the grammar world, you can't mix singular and plural without risking war.

Two spots call for agreement (I know I said I wouldn't throw grammar terms at you, but a couple are indispensable!):

- Subject-verb pairs
- Pronoun-antecedent pairs.

Subject-verb agreement

A *verb* expresses action or state of being; the *subject* is whoever or whatever is *doing* the action or *in* the state of being. Think of the subject-verb pair as a marriage: The two have to be compatible or potted plants start sailing across the room. In grammarland, compatibility means that a singular subject takes a singular verb and a plural subject takes a plural verb. Check out these examples:

Felicia flounders in the face of an SAT test. (*Felicia* = singular subject, *flounders* = singular verb)

All Felicia's friends happily help her. (*friends* = plural subject, *help* = plural verb)

The SAT doesn't spend much time on the simple subject-verb pairs. Instead, the exam concentrates on the ones that may be confusing, such as the following:

CONFUSING: *There is, there are, here is, here are*

WHY THEY'RE CONFUSING: *There* and *here* aren't subjects. The real subject comes after the verb.

GUIDELINE TO END CONFUSION: Look for the real subject and match the verb to it.

WRONG: There is three chipmunks on the desk. Here's two gerbils.

RIGHT: There are three chipmunks on the desk. Here are two gerbils.

WHY THEY ARE RIGHT: *chipmunks are, two gerbils are* (plural subjects and verbs match)

CONFUSING: *Neither/nor* and *either/or* sentences.

WHY THEY'RE CONFUSING: You have two subjects for every verb. When one subject is singular and the other plural, mayhem ensues.

GUIDELINE TO END CONFUSION: Match the verb to the closest subject.

WRONG: Neither Brunhilda nor her parakeets is eating much these days.

WHY IT'S WRONG: *parakeets* is closer to the verb than *Brunhilda,* and *parakeets* is plural.

RIGHT: Neither Brunhilda nor her parakeets are eating much these days.

WHY IT'S RIGHT: *parakeets are* (plural subject matches plural verb)

CONFUSING: Sentences with interrupters (*as well as, along with, in addition to, not*) between the subject and verb.

WHY THEY'RE CONFUSING: The interrupters, like rude people in a conversation, take your attention away from the important stuff. In terms of subject-verb agreement, they're irrelevant.

GUIDELINE TO END CONFUSION: Ignore the interrupters and match the subject-verb pair.

WRONG: Brunhilda, as well as her parakeets, like honey-flavored seed.

ALSO WRONG: Brunhilda, not her parakeets, like honey-flavored seed.

WHY THEY'RE WRONG: The two interrupters, *as well as her parakeets* and *not her parakeets,* should be ignored

RIGHT: Brunhilda, as well as her parakeets, likes honey-flavored seed.

ALSO RIGHT: Brunhilda, not her parakeets, likes honey-flavored seed.

WHY THEY'RE RIGHT: *Brunhilda likes* (singular subject matches singular verb)

Bottom line: In checking subject-verb agreement, look for the real subject and ignore distracting words. Match the verb to the subject and you're all set.

Pronoun-antecedent agreement

An *antecedent* is a word that a pronoun replaces. In the sentence "Mary told John that he was a drip," *he* is a pronoun and *John* is the antecedent because *he* stands for *John.* The rule on antecedents is super-simple: Singular goes with singular and plural with plural. You already know all the easy applications of this rule. In the *Mary/John* sentence, you'd never dream of replacing *John* with *they.* The SAT-makers, however, go for the confusing spots, and so do I.

CONFUSING: These antecedents: *everyone, someone, anyone, everybody, somebody, anybody*

WHY THEY'RE CONFUSING: Most people want to match them with the plural pronoun *their.*

GUIDELINE TO END CONFUSION: All the "ones" and all the "bodies" are singular, all the time.

WRONG: Everybody brought their cheat sheets to the SAT.

WHY IT'S WRONG: *Everybody* = singular and *their* = plural

RIGHT: Everybody brought his or her cheat sheet to the SAT.

WHY IT'S RIGHT: All the "bodies" are singular, so *everybody* matches the singular pronouns *his* and *her.*

CONFUSING: Sentences with *either* and *neither.*

WHY THEY'RE CONFUSING: *Either* and *neither* may be followed by phrases that make them sound plural.

GUIDELINE TO END CONFUSION: *Either* and *neither* are always singular when they show up without their usual dates, *or* and *nor.*

WRONG: Neither of my friends brought their two-way radios to the SAT.

WHY IT'S WRONG: *neither* = singular and *their* = plural

RIGHT: Neither of my friends brought her two-way radio to the SAT.

WHY IT'S RIGHT: *neither* = singular and *her* = singular

Dateless *either* and *neither* (their partners *or* and *nor* are seeing someone else on the sly) are always singular, so match them with singular, not plural verbs, as in "neither of my friends wants to take the SAT" (*neither* and *wants* are both singular).

CONFUSING: Sentences with *the only one who* and *one of the few . . . who*.

WHY THEY'RE CONFUSING: *One* implies singular, but you have to analyze what the sentence is really saying in order to find the proper verb and pronoun.

GUIDELINE TO END CONFUSION: *the only one who* (or, *the only one that*) is singular and calls for a singular verb and singular pronoun and *one of the few . . . who* (or *one of the few . . . that*) is plural and calls for a plural verb and plural pronoun.

WRONG: Dentalia is the only one of the SAT takers who gnash their teeth.

WHY IT'S WRONG: The expression *the only one* is singular, and *gnash* is a plural verb. *Their* is a plural pronoun.

RIGHT: Dentalia is the only one of the SAT takers who gnashes her teeth.

WHY IT'S RIGHT: Everything's singular now — *the only one, gnashes,* and *her.*

As in the preceding example, when you're deciding singular/plural for a pronoun, you may be deciding the same issue for a verb. Check both!

Tensing up

On the SAT Writing section, tense isn't just what's happening to your muscles. Tense is the quality of verbs that indicates time. The English language has a ton of rules regulating tense, but I just hit the biggies, at least in terms of the SAT.

CONFUSING: The difference between past (*Rodney bubbled*) and present perfect tense (*Rodney has bubbled*).

WHY THEY'RE CONFUSING: Both refer to the past.

GUIDELINES TO END CONFUSION: Present perfect — the one with *has* or *have* attached — refers to something that began in the past and is connected to the present.

WRONG: As of now, Rodney bubbled only three answers, but the test runs for another half minute.

WHY IT'S WRONG: The word *now* tells you that the action is connected to the present. You need present perfect tense.

RIGHT: As of now, Rodney has bubbled only three answers, but the test runs for another half minute.

WHY IT'S RIGHT: The verb *has bubbled* shows that Rodney is still bubbling.

CONFUSING: The difference between past (*Rodney bubbled*) and past perfect tense (*Rodney had bubbled*).

WHY THEY'RE CONFUSING: Both refer to the past.

GUIDELINES TO END CONFUSION: Past perfect — the one with *had* attached — shows up when you have two actions in the past and you need to place one earlier than the other. The *had* belongs to the earlier of the two actions.

WRONG: Rodney bubbled only three answers when the proctor called time.

WHY IT'S WRONG: The bubbling took place before the time calling, but both verbs are in past tense.

RIGHT: Rodney had bubbled only three answers when the proctor called time.

WHY IT'S RIGHT: The verb *had bubbled* shows that Rodney bubbled before the proctor called time.

 Verbs also have moods. The only mood you have to worry about on the SAT is subjunctive (forget the name) and in only one situation: condition contrary to fact. Look for sentences that make statements that aren't true. ("If I were making the SAT, I would dump all the grammar questions. If I had known about the grammar, I would not have burned my English textbook.") The *if* part of the sentence — the untrue part — gets *were* or *had* and the other part of the sentence features *would*. The SAT-demons like to place a *would* in the *if* part of the sentence in order to trip you up.

Casing the joint

Pronouns, bless their little hearts, have case. Case makes the difference between *me* and *I*, *him* and *his*, and (gasp) *who* and *whom*, not to mention *whose*. The rule is actually quite easy: Use a subject pronoun (*I, he, she, we, they, who, whoever*) when you need a subject. Object pronouns (*me, him, her, us, them, whom, whomever*) cover almost everything else. To show possession, try *my, his, her, its, our, your, their,* and *whose*.

CONFUSING: Sentences with pairs.

WHY THEY'RE CONFUSING: The pronoun gets lost in the shuffle.

GUIDELINE TO END CONFUSION: Isolate the pronoun and check it for errors.

WRONG: The proctor gave Dentalia and I a dirty look when the teeth-gnashing got too loud.

WHY IT'S WRONG: *I* is a subject pronoun, but *proctor* is the subject.

RIGHT: The proctor gave Dentalia and me a dirty look when the teeth-gnashing got too loud.

HOW YOU KNOW IT'S RIGHT: Cover *Dentalia and* with your finger. *The proctor gave I?* I don't think so. *The proctor gave me*.

CONFUSING: The whole *who/whom* universe.

WHY IT'S CONFUSING: Most people throw in *whom* whenever they want to sound educated, but *whom* may serve as an object and *not* as a subject.

GUIDELINE: Choose *who* for subject and *whom* for everything else.

WRONG: Whom shall I say is calling?

WHY IT'S WRONG: When you untangle the sentence you get *I shall say whom is calling? Whom* can't be the subject of *is*.

RIGHT: Who shall I say is calling?

WHY IT'S RIGHT: You need a subject pronoun to partner *is*.

To crack a *who/whom* problem, make sure all the verbs in the sentences are paired with subjects. If you have a verb flapping around with no subject, you probably need *who* for its partner. Also, if the *who/whom* issue shows up in a question, change the question to a statement and then make the pronoun decision.

CONFUSING: Pronouns and nouns preceding *-ing* words such as *swimming, skiing, crying,* and so forth.

WHY THEY'RE CONFUSING: You need a possessive pronoun or noun in order to place the emphasis on the *-ing* word.

GUIDELINE TO END CONFUSION: Decide what you're emphasizing. If you're emphasizing the activity, go for a possessive. If you're emphasizing the person doing the activity, don't use a possessive.

WRONG: Gonzaio's parents did not object to him taking the SAT fifteen times.

WHY IT'S WRONG: You should never take fifteen SATs. Also, *him* is a strong pronoun and grabs the attention from *taking.* The sentence clearly means that the parents did not object to the *taking.*

RIGHT: Gonzaio's parents did not object to his taking the SAT fifteen times.

ALSO RIGHT: Those crazy parents did not object to Gonzaio's taking the SAT fifteen times.

WHY THEY'RE RIGHT: The possessives (*his, Gonzaio's*) are weak and don't take the attention away from *taking,* where it should be.

A couple other tricks the SAT-writers have up their sleeves concern the following:

✔ *Between you and I* is a common error, so they like placing it on the test. The correct phrase is *between you and me.* If you have to know why, read on: *Between* is a preposition, a preposition needs an object, and *me* is an object pronoun.

✔ *Whose* and *its* are possessives. *Who's* means *who is* and *it's* means *it is.*

One cardinal rule of Pronoun-land: Be sure that every pronoun you place in a sentence refers to one, and only one noun. Confusing pronouns (*she* in a sentence with two female names, perhaps) are a no-no. Also avoid plopping *this, that,* or *which* into a sentence to refer to an entire sentence. Pronouns are like algebra equations: One noun out, one pronoun in.

Punctuating your way to a perfect score

Not a whole lot of punctuation shows up on the SAT, but you do find a couple of common errors.

CONFUSING: Sentences joined together.

WHY IT'S CONFUSING: Sometimes a comma and a joining word — what grammarians call a *conjunction* — do the job, and sometimes you need a semicolon.

GUIDELINE TO END CONFUSION: Joining words include *and, or, so, but, nor, for.* When these guys glue one complete sentence to another, place a comma in front of the joining word. Some tricksters (*consequently, therefore, nevertheless, however*) look like they're strong enough to join two sentences, but they really aren't. When you have one of these guys stuck between two sentences, add a semicolon.

WRONG: Oxford threw the SAT booklet into the trash, consequently he took a guess on every question.

WHY IT'S WRONG: Guessing is okay only in certain circumstances, which I explain in Chapter 1. Also, *consequently* isn't strong enough to join two sentences.

RIGHT: Oxford threw the SAT booklet into the trash; consequently he took a guess on every question.

WHY IT'S RIGHT: The semicolon is strong enough to connect the two sentences.

CONFUSING: Commas in two-verb sentences.

WHY IT'S CONFUSING: As they say in New York City, "oy vey." Commas come with more rules than the IRS. One that shows up fairly frequently is a comma between two verbs that are paired with one subject.

GUIDELINE TO END CONFUSION: Subject/verb + verb = no comma. In other words, don't put a comma between compound verbs.

WRONG: Archibald sneezed, and sighed, during the writing section.

WHY IT'S WRONG: The verbs *sneezed* and *sighed* are paired with *Archibald.* Don't place a comma in a compound verb.

RIGHT: Archibald sneezed and sighed during the writing section.

CONFUSING: Where to place commas in sentences with descriptions.

WHY IT'S CONFUSING: Commas are always confusing. Get used to it.

GUIDELINE TO END CONFUSION: If the description is essential to the meaning of the sentence — you don't know what you're talking about without the description — don't use commas. If the description is interesting but nonessential, place commas around it.

WRONG: The play, that Dentalia wrote, makes no mention whatsoever of the SATs.

WHY IT'S WRONG: *The play* is vague. The description *that Dentalia wrote* is essential to identifying which play you're talking about.

RIGHT: The play that Dentalia wrote makes no mention whatsoever of the SATs.

WHY IT'S RIGHT: Don't set off identifying descriptions with commas. (Use detonators instead. Just kidding.)

CONFUSING: Apostrophes.

WHY THEY'RE CONFUSING: Beats me. I think they're pretty simple, but every day I see tons of mistakes on signs all over New York City.

GUIDELINE TO END CONFUSION: Place an apostrophe to show that letters are missing (*they're* instead of *they are*) or to show possession *(Dentalia's, students')*. The apostrophe comes before the "s" with singular possessives and after the "s" with plural possessives.

WRONG: The girl's locker room smells like old socks.

WHY IT'S WRONG: No matter how important she is, no one girl gets her own locker room. A star football player, maybe. . . . In a plural possessive, the apostrophe comes after the "s."

RIGHT: The girls' locker room smells like old socks.

No possessive pronoun (whose, its, theirs, his, hers, our, and so on) ever has an apostrophe in it.

Time statements sometimes call for apostrophes: one hour's work, two weeks' salary.

Choosing the right word

The SAT-devils love to throw words at you that are almost right. Unfortunately, in grammar-land, not quite right is completely wrong. In this section, I take you on a quick tour of the most common sights in the SAT Writing section, at least in terms of word choice.

- **Affect and effect:** The SAT *affects* your life; its influence is inescapable. The *effect* of all this SAT prep is a high score. See the difference? The first is a verb and the second a noun. But — and the SAT loves this trick — *effect* can sometimes be a verb meaning "to bring about" as in *Pressure from the colleges effects change.*

- **Continuous and continual:** The first of this pair describes something that never stops, and the second describes something that stops and starts. So a baby needs *continuous* care, but a refrigerator's freezing cycle is *continual.*

- **Disinterested and uninterested:** The first means fair, as in *the SAT is supposed to be a disinterested measure of your ability.* The second means you're yawning because you couldn't care less.

- **Except and accept:** I *accept* all the awards offered to me *except* the one for Nerd of the Year.

- **Farther and further:** *Farther* is for distance and *further* for time and intensity.

- **Fewer and less:** *Fewer* is for stuff you can count (shoes, pimples, cavities) and *less* for stuff you measure (sugar, ability, toothache intensity).

- **Good and well:** *Good* describes nouns, and *well* describes verbs. To put it another way, a person or thing is *good,* but you do something *well.* The SAT is *good,* and you study *well* for the exam.

- **Lie and lay:** Two words created by the devil. You *lie* down when you plop yourself on the sofa, and you *lay* a book on a shelf. But in the past tense, you *lay* down for a few hours yesterday, and you *laid* your SAT prep book on the bonfire.

- **Like and as:** The first one can be used with a noun but not with a subject-verb pair. (Think of Madonna's old song "*Like* a Virgin.") The second is the one you want for a subject-verb pair. (Do *as you like.*)

- **Sit and set:** *Sit* is what you do to yourself, and *set* is what you do to something else. Therefore, *Maybelle sits down as soon as Abner sets a chair on the floor.*

These pairs of commonly confused words are joined by "words" or phrases that you should never use because they don't exist in standard English:

Irregardless (use *regardless*)

Different than (correct version = *different from*)

The reason is because (should be *the reason is that*)

Could of/should of/would of (use *could have, would have, should have*)

This list obviously doesn't contain all the errors you may encounter on the SAT tests, because English has a couple of hundred thousand words and a lot can go wrong. But the traps outlined in this grammar review go a long way toward a better writing score. Now you know what to expect on the SAT grammar questions — Error Recognition, Sentence Revision, and Passage Revision. Practice makes perfect, so check out the examples in Chapter 12.

Chapter 12

Recognizing Your Mistakes: Practice Grammar Problems

In This Chapter

▶ Practicing Error Recognition problems
▶ Revising sentences
▶ Revising paragraphs

The old SAT II W (the Writing and Grammar Subject Area Test) wasn't much fun, and don't expect to bounce off the walls during the Writing section of the new SAT Reasoning Test either. This chapter helps you get in the mood (terminally bored, ready to have root canal rather than think about grammar *one more minute*). You find Error Recognition, Sentence Revision, and Paragraph Revision sample questions. All are accompanied by answers and explanations. I promise not to say, "Because I said so," when I explain why a particular answer is correct.

Error Recognition Questions: Set One

The SAT (**S**low **A**nd **T**ime-consuming) directions tell you to choose an underlined portion of the sentence that contains an error and to bubble in the corresponding letter. The last choice — (E) — always stands for "no error." As you work on these sample problems, keep in mind that you're checking for grammar, punctuation, and word use. Forget about capital letters and spelling, which aren't covered on this exam. Also, assume that everything that is *not* underlined is correct. Answers immediately follow each question. Use a piece of paper to cover up the answer while you work on the question.

After you finish questions 1 through 10, check your answers. Even if you answered the question correctly, take a moment to read the explanation; it may help you with future problems.

After each explanation, I state in parentheses which grammar principle is being tested. If you need a more complete review, turn back to Chapter 11 and review the relevant section.

1. At least a year <u>before the race.</u> Kaitlin, <u>as well as</u> all the other drivers, <u>need to assemble</u> a

                             A   B   C
   staff of qualified <u>mechanics who</u> can assist her in preparing the vehicle. <u>No error.</u>

                       D   E

The portion of the sentence set off by commas (*as well as all the other drivers*) is an interrupter. Ignore it when matching a subject to a verb. If you cover the interrupter and examine the sentence without it, here's the naked subject-verb pair: *Kaitlin need.* Sounds wrong, right? *Kaitlin* is singular and takes the singular verb *needs.* (C) is correct. (subject-verb agreement)

2. According to our friends at the Internal Revenue Service, the problem with uncollected
   <u>A</u>   <u>B</u>
   taxes is when other taxpayers have to pay more. No error.
   <u>C</u>   <u>D</u>   <u>E</u>

The verb *is* acts as a giant equal sign, so the stuff on each side of *is* must match. Grammatically, *problem* is the important word in front of *is* because *problem* is the subject. *Problem* should match *that,* not *when,* because *problem* is a general word — a noun — and doesn't refer specifically to time. *When* is a time word. The correct sentence would read *the problem with uncollected taxes is that . . . .* (C) is correct. (word choice)

3. Awed by the power of the New York Yankees, Dan, whom everyone believes is the most
                                                        <u>A</u>
   committed fan, purchased a banner proclaiming the fact that "Bombers Rule!" No error.
             <u>B</u>   <u>C</u>   <u>D</u> <u>E</u>

Who is for subjects and *whom* takes on all the other jobs in the sentence (direct object, bricklayer, dental floss untangler, and so forth). Every verb in the sentence has to have a subject. The subject verb pairs are *everyone believes, who is,* and *Dan purchased.* (A) is correct. (pronoun case)

4. If I would have known about the possibility of a volcanic eruption, I would have stayed away
        <u>A</u>   <u>B</u>   <u>C</u>   <u>D</u>
   from the area. No error.
                  <u>E</u>

This sentence falls into a category labeled "condition contrary to fact" because the speaker in the sentence *didn't* know about the eruption. In a contrary-to-fact sentence, use *had* or *were* in the "if" part of the sentence and *would* in the other part of the sentence. The correct version: *If I had known about . . . .* (A) is correct. (verb tense and mood)

5. Lakshman donated the violins to the senior orchestra members and to we freshmen so that
                                                       <u>A</u>   <u>B</u>   <u>C</u>
   all talented musicians could play with top-notch instruments. No error.
                            <u>D</u>   <u>E</u>

Take your fingers and cover *the senior orchestra members* and *freshmen.* Now read the sentence. *Donated the violins to . . . we?* I don't think so. *Donated . . . to us* sounds better. The grammatical explanation: *to* is a preposition and needs an object pronoun. *Us* = object pronoun, *we* = subject pronoun. (B) is right. (pronoun case)

6. Sitting on the dock, the patient boy watched his father row the boat toward the shore.
   <u>A</u>   <u>B</u>   <u>C</u>   <u>D</u>
   No error.
   <u>E</u>

(E) is correct. No error.

7. Phil exclaimed, "Don't call me 'Philly' unless you want a black eye"! No error.
        <u>A</u>   <u>B</u>   <u>C</u>   <u>D</u> <u>E</u>

The quoted remarks are an exclamation, so the exclamation point should be placed inside the quotation marks. Bravo if you picked (D). (punctuation)

8. Irregardless of your feelings about museum visits, you must take the time to see the new
   <u>A</u>   <u>B</u>   <u>C</u>   <u>D</u>
   exhibit on the Byzantine Empire. No error.
                                    <u>E</u>

Regardless of what you think, *irregardless* isn't a word. (A) is correct. (word choice)

9. <u>The teachers can't</u> understand why the <u>boy's lavatory</u> is always filled with <u>smoke,</u> despite
    A   B   C

the <u>principal's efforts</u> to enforce the ban on tobacco. <u>No error</u>.
        D   E

The lavatory belongs to all the boys, so the apostrophe should go after the letter *s*. (B) is correct. (punctuation)

10. <u>There are</u> <u>less</u> shoes today in that cabinet <u>than</u> there <u>were</u> yesterday because the shoe-
     A   B   C   D

maker has taken some to be repaired. <u>No error</u>.
                                     E

Less is for stuff you measure (air, loneliness, mustard) and *fewer* for stuff you count. (B) is right. (word choice)

Okay, if you correctly answered about 50 percent, you're on track for a fairly good score. Of course, keep at it and aim for higher. Analyze your mistakes, reread the appropriate explanations in Chapter 11, and then hit set two.

Error Recognition Questions: Set Two

Try these on for size. No fair peeking at the answers. Once again I indicate in parentheses which grammar principle is involved. Turn to Chapter 11 for a full explanation.

1. That store <u>is selling</u> <u>their best wool sweaters</u> at a large <u>discount; Kirsten</u> may purchase one
           A   B   C

pullover for <u>each day</u> of the week. <u>No error</u>.
             D   E

The store is singular, so *their* (which is plural) doesn't match. The correct pronoun is *its*. (B) is right. (pronoun-antecedent agreement)

2. The complete <u>affect</u> of global warming on the environment <u>is</u> still <u>unknown;</u> <u>nevertheless,</u>
               A   B   C   D

the nation must take steps to reduce carbon fuel consumption. <u>No error</u>.
                                                 E

Affect means "to influence" and *effect* means "a result." In this sentence, *effect* is the one you want. Ring one up for (A). (word choice)

3. Did Zane <u>really state</u> that the Mets are <u>"not</u> nearly <u>as good</u> as the <u>Yankees?"</u> <u>No error</u>.
               A   B   C   D   E

In this sentence the quoted words aren't a question, so the question mark should go outside the quotation marks. (D) is correct. (punctuation)

4. <u>Defiant</u> to the <u>end,</u> the convicted revolutionary <u>refuses</u> to <u>except</u> his fate. <u>No error</u>.
   A   B   C   D   E

Except means "all but" and *accept* means "to receive willingly." In this sentence, *accept* makes more sense. Three cheers for (D). (word choice)

5. The <u>packet of multicolored</u> jellybeans, won by our combined <u>efforts,</u> should be divided
   $\overset{\text{A}}{}$ $\overset{\text{B}}{}$ $\overset{\text{B}}{}$

   <u>between you and I</u> and not shared with the <u>slackers who</u> skipped the final competition.
   $\overset{\text{C}}{}$ $\overset{\text{D}}{}$

   <u>No error</u>.
   $\overset{\text{E}}{}$

   The correct expression is *between you and me. Between* is a preposition and must be followed
   by an object, not a subject pronoun. (C) is right. (pronoun case)

6. Ashley <u>gave</u> a portion of salad <u>to we men</u> and <u>then</u> began to distribute the napkins <u>and forks</u>.
   $\overset{\text{A}}{}$ $\overset{\text{B}}{}$ $\overset{\text{C}}{}$ $\overset{\text{D}}{}$

   <u>No error</u>.
   $\overset{\text{E}}{}$

   Cover *men* with your finger and read the sentence. *To we?* Uh uh. *To us.* (B) is correct.
   (pronoun case)

7. <u>Distressed</u> by rumors about a large number of fatal <u>crashes, her</u> parents firmly <u>objected to</u>
   $\overset{\text{A}}{}$ $\overset{\text{B}}{}$ $\overset{\text{C}}{}$

   <u>Alexa's skydiving</u> without a generous insurance policy. <u>No error</u>.
   $\overset{\text{D}}{}$ $\overset{\text{E}}{}$

   Everything is hunky dory in this statement! (E) is correct No error.

8. Annie <u>feels badly</u> about the mistake <u>she made</u> <u>when preparing</u> oxtail stew <u>for her friends</u>.
   $\overset{\text{A}}{}$ $\overset{\text{B}}{}$ $\overset{\text{C}}{}$ $\overset{\text{D}}{}$

   <u>No error</u>.
   $\overset{\text{E}}{}$

   Badly describes an action and *bad* describes a person or thing. In this sentence you need *bad*
   to explain Annie's mood. (A) is correct. (word choice)

9. Miranda<u>, to her amazement</u>, is the only one attending <u>this year's</u> French Day Festival <u>who is</u>
   $\overset{\text{A}}{}$ $\overset{\text{B}}{}$ $\overset{\text{C}}{}$

   able to pronounce her <u>teacher's</u> name correctly. <u>No error</u>.
   $\overset{\text{D}}{}$ $\overset{\text{E}}{}$

   Nothing wrong with this statement. (E) is correct. No error.

10. <u>Who</u> shall <u>I</u> say is <u>calling,</u> assuming that I agree <u>to relay</u> the message? <u>No error</u>.
    $\overset{\text{A}}{}$ $\overset{\text{B}}{}$ $\overset{\text{C}}{}$ $\overset{\text{D}}{}$ $\overset{\text{E}}{}$

    (E) is correct. No error.

    Once more onto the analyst's couch: Check what type of question tripped you up and go
    back over the explanations in Chapter 11.

Sentence Revision Questions: Set One

In this sort of question you're not just looking for grammar mistakes; you're also aiming for
style. (A) is always the underlined part of the sentence, repeated as is. If you think the sentence sounds fine, bubble in (A) and be done with it. Otherwise, reword the sentence in your
mind and try to find an answer that fits. If nothing fits your imaginary revision, check out the
SAT's offerings and choose a letter.

Even after you've found the correct answer, squeeze out a couple of seconds so you can review the explanations immediately following each question. I have taken care to include a couple of frequently tested ideas in this section that didn't merit a full-blown discussion in Chapter 11. So if you read the explanation, you may pick up a grammar issue that shows up on your SAT. Don't cheat. Keep a piece of paper over the specific answer until you complete each question.

1. Dancing in local productions, singing in the homecoming show, <u>and music lessons all</u> paved the way for her career in the arts.

   (A) and music lessons all

   (B) as well as music lessons all

   (C) and teaching music, all

   (D) and teaching music all

   (E) and lessons in music

All the items in a list should resemble each other, at least in terms of grammar. *Dancing* and *singing* should be matched with *teaching*. No comma is needed at the end of a list, so (C) hits the reject pile. (D) is correct. (This one doesn't fit neatly into any category of grammar that I describe in Chapter 11. It has to do with balance and symmetry in the sentence — things the SAT Writing evaluates.)

2. <u>In the newspaper it says that</u> the egg hunt will be held outdoors only if the weather cooperates.

   (A) In the newspaper it says that

   (B) According to the newspaper, it says that

   (C) According to the newspaper,

   (D) In the newspaper it reports that

   (E) The newspaper says that

The *newspaper* doesn't *say,* and neither does *it.* (C) is right. (word choice)

3. The plot of the drama was so intriguing that Annie didn't realize until the final curtain <u>how much time it was that had passed.</u>

   (A) how much time it was that had passed.

   (B) how much time it was that passed.

   (C) how much time passed.

   (D) how much time had passed.

   (E) how late it had been.

First of all, you don't need *it,* so you can immediately rule out (A), (B), and (E). Of the two remaining, (D) is better because the *realizing* and the *passing* take place at two separate times in the past. To show that the *passing* was earlier, use *had.* (D) is correct. (verb tense)

4. Stirring the batter vigorously, <u>a tasty cake will result, even for amateur bakers.</u>

   (A) a tasty cake will result, even for amateur bakers.

   (B) even amateur bakers can make a tasty cake.

   (C) a tasty cake will be made by amateur bakers.

   (D) amateur bakers will result in a tasty cake.

   (E) a cake that tastes good will be the result for amateur bakers.

The sentence begins with a verb form *(stirring)*, but the next subject up — *a tasty cake* — obviously isn't doing the stirring. By the laws of grammar, a verb form beginning a sentence must be an action performed by the subject. (A), (C), and (E) are out on those grounds. (D) bites the dust because it doesn't make sense. Give it up for (B). (This one doesn't fit the categories from Chapter 11, but it's good to know anyway because the SAT likes to throw this kind of question into the mix.)

5. Either the puppies or the dog trainer is to be commended for the excellent behavior of the pack.

    (A) Either the puppies or the dog trainer is

    (B) Either the puppies or the dog trainer are

    (C) The puppies, along with the dog trainer is

    (D) The dog trainer, and the puppies too, is

    (E) Either the puppies, or the dog trainer is

When you're confronted with an *either/or* sentence, match the verb to the closest subject. In this sentence, the closest subject is *trainer,* which pairs nicely with *is.* Also, avoid separating two subjects with commas, as in (E). (A) is right. (subject-verb agreement)

6. The mayor told us citizens that the responsibility for public safety was to be shouldered by him.

    (A) was to be shouldered by him.

    (B) he was to shoulder.

    (C) he would have shouldered.

    (D) was his.

    (E) was to be his.

What's with the shoulders? The other choices are overly long. Go for the concise version wherever possible. (D) is correct. (The SAT often tests for conciseness.)

7. Alex told us that there is a good reason for him accepting blame for the fire.

    (A) there is a good reason for him accepting

    (B) there is a good reason for he not accepting

    (C) there is a good reason, he accepts

    (D) he has a good reason to accept

    (E) there is good reason, for him to accept

There is helps out in some sentences, but often it's unnecessary. (D) does the job in fewer words. (conciseness)

8. Rodrigo maintains that only the painter can interpret his work, consequently the art gallery must use the catalog Rodrigo prepared or nothing at all.

    (A) can interpret his work, consequently

    (B) can interpret his work; consequently

    (C) can have interpreted his work; consequently

    (D) can have interpreted his work, and consequently

    (E) can be interpreting his work; consequently

Consequently, a nice mouthful that looks important, is actually a weak, never-goes-to-the-gym sort of word. The rules of grammar don't allow *consequently* to join two complete sentences. If you want to glue two sentences together, you need a semicolon or a conjunction — a true joining word — in front of *consequently.* (A) is out. Choices (C), (D), and (E) lose the race because the verb tense is wrong. If you selected (B), pat yourself on the head. (punctuation)

Sentence Revision Questions: Set Two

Once more into the battle. Again, choose the correct revision of the underlined portion of the sentence.

Making a list (of answers) and checking it twice is a great idea; Santa will reward you with a nice bag of SAT scores. Just don't peek at the answers or Santa may just leave some coal (or a bad SAT score) in your stocking.

 After you check the answers, take note of your problem areas (flabby abs? saddlebag thighs?) and turn back to the corresponding explanations in Chapter 11. Because this sort of question checks style as well as grammar, not every answer has a corresponding section in Chapter 11. Fortunately for you, I tell you something's right (or wrong) in the explanation.

1. The business executive <u>spoke continually for seven hours with whomever</u> would listen until the problem with the company's cash shortage was resolved.

    (A) spoke continually for seven hours with whomever

    (B) spoke continuously for seven hours with whomever

    (C) spoke continually for seven hours with whoever

    (D) spoke continuously for seven hours with whoever

    (E) had spoken continually for seven hours with whoever

Continually means "stopping and starting endlessly." *Continuously* means "ongoing without a pause." In this sentence the executive (who now has a severe case of laryngitis) didn't stop talking at all for seven hours. Hence (B) and (D) are in the running, but (D) wins because *whoever* is needed as the subject of *would listen.* (D) is correct. (pronoun case, word choice)

2. My sister, barely able to speak and sniffing furiously, <u>told me that she has a cold</u>.

    (A) told me that she has a cold.

    (B) has told me that she has a cold.

    (C) told me that she had a cold.

    (D) will have told me that she had a cold.

    (E) told me, that she had a cold.

When you relate what someone said, use past tense unless you're stating something that is always true (the sort of thing you'd read in an encyclopedia). (C) is correct. (verb tense)

3. Everyone <u>should have brought their best</u> clothes to the dance competition in order to make a good impression on the judges.

    (A) should have brought their best

    (B) should of brought his or her best

    (C) should have brought his or her best

    (D) could've brought their

    (E) should've brought their

Should of (along with its pals *could of* and *would of*) is a big no-no. Strike these expressions from your vocabulary. The *of* should be *have,* as in *should have, could have, would have. Everyone* is singular, so *their* changes to *his or her.* (C) is right. (word choice, pronoun-antecedent agreement)

4. <u>Give this trophy to whoever</u> amasses the most points in the target-shooting competition.

   (A) Give this trophy to whoever

   (B) Give this trophy to whomever

   (C) Give this trophy, to whoever

   (D) You give this trophy to whomever

   (E) You should give this trophy to whomever

Whoever is the pronoun you want because it must act as the subject of *amasses.* No *you* is needed because in the sentence as it is now, *you* is understood. (A) is correct. (pronoun case)

5. <u>When one is ready to enter college, you</u> should have the ability to write a good essay.

   (A) When you is ready to enter college, you

   (B) When you are ready to enter college, you

   (C) When one is ready to enter college you

   (D) When one is ready to enter college, they

   (E) When one is ready to enter college they

A shift in a car gives you the right gear at the right time (except when I'm driving a manual, in which case I buck all over the road and then stall). A shift in a sentence is a grammatical *faux pas* (error). Grammar rests upon a basis of consistency. This sentence has a shift from *one* to *you.* Oops. Gotta go to (B), which stays with *you.* (Don't look for this material in Chapter 11.)

6. Mary told her aunt that <u>she should not wear black because it</u> is a gloomy color.

   (A) she should not wear black because it

   (B) she should not wear black, because it

   (C) her aunt should not wear black, it

   (D) her aunt should not wear black, it.

   (E) her aunt shouldn't wear black because it

The original sentence doesn't tell you who needs the pink scarf instead of funeral colors — Mary or the aunt? (C), (D), and (E) clarify the situation, but (C) and (D) are run-on sentences (two sentences glued together without a legal joining word or a semicolon). (E) is correct. (pronouns, punctuation)

7. The <u>principle of the school must maintain an attitude</u> of dignity, even when pupils misbehave.

   (A) principle of the school must maintain an attitude

   (B) principal of the school must maintain an attitude

   (C) principle of the school should maintain an attitude

   (D) principle of the school, he must maintain an attitude

   (E) principal of the school he must maintain an attitude

The *principal* is your *pal,* so you need to dump (A), (C), and (D). (E) adds an unnecessary *he.* (B) is correct. (word choice)

8. <u>Having read the report, John immediately took</u> steps to correct the problem.

   (A) Having read the report, John immediately took

   (B) Reading the report, John immediately had taken

   (C) Reading the report John immediately took

   (D) Having read the report, John immediately will take

   (E) Having read the report John immediately will take

Verb tense and commas are both issues in this sentence. Verb tense errors rule out (B), (D), and (E). The tenses in (A) and (C) are okay, but (C) is missing a comma. (A) is correct.

Paragraph Revision

This section presents a piece of writing that a fellow student may have produced. As a first draft, it has some grammar and style problems. Each sentence is numbered, and the whole thing is followed by a set of questions.

1 When I was about two years old, my mother made me eat lima beans, which apparently annoyed me so much that I frowned at her the rest of the day. 2 That's what my family says, as I don't remember myself. 3 Now I like lima beans, therefore my tastes have changed. 4 Your preferences one day may be different at another time. 5 No one can tell what they will think in the future, so everyone should be careful not to rule out the possibility of change.

6 This is particularly important in the world of ideas. 7 If someone presents an idea that you don't like, you shouldn't put it aside and never think about it again. 8 After all, new information may change your mind. 9 Different experiences can also change the way you think. 10 Many ideas that were once accepted by almost everyone – slavery, the absolute right of a king to rule his country and other ideas – are now considered wrong.

11 Being in a democracy, openness to ideas is more important than anything else. 12 A political candidate may seem too radical or too conservative the first time you listen, but later they start to appear more logical. 13 Thinking and probing for information makes the difference. 14 Last election day when I went to the polls, I had thought before about whom to vote for and why. 15 If I would have chosen without thought, I would not have done my duty as a citizen. 16 Like lima beans, ideas can grow on you. 17 So everyone has the obligation to be open and thoughtful.

1. Which of the following is the best revision of the underlined portion of sentence 1?

   When I was about two years old, my mother made me eat <u>lima beans, which apparently annoyed me so much that</u> I frowned at her the rest of the day.

   (A) lima beans that apparently annoyed me so much that I

   (B) lima beans. I was so annoyed that

   (C) lima beans, however they annoyed me so much that

   (D) annoying lima beans, and

   (E) lima beans, apparently annoyed me so much that

   Pronouns have a lot in common with algebra equations: Each pronoun may replace *one* noun and only one noun. In the original sentence, *which* is replacing a bunch of words *(my mother made me eat)*. Penalty box. Changing *which* to *that* in (A) doesn't solve the problem because *that* is also a pronoun. (C) is a run-on because *however* isn't a legal joining word. (D) and (E) are awkward. (B) is correct.

2. In the context of paragraph one, how should sentence 5 be revised?

   (A) You can't tell what you will think in the future, so you should be careful not to rule out the possibility of change.

   (B) No one can tell what he or she will think in the future, so everyone should be careful not to rule out the possibility of change.

   (C) What you think might be a mystery tomorrow, so don't rule out change.

   (D) You may change in ways you can't foresee, don't rule out new ideas.

   (E) No one knows how they will change, especially in terms of ideas.

   One and *they* are a mismatch because *one* is singular and *they* is plural. Also, the rest of the paragraph — and the question specifically tells you to look at the rest of the paragraph — deals with *you*. A paragraph needs consistency, and shifting from *one* or *they* to *you* is inconsistent. Go for (A) instead of (C) or (D) because (A) keeps the original meaning of the sentence.

3. How may sentences 8 and 9 best be combined?

   (A) After all, new information may change your mind and different experiences can also change the way you think.

   (B) After all, new information may change your mind, and different experiences can also change the way you think.

   (C) After all, new information may change your mind; different experiences can also change the way you think.

   (D) After all, new information and experiences may change the way you think.

   (E) After all, new information may change your mind, like different experiences do.

   Wordiness is a pain. Why? Have you ever sat through a 20-minute speech containing three minutes' worth of information? (D) is the most concise.

4. What is the best revision of sentence 11?

   (A) Being in a democracy, openness to ideas are more important than anything else.

   (B) Openness to ideas is more important than anything else because of democracy.

   (C) Being in a democracy, you should have openness to ideas more than anything else.

   (D) In a democracy, openness to ideas is an extremely important quality.

   (E) Being in a democracy, openness to ideas is needed more than anything else.

Being is a verb form, and when you begin a sentence with a verb form, the subject of the sentence should be doing the action expressed by the verb form. (A) and (E) bite the dust because *openness* isn't the person who is *being* in a democracy. (B) and (C) are wordy and awkward. (D) is correct.

5. What is the best revision of sentence 15?

   (A) If I would choose without thought, I would not have done my duty as a citizen.

   (B) If I had chosen without thought, I would not have done my duty as a citizen.

   (C) Choosing without thought had been wrong, as a citizen.

   (D) If I would have chosen without thought, I should not have done my duty as a citizen.

   (E) Had I chosen without thought, my duty as a citizen would not have been done.

Sentence 15 expresses what grammarians call "condition contrary to fact" — something that isn't true. In this sort of sentence, the "if" part should have *were* or *had* as part of the verb, never *would*. The *would* belongs in the other half of the sentence. (B) is right.

6. The writer's reference to lima beans in paragraph three is intended to

   (A) show personal growth

   (B) introduce a note of humor

   (C) compare election choices to food

   (D) relate to the reader's personal experience

   (E) unify the passage by brining it full circle

A fine design for essays is that of a circle, to end where you began. Very deep and philosophical, also unified! (E) is correct.

If you've worked your way through all the questions in this chapter, take two aspirin and call me in the morning. Just kidding. But you do need a break — in a minute! However many problems you plowed through, take a few moments to chart your errors. The answer key tells you what type of grammatical principle is involved in most questions. Find out your strengths and weaknesses and study accordingly.

Here's looking at *Eu, Anthro*

The *eu* family has nothing in common with *ew,* the sound you make when a bug crawls up your sleeve. *Eu* is a Greek prefix that means "good" or "pleasant." Easy-listening tunes are *euphonious* (they sound good) and *eulogies* are speeches in which all (and only) good things are said about someone who's died. A *euphemism* is a more pleasant term that may substitute for a word you don't like to say ("restroom" is a euphemism for toilet).

The *anthros* are the family of man (and woman). An *anthropologist* studies human behavior and society, but a *misanthrope* hates people. If you dress your dog in little dresses (pause for a shudder and a call to the humane society), you're guilty of *anthropomorphism* — projecting human qualities onto non-humans.

Part IV
Take a Number: The Math Section

The 5th Wave   **By Rich Tennant**

TAKING THE MATH PORTION OF THE SAT WAS PARTICULARLY EMBARRASSING FOR MR. ED BECAUSE OF HIS INABILITY TO KEEP HIS CALCULATIONS TO HIMSELF.

@RICHTENNANT

In this part . . .

In my experience, two types of people inhabit the world: Those who say disdainfully, "Math? My accountant will take care of that stuff!" and those who gleefully declare, "Ooh, more numbers!" No matter which camp you belong to, after you read this part, you can find SAT math approachable and, perhaps, easier than you anticipate. This part begins with a brief fly-by of the exam's math portion, all 70 glorious minutes of it, and moves on to more in-depth analysis and techniques for each math topic covered by the **S**electively **A**sinine **T**ummy-troubler. To ruin just a tiny bit more of your life, I also include practice questions.

Chapter 13

Picking a Number, Any Number: The SAT Math Sections

. . . .

In This Chapter

▶ Surveying the math portion of the SAT

▶ Choosing the right calculator and using it efficiently during the exam

▶ Tackling time constraints

▶ Getting good at grid-ins

▶ Adopting the best strategies for SAT math questions

. . . .

*I*f you're one of those people who whined to your ninth grade math teacher, "No one in the real world *ever* has to calculate the value of $6x - y$," the SAT is about to prove you wrong. You can't get much more real world than a test that helps to determine where you go to college and maybe even what sort of job you get afterwards. And on the SAT, the value of $6x - y$ is fair game. So is absolute value (and I'm not talking about the great price you got on that orange sweater), exponential growth (the kind your tuition payments will display), and plenty of other fun stuff. In this chapter I show you what's where, how to prepare, and most important, how to survive SAT math.

Adding and Subtracting: What's New in the SAT Math Section

The SAT booklet you open with sweaty, trembling fingers one morning in the near future will resemble the "old" SAT in many ways. The new SAT Reasoning Test contains three portions of math that count toward your score: two 25-minute sections and one 20-minute section. As in the past, you may also encounter a math "equating" section that allows the SAT-makers to try out new questions. You pay them to take the test and they treat you like a lab rat. Nice, huh?

The equating section doesn't count toward your final score, but because you never know which section is equating, don't blow anything off. You may end up ignoring a section they score, and then *you* won't score very well. (For more information on the SAT equating section, see Chapter 1.)

Each math section begins with a little gift basket: A set of formulas to help you solve the problems — the area and circumference of a circle, the area of a square, the angles and sides of "special" triangles, and so forth. As you plod through an SAT math section, look back whenever you need this information so you're sure that your nerves haven't changed say, the area of a rectangle from $a = lw$ to $a = lw^2$.

What's still around

The math SAT sections, minus Quantitative Comparisons (QCs), are mostly five-answer multiple-choice questions. (QCs were tricky little inquiries that asked you whether A was greater than, less than, or the same as B or could not be determined from the information given.) Ten questions are *grid-ins,* which require you to bubble in the numbers you came up with and thus give you no hint whatsoever about the correct answer. (Check out "Getting Good at Grid-Ins" later in this chapter for everything you need to know about these questions.)

The SAT-makers see math as a sort of intellectual chocolate and subscribe to the "you-can-never-have-too-much-of-a-good-thing" theory of testing. In terms of content, they've added some topics (described in "What's New" later in this chapter) and dropped nothing, at least in terms of content. Nada. Zilch. Zippo. So you have to be sharp about everything you learned in nine and tenth grade math *as well as* the stuff your teachers cram into you during junior year. Here are the holdover topics:

- ✔ **Areas and perimeters:** The basic how-much-carpet-and-wallboard-to-buy question, for common shapes as well as weird forms. Also, you may find questions on volume.

- ✔ **Arithmetic:** You have to add, subtract, divide, and multiply and know the difference between even and odd numbers (the odd ones wear weird clothes and talk funny), positive and negative numbers, and primes.

- ✔ **Averages:** Make friends with the three Ms — median, mode, and mean.

- ✔ **Equations and inequalities:** Fun with equal signs, as in $3q + 4(6w - 8)$ = the number of hours you waste learning stuff like this. Also, quadratic equations, which have things like x^2 in them, such as $x^2 + 8 + 15$.

- ✔ **Exponents:** The little numbers that tell you how many times to multiply something by itself, as in x^4.

- ✔ **Factoring:** The math equivalent of extracting the cocoa powder and flour from a brownie after it's baked. Typical factoring problem: If a rectangle has a length of $x + 3$ and an area of $x^2 + 8 + 15$, what is its width, in terms of x? Best way to find the answer: Grab a ruler and measure the thing.

- ✔ **Logic:** Those horrible problems you never see in real life, such as *What is the seating plan if Mr. Green can't sit next to Ms. Red but must sit across from Violet and behind Orchid or he throws popcorn . . .* Wait, I just flashed back to the seating plan at my wedding. You *do* use this stuff in real life!

- ✔ **Parallel and perpendicular lines:** What they do when they're alone in the dark, what kind of angles cut into them, how they behave under pressure (when they have to take the SATs, for example), and so forth.

- ✔ **Percents:** How much you pay if your book bill increases by 4,000 percent and similar queries.

- ✔ **Probability:** If you wash 12 pairs of black socks and a pair of white socks, what is the likelihood that you'll match two socks right out of the drawer? (In my house, zero, given that I always forget to take the clothes out of the dryer.)

- ✔ **Ratios and proportions:** If the ratio of tuba players that try for Prestigious University to those that get in is 2,000 to 3, how many tuba players are accepted out of the 4,000 that apply?

- ✔ **Sequences:** If you get 20, 24, 28, 32, and 36 on your five most recent math quizzes, what will you get next, assuming that the sequence stays the same? And will you ever *not* be grounded again in this lifetime, after your parents see your report card?

- ✔ **Special symbols:** Strange figures created just for the SAT that don't exist in normal math. You have to figure out, given the definition, how to manipulate these symbols.

✔ **Triangles:** Everything you ever wanted to know about them, especially the properties of right, isosceles (Sounds like a disease, doesn't it? *Doctor, he's isosceles. Should we inform the family?*), and equilateral.

 Anything in the preceding list resemble a foreign language? Probably, because math is a kind of language. If you need to brush up, check out the relevant chapters in Part IV for review and practice problems.

What's added

From 12 to 15 percent of the math questions facing you are the new and improved (on sale now!) version of the SAT, including the following:

✔ **Absolute value:** How far away from a particular point on the number line is another number? That's the absolute value, and it may show up in equations or functions on the new SAT.

✔ **Coordinate geometry:** As if triangles weren't bad enough, the new SAT asks about slopes of parallel and perpendicular lines. For example, if G has the coordinates (x_1, y_1) and W has coordinates (x_2, y_2), what is the midpoint when I spread cream cheese on a bagel? Just kidding about the bagel, but you do have to know midpoint. You may also have to interpret the graph of a function and to answer questions about transformations of a function. An example: If $f(x)$ measures how much time a student spends on her cellphone, how will $f(x)$ change the day after her unlimited calling plan starts?

✔ **Equations and exponents:** The variety of equations is expanded. You may find radicals (not the long-haired hippie type) and fractional or negative exponents. (The old SAT stuck to positive, whole number exponents, but the new SAT is more daring.)

✔ **Exponential growth sequences, also known as geometric sequences:** These questions require you to multiply by a certain number in order to get to the next term in the sequence. For example, the number of bent wire hangers at the bottom of my closet on consecutive days is 4, 12, 36, 108, 324 . . . you get the idea. (I think the little devils get cozy when I shut the closet door and pretty soon, baby hangers appear.) You may be asked to create a mathematical statement expressing the way my wire hanger collection grows.

✔ **Functions:** Not my cousin Thelma's fundraiser for impoverished beekeepers, but problems in which you take a number, do some stuff to it, and end up with a new number. Functions have been on the SAT for a long time, in disguise. Now the SAT-makers come right out and say $f(x)$ without any embarrassment. The nerve. They also ask you to do a bit more with functions, including questions about domain and range (*not* as in "home on the . . ."). They also quiz you about graphs of linear functions.

✔ **Geometric probability:** If I'm hanging a picture on my kitchen wall, what's the probability that I'll drive the nail right through a hot-water pipe? Questions like this one address geometric probability, and you may find some on the new SAT.

✔ **Scatterplots:** No, the term doesn't refer to incompetent mystery writers. Scatterplots are bits of data represented on a graph. The test-writers may show you a bunch of dots, where the x-axis represents the amount of time spent reading this book and the y-axis shows students' SAT scores. You may have to answer questions about the data, such as exactly how brilliant you were to buy *The SAT I For Dummies,* 6th Edition.

✔ **Sets, including union, intersection, and elements:** The set of all the parakeet treats I buy and the set of all the parakeet treats that my birds will actually eat (instead of strew around my living room) overlap slightly. The SAT may ask you to identify common elements or ask other questions about two or more sets.

✔ **Triangles:** The new SAT ups the trigonometry content, throwing more questions about "special" (30-60-90 or 45-45-90) triangles at you.

X^{-2}: Why SAT math got harder

The "old" SAT math

(A) was carved on wax tablets by hairy-legged guys in togas

(B) could be computed only by people who sleep with algebra books under their pillows

(C) covered nothing but the first two years of high school math

(D) was best approached with a whip and protective body armor

(E) received rave reviews from exam-takers whose eyeglasses are held together by tape

Answer: (C). Yes, SAT math used to be a lot simpler. A pinch of arithmetic, one year of algebra, and some introductory geometry, and you were all set. But now (sigh), the stakes are higher. Bowing to pressure from colleges (who want their freshmen class to calculate the lifetime compounded return of salary increases relative to their sky-high tuition payments) and from high school math teachers (who want you to at least *pretend* to pay attention to the material taught in junior year), the new SAT includes some higher level math, typically taught in the third year of high school. Don't you wish you'd been born a little earlier?

Confused by any of the terms in the preceding list of new SAT math topics? Not to worry. First, the new math is a relatively small portion of the exam. Second, other chapters in Part IV explain the best way to approach and solve these problems.

Calculating the Odds of SAT Success

When *pundits* (wise guys, like the intellectuals sitting around tables discussing politics on TV) blather on about the decline of civilization, they often mention the fact that students today are allowed to bring calculators to the SAT and other standardized tests. In our day, they say, we had to work with our heads, not with machines. Yeah, right. As if any of them even knew how to turn on a calculator, let alone figure out the square root of 324. (P.S. It's 18.)

So you can bring a calculator. Big deal. The SAT-makers declare that you can solve every problem on the test with brainpower alone, and they're right. But you're not allergic to a little help, are you? In fact, a calculator may not be the absolute No. 1 requirement for doing well on the math section, but it's pretty high on the list. Let me tell you a little secret: Become best friends with your calculator *before* the exam. Don't walk into the testing site and say the equivalent of "Hi, my name is Fred! What's yours?" to a calculator on SAT-day.

You're allowed to bring a battery-operated, four-function, graphing, or scientific calculator to the exam. For the new SAT, the test-makers recommend a scientific calculator. In addition to the four functions (addition, subtraction, multiplication, and division), a scientific calculator also lets you figure out cool stuff like square roots, combination problems involving π, and more. Most also calculate fractions, so adding ¼ and ½ is less traumatic.

A graphing calculator, in addition to everything a scientific calculator accomplishes, also lets you draw graphs. If you have one you're comfortable with, bring it along to the test. If you don't own a graphing calculator, don't rush out and buy one because the instruction manual is about 100 pages long (I'm not joking) and you don't really need graphing capability on the SAT.

All calculators come with instruction manuals. After you find your manual, read it. Practice the more complicated-looking procedures with problems from a math book or from this book. Fractions, decimals, and percents should be first on your list; you may also want to become familiar with combinations and permutations, which I discuss at length in Chapter 20. If you're not getting the right answers, ask a fellow student or your math teacher for help. Knowing in advance how to push the right buttons can save you time and give you more right answers, and that's why you're taking the test.

If you've lost your manual, get a copy from the manufacturer. (Check the calculator's serial number and the Web site or information telephone line of the company that made it.) Or buy a new calculator if you can possibly afford one. Remember: Higher SAT scores equal better colleges. Better colleges equal better jobs. Better jobs equal more money. Spending a few bucks on a new calculator now will pay off big time down the line.

If you don't own a calculator, don't worry. Although the SAT doesn't supply calculators, some schools do provide "loaners" to students who don't have their own. Talk with your math teacher. (Home schoolers, call the local high school to inquire about access to their supply.)

Knowing when *not* to use a calculator is almost as important as knowing when to start tapping in numbers. Sometimes a question presents you with a long string of numbers. You *can* find the answer by calculating, *if* you type in everything accurately and *if* you have time to do so. But often the long-string-of-numbers question can be solved much more quickly, without a calculator, by a simple math operation. As you work the practice problems in Part 4, read the explanations that accompany the answers, even if you correctly answered the problem. Tucked into the explanation you may find a statement telling you how a calculator could have helped.

If your batteries run out during the test, too bad. Don't expect the proctor to plunk a double-A on your desk. Moral of the story: Have fresh batteries in your calculator before SAT-day morning.

Taking Your Time versus Getting It Right

Finishing every problem on the math sections of the SAT in the time you're given is certainly possible. After all, you may be this century's Einstein. However, finishing every SAT math question the SAT-makers hit you with *and* getting them all correct is extremely unlikely. Furthermore, if you're in a mad rush to finish a section, you're going to make some mistakes that you would never have made had you worked at a slower pace.

Is it just me, or are there more exponents on the bottom of the page?

SAT math problems are placed in order

(A) so that the answer letters spell out the name of the test-maker's boyfriend

(B) with the hardest topics last

(C) by grade level, with ninth grade material first and 11th grade material last

(D) by throwing the questions down a flight of stairs

(E) from easiest to hardest

Answer: (E). The SAT-makers arrange the problems roughly in the order of difficulty. (How do they know

what's difficult and what's easy? They make you slog through equating sections and gather data on the number of wrong answers, that's how.) Don't assume that all the arithmetic questions are easy and all the third-year math problems are tough. The SAT-makers try to include varying levels of difficulty for each topic, regardless of when it shows up in your high school curriculum.

Take a shot at all the questions in the first third of each math set and attempt to figure out the middle third, if you can. Hit the last third of a set of problems only as time allows.

Right now, resolve that you're not going to worry about getting to all the problems. Decide instead to spend as much time as you need on each problem to be reasonably sure that you answer it correctly. Also, cut your losses. Give up on a problem if you spend two or three minutes on it without getting anywhere. Finally, if a problem makes absolutely no sense to you, skip it. Put a big circle around the question in the booklet, and take pains to skip the proper line on the answer sheet. If you find yourself with an extra nanosecond at the end of the section, go back to the problems you skipped. Follow the usual guessing rules. (See Chapter 1 for more information on guessing.)

Knowing When to Grid and Bear It

Ten of the most fun questions (just kidding — they're as boring as everything else on the exam) are grid-ins. You don't get five convenient multiple choices for a grid-in. On the other hand, you don't lose any points for a wrong answer, so guess as much as you want. Figure 13-1 shows a sample blank grid-in.

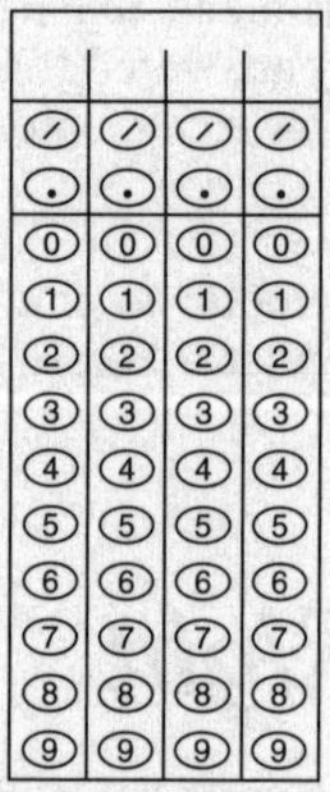

Figure 13-1:
A blank
grid-in.

The grid-in problems are normal questions of any type and all levels of difficulty. After you solve the problem, you have to darken the ovals that correspond to your answer. (Notice that the SAT-makers cleverly avoid writing checks to math teachers who could actually evaluate your ability to solve a math problem.) Those little ovals come with some built-in traps. Beware of the following:

- ✔ **Write your answer and then darken the ovals.** Grid-ins have little boxes in which you can write your answer, but the scanner doesn't read the boxes, just the darkened ovals. Don't skip the writing part because you may "bubble" inaccurately. Don't skip the bubbling because the boxes don't count.

- ✔ **You can't grid in negative numbers.** There's no minus sign in the grid. Hence, all answers are positive.

- ✔ **Gridding in mixed numbers is impossible.** If you grid in 5½, the scanner reads "51 over 2," not "five and one half." Solution: Convert your answer to an improper fraction (one that has absolutely no manners and behaves scandalously on Saturday night). In the preceding example, grid in ¹¹⁄₂ (eleven over two) as shown in Figure 13-2a.

- ✔ **You can start from the extreme left or right, and the middle too.** Just be sure that you have enough boxes for the answer you want to record.

- ✔ **Don't place zeroes before a decimal point.** If your answer is .5, darken the oval for the decimal point and the five, not 00.5, as shown in Figure 13-2b.

✔ **If your answer is a repeating decimal, fill in all the boxes, rounding off as necessary.** In other words, darken the ovals for .333 or .667 (⅓ and ⅔ expressed as decimals), not .3 or .67, as shown in Figure 13-2c.

✔ **If your answer isn't a repeating decimal (.4, for example), you don't have to fill all the boxes.** Just darken a decimal point and a four.

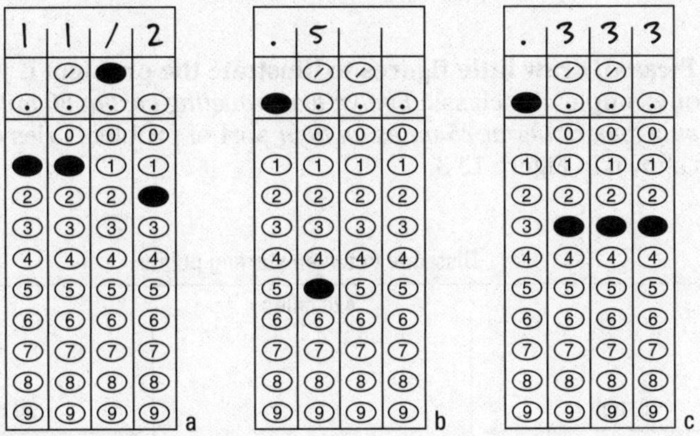

Figure 13-2:
Three
grid-ins,
properly
filled in.

a   b   c

TIP

Don't agonize over *the* perfect, correct answer. Some grid-ins have several possible right answers. (Usually those problems say something like "a possible value for *x* is . . .") Just find one of them and you're all set.

Planning for the Battle: Some Math Strategies That Work

In Part IV, I show you the best way to attack each type of SAT math question. But some general math strategies help you get off on the right foot. Try these on for size:

✔ **Read the question and figure out what the SAT-makers want to know.** Circle significant words such as "greater than," "percentage," and so forth.

✔ **Use the booklet as scrap paper.** Write your calculations in the extra blank space, but no matter what, take time to bubble in your answers. Even though the proctor collects the test booklet, the information in it doesn't count toward your score.

✔ **Don't overuse the calculator.** See if a simple math approach gets you to the right answer.

✔ **Keep an eye on the clock.** You get as many points (about ten, in the converted score) for each correct answer to an easy question as you do for a correct answer to a hard question. Don't spend five minutes on one hard question and skip 11 easy questions because you've run out of time.

✔ **Follow the guessing guidelines outlined in Chapter 1.** You lose a quarter point for each incorrect multiple-choice answer. Grid-ins take nothing away from your score if you're wrong, so guess as much as you want.

✔ **Try out the multiple-choice answers and see which one works.** If the SAT-writers ask something like "which number is divisible by both 13 and 14," start plugging in the answers until one of them works. SAT multiple-choice answers are usually in order from smallest to largest. When you plug in, start with (C), and see whether you've ended up above or below the target. Then try (B) or (D), depending on the direction you need to go.

✔ **Think of realistic answers.** SAT math isn't tied tightly to the real world, but it's not from Mars either. If you're looking for a weight, don't choose "5,098 pounds" unless you have a truck on the scale. Think about the range of human body sizes and concentrate on answers in that category. Similarly, if you're looking for a discount and come up with a negative sale price, you've done something wrong. Try again.

✔ **Don't assume that the provided diagram will solve the problem.** SAT figures aren't created purposely to deceive you, but they may not be drawn to scale. (Look for a note stating this.)

✔ **Even if you're not Picasso, draw little figures to illustrate the problem if you need help visualizing.** For example, the classic *Evelyn was traveling east at 60 miles an hour and Robert was moving toward her at 25 miles an hour* sort of problem cries out for arrows and lines as shown in Figure 13-3.

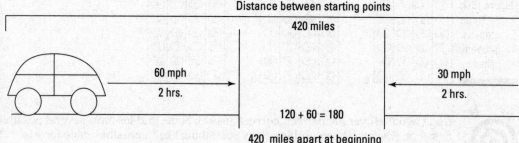

Figure 13-3: A diagram such as this one may help you solve SAT math problems.

Distance between starting points
420 miles
60 mph
2 hrs.
30 mph
2 hrs.
120 + 60 = 180
420 miles apart at beginning

Multiplying your vocabulary

Basic number operations multiply your vocabulary skill:

✔ *Multi*-plying and *div*-iding. Think *multiply*, when you encounter **multinational** (many nations involved), **multilateral** (many sides), **multifarious** (many different types, various) and any other *multi* word. Similarly, *division* will help you tackle **diversify** (to split or to branch out into many paths) and **divergent** (splitting in different directions, differing, contradictory).

✔ Sub*traction* has a root word — *trac* or *tract* — to pull. With the same root word you've got **contract** (to pull together, to shrink in on itself) and **retract** (literally, "to pull back"; to take back words you've already said) and **detract** (literally, "to pull down"; to take away from someone's reputation) and **extract** (to pull from, the way a dentist *extracts* your teeth).

Chapter 14

Numb and Numbering: Everything You Need to Know About Numbers and Operations

*O*nce upon a time you could take care of all the numbers you needed for school purposes with ten fingers and, in a pinch, a couple of toes. Sadly, life has changed. Now you need to know what's prime and what's not, as well as how to calculate and manipulate percents, ratios, means, and the like. Not to mention sets and sequences! Never fear. Even though you've moved way beyond body-part math, this chapter tells you everything you need to know about numbers and operations, at least as they appear on the SAT.

Meeting the Number Families

Mathematics starts with numbers. (Wouldn't life be grand if math also ended with numbers?) Numbers come in various "flavors," but few are as tasty as, say, anchovy ice cream. Nevertheless, you need to nibble a bit of several types of numbers before you hit SAT-day. In this section I present a buffet of numbers.

You may be wondering why you need a vocabulary lesson in order to do well on SAT math. The SAT-makers love to tuck these terms into the questions, as in "How many prime numbers are . . ." or "If the sum of three consecutive integers is 102, what is . . ." and the like. If you don't know the vocabulary, you're sunk before you start.

Check out this "menu" of *toothsome* (good-tasting) numbers:

- **Whole numbers:** The number, the whole number, and nothing but the number. Actually, whole numbers aren't very well named, because they include zero, which isn't a whole lot of anything. The whole numbers are the ones you (hopefully) remember from grade school: 0, 1, 2, 3, 4, 5, 6 . . . you get the idea. Whole numbers, by definition, *don't* include fractions or decimals.

- **Even and odd numbers:** Whole numbers can be *even* or *odd*. *Even* numbers are divisible by two, and *odd* numbers aren't.

- **Prime numbers:** Prime numbers are numbers that are divisible only by themselves and by one. The first few prime numbers are 2, 3, 5, 7, 11, 13, 17, and 19. Zero and one *aren't* prime numbers. They're considered "special." (The kids in grade school said that about me, too.) Two is the only even prime number. No negative number is ever prime because all negative numbers are divisible by negative one.

One common misconception is that all odd numbers are prime. Don't fall into that trap. Tons of odd numbers (9 or 15, for example) aren't prime, because they're divisible by another number.

- **Composite numbers:** Anything that's not prime or special is *composite*. If you can divide a number by some smaller number (other than one) without getting a remainder, you have a composite. A few composite numbers are 4, 6, 8, 9, 10, 12, 14, 15, 16, 18, 20, 21, and so on. (I could go on to add zillions more, but you get the idea.) To define composite numbers still another way: They're evenly divisible by a number other than one.

Speaking of divisibility, keep these points in mind:

- All numbers whose digits add up to a multiple of 3 are also divisible by 3. For example, the digits of 789 add up to 24 (7 + 8 + 9 = 24); because 24 is divisible by 3, so is 789.

- Ditto for multiples of 9. If the digits of a number add up to a multiple of 9, you can divide the number itself by 9. For example, the digits of 729 add up to 18; because 18 is divisible by 9, so is 729.

- All numbers ending in 0 or 5 are divisible by 5.

- All numbers ending in 0 are also divisible by 10.

These divisibility rules work backwards, too. Consider the number 365. It's not even, so it can't be divided by 2. Its digits add up to 14, which isn't divisible by 3 or 9, so it's not divisible by either 3 or 9. Because 365 ends in 5, it's divisible by 5. Because it doesn't end in 0, it's not divisible by 10.

- **Integers:** The whole numbers and all their opposites — also known as *negative* numbers — are *integers*. The whole numbers go all the way up to infinity, but the integers are even more impressive. Integers reach infinity in *both* directions, as the number line in Figure 14-1 shows.

Figure 14-1:
Integers go
on forever
and ever.

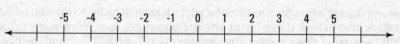

When you're asked to compare integers, remember that the farther to the right a number is, the greater it is. This joke may help you remember. Once, the numbers –5 and 3 were having an argument about which one was greater. Finally, number 3 said, "Wait a minute, I *must* be greater than you, because I'm greater than zero!" The number –5 looked doubtful. "I'm not just sure," protested number 3. "I'm positive!"

✔ **Rational numbers:** Numbers for whom a padded room without a view isn't necessary. Just kidding. All integers are rational numbers. In addition, any number that can be written as a fraction — proper or improper — is a rational number. (In a *proper* fraction, the number on top is smaller than the number on the bottom, and in an *improper* fraction, the top number is greater than the bottom number.) Plus, any decimal that either ends or repeats like $0.1\overline{6}$, the decimal for $\frac{1}{6}$, or $0.\overline{142857}$, the decimal for $\frac{1}{7}$, is a rational number. The following are rational: -2, 0.234, $^{73}\!\%_3$, $5.8\overline{53}$.

✔ **Irrational numbers:** Irrational numbers are decimals that never end or repeat. Practically speaking, there are only two kinds of irrational numbers that you need to worry about:

   • Radicals (such as $\sqrt{2}$ and $\sqrt{3}$)

   • π, which you've probably heard of because it appears in the formula for the area of a circle. Like Mom's apple dessert, π is in a class by itself.

Every type of number I mention in this chapter is a *real* number. Right about now you're probably asking whether some numbers aren't real. The bad news: Yes, and you may have to figure them out some day, perhaps in the college you're sending your SAT scores to. The good news: That day isn't today, because every number on the SAT is real.

Getting Your Priorities Straight: Order of Operations

How many times has your mom told you to turn off the XBox and start on your homework because, "You have to get your priorities straight." I'm not going to comment on the annoyance that authority figures generate, especially when they're right, but I am going to tell you that in math, priorities matter.

Consider the problem $3 + 4 \times 2$. If you add $3 + 4$, which of course equals 7, and multiply by 2, you get 14. Nice answer, but wrong, because you forgot about Aunt Sally. "Aunt Sally," or more accurately, "**P**lease **E**xcuse **M**y **D**ear **A**unt **S**ally," or PEMDAS, is a device to help you remember what mathematicians call "Order of Operations." When faced with a multipart problem, just do what "Aunt Sally" says to do. Follow the order of operations. Note the italicized letters in the following list, which tell you what "Aunt Sally" really means:

1. **Do everything in *P*arentheses.**

2. **Next calculate all *E*xponents.**

3. ***M*ultiply and *D*ivide, *from left to right*.**

4. ***A*dd and *S*ubtract, *from left to right*.**

Back to the sample problem, $3 + 4 \times 2$. No parentheses or exponents, so the first operation up is multiplication and division. Because there's no division, you're left with 4×2, which equals 8. Onward to addition and subtraction (in this problem, subtraction isn't present, so forget about it). Just add 3 to 8, at which point you arrive at 11, the correct answer.

When using a calculator, input the numbers according to the "Aunt Sally" rules to ensure the right answer.

She's lonely, so here's another chance to visit "Aunt Sally":

The expression $20 - (40 \div 5 \times 2) + 3^2$ is equal to:

(A) –5

(B) 7

(C) 10

(D) 13

(E) 25

Answer: (D). Start with what's in the parentheses: $40 \div 5 \times 2$. Don't fall into the trap of multiplying 5×2 first; proceed from left to right: $40 \div 5 = 8$ and $8 \times 2 = 16$. Next, tackle the exponent: $3^2 = 9$. At this stage you have $20 - 16 + 9$. Again, resist the temptation to start by adding; just go left to right ($20 - 16 = 4$ and then $4 + 9 = 13$).

Playing Percentage Games

The SAT loves percentages, perhaps because math teachers who are sick of the question "Am I ever going to use this stuff in real life?" actually write the math portion of the exam. With percentages, the answer is yes if you're taking out a loan (interest rates) or investing your part-time job's earnings in mutual funds (still interest, but this time it's a good thing). *Percents* represent how much of each hundred you're talking about.

Taking a percentage of a number is a simple task if you're using a calculator with a "%" button. Just hit the "%" and "×" buttons. For example, to find 60 percent of 35, multiply 60% by 35. The answer is 21. If you're not blessed with such a calculator, you can turn a percent into a decimal by moving the decimal point two spaces to the left, as in 60% = .60. (Other examples of percents include 12.5% = .125, 0.4% = 0.004, and so on.) Or, turn the percent into a fraction. The "cent" in *percent* means hundred, so 60 percent = $^{60}\!/_{100}$.

For more complicated problems, fall back on the formula you mastered in grade school:

$$\frac{\text{is}}{\text{of}} = \frac{\%}{100}$$

Suppose you're asked "40% of what number is 80?" The number you're looking for is the number you're taking the percent *of*, so x will go in the "of" space in the formula:

$$\frac{80}{x} = \frac{40}{100}$$

Now cross-multiply: $40x = 8000$. Dividing by 40 gives $x = 200$.

A particularly annoying subtopic of percentages is a problem that involves a percent increase or decrease. A slight variation of the percentage formula helps you out with this type of problem. Here's the formula and a typical problem:

$$\frac{\text{amount of change}}{\text{original amount}} = \frac{\%}{100}$$

The value of your investment in the winning team of the National Spitball League increased from $1,500 to $1,800 over several years. What was the percentage increase of the investment?

(A) 300

(B) 120

(C) 83⅓

(D) 20

(E) 16⅔

Answer: (D). The key here is that the number 1,800 shouldn't be used in your formula. Before you can find the *percent* of increase, you need to find the *amount* of increase, which is 1,800 – 1,500 = 300. To find the percentage of increase, set up the equation:

$$\frac{300}{1500} = \frac{x}{100}$$

Cross-multiply to get 1,500x = 30,000. Dividing tells you that x = 20 percent.

The SAT-devils often try to confuse you by asking about something that doesn't appear in the original question, as in this example:

The New York Yankees won 60 percent of their games. The Yanks lost 30 times and never tied. (As you know, there are no ties in the world's noblest sport, baseball. No crying either.) How many games did the team play?

(A) 12

(B) 18

(C) 50

(D) 75

(E) 90

Answer: (D). Did you find the catch? The winning percentage was 60 percent, but the question specified the number of losses. What to do? Well, because ties don't exist, the wins and losses must have represented all the games played, or 100 percent. Thus the percentage of losses must be 100% – 60%, which is 40%. Putting the formula to work:

$$\frac{30}{x} = \frac{40}{100}$$

As always, cross-multiply: 40x = 3000, and x = 75.

Keeping It in Proportion: Ratios

After you know the tricks, ratios are some of the easiest problems to answer quickly. I call them "heartbeat" problems because you can solve them in a heartbeat. Of course, if someone drop-dead gorgeous sits next to you and makes your heart beat faster, it may take you two heartbeats to solve a ratio problem. So sue me. Here are the points to remember:

✔ A ratio is written as $\frac{\text{of}}{\text{to}}$ or of:to.

- The ratio *of* sunflowers *to* roses = $\frac{\text{sunflowers}}{\text{roses}}$.

- The ratio *of* umbrellas *to* heads = umbrellas:heads.

✔ A possible total is a multiple of the *sum* of the numbers in the ratio.

You may confront a problem like this:

> At a party, the ratio of blondes to redheads is 4:5. What could be the total number of blondes and redheads at the party?

Mega-easy. Add the numbers in the ratio: 4 + 5 = 9. The total must be a multiple of 9, like 9, 18, 27, 36, and so on. If this "multiple of" stuff is confusing, think of it another way: The sum must divide evenly into the total. That is, the total must be divisible by 9. Can the total, for example, be 54? Yes, 9 goes evenly into 54. Can it be 64? No, 9 doesn't go evenly into 64.

Check out another example.

Trying to get Willie to turn down his stereo, his mother pounds on the ceiling and shouts up to his bedroom. If she pounds seven times for every five times she shouts, which of the following can be the total number of poundings and shouts?

(A) 75

(B) 57

(C) 48

(D) 35

(E) 30

Answer: (C). Add the numbers in the ratio: 7 + 5 = 12. The total must be a multiple of 12. (It must be evenly divisible by 12.) Here, only 48 is evenly divisible by 12. The correct answer is (C). Of course, 75 and 57 try to trick you by using the numbers 7 and 5 from the ratio.

Notice how carefully I have been asking which *can be* the *possible* total. The total can be *any* multiple of the sum. If a question asks you which of the following *is* the total, you have to answer, "It cannot be determined." You know only which *can be* true.

Another ratio headache strikes when you're given a ratio and a total and asked to find a specific term. Do the following, in order:

1. **Add the numbers in the ratio.**

2. **Divide that sum into the total.**

3. **Multiply that quotient by each term in the ratio. (The *quotient* is the answer when you divide.)**

4. **Add the answers to double-check that they sum up to the total.**

Pretty confusing stuff. Take it one step at a time. Look at this problem:

Yelling at the members of his team, whose record was 0 for 21, the irate coach pointed his finger at each member of the squad, calling everyone either a wimp or a slacker. If he had 3 wimps for every 4 slackers, and every member of the 28-man squad was either a wimp or a slacker, how many wimps were there?

1. **Add the numbers in the ratio: 3 + 4 = 7.**

2. **Divide that sum into the total: $^{28}\!/_7 = 4$.**

3. **Multiply that quotient by each term in the ratio: $4 \times 3 = 12$; $4 \times 4 = 16$.**

4. **Add to double-check that the numbers sum up to the total: 12 + 16 = 28.**

Now you have all the information you need to answer a variety of questions: How many wimps were there? 12. How many slackers were there? 16. How many more slackers than wimps were there? Four. How many slackers would have to be kicked off the team for the number of wimps and slackers to be equal? Four. The SAT-writers can ask all sorts of things, but if you have this information, you're ready for anything they throw at you.

Be sure that you actually do Step 4, adding the terms to double-check that they sum up to the total again. Doing so catches any careless mistakes you may have made.

The SAT-writers often throw in extra numbers that aren't used at all to solve the problem. In the preceding example, the team's not-quite-World-Series-quality 0 and 21 won/lost record is interesting, but irrelevant in terms of the question you're answering. Don't get distracted by extra information.

Getting DIRTy: Time, Rate, and Distance

Time to dish the dirt, as in D.I.R.T. Distance Is Rate × Time. $D = RT$. When you have a time, rate, and distance problem, use this formula. Make a chart with the formula across the top and fill in the spaces on the chart.

Jennifer drives 40 miles an hour for 2½ hours. Her friend Ashley goes the same distance but drives at 1½ times Jennifer's speed. How many *minutes* longer does Jennifer drive than Ashley?

Don't start making big, hairy formulas with *x*'s and *y*'s. Make the DIRT chart.

Distance = Rate × Time

When you fill in the 40 mph and 2½ hours for Jennifer, you can calculate that she went 100 miles. Think of it this simple way: If she goes 40 mph for one hour, that's 40 miles. For a second hour, she goes another 40 miles. In a half hour, she goes ½ of 40, or 20 miles. (See? You don't have to write down 40 × 2½ and do all that pencil-pushing; use your brain, not your yellow No. 2 pencil or your calculator.) Add them together: 40 + 40 + 20 = 100. Jennifer has gone 100 miles.

Distance = Rate × Time

100 (Jennifer)   40 mph   2½ hours

Because Ashley drives the same distance, fill in 100 under distance for her. She goes 1½ times as fast. Uh-uh, put down that calculator. Use your brain! 1 × 40 is 40; ½ × 40 is 20. Add 40 + 20 = 60. Ashley drives 60 mph. Now this gets really easy. If she drives at 60 mph, she drives one mile a minute. (60 minutes in an hour, 60 miles in an hour.) Therefore, to go 100 miles takes her 100 minutes. Because your final answer is asked for in minutes, don't bother converting this to hours; leave it the way it is.

Distance = Rate × Time

100 (Ashley)   60 mph   100 minutes

Last step. Jennifer drives 2½ hours. How many minutes is that? Do it the easy way, in your brain. One hour is 60 minutes. A second hour is another 60 minutes. A half hour is 30 minutes. Add them together: 60 + 60 + 30 = 150 minutes. If Jennifer drives for 150 minutes and Ashley drives for 100 minutes, Jennifer drives 50 minutes more than Ashley. However, Ashley gets a speeding ticket.

Distance	= Rate	× Time
100 (Jennifer)	40 mph	150 minutes
100 (Ashley)	60 mph	100 minutes

Be careful to note whether the people are traveling in the *same* direction or *opposite* directions. Suppose you're asked how far apart drivers are at the end of their trip. If you're told that Jordan travels 40 mph east for 2 hours and Connor travels 60 mph west for 3 hours, they're going in opposite directions. If they start from the same point at the same time, Jordan has gone 80 miles one way, and Connor has gone 180 miles the opposite way. They're 260 miles apart. The trap answer is 100, because careless people (not *you!*) simply subtract 180 – 80.

Demonstrating the Value of Radicals

Knowing how to manipulate radicals can help you get around in Berkeley, California. Radical knowledge also helps with the SATs. In math-speak, a *radical* is a square root, as well as the sign indicating square root. The square root of number x, written $\sqrt{x}$, is the positive number which, multiplied by itself, gives x. As a classic example, $\sqrt{9} = 3$, because $3 \times 3 = 9$. If only radicals were always that easy. Unfortunately, most numbers have square roots that are decidedly not pretty. $\sqrt{7}$, for example, equals approximately 2.645751311.

The rules for multiplication and division of radicals are simple. Just multiply and divide the numbers normally:

$$\sqrt{5} \times \sqrt{6} = \sqrt{30} \text{ or } \sqrt{55} \div \sqrt{5} = \sqrt{11}$$

Addition and subtraction are trickier. You can't just add and subtract the numbers and plop the result under a square root sign. For example, $\sqrt{3} + \sqrt{5}$ doesn't equal $\sqrt{8}$. You can add or subtract radicals only if they have the same number under the symbol, so $\sqrt{27} + \sqrt{12}$ is impossible as written. However, you can break down any radical by factoring out a perfect square and simplifying it, so $\sqrt{27} = \sqrt{9}\sqrt{3} = 3\sqrt{3}$, and $\sqrt{12} = \sqrt{4}\sqrt{3} = 2\sqrt{3}$; then, $3\sqrt{3} + 2\sqrt{3} = 5\sqrt{3}$.

A few squares show up all the time on the SAT. Scan Table 14-1 so you're familiar with these numbers when you see them:

Table 14-1				Simple Square Roots								
Numbers	$-x$	−1	0	1	2	3	4	5	6	7	8	9	x
Squares	x^2	1	0	1	4	9	16	25	36	49	64	81	x^2

Notice how the square of both x and $-x$ is x^2? Conveniently, when you multiply two negative numbers, the result is positive, as it is when you multiply two positive numbers. So the square of the same negative and positive number will always be the same: $(-8)^2 = 64$ and $(+8)^2 = 64$.

Computing Absolute Value

Absolute value is a simple concept that's annoyingly easy to mess up. *Absolute value* is the number, shorn of its positive or negative value. The symbol looks like a Superman phone booth without a roof. The absolute value of 3 is written $|3|$, which equals 3; the absolute value of −3 is written $|-3|$, which also equals 3.

On the SAT you may see a number or algebraic expression inside the absolute value symbol. If you do, follow these steps.

1. **Simplify whatever is inside the absolute value symbol, if possible.**

2. **If the answer is negative, switch it to positive.**

Some people have the (incorrect) idea that absolute value changes subtraction to addition. Nope. If you're working with $|3 - 4|$, don't change the quantity to $3 + 4$. Calculate whatever is inside the absolute value symbols first, $|3 - 4| = |-1|$, and only *then* change the result to a positive number, in this case 1.

Saying "MMM" Mean, Median, Mode

Sometimes the SAT-writers give you a group of numbers and ask you to find their average. This sort of problem is probably familiar to you, especially if you're into computing your grade-point average or your favorite player's batting average. To find the average, just add up the numbers and divide the total by the number of numbers you just added. For example, to find the average of 2, 4, and 9, add those three numbers (total = 15) and divide by three. The average is 5.

When you calculate an average, don't fall into the trap of dividing by 2 all the time. You must divide by the number of terms you're averaging.

This old-fashioned average is officially called the *mean* of the numbers (or sometimes the *arithmetic mean*). If a group of numbers is evenly spaced, the mean is the middle number (assuming there is one).

Suppose you're asked to find the arithmetic mean of the numbers from 1 to 19. Even with a calculator, adding up all the numbers and then dividing is time-consuming, not to mention easy to mess up. But of the 19 numbers — which are, of course, evenly spaced — 10 is the middle. No matter which way you start, from one or from 19, you find nine numbers on either side of 10. Bingo. Ten is the average, the mean, and the arithmetic mean. (Use any term you want.) Remember that this trick works only when the numbers are evenly spaced. If you're told to find the average of 3, 5, 7, 12, and 18, you have to compute the long way.

Despite what common sense may tell you, only an *odd* number of things has a middle. For example, this trick doesn't quite work for a list like 3, 4, 5, 6, 7, 8; there's no middle term when you have an even number of terms in the list. Remember, I'm not talking about the average here, I'm talking about the middle term.

Moving on beyond mean (to nice and friendly or *affable* and *amiable*, which are variations on the nice/friendly theme), SAT mathematicians also want you to understand *median*. The *median*, as those of you with drivers' licenses already know, is the strip down the middle of the road. In math, the *median* is defined as the middle number in a list, when the list is in numerical order. That last bit is important, because you may have a list like 2, 5, 3, 7, 8 and need to find the median. It's not 3, but 5. When you put the numbers in order, the list reads 2, 3, 5, 7, 8, with 5 sitting right in the center.

If you have an even number of numbers (say, 3, 5, 6, 7, 8, 10), there is no middle number, so mathematicians cheat a little. The median is the mean (Remember the mean? It's an average.) of the two numbers closest to the middle. In this example, the two numbers in question are 6 and 7, so the median is 6.5.

The last of the three Ms is the *mode*, the easiest to find. In a mixed bag of numbers, the *mode* is the number or numbers that pop up most frequently. So if you have a set with three 4s and three 8s, plus pairs of a bunch of other numbers, you have two modes, 4 and 8, in that set. You can also have a set with no mode at all if everything shows up the same number of times.

Which of the following is true for the set of numbers 3, 4, 4, 5, 6, 8?

(A) Mean > Mode

(B) Median > Mean

(C) Mode > Median

(D) Median = Mode

(E) Median = Mean

Answer: (A). If you average the terms, you get 30 ÷ 6, or 5, which is the mean. The median is 4.5 (halfway between the third and fourth term), and the mode is 4. So (A) is the only one that fits.

Finding the Pattern: Though This Be Madness, Yet There Is Method in It

Sorry about the heading. As an English teacher, I can't resist quoting *Hamlet,* especially when I can throw an English lesson in a math chapter. Nor can I resist asking what separates mathematicians from the rest of humanity. (Insert your own sarcastic remark here.) Joking aside, mathematicians are very good at recognizing patterns and seeing where those patterns lead. The SAT occasionally asks you to play mathematician with two types of patterns: *arithmetic* and *geometric.* The math word for pattern, by the way, is *sequence.*

Check out this arithmetic sequence: 2, 5, 8, 11, 14, . . . Notice how each number is obtained by adding 3 to the previous number? In an arithmetic sequence, you always add or subtract the same number to the previous term to get the next term. Another example of an arithmetic sequence is 80, 73, 66, 59, . . . In this one, you're subtracting 7 from the previous term.

A geometric sequence is similar to an arithmetic sequence, but it works by multiplication or division. In the sequence 2, 6, 18, 54, . . . every term is multiplied by 3 to get the next term. In 100, 50, 25, 12½, . . . each term is divided by 2 to get the next term.

Often, the best way to solve these problems is just to make a list and follow the pattern. However, if the test-writers ask you for something like the 20th term of the sequence, this process can take forever. There is a useful formula for each type of sequence, which is worth memorizing if you have the time and the room in your head:

For an arithmetic sequence, the nth term is the first term plus $(n-1)$ times d, where d is the difference between the terms. In the sequence 2, 5, 8, 11, 14, the difference between terms is +3, because you add 3 each time. What would be the 20th term? Take 2, the first term, and add 3 19 times, so it's $2 + 19(3) = 2 + 57 = 59$.

For a geometric sequence, the nth term is the first term, *times r* to the $(n-1)^{th}$ power, where r is the ratio of one term to the next. Huh? Well, you probably remember that taking something to a power means multiplying it by itself a bunch of times. For example, 4 to the 5th power $= 4 \times 4 \times 4 \times 4 \times 4$, which equals 1,024. (Powers get big really fast.) You can do powers on most calculators by using either the "y^x" or the "$\wedge$" button. On mine, I do 4 to the 5th by typing $4\ y^x\ 5 =$.

Check out this sequence: 2, 6, 18, 54. The ratio was 3, because you multiplied by 3 each time. To find the tenth term (the 20th would be way too big to handle), take 2 times 3 to the 9th power. 3^9 = 19,683, and $2 \times 19,683$ = 39,366, so that's the answer.

As if your life weren't tough enough, the SAT-folks often hide these sequences inside a word problem, such as the following:

The bacteria population in my day-old wad of chewing gum doubles every 3 hours. If there are 100 bacteria at 12:00 noon on Friday, how many bacteria will be present at midnight of the same day?

(A) 200

(B) 300

(C) 800

(D) 1,600

(E) 409,600

Answer: (D). To solve this, make a chart. Because the population doubles every 3 hours, count off three-hour intervals, doubling as you go:

12:00(noon) = 100 bacteria

3:00 = 200 bacteria

6:00 = 400 bacteria

9:00 = 800 bacteria

12:00 (midnight) = 1,600 bacteria

And here's a little fantasy where the formulas come in handy:

Author A, an extraordinarily fast writer who zips through a chapter a day, gets paid $100 for her first chapter, $200 for her second, $300 for her third, and so on. Author B, also a member of the chapter-a-day club, gets paid $1 for his first chapter, $2 for his second, $4 for his third, $8 for his fourth, and so on. On the 12th day,

(A) Author A is paid $76 more.

(B) Author B is paid $24 more.

(C) They are paid the same amount.

(D) Author A is paid $1,178 more.

(E) Author B is paid $848 more.

Answer: (E). Author A's plan is an arithmetic sequence, increasing by $100 each time, so on the 12th day she's paid 100 + 11(100) = 100 + 1,100 = $1,200. Author B's plan is a geometric sequence, multiplied by 2 each time, so on the 12th day, he's paid 1×2^{11} = 1 × 2,048 = $2,048. So Author B is paid $848 more.

Setting a Spell

A *set* is just a collection of things — shrunken heads, leftover hockey pucks, Barbie outfits, whatever. In math, a set is a collection of *elements*, usually numbers, which you find inside brackets: { . . . }. For example, the set of whole numbers less than 6 is a set with six elements: {0, 1, 2, 3, 4, 5}. Some sets go on forever, and three dots at the end tell you so. The set of positive odd numbers is {1, 3, 5, 7, . . . } because it reaches infinity. It's also possible for a set to have nothing inside of it; this is the "empty set," and it's written either { } or (more commonly) Ø.

You can do a lot of stuff with sets, including auctioning them on eBay. The SAT-folks love to ask about two specific things — the union and the intersection of sets. The *union* of two sets is just the two sets put together; thus, the union of {1, 2, 3} and {5, 7, 8} is {1, 2, 3, 5, 7, 8}.

Even if something shows up in both sets, it shows up only once in the union. Thus, the union of (2, 3, 4) and {3, 4, 5} is {2, 3, 4, 5}, NOT {2, 3, 4, 3, 4, 5}. A useful formula helps you find the number of elements in the union of two sets:

1. **Add up the number of elements in each set.**

2. **Then subtract the number of elements that show up in both.**

In the preceding example, 3 + 3 = 6; but because 3 and 4 show up in both sets, you have to subtract 2. The union has 4 elements.

The *intersection* of two sets, on the other hand, contains only those elements that show up in both of them. The intersection of {1, 2, 4} and {4, 6, 7} is {4}; the intersection of {3, 5, 7} and {2, 4, 6} is Ø, also known as "empty."

Chapter 15

Practice Problems in Numbers and Operations

In This Chapter

▶ Trying SAT problems involving numbers and operations

▶ Focusing on numbers and operations problems that give you trouble

*T*hat old saying, "Practice makes perfect," is annoying yet true. In this chapter, I hit you with two sets of numbers and operations questions along with explanations of the answers. After you practice the first set, check your answers and read the explanations of any you answered incorrectly. (The answers immediately follow each question. Use a piece of paper to cover the answers as you work.) If you're confused about any point, turn back to Chapter 14 for more detail on the kind of problem that's stumping you. Sorry, I can't help you with what to get Aunt Agnes for her birthday, whether to dump your tech stocks, and how to get even with your little brother.

Practice Set One

1. If you invest $2,000 for one year at 5% annual interest, the total amount you would have at the end of the year would be:

    (A) $100

    (B) $2,005

    (C) $2,100

    (D) $2,500

    (E) $3,000

    Solve it like this: 5% = .05, so 5% of 2000 = .05 × 2000 = 100. But wait! Before you choose 100 as your answer, remember that you still have the $2,000 that you originally invested, so you now have 2,000 + 100 = $2,100. You can also solve this problem with the is/of method. You're basically being asked, "What is 5% of 2000," so you write $\frac{x}{2000} = \frac{5}{100}$. Cross-multiplying gives 100x = 10,000, so x = $100. Of course, you still need to add in the original $2,000 to get your answer, so (C) is correct.

2. Which number is an element of the set of prime numbers but not of the set of odd numbers?

   (A) 0

   (B) 1

   (C) 2

   (D) 3

   (E) 9

   Because 2 is the only prime number that isn't odd, (C) is correct.

3. 100 percent of 99 subtracted from 99 percent of 100 equals:

   (A) –1

   (B) 0

   (C) 0.99

   (D) 1

   (E) 1.99

   Keep in mind that 100 percent of anything is itself, so 100 percent of 99 is 99. 99 percent of 100 equals 0.99 x 100 = 99 (not a big surprise, because percent means "out of one hundred"). And 99 – 99 = 0. (B) is the correct answer.

4. The tenth number of the sequence 50, 44.5, 39, 33.5, . . . would be:

   (A) –4

   (B) 0.5

   (C) 1

   (D) 1.5

   (E) 6

   The numbers decrease by 5.5 every time. The simplest way to do this problem is to continue the pattern: 50, 44.5, 39, 33.5, 28, 22.5, 17, 11.5, 6, 0.5. You can also use the formula: The tenth term is $50 + 9(-5.5) = 50 - 49.5 = 0.5$. Hooray for (B), the correct answer.

5. If E represents the set of even numbers, and N represents the set of numbers divisible by nine, which number is in the intersection of E and N?

   (A) 99

   (B) 92

   (C) 66

   (D) 54

   (E) 9

   An element is in the intersection of two sets only if it is in both of them. You can go through the choices until you find the right one: 99 isn't even; 92 isn't divisible by 9; 66 isn't divisible by nine; 54 is even *and* divisible by nine; 9 isn't even. Thus 54 is the only one that works. (D) is the right answer.

6. The first three elements of a geometric sequence are 1, 2, and 4. What is the eighth element of the sequence?

   (A) 14

   (B) 16

   (C) 29

   (D) 128

   (E) 256

   The formula for geometric sequences tells you that the answer is $1 \times 2^7 = 1 \times 128 = 128$. Remember, if you use these formulas, always subtract one from the number of the term you're being asked for. Three cheers for (D).

7. The expression $3^2 - 4 + 5(\%)$ equals

   (A) –27

   (B) –15

   (C) 5

   (D) 22

   (E) 25

   Aunt Sally to the rescue! (See Chapter 14 for the lowdown on my favorite relative.) First do the operation in parenthesis, $\% = 4$, and then calculate 3^2, which equals 9. That leaves you with $9 - 4 + 5(4)$. Next, multiply $5 \times 4 = 20$. Now the expression is $9 - 4 + 20$. You have a trap to avoid: Did you see it? Don't do addition before subtraction; just go left to right: $9 - 4 = 5$, and $5 + 20 = 25$. Give it up for (E).

8. Which of the following numbers is rational?

   (A) π

   (B) $0.12112111211112\ldots$

   (C) $\sqrt{8}$

   (D) $\sqrt{9}$

   (E) $\sqrt{10}$

   To do this problem, you need to remember the definitions of rational and irrational numbers. π is irrational by definition. (Yes, it's worth memorizing this fact.) The number $0.12112111211112\ldots$ is irrational because the decimal never ends or repeats. (For those of you who are still awake, it doesn't repeat because the number of 1's keeps increasing.) All radicals are irrational if the number underneath isn't a perfect square: So $\sqrt{8}$ and $\sqrt{10}$ are both irrational. However, because $\sqrt{9} = 3$, it's rational. (D) is correct.

9. A student has taken three tests, with an average (arithmetic mean) of 82. What grade must she receive on her next test in order to have an overall average of 85?

   (A) 85

   (B) 88

   (C) 90

   (D) 94

   (E) 97

The formula (total) = (average) × (number) helps with this problem. The student's total number of points on the first three tests is 82 × 3 = 246. She wants to end up with an 85 average on four tests, for a total of 85 × 4 = 340. So she needs 340 − 246 = 94 points on her next test to get (1) the car keys and (2) permission to stay out past 7 p.m. (D) is correct.

10. At a sale, a shirt normally priced at $60 was sold for $48. What was the percentage of the discount?

    (A) 12%

    (B) 20%

    (C) 25%

    (D) 48%

    (E) 80%

Use the percentage formula: $\frac{is}{of} = \frac{\%}{100}$. But, as usual, be careful. The problem asks for the percentage of the discount, so don't just plug in 48. Instead, first figure out the amount of the discount, which was 60 − 48 = 12. Using 12, write $\frac{12}{60} = \frac{p}{100}$, where p is the percentage of the discount. Cross-multiplying, you get 1200 = 60p, and p = 20. You could still get the right answer using 48. If you used 48 in the formula, you'd get 80%. Because the shirt now costs 80% of what it used to, the discount is 100% − 80% = 20%. (B) is correct.

Practice Set Two

If practice set one was a breeze, go golfing. If you got stuck, try this set.

Two questions (2 and 6) are grid-ins. On the blank grids in this section, bubble in your answers. (See Chapter 13 for the proper way to bubble in your answers with grid-ins.)

1. The total number of even three-digit numbers is

    (A) 49

    (B) 100

    (C) 449

    (D) 450

    (E) 50

Counting them all would take a really long time, so try to figure it out logically. The three-digit numbers start with 100 and end with 999. How many numbers do you have? It's 900, not 899. (Yes, there is a formula you can use here: Subtract the numbers and add 1. Works every time.) How many of these numbers are even? Well, because even and odd numbers alternate on this list, half of them are even, and half are odd. So you have 450 of each type. (D) is right.

2. Evaluate $\left|10 - \left(42 \div |1 - 4|\right)\right|$

When doing an absolute value problem, treat the absolute values as parentheses when trying to figure out the order of operations. Because this problem has a bunch of parentheses and

$$\left|10 - \left(42 \div |1 - 4|\right)\right|$$

$$\left|10 - \left(42 \div |-3|\right)\right|$$

absolute values, work from the inside out. So $\left|10 - \left(42 \div 3\right)\right|$, and 4 is the correct answer.

$$\left|10 - \left(14\right)\right|$$

$$\left|-4\right|$$

$$4$$

3. A disease is killing the fish in a certain lake. Every 8 days, half of the fish in the lake die. If there are 1,000 fish alive on March 3, how many are still alive on March 19?

(A) 0

(B) 100

(C) 125

(D) 250

(E) 500

On March 3: 1,000 fish are alive. March 11: 500 fish. On March 19: 250 fish. (D) is correct.

4. If a number n is the product of two distinct primes, x and y, how many factors does n have, including 1 and itself?

(A) 2

(B) 3

(C) 4

(D) 5

(E) 6

Prime numbers have only two factors: one and themselves. Pretend in your problem that $x = 5$ and $y = 7$. Then $n = 5 \times 7 = 35$. The factors of 35 are 1, 5, 7, and 35. Because you can't break down 5 or 7, there are no other factors. As long as you picked prime numbers for x and y, you would always get four factors for n. (D) is correct.

5. Which number is 30% greater than 30?

   (A) 27

   (B) 33

   (C) 36

   (D) 39

   (E) 60

   Solve it like this: 30% of 30 = 0.30 × 30 = 9. Because the answer is 30% greater than 30, add 30 + 9 = 39. Three cheers for (D).

6. A recipe for French toast batter calls for ½ teaspoon of cinnamon for every 5 eggs. How many teaspoons of cinnamon would be needed if a restaurant made a huge batch of batter using 45 eggs?

   If you set up a ratio, you would write $\frac{cinnamon}{eggs} = \frac{cinnamon}{eggs} : \frac{\frac{1}{2}}{5} = \frac{x}{45}$. Cross-multiplying: 22.5 = 5x, and x = 4.5. You could also have reasoned as follows: The number of eggs was multiplied by 9, so the amount of cinnamon should be, too. Okay, ½ × 9 = 4½ = ⁹⁄₂ or 4.5. The answer is 4.5 or ⁹⁄₂. (Don't grid 4½.)

7. Which of the following is <u>not</u> equivalent to $\sqrt{40}$?

   (A) $2\sqrt{10}$

   (B) $\sqrt{30} + \sqrt{10}$

   (C) $\sqrt{5}\sqrt{8}$

   (D) $\sqrt{90} - \sqrt{10}$

   (E) $\sqrt{160} + 2$

   You could use a calculator to figure out what each choice equals, but this problem gives you a chance to practice working with radicals. Start with $2\sqrt{10}$. This doesn't equal $\sqrt{20}$, because you can't multiply a whole number and a radical. In order to multiply these, you must turn 2 into $\sqrt{4}$; now, $\sqrt{4}\sqrt{10} = \sqrt{40}$. On to (B): It's "illegal" to add radicals that don't have the same number inside (penalty = 5 to 10 years of multiplication tables). Also, there's no way to break down $\sqrt{30}$ or $\sqrt{10}$, because there's no perfect square that goes into either one. So you're stuck on this one. In (C), $\sqrt{5}\sqrt{8} = \sqrt{40}$. In (D), you can break down $\sqrt{90}$ to $\sqrt{9}\sqrt{10} = 3\sqrt{10}$. Then $3\sqrt{10} - \sqrt{10} = 2\sqrt{10}$ (remember that $\sqrt{10}$ has an "invisible one" in front of it). And you saw in (A) that $2\sqrt{10} = \sqrt{40}$. For (E), use the same trick as in (A): Change 2 into $\sqrt{4}$, so $\sqrt{160} + 2 = \sqrt{160} + \sqrt{4} = \sqrt{40}$.

Bottom line: They all equal $\sqrt{40}$, except for (B). If you check it out on a calculator, $\sqrt{40} \approx 6.32$, but $\sqrt{30} + \sqrt{10} \approx 8.64$. Thus, (B) is correct.

8. Janice wrote down all the numbers from 11 to 25. Darren wrote down all the positive numbers less than 50 that are divisible by 6. How many numbers are in the union of their two lists?

   (A) 3

   (B) 8

   (C) 15

   (D) 20

   (E) 23

   Janice's list has 15 numbers: {11, 12, 13, 14, 15, 16, 17, 18, 19, 20, 21, 22, 23, 24, 25}. Darren's list has 8 numbers: {6, 12, 18, 24, 30, 36, 42, and 48}. Now, don't fall into the trap of thinking that there are 23 numbers in the union; even though 12, 18, and 24 show up in both sets, you're not allowed to count them twice in the union. The total number of elements in the union is $23 - 3 = 20$. Thus, (D) is correct.

9. Preparing for a marathon, Steven jogged 2 miles on April 10, 2.5 miles on April 11, 3 miles on April 12, and so on, increasing by half a mile each day, until April 25. The <u>median</u> number of miles he jogged per day was

   (A) 5 miles

   (B) 5.5 miles

   (C) 5.75 miles

   (D) 6 miles

   (E) 9.5 miles

   Although it's time-consuming, list the number of miles Steven ran each day:

10th	11th	12th	13th	14th	15th	16th	17th	18th	19th	20th	21st	22nd	23rd	24th	25th
2	2.5	3	3.5	4	4.5	5	5.5	6	6.5	7	7.5	8	8.5	9	9.5

   This list has 16 numbers. If a list contains an even number of terms, there is no middle term. The two terms that are the closest to the middle are 5.5 and 6, so you must average them: $\frac{5.5 + 6}{2} = 5.75$. (C) is correct.

10. In the correctly solved subtraction problem below, A, B, and C all stand for different numbers from 1 to 9. The value of C must be

    $$\begin{array}{r} 1B5A \\ -\ 6BC \\ \hline ABC \end{array}$$

    (A) 9

    (B) 8

    (C) 7

    (D) 6

    (E) 3

Doing this problem is easier if you think of addition instead of subtraction. If the equation the SAT-writers give you is true, then $\begin{array}{r} ABC \\ + \ 6BC \\ \hline 1B5A \end{array}$. A must be an even number, because you get it by adding C + C. It can't be 2, because then your two numbers wouldn't add up to something bigger than 1,000. So A is 4, 6, or 8.

Now look at the tens column. The sum of B + B can't be 5 unless you carried a "1" from the ones column. That means that C + C equals either 14, 16, or 18, so C equals 7, 8, or 9.

What about B? B + B +1 (you carried, remember) gives you 5. So B could be either 2 or 7, because 7 +7 + 1 = 15. But if B is 7, then the hundreds column makes no sense. (Try it and you'll see why.) So B must be 2. Because B is 2, A must be 6, to make the hundreds column work, and that makes C equal 8. Check the original problem: $\begin{array}{r} 1256 \\ - \ 628 \\ \hline 628 \end{array}$ It works! (B) is correct.

Hitting a vocabulary homer

Had enough math for the moment? Take a TV break. Have you ever seen anyone less *hirsute* (hairy) than Homer Simpson? This famous *gourmand* (someone who loves to eat and drink a large quantity) isn't exactly a fan of *gourmet* cooking (featuring excellent or high quality food and drink). Homer spends so much time gobbling down doughnuts that he's made himself *rotund, obese,* and not at all *agile* or *lithe* (the first two mean "fat" and the second two "graceful in movement"). Homer's also *gullible* (he'll believe anything) and *indolent* (don't wake him up when he's "working"). Two words you'll never use to describe Homer: *svelte* (fashion-model thin) and *emaciated* (thin to the point of starvation).

Chapter 16

X Marks the Spot: Algebra and Functions

In This Chapter

▶ Dealing with exponents

▶ Figuring out factoring

▶ Unraveling equations

▶ Understanding functions

1f x is the value of the present your mom expects for her birthday and y is the amount of money in your piggybank, what equation best represents your chances of staying on her good side this year? Don't worry. This problem won't appear on the SAT, but it's a good example of why I love algebra: You get to play with little letters, even though you're solving a math problem.

If you love algebra, or even if you'd prefer to shred the pages of your algebra text, this chapter's for you. In this chapter you find a quick and dirty review of the basics of SAT algebra, plus a spin through function-land, where $f(x)$ rules.

Powering Up: Exponents

Many SAT questions require you to know how to work with bases and exponents. Here's the lowdown on some of the most important concepts.

✔ The *base* is the big number (or letter) on the bottom. The *exponent* is the little number (or letter) in the upper right corner.

- In x^5, x is the base; 5 is the exponent.

- In 3^y, 3 is the base; y is the exponent.

✔ A base to the zero power equals one.

✔ $x^0 = 1$

- $5^0 = 1$

- $129^0 = 1$

I could give you a long, *soporific* (sleep-causing) explanation as to why a number to the zero power equals one, but you don't really care, do you? For now, just memorize the rule.

✔ A base to the first power is just the base. In other words, $4^1 = 4$.

✔ **A base to the second power is *base* × *base*.** Do you remember that from ninth-grade algebra?

- $x^2 = x \times x$
- $5^2 = 5 \times 5$
- $129^2 = 129 \times 129$

✔ **The same is true for bigger exponents.** The exponent tells you how many times the number repeats. For example, 5^6 means that you write down six 5s and then multiply them all together.

- $5^6 = 5 \times 5 \times 5 \times 5 \times 5 \times 5$, which equals 15,625.

- Remember that an exponent tells you to multiply the base times itself as many times as the exponent, so 2^3 does *not* equal 6. $2 \times 2 \times 2 = 8$.

On most calculators, you can do powers with either the "y^x" or the "^" button. Just type the base, the appropriate button, the exponent, and the good ol' "=" button.

✔ **A base to a negative exponent is the reciprocal of the base to a positive exponent.**

This one is a little more confusing. A *reciprocal* is the upside-down version of something. (Here's a *conundrum*, or riddle: Is the North Pole the reciprocal of the South Pole?) When you have a negative exponent, just put base and exponent under a 1 and make the exponent positive again.

- $x^{-4} = \frac{1}{x^4}$
- $5^{-3} = \frac{1}{5^3}$
- $129^{-1} = \frac{1}{129^1}$

The *number isn't* negative. When you flip it, you get the reciprocal, and the negative just sort of fades away. *Don't* fall for the trap of saying that $5^{-3} = -\frac{1}{5^3}$ or $-\frac{1}{25}$.

✔ **A base to a fractional exponent is a root of the base.** Ah, more confusion. You're already familiar with the standard square root of a number: $\sqrt{25} = 5$ because $5^2 = 25$. Because it takes two 5s to make 25, we can also write $25^{\frac{1}{2}} = 5$.

It works the same way with other powers. $5^3 = 5 \times 5 \times 5 = 125$, so you can say that $125^{\frac{1}{3}} = 5$. $64^{\frac{1}{6}} = 2$, since $2^6 = 64$.

You can also do fractional powers on your calculator, either by using "y^x" and typing the fraction, or by the $\sqrt[x]{y}$ button, which is usually accessed by using the 2nd function key.

When you take a base of 10 to some power, the number of the power equals the number of zeros in the number.

- $10^1 = 10$ (one zero)
- $10^4 = 10,000$ (four zeros)
- $10^0 = 1$ (zero zeros)

✔ **To multiply like bases, add the exponents.** You can multiply two bases that are the same; just add the exponents.

- $x^3 \times x^2 = x^{(3+2)} = x^5$
- $5^4 \times 5^9 = 5^{(4+9)} = 5^{13}$
- $p^3 \times p = p^3 \times p^1 = p^{(3+1)} = p^4$
- $129^3 \times 129^0 = 129^{(3+0)} = 129^3$

You can't multiply *unlike* bases. Think of it as trying to make dogs and cats multiply — it doesn't work. All you end up with is a miffed meower and a damaged dog.

- $x^2 \times y^3 = x^2 \times y^3$ (no shortcuts)
- $5^2 \times 129^3 = 5^2 \times 129^3$ (you actually have to work it out)

✔ **To divide like bases, subtract the exponents.** You can divide two bases that are the same by subtracting the exponents.

- $x^5 \div x^2 = x^{(5-2)} = x^3$
- $5^9 \div 5^3 = 5^{(9-3)} = 5^6$
- $q^3 \div q^5 = q^{(3-5)} = q^{-2} = \frac{1}{q^2}$
- $129^4 \div 129^0 = 129^{(4-0)} = 129^4$

(Did I get you on that last one? It should make sense. Any base to the zero power is 1. Any number divided by 1 is itself.)

Did you look at the second example, $5^9 \div 5^3$, and think that it was 5^3? Falling into the trap of dividing instead of subtracting is easy, especially when you see numbers that just beg to be divided, like 9 and 3. Keep your guard up.

✔ **Multiply the exponents of a base inside and outside the parentheses.** That's quite a mouthful. Here's what it means:

- $(x^2)^3 = x^{(2 \times 3)} = x^6$
- $(5^3)^3 = 5^{(3 \times 3)} = 5^9$
- $(129^0)^3 = 129^{(0 \times 3)} = 129^0$

✔ **To add or subtract like bases to like powers, add or subtract the numerical coefficient of the bases.** The *numerical coefficient* (a great name for a rock band, don't you think?) is simply the number *in front of* the base. Notice that it isn't the little exponent in the right-hand corner but the full-sized number to the left of the base.

- $31x^3$: 31 is the numerical coefficient.
- $-8y^2$: –8 is the numerical coefficient.
- x^3: What is the numerical coefficient? 1, because any number is itself times 1; the 1 isn't always written out. Good trap.
- $37x^3 + 10x^3 = 47x^3$: Because the bases are the same and the exponents are the same, just add the numerical coefficients: $37 + 10 = 47$.
- $15y^2 - 10y^2 = 5y^2$: Just subtract the numerical coefficients: $15 - 10 = 5$.

You can't add or subtract terms with like bases with *different exponents.* In other words, $13x^3 - 9x^2$ isn't equal to $4x^3$ or $4x^2$ or $4x$. All it is equal to is $13x^3 - 9x^2$. The bases *and* exponents must be the same for you to add or subtract the terms.

✔ **You can't add or subtract the numerical coefficients of unlike bases.**

- $16x^2 - 4y^2 = 16x^2 - 4y^2$
- It isn't $12x^2$ or $12y^2$ or $12xy^2$ or $12x^2y$

Putting It Together and Taking It Apart: FOIL and Factoring

One of the most common tasks that you probably remember from algebra class (What? You were playing fantasy baseball that Thursday? Well, because it was baseball you're forgiven!) is the multiplication of expressions. These come in several varieties:

One term times one term: To multiply two terms, multiply their coefficients, and *add* the powers of any common variables being multiplied. You can encounter these in "Powering Up: Exponents" earlier in this chapter; for example, $(3a^3)(-2a) = (3 \times -2)(a^{(3+1)}) = -6a^4$.

One term times two (or more) terms: Here, use the familiar distributive law: Multiply the single term by each of the terms in parentheses. Be sure to take your time and work out each product individually, before combining them for the final answer. To do $3b^3(2b^2 - 5)$, write:

$3b^3 \times 2b^2 = 6b^5$

$3b^3 \times -5 = -15b^3$

And your answer is $6b^5 - 15b^3$.

Two terms times two terms: Now, use my favorite four-letter word starting with "f." Shame on you! I mean FOIL, of course. Multiply in the order *First, Outer, Inner, Last*.

To work out $(x - 3)(2x + 5)$:

1. **Multiply the *First* terms:** $x \times 2x = 2x^2$.

2. **Multiply the *Outer* terms:** $x \times 5 = 5x$.

3. **Multiply the *Inner* terms:** $-3 \times 2x = -6x$.

4. **Multiply the *Last* terms:** $-3 \times 5 = -15$.

5. **Combine like terms:** $5x + -6x = -1x$ or $-x$.

Solution: $2x^2 - x - 15$.

You should out-and-out memorize the following two special cases of FOIL. Don't bother to work them out every time; know them by heart.

✔ $(a + b)(a - b) = a^2 - b^2$. You can use this shortcut only when the two terms are exactly the same *except for their signs*. For example, $(x + 5)(x - 5) = (x)^2 - (5)^2 = x^2 - 25$. Because this method uses only the first and the last terms from FOIL, I like to call it the FL method. (Try not to spit on your friends when you pronounce it.)

✔ $(a + b)^2 = (a + b)(a + b) = a^2 + 2ab + b^2$. If I had a nickel for every time a student has messed this one up, I wouldn't need the meager cash I'm making from writing this book. (Of course, I'd still be writing it; I'm here for you!) Here's the rule in action:

The expression $(x - 3)^2$ is equivalent to:

(A) $x^2 - 9$

(B) $x^2 + 9$

(C) $x^2 + 6x - 9$

(D) $x^2 - 6x + 9$

(E) $x^2 - 6x - 9$

Answer: (D). Say it with me: "FL" doesn't work here! Answer choices (A) and (B) are just wrong. If you do "FOIL" the long way, you get $(x - 3)(x - 3) = x^2 - 3x - 3x + 9 = x^2 - 6x + 9$. Or you could just use the formula: $(x - 3)^2 = (x)^2 + 2(-3)x + (-3)^2 = x^2 - 6x + 9$.

Memorize these two formulas. Doing so saves you time, careless mistakes, and acute misery on the actual exam.

Now that you know how to do algebra forward, are you ready to do it backward? You need to be able to factor down a quadratic equation, taking it from its final form back to its original form of two sets of parentheses.

Given $x^2 + 13x + 42 = 0$, solve for x. Take this problem one step at a time.

1. **Draw two sets of parentheses.**

   ( )( ) = 0.

2. **To get x^2, the *First* terms have to be x and x. Fill those in.**

   $(x)(x) = 0$.

3. **Look now at the *Outer* terms.**

   You need two numbers that multiply together to be +42. Well, there are several possibilities such as 42×1, 21×2, or 6×7. You can even have two negative numbers: -42×-1, -21×-2, or -6×-7. You aren't sure which one to choose yet. Go on to the next step.

4. **Look at the *Inner* terms.**

   You have to add two values to get +13. What's the first thing that springs to mind? Probably $6 + 7$. Hey, that's one of the possibilities in the preceding step! Plug it in and try it.

   $(x + 6)(x + 7) = x^2 + 7x + 6x + 42 = x^2 + 13x + 42$.

Great, but you're not done yet. The whole equation equals zero, so you have $(x + 6)(x + y) = 0$. So either $(x + 6) = 0$ or $(x + 7) = 0$. That's because any number times zero equals zero. Therefore, x can equal -6 or -7.

You may also have to factor an expression like $y^2 - 49$. This sort of problem probably looks familiar to you if you remember the "FL" formula (see earlier in this section): $(a + b)(a - b) = a^2 - b^2$. $y^2 - 49$ is known as a "difference of squares," because it equals $(y)^2 - (7)^2$. Any difference of squares can be factored into an "FL" product; in this case, $y^2 - 49 = (y + 7)(y - 7)$.

Solving Equations: Why Don't They Just Tell Me What X Is?

You've probably spent a lot of time in school solving the two most basic types of equations: *linear* (for example, $3x + 5 = 5x - 7$, whose solution is $x = 6$) and *quadratic* (for example, $x^2 + 13x + 42 = 0$, which is solved in the preceding section by factoring). But post-2005 SATs hit you with more complex algebraic equations: absolute-value equations, rational equations, and radical equations.

Remember that the SAT — most of it, at least — is a multiple-choice test. When you're presented with an equation that you're not sure how to solve, you can always fall back on the ancient strategy of plugging in the answers one at a time.

Absolute value

Absolute value presents you with a number stuck inside a phone booth (the full-length, Superman type of booth). I explain absolute value in Chapter 14. Here I tell you what to do when one pops up in an equation. Check out this problem:

The equation $|x - 4| = 3$ has the solution(s):

(A) 7 only

(B) 1 only

(C) −1 only

(D) 7 and 1

(E) 7 and −1

Answer: (D). Because an absolute value symbol turns everything into a positive number, the expression inside the absolute value could equal either 3 or –3. This is the key to solving an equation with an absolute value. If $|something| = n$, then either $something = n$ or $something = -n$. You must solve each of these equations separately to get two answers. But there's a catch: You also must check each answer in the original equation. Only solutions that make the original equation true count in your final answer. Back to the preceding problem:

$$|x - 4| = 3$$
$$x - 4 = 3 \quad \text{or} \quad x - 4 = -3$$
$$+4 \quad +4 \qquad \qquad +4 \quad +4$$
$$x = 7 \quad \text{or} \quad x = 1$$

Check:

$$|(7) - 4| = 3 \qquad |(1) - 4| = 3$$
$$|3| = 3 \qquad \qquad |-3| = 3$$
$$3 = 3 \qquad \qquad 3 = 3$$

Because both checks work, your answer is (D): 7 and 1.

You can plug in the choices to solve the problem. Remember those pesky grid-ins, though! Because not every problem is multiple choice, take the time to figure out how to solve each type of equation from scratch.

Radical equations

Not a fringe group of equations that the FBI is monitoring, radical equations are those that contain square roots. Check out this example, with a handy radical.

Find the solution to the equation $3\sqrt{x} + 5 = 17$.

Because this question isn't multiple choice, you have to solve this problem the long way. In a normal linear equation, you start by isolating x; here, you must first isolate $\sqrt{x}$.

$$3\sqrt{x} + 5 = 17$$
$$-5 \quad -5$$
$$\frac{3\sqrt{x}}{3} = \frac{12}{3}$$
$$\sqrt{x} = 4$$

Now don't make the mistake of thinking that x should be 2; $\sqrt{2}$ doesn't equal 4. Instead, x is 16, because $\sqrt{16} = 4$.

Rational equations

Rational equations have fractions in them. Sometimes, when there are only numbers in the denominators of the fractions, removing the fractions and dealing with a simpler problem is easier. To solve $\frac{x}{3} + 1 = \frac{x}{2} - 3$, you multiply every term by 6, because that's the smallest number that eliminates both the 2 and the 3 (officially, 6 is the *least common denominator,* or LCD, of 2 and 3). Assuming you cancel correctly, your new equation is $2x + 6 = 3x - 18$, and x will equal 24. (I'm letting you do the steps by yourself; practice makes perfect scores.)

When the denominator contains variables, your best bet is to combine terms with like denominators and then cross-multiply:

$$\frac{12}{x} + \frac{15}{x-1} = \frac{25}{x-1}$$
$$\phantom{\frac{12}{x}} -\frac{15}{x-1} \quad -\frac{15}{x-1}$$
$$\frac{12}{x} = \frac{10}{x-1}$$

Cross-multiplying gives $12(x-1) = 10(x)$. Then $12x - 12 = 10x$, and x equals 6. If you plug back into the original equation, you get $^{12}/_6 + {}^{15}/_5 = {}^{25}/_5$, or $2 + 3 = 5$, which means that your answer checks out.

Direct and inverse variation

Variety may be the spice of life, but direct and inverse variation is an SAT math topic waiting to bring joy to your life. Instead of being given an equation to work with, you'll be told that two quantities "vary directly" or "vary inversely." These expressions represent two specific types of equations that you're already familiar with under other names.

A *direct variation* problem is just another type of ratio problem. If a and b vary directly, then the ratio $\frac{a}{b}$ is always equal to a certain constant. Thus, you can solve a direct variation problem by setting up the ratio $\frac{a_1}{b_1} = \frac{a_2}{b_2}$, cross-multiplying, and solving as usual:

x and y vary directly. If $x = 10$ when $y = 6$, what does x equal when $y = 21$?

Let $x_1 = 10$ and $y_1 = 6$. Then x_2 is what you're looking for, and $y_2 = 21$. Set up the ratio $\frac{x_1}{y_1} = \frac{x_2}{y_2}$ or $\frac{10}{6} = \frac{x_2}{21}$, and cross-multiply to get $6x_2 = 210$, so $x_2 = 35$.

Notice that, when one variable increases, the other variable increases, as well. This feature of direct variation problems helps you do a "common-sense check" of your answer.

When two variables vary *inversely*, their product is always equal to the same number. For example, suppose that p and q vary inversely, and $p = 3$ when $q = 12$. Since $pq = (3)(12) = 36$ in this case, pq must equal 36 for all values of p and q. When $p = 2$, $q = 18$ (and vice-versa); when $p = 6$, $q = 6$, as well. This strategy works for all inverse variation problems.

Barely Functioning

By the time you get to functions on the SAT, you may think that you can't . . . function, that is. But think of a function as a simple computer program: You give it an input and it produces an output. For example, $x \rightarrow 2x - 1$ is a function. The arrow means that you put in a number for x (5, for example), and get out one less than twice that number as the result (9, in this case). The input and output can then be written as an ordered pair: $(5, 9)$ is a member of this function, as are the pairs $(1, 1)$ and $(0.5, 0)$, along with many others.

You're most likely to see functions written as $f(x)$. This expression, pronounced "eff of x" is somewhat misleading, because it looks as though multiplication of some sort is going on, which isn't necessarily the case. For example, $f(x) = x - 4$ is a function for which $f(9) = 5$, $f(4) = 0$, and $f(1) = -3$. When you put in 9 for x, you get out 5; when you put in 4, you get out 0; and when you put in 1, you get out -3. Notice that $f(x)$ and y are the same thing.

Notice that the number replaces x when evaluating the function. That is, $f(9) = (9) - 4 = 5$. Some students like the notation $f(\square) = \square - 4$, because the box shows where the input goes. This is especially useful for complicated-looking functions, such as $f(x) = 3x^2 - 2^x + x$. What's $f(3)$ in this case? Well, if you write $f(\square) = 3\square^2 - 2\square + \square = 3(3)^2 - 2^{(3)} + (3) = 3(9) - 8 + 3 = 27 - 8 + 3 = 22$, you have the answer.

For many functions, only a limited number of possible inputs and outputs exists. The set of all possible inputs is referred to as the *domain* of the function; the set of all possible outputs is the function's *range*. In terms of variables, the domain represents all the possible *x*-values, while the range represents all the possible *y*-values.

On the SAT, you may be given a function and asked about possible or impossible values for the domain and range. Usually, deciding what's impossible is easier. Keep in mind two things that you can't do in a function:

✔ Divide by zero.

✔ Take the square root of a negative number.

So if you see a function like $y = \sqrt{x - 4}$, numbers like 4, 5, 6, and so on are in the domain, but numbers less than 4 aren't, because then you'd have a negative number under the radical. For a function like $f(x) = \dfrac{x + 2}{(x - 4)(x + 1)}$, *x* could be any number except 4 or –1, because plugging in those numbers gives you a denominator of zero, which is a no-no. Notice, by the way, that plugging in –2 is fine, because it's okay for the *numerator* of a fraction to be zero.

Functioning at a Higher Level

At this point, you may be wondering, "Why are functions such a big deal?" After all, function seems like a pretty abstract concept. However, it turns out that a huge number of real-life situations can be modeled using functions. On the SAT you have to be good friends with three of the most common types of functions: linear, quadratic, and exponential.

Linear functions

You've probably worked a lot with linear functions, especially in graphing. All linear functions have the form $y = mx + b$ or $f(x) = mx + b$. In graphing terms, m represents the slope of the line being drawn, while *b* represents its *y*-intercept. Take a look at this example of a linear function:

If *f*(*x*) is a linear function with a slope of 2, passing through the point (–2, –3), *f*(*x*) must also pass through the point:

(A) (1, 2)

(B) (1, 3)

(C) (2, 2)

(D) (2, 3)

(E) (0, 2)

Answer: (B). The best way to solve this problem is to draw a graph. In order to get it right, you have to remember the meaning of slope: slope $= \dfrac{\text{rise}}{\text{run}}$. A slope of ⅖, for example, tells you to move 2 spaces up (the rise) and 5 spaces to the right (the run). This function has a slope of 2, which is the same as ⅖. Starting at (–2, –3) and following these directions yields this graph:

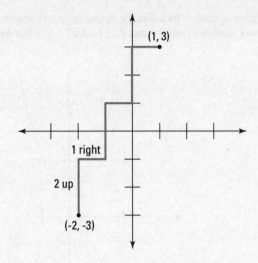

Instead of simply giving you numbers, the SAT-writers may present a real-world situation and ask you to model it with a function. For example, if an express mail package costs $1.50, plus 40 cents per pound, you can write $c = 1.50 + .40p$, where c is the cost, and p represents the number of pounds.

Quadratic functions

Quadratic functions, on the other hand, have the form $y = ax^2 + bx + c$ or $f(x) = ax^2 + bx + c$. Graphically, they can be represented by a *parabola*, a shape that resembles the basic roller-coaster hump. You certainly won't be asked to graph any of these, but you may be asked some graph-based questions. Keep these points in mind:

✔ The roots or solutions of a function are the x-values that make $f(x) = 0$. On a graph, the roots are the points where the graph crosses the horizontal x-axis.

✔ The number of solutions of $f(x) = a$ is the number of points where the graph has a height of a. On the following graph, $f(x) = 3$ twice, at the circled points.

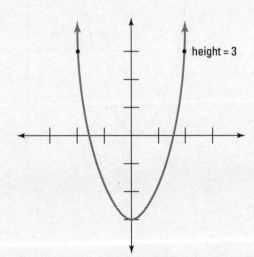

✔ If a number is added to a function, the graph is moved up that many units. If the function above were changed from *f*(*x*) to *f*(*x*) + 4, the new graph would be:

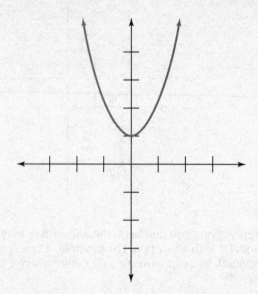

Note that subtracting a number from a function moves the graph down.

✔ If a number is added to *x* in a function, the graph is moved that many units *to the left*. This rule is tricky, because you may guess that the graph moved the other way. If the original function were changed to *f*(*x* + 4), it would look like the following graph. Notice that this rule is used when you're adding to *x*, not to the whole function. As you may guess, if you were to graph *f*(*x* – 4), you'd move four units to the right.

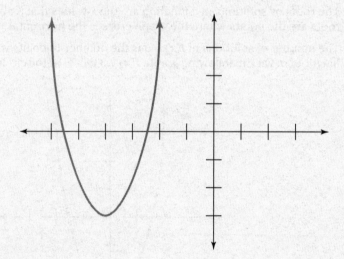

Some graphing problems don't involve equations; instead, you could be given a pair of points and asked about the line connecting them. In problems like these, three formulas are crucial :

The slope of the line connecting the points (x_1, y_1) and (x_2, y_2) is $\frac{y_2 - y_1}{x_2 - x_1}$.

The distance between the points (x_1, y_1) and (x_2, y_2) is $\sqrt{(x_2 - x_1)^2 + (y_2 - y_1)^2}$.

The midpoint of the line connecting the points (x_1, y_1) and (x_2, y_2) is $\left(\frac{x_2 + x_1}{2}, \frac{y_2 + y_1}{2} \right)$.

You probably learned these formulas some time during tenth grade. They're not exciting, but they are useful. Try using them on the points $(-1, 2)$ and $(5, -6)$:

$$\text{Slope} = \frac{(-6) - (2)}{(5) - (-1)} = \frac{-8}{6} = -\frac{4}{3}$$

$$\text{Distance} = \sqrt{\left((5) - (-1)\right)^2 + \left((-6) - (2)\right)^2} = \sqrt{(6)^2 + (-8)^2} = \sqrt{36 + 64} = \sqrt{100} = 10$$

$$\text{Midpoint} = \left(\frac{(5) + (-1)}{2}, \frac{(-6) + (2)}{2} \right) = \left(\frac{4}{2}, \frac{-4}{2} \right) = (2, -2)$$

Exponential functions

Exponential functions are closely related to the geometric sequences I explain in Chapter 14. In an exponential function, the y-value is multiplied by a "growth factor" every so often. Exponential functions are often written in the form $y = A(r)^{x/t}$, where A is the amount you start with, r is the "growth factor," and t represents how long it takes for the function to grow.

Take a look at this problem. A bacteria population in a science lab experiment doubles every 3 hours. If there are 100 bacteria at 12:00 noon one day, the number of bacteria that will be present at midnight would be:

Here, $A = 100$, $r = 2$, and $t = 3$ (because the doubling happens every three hours), so you can write $y = 100(2)^{x/3}$. To solve the problem, plug in $x = 12$, because midnight is 12 hours after noon: $y = 100(2)^{12/3} = 100(2)^4 = 100(16) = 1600$. Notice that, following the rules of PEMDAS, I did the exponent first, and only multiplied by 100 at the very end.

Decoding symbolism

One of the most popular (to the test-makers, that is) types of function problems on the SAT involves symbolism. In these problems, the SAT-makers create a new symbol for a function. Look over this example, which uses < and > as symbols.

If $<n> = n^2 - n$, then which of the following is equal to $<3> + <3>$?

(A) $<3>$

(B) $<4>$

(C) $<6>$

(D) $<9>$

(E) $<12>$

Answer: (B). This problem is just like a normal function problem, except that instead of writing $f(n) = n^2 - n$, the problem uses the symbol $<n>$. This is also one of those annoying problems where you have to try out all the possibilities until one of them works.

$<3> = 3^2 - 3 = 9 - 3 = 6.$

$<4> = 4^2 - 4 = 16 - 4 = 12.$ This looks like the answer, because it equals $6 + 6$.

$<6> = 6^2 - 6 = 36 - 6 = 30.$

$<9> = 9^2 - 9 = 81 - 9 = 72.$

$<12> = 12^2 - 12 = 144 - 12 = 132.$

Because $<3> + <3> = <4>$, the answer is (B).

Thanks, you've been *Grat*

Did your favorite grandparent send you a lucky rabbit's foot (from a very unlucky rabbit) to insure success on the math portion of the SAT? If so, you probably expressed your *gratitude* (thanks) because you were *grateful* (thankful) and not an *ingrate* (someone who thinks the whole world owes him or her a living and therefore never appreciates anything). Waiters and bartenders, on the other hand, always appreciate *gratuities* (tips). Other *grat* words include *gratis* (free — you'll be thankful for the gift, right?) and *gratuitous* (given freely but not necessary, like your mom's criticism of your latest dating partner). You may find the *grat* family *gratifying* (filling one's needs or desires) when they show up on the SAT.

Chapter 17

Practice Problems in Algebra and Functions

In This Chapter

▶ Practicing algebra and function problems
▶ Troubleshooting your problem areas

1n this chapter you get to hone your skills for SAT algebra and function problems. Try ten, see how you did, and then try ten more if you're a glutton for punishment (or algebra, which in some people's minds is the same thing).

Check your answers against mine. Don't neglect the explanations, which may help you understand what went wrong besides your answer. Remember each answer immediately follows the question. Don't cheat. Cover the answer with a piece of paper until you're ready to read the explanation. For more information on any of these topics, check out Chapter 16.

Practice Set One

Most of these problems are multiple choice, but just to keep you interested, I throw in a grid-in (question three). (See Chapter 13 for more on answering grid-ins correctly.) Have fun.

1. If k is a positive integer, which of the following is a possible value for k^2?

    (A) –1

    (B) 0

    (C) 2

    (D) 6

    (E) 9

(A) is impossible, because any number, when squared, is positive. (B) is zero squared, but the problem said that our original number had to be positive. (C) and (D) aren't perfect squares; no number multiplied by itself gives you 2 or 6 as an answer. That leaves you with (E), which is 3^2.

2. If $y = \frac{x+5}{2}$, then increasing the value of y by 2 will increase x by

   (A) 1

   (B) 2

   (C) 3

   (D) 4

   (E) 5

This problem is good for picking your own numbers. For example, say that y was originally 10; then you would have $10 = \frac{x+5}{2}$. Multiplying both sides by 2 gives $20 = x + 5$, or $x = 15$. Now the problem tells you to increase y by 2, making it 12. If you do the math (I'm trusting you here), you find that x is now 19, so it increased by 4. This result makes sense, because the equation tells you that you need to divide $x + 5$ by 2 in order to get y; y increases half as quickly as x. Your answer is (D).

3. In his will, a man left his land to his three children: ⅗ of the estate to his oldest child, ¼ to his middle child, and 15 acres to his youngest. How many acres were in the original estate?

A word problem? With no multiple-choice answers? And fractions? Okay, deep breaths. Repeat quietly to yourself: Don't panic. Don't panic. Don't panic. Feeling better? Then get to work. In any word problem, list the various things you need to know in order to solve the problem. Four important things pop up in this one: the original estate and the amount left to the three children. Because the original estate is what you're looking for, call it x. Remembering that "of" usually indicates multiplication, you can then make a list:

   x = original estate

   ⅗x = oldest child

   ¼x = middle child

   15 = youngest child

Because the three children's shares made up the whole estate, you can write: $\frac{2}{3}x + \frac{1}{4}x + 15 = x$.

With a common denominator of 12:

$$\frac{8}{12}x + \frac{3}{12}x + 15 = x$$

$$\frac{11}{12}x + 15 = x$$

$$-\frac{11}{12}x \qquad -\frac{11}{12}x$$

$$15 = \frac{1}{12}x$$

Finally, multiplying both sides by 12, you get $x = 180$.

That's a lot of work for one problem. If you're a visual person, you may prefer to do it with a graph:

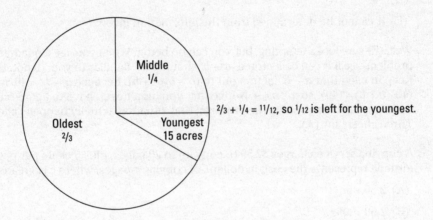

$\frac{2}{3} + \frac{1}{4} = \frac{11}{12}$, so $\frac{1}{12}$ is left for the youngest.

4. If x and y are both integers, $x > 3$, and $y < 2$, then $x - y$ could be

   (A) 3
   (B) 2
   (C) 1
   (D) 0
   (E) –1

After the last problem, this one's a breeze. x is an integer greater than 3, so it must be at least 4. y is an integer less than 2, so it must be at most 1. $4 - 1 = 3$, so (A) is correct. Notice that making x bigger or y smaller would make $x - y$ bigger than 3, so all the other choices are impossible.

5. If n and p vary directly, and $n = 12$ when $p = 9$, which of the following pairs is a possible set of values for n and p?

   (A) $n = 9, p = 12$
   (B) $n = 18, p = 15$
   (C) $n = 18, p = 6$
   (D) $n = 20, p = 15$
   (E) $n = 10, p = 8$

When quantities vary directly, their ratio — in this case $\frac{9}{6}$ — must always remain the same. There are two ways to solve this problem. One way is to set up the ratios one at a time, cross-multiplying to see which answer works. For example, for (A) write $\frac{12}{9} = \frac{9}{12}$. Cross-multiplying gives $144 = 81$, so this answer doesn't work. Repeating this process shows that (D) works.

The other way is to find the original ratio on your calculator. $\frac{12}{9} = 1.3333 \ldots$ or $\frac{4}{3}$. Trying all of the other pairs shows you that only $\frac{20}{15}$ gives the same ratio.

6. If $a^2 - b^2 = 40$ and $a - b = 10$, then $a + b =$

   (A) 4

   (B) 10

   (C) 14

   (D) 30

   (E) It cannot be determined from the information given

Well, (E) sure looks tempting, but you can do better. When you see a quadratic expression in a problem, see if it can be factored. $a^2 - b^2$ should look familiar to you. (If not, turn to Chapter 16.) Keep in mind that $a^2 - b^2$ factors out to $(a - b)(a + b)$. Because $a^2 - b^2 = 40$ and $a - b = 10$, $(10)(a + b) = (40)$, so $a + b = 4$. Notice that you didn't even have to figure out the value of the variables in order to solve the problem; that situation actually happens a lot on the SAT. Three cheers for (A).

7. A copying service charges \$2.50 to copy up to 20 pages, plus 5 cents per page over 20. Which formula represents the cost, in dollars, of copying c pages, where c is greater than 20?

   (A) $2.50 + 5c$

   (B) $2.50 + .05c$

   (C) $(2.50)(20) + .05c$

   (D) $2.50 + .05(c - 20)$

   (E) $.05(2.50 + c)$

As is often the case, one good approach is to pick a number for c, and then to see which formula works. Try $c = 28$. (Remember, c has to be greater than 20). The cost for 28 pages would be \$2.50 for the first 20, plus \$.05 times the 8 remaining pages, which is \$.40, for a total of \$2.90. Plugging 28 into the various formulas (using a calculator, of course) yields \$142.50 for (A), \$3.90 for (B), \$51.40 for (C), \$2.90 for (D), and \$1.525 for (E). (D) is correct.

8. Let a be defined as one more than a if a is odd, and as one less than a if a is even. Which of the following would result in the *smallest* number?

   (A) −2

   (B) −1

   (C) 0

   (D) 1

   (E) 2

Because −2 is even, '−2' is one less than −2, which is −3. The other choices would give us 0, −1, 2, and 1, in that order. Thus (A) is correct.

9. If $(2g - 3h)^3 = 27$, then $(2g - 3h)^{-2} =$

    (A) 9

    (B) ⅙

    (C) ⅑

    (D) –6

    (E) –9

First, give up on trying to figure out the value of g and h. The key is the expression $(2g - 3h)$, which shows up in both parts of the problem. Replace it with something simpler, like q. (I got tired of using x all of the time.) So you know that $q^3 = 27$. A little trial and error (or your calculator) reveals that $q = 3$. Now you need to find $q^{-2} = (3)^{-2} = 1/(3)^2 = \frac{1}{9}$. (C) is correct.

10. A party supplier charges a flat rate, plus a certain amount for each person. If supplies for 12 people cost $140, and supplies for 20 people cost $180, then supplies for 40 people would cost:

    (A) $220

    (B) $280

    (C) $300

    (D) $360

    (E) $400

The set-up for this problem is a classic linear-equation model. The flat rate is the y-intercept, while the amount per person is the slope. Therefore you can write $y = mx + b$, using the number of people as x and the cost as y. When you're solving a problem like this, find the slope first, using the formula $m = \frac{y_2 - y_1}{x_2 - x_1} = \frac{180 - 140}{20 - 12} = \frac{40}{8} = 5$. Bingo, the cost per person is $5. You can now figure out b by using either pair of numbers. Because supplies for 12 people cost $140, and $5 × 12 people = $60, the flat rate was $80. (You'd get the same answer if you used 20 people and $180.) Your equation is $y = 5x + 80$. Plugging in 40 for x gives $y = 280$. (B) is correct.

By the way, another way to do this problem is to play "find the pattern." When the number of people went up by 8 — from 12 to 20 — the cost went up by $40. You could make a chart like this:

people	12	20	28	36	44
cost	$140	$180	$220	$260	$300

The cost for 40 people would be halfway between $260 and $300 — in other words, $280.

Practice Set Two

Willing to ruin still more of your life with algebra? Then you'll be happy to know that ten more problems await you. You have to grid (Aren't you excited?) question 1. Break out the red pencil (teachers' revenge color) and correct your mistakes.

1. If $(x + 2)^2 + (x - 1)^2 = ax^2 + bx + c$, find the value of b.

The answer is 2. This problem is an easy one to mess up, but not if you remember the formulas I explain in Chapter 16: $(a + b)^2 = a^2 + 2ab + b^2$. It's also fine to just do FOIL, rewriting the problem as $(x + 2)(x + 2) + (x - 1)(x - 1)$. Either way, the problem becomes $x^2 + 4x + 4 + x^2 - 2x + 1$, which equals $2x^2 + 2x + 5$, so $b = 2$.

2. The pressure of a gas and its volume vary inversely. If a certain gas has a pressure of 120 kilopascals (kPa) when its volume is 250 cubic centimeters (cc), what is its pressure when its volume is 200 cc?

   (A) 170 kPa

   (B) 150 kPa

   (C) 100 kPa

   (D) 96 kPa

   (E) 70 kPa

When two quantities "vary inversely," their product is always the same number. Usually, finding that number is the key to getting the right answer. You're told that a pressure of 120 corresponds to a volume of 250, and $120 \times 250 = 30,000$. Thus, your missing pressure (call it p), times 200, must equal 30,000. Solving $200p = 30,000$ gives $p = 150$. Common sense double-check: If quantities vary inversely, one of them should go up when the other goes down. Notice that the volume went down from 250 cc to 200 cc, and the pressure went up from 120 kPa to 150 kPa. Take a second to make sure that your answer makes sense. (B) is correct.

3. Given the function $f(x) = \dfrac{5x}{x^2 - 4x + 4}$, which number is *not* in the domain of $f(x)$?

   (A) -4

   (B) -2

   (C) 0

   (D) 2

   (E) 4

The domain of a function is the set of all the numbers that can be plugged in for x. If something isn't in the domain, that means that plugging it in would force you to do something against the rules. In this case, you know that dividing by zero is against the rules. The denominator can be factored to $(x - 2)(x - 2)$, which means that 2 is the only number that would make the denominator zero, so it's the only number that's not in the domain. Thus, (D) is correct.

4. At right is the graph of the equation $y = -x^2$.

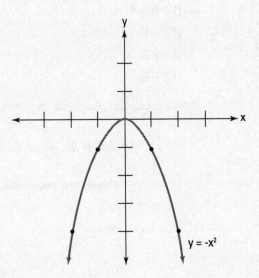

$y = -x^2$

Which of the following choices represents the graph of $y = -x^2 + 4$?

A

B

C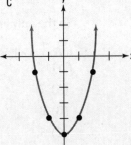

D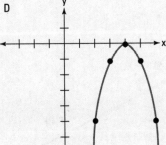

E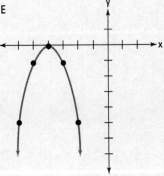

Adding 4 to a function raises its graph by four units. (B) is correct.

5. The solution set to the equation $|w| - 6 = 2w$ is

   (A) {6}

   (B) {6, –6}

   (C) {–6}

   (D) {–2, –6}

   (E) {–2}

You could just plug in all the choices, but go through the official steps. (E) is correct.

$$|w| - 6 = 2w$$

Isolate the absolute value: $+ 6 \quad + 6$

$$|w| = 2w + 6$$

Create two equations: $w = 2w + 6$ or $w = -2w - 6$

$\qquad\qquad\qquad\qquad -2w \ -2w \qquad\qquad\quad +2w \quad +2w$

Solve: $\dfrac{-w}{-1} = \dfrac{6}{-1} \qquad\qquad \dfrac{3w}{3} = \dfrac{-6}{3}$

$\qquad\qquad\quad w = -6 \qquad\qquad\qquad\quad w = -2$

Check: $|(-6)| - 6 = 2(-6) \qquad |(-2)| - 6 = 2(-2)$

$\qquad\qquad\quad 6 - 6 = -12 \qquad\qquad\quad 2 - 6 = -4$

$\qquad\qquad\qquad\ 0 = -12 \qquad\qquad\qquad -4 = -4$

$\qquad\qquad\qquad\quad$ No $\qquad\qquad\qquad\qquad$ Yes

So the only answer that works is –2.

6. If $f(x)$ is a linear function passing through the points (2, 5) and (6, 3), then the *y*-intercept of $f(x)$ is

   (A) 7

   (B) 6

   (C) 5

   (D) 4

   (E) 3

If you find a sketch helpful (I know I do), draw something like the following graph. That graph can convince you that the answer is either (A) or (B).

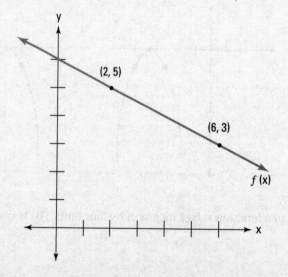

To be sure, use your formula for linear equations, $y = mx + b$. First, find the slope of your line:

$$m = \frac{y_2 - y_1}{x_2 - x_1} = \frac{3 - 5}{6 - 2} = \frac{-2}{4} = -\frac{1}{2}$$

So the equation is $y = -\frac{1}{2}x + b$. Use $(2, 5)$ to find b: $5 = -\frac{1}{2}(2) + b$

$5 = -1 + b$

$+1 \quad +1$

$6 = b$

So your y-intercept is 6, and the answer is (B).

7. If $x\backslash\backslash y$ is defined as $x^2 - y$, which statement is *always* true?

   (A) $0\backslash\backslash y = y$

   (B) $x\backslash\backslash 1$ is positive

   (C) $x\backslash\backslash 4 = x\backslash\backslash(-4)$

   (D) $x\backslash\backslash y = y\backslash\backslash x$

   (E) $4\backslash\backslash y = (-4)\backslash\backslash y$

No cool solving methods here. You just have to check all of the possibilities:

(A): $0\backslash\backslash y = (0)^2 - y = 0 - y = -y$. Nope. Onward to (B): $x\backslash\backslash 1 = (x)^2 - 1 = x^2 - 1$. This is usually positive, but if x is zero (or a fraction), then it's negative. Moving on to (C): $x\backslash\backslash 4 = (x)^2 - 4 = x^2 - 4$. $x\backslash\backslash(-4) = (x)^2 - (-4) = x^2 + 4$. They're not equal. Now for (D): $x\backslash\backslash y = x^2 - y$, and $y\backslash\backslash x = y^2 - x$. These don't look equal, and plugging in two different numbers for x and y should convince you that they're not. Which leaves (E): $4\backslash\backslash y = (4)^2 - y = 16 - y$. $(-4)\backslash\backslash y = (-4)^2 - y = 16 - y$. At last!

8. If $k^{1/2} - 3 = 5$, then $k =$

   (A) 64

   (B) 16

   (C) 8

   (D) 4

   (E) 2

$$k^{1/2} - 3 = 5$$

The official way: $\quad +3 \quad +3$

$$k^{1/2} = 8$$

Because $k^{1/2}$ means $\sqrt{k}$, square both sides:

$$k = 8^2 = 64$$

Of course, you could also just plug in all the choices to see which one worked. The key is knowing what $k^{1/2}$ means. Give it up for (A).

9. The population of a certain city can be modeled by the function $p(y) = 20,000(2)^{y/20}$, where $p(y)$ represents the population, and y measures years since 1976. If the city had a population of 32,490 in 1990, then its population in 2030 will be:

   (A) 30,000

   (B) 64,980

   (C) 80,000

   (D) 108,000

   (E) 129,960

When you're given a problem like this one, it helps to pause for a moment and see if you can figure out what the function really means. This function is an exponential growth situation. The initial population (in 1976) was 20,000, and the function doubles (the growth factor is 2) every 20 years. If you understand this concept, you can figure out the answer without actually plugging the numbers into the function. Because the population doubles every 20 years, it doubles from 1990 to 2010, and doubles again from 2010 to 2030. $32,490 \times 2 \times 2 = 129,960$. (E) is correct.

You can also solve the problem by plugging the right numbers into your calculator. Because $2030 - 1976 = 54$ years, plug in 54 for y. $20,000(2)^{54/20} = 20,000(2)^{2.7} = 20,000(6.4980) = 129,960$.

10. The solution set to the equation $5 - \dfrac{2x+2}{x+1} = \dfrac{9}{x+1}$ is

    (A) { }

    (B) {−1}

    (C) {−1, 2}

    (D) {2}

    (E) {8}

The best way to do this problem is to start by noticing that the two fractions have common denominators. Therefore they can be combined if you get them on the same side:

$$5 - \frac{2x+2}{x+1} = \frac{9}{x+1}$$
$$+\frac{2x+2}{x+1} \quad +\frac{2x+2}{x+1}$$
$$5 = \frac{9}{x+1} + \frac{2x+2}{x+1}$$
$$5 = \frac{2x+11}{x+1}$$

Now, if you multiply by $x + 1$ on both sides:

$$(x+1)5 = \frac{2x+11}{x+1}(x+1)$$
$$5x + 5 = 2x + 11$$
$$\underline{-2x \qquad -2x}$$
$$3x + 5 = 11$$
$$\underline{-5 \quad -5}$$
$$\frac{3x}{3} = \frac{6}{3}$$
$$x = 2$$

(D) is correct.

Chapter 18

Checking More Figures Than an IRS Agent: Geometry Review

- -

In This Chapter

▶ Getting to the point with angles

▶ Taming triangles

▶ Sizing up quadrilaterals

▶ Playing with polygons

▶ Running in circles

▶ Thinking in 3-D

- -

Think of geometry as a mini art lesson. The No.1 key to doing well on geometry problems is this: *Draw and label a diagram for every geometry problem that you face.* Include every measurement that you know on the diagram. Use a variable to label anything you're looking for.

After you get a nice little illustration, you're ready to rumble. But without that drawing, you're primed for a fall. Even if you think that a problem is incredibly easy, draw a quick diagram. Beauty isn't what counts; getting the right answer is.

Also, fair warning: This chapter has a lot of information to memorize. I do have some good news, too. A lot of what I review in this chapter appears in the "cheat sheet" that is printed at the beginning of every section on the real SAT. Here's a copy:

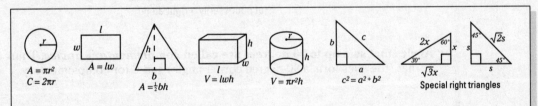

There are 360 degrees of arc in a circle.

There are 180 degrees in a straight line.

There are 180 degrees in the sum of the interior angles of a triangle.

Playing the Angles

Angles are a big part of the SAT geometry problems. Finding an angle is usually a matter of simple addition or subtraction, provided you remember the key facts listed in this section.

These three rules generally apply to the SAT:

- ✔ There are no negative angles.

- ✔ There are no zero angles.

- ✔ Meeting a fractional angle on the test is extremely unlikely. (For example, an angle won't measure 45½ degrees or 32¾ degrees.)

Now that you know what you won't find in the SAT geometry questions, take a look at the important bits of information you need to remember for the problems you'll find on the SAT:

- ✔ **Angles equal to 90 degrees are called *right angles*.** They're formed by perpendicular lines and are indicated by a box in the corner of the two intersecting lines.

Right

WARNING!

A common SAT trap is to have two lines appear to be perpendicular. Don't assume you're looking at a right angle. A diagram shows a right angle *only* if

- • You're expressly told, "This is a right angle."

- • You see the perpendicular symbol (⊥) indicating that the lines form a 90-degree angle; or

- • You see the box in the angle.

If you don't see one of these three "disclaimers," you may be headed for a trap!

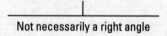

Not necessarily a right angle

- ✔ **Angles that sum up to 90 degrees are called *complementary angles*.** Think of C for corner (the lines form a 90-degree corner angle) and C for complementary.

Complementary

- ✔ **Angles that sum up to 180 degrees are called *supplementary angles*.** Think of S for a straight line (180 degrees) and S for supplementary angles.

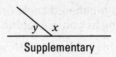
Supplementary

Be careful not to confuse complementary angles (C for complementary; C for corner) with supplementary angles (S for supplementary; S for straight).

✔ **Angles around a point sum up to 360 degrees.** Think of the angles as forming a complete circle around a center point.

360 degrees

✔ **Angles that are opposite each other are** *congruent* **(they have equal measures) and are called** *vertical angles.* Note that vertical angles may actually be horizontal.

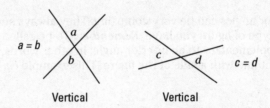
Vertical   Vertical

Just remember that vertical angles are across from each other, whether they are up and down (vertical) or side by side (horizontal).

✔ **Angles in the same position —** *corresponding angles* **— around two parallel lines and a transversal have the same measures.** When you see two parallel lines and a transversal, number the angles. Start in the upper right corner with 1 and go clockwise. For the second batch of angles, start again in the upper right corner with 5 and proceed clockwise. The numbers will help you keep track.

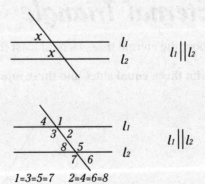
$1=3=5=7 \quad 2=4=6=8$

Note that all the odd-numbered angles are congruent and all the even-numbered angles are congruent, as long as you are told that the lines are parallel.

Be careful not to zigzag back and forth when numbering, like this:

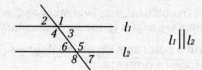

If you zig when you should have zagged, you can no longer use the tip that all even-numbered angles equal one another and all odd-numbered angles equal one another.

✔ The *exterior angles* of any figure are supplementary to the interior angles and sum up to 360 degrees.

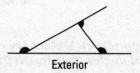

Exterior

Exterior angles can be very confusing. They always sum up to 360 degrees, no matter what type of figure you have. ***Remember:*** To be called an exterior angle, an angle must be supplementary to an interior angle; in other words, the two angles must form a straight line with a side of the figure. This example *isn't* an exterior angle:

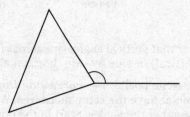

Chasing the Eternal Triangle

Some fun facts about the eternal triangle, or at least the triangles you'll see on the SAT:

A triangle with three equal sides and three equal angles is called *equilateral*.

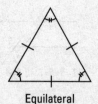

Equilateral

A triangle with two equal sides and two equal angles is called *isosceles*.

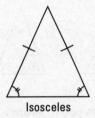

Isosceles

Angles opposite equal sides in an isosceles triangle are also equal.

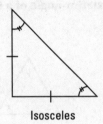

Isosceles

A triangle with no equal sides and no equal angles is called *scalene*.

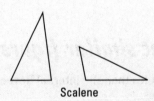

Scalene

In any triangle, the largest angle is opposite the longest side.

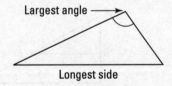

In any triangle, the sum of the lengths of two sides must be greater than the length of the third side.

This is often written as $a + b > c$, where a, b, and c are the sides of the triangle.

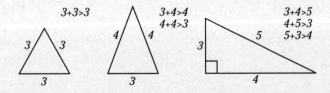

In any type of triangle, the sum of the interior angles is 180 degrees.

  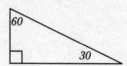

Often, a trap question wants you to assume that different-sized triangles have different angle measures. Wrong! A triangle can be seven stories high and have 180 degrees or be microscopic and have 180 degrees. The size of the triangle is irrelevant; every triangle's internal angles sum up to 180 degrees.

The measure of an exterior angle of a triangle is equal to the sum of the two remote interior angles.

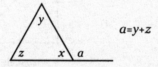

When you think about this rule logically, it makes sense. The sum of supplementary angles is 180. The sum of the angles in a triangle is 180. Therefore, angle $x = 180 - (y + z)$ or angle $x = 180 - a$. That must mean that $a = y + z$.

Psyching out similar figures

This topic has more rules than the Internal Revenue Service, don't you think? Here are some "laws" of similar figures:

The sides of similar figures are in proportion. For example, if the heights of two similar triangles are in a ratio 2:3, then the bases of those triangles are in a ratio of 2:3, as well.

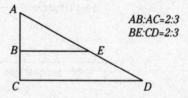

The ratio of the areas of similar figures is equal to the square of the ratio of their sides. For example, if each side of Figure A is ⅓ the length of each side of similar Figure B, then the area of Figure A is ⅑ (which is [⅓]^2) the area of Figure B.

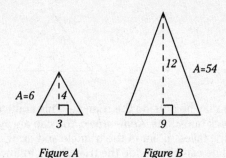

Figure A   Figure B

Time to apply the rules. Take a crack at this example:

Two similar triangles have bases 5 and 25. Which of the following expresses the ratio of the areas of the two triangles?

(A) 1:5

(B) 1:15

(C) 1:25

(D) 2:15

(E) It cannot be determined from the information given.

Answer: (C). The ratio of the sides is ⁵⁄₂₅ = ⅕. The ratio of the areas is the *square* of the ratio of the sides: ⅕ × ⅕ = ¹⁄₂₅. Note that (E) is a trap for the unwary. You can't figure out the exact area of either figure because you don't know the height (the area of a triangle is ½ base × height). However, I didn't ask you for an area, only for the ratio of the areas, which you *can* find.

Tired yet? I hope not, because you can travel this logical road a bit farther: What do you suppose is the ratio of the *volumes* of two similar figures? Because volume is found in cubic units, the ratio of the volumes of two similar figures is the *cube* of the ratio of their sides. If Figure A has a base of 5 and similar Figure B has a base of 10, then the ratio of their volumes is 1:8 (½³, which is ½ × ½ × ½ = ⅛).

Don't assume that figures are similar; you must be told that they are.

Area

The area of a triangle is ½ *base* ¥ *height*. The height is always a line perpendicular to the base. The height may be a side of the triangle, as in a right triangle.

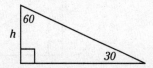

The height may be inside the triangle. It is often represented by a dashed line and a small 90-degree box.

The height may be outside the triangle. This configuration is very confusing and can be found in trick questions. *Remember:* You can always drop an altitude. That is, put your pencil on the tallest point of the triangle and draw a line straight from that point to the base. The line can be outside the triangle, as follows.

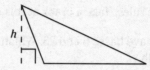

Pythagorean theorem

You have probably studied the Pythagorean theorem (known colloquially as PT). Keep in mind that it works only on *right* triangles. If a triangle doesn't have a right or 90-degree angle, you can't use any of the following information.

In any right triangle, you can find the lengths of the sides with the formula:

$$a^2 + b^2 = c^2$$

where a and b are the legs of the triangle and c is the hypotenuse. The *hypotenuse* is always opposite the 90-degree angle and is always the longest side of the triangle.

Pythagorean triples

Doing the whole PT formula every time you want to find the length of a side is a pain in the posterior. You'll find four very common PT ratios in triangles.

✔ **Ratio 3:4:5.** In this ratio, if one leg of the triangle is 3, the other leg is 4 and the hypotenuse is 5.

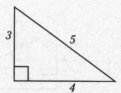

Because this is a ratio, the sides can be in any multiple of these numbers, such as 6:8:10 (twice 3:4:5), 9:12:15 (three times 3:4:5), 27:36:45 (nine times 3:4:5), and so on.

✔ **Ratio 5:12:13.** In this ratio, if one leg of the triangle is 5, the other leg is 12 and the hypotenuse is 13.

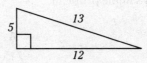

Because this is a ratio, the sides can be in any multiple of these numbers, such as 10:24:26 (twice 5:12:13), 15:36:39 (three times 5:12:13), 50:120:130 (ten times 5:12:13), and so on.

✔ $s : s : s\sqrt{2}$, **where s stands for the side of the figure.** Because two sides are congruent, this formula applies to an isosceles right triangle, also known as a 45:45:90 triangle. If one side is 2, then the other leg is also 2, and the hypotenuse is $2\sqrt{2}$.

This formula is great to know for squares. If a question tells you that the side of a square is 5 and wants to know the diagonal of the square, you know immediately that it is $5\sqrt{2}$. Why? A square's diagonal cuts the square into two isosceles right triangles (*isosceles* because all sides of the square are equal; *right* because all angles in a square are right angles). What is the diagonal of a square of side 64? $64\sqrt{2}$. What is the diagonal of a square of side 12,984? $12,984\sqrt{2}$.

✔ $s : s\sqrt{3} : 2s$. This equation is a special formula for the sides of a 30:60:90 triangle.

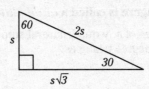

This type of triangle is a favorite of the test-makers. The important thing to keep in mind here is that the hypotenuse is twice the length of the side opposite the 30-degree angle. If you get a word problem saying, "Given a 30:60:90 triangle of hypotenuse 20, find the area" or "Given a 30:60:90 triangle of hypotenuse 100, find the perimeter," you can do so because you can find the lengths of the other sides.

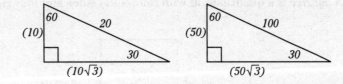

Two 30:60:90 triangles are formed whenever an equilateral triangle is cut in half. If an SAT question mentions the altitude of an equilateral triangle, it's virtually guaranteed that you'll use a 30:60:90 triangle to solve it. Time to stretch those mental triangular muscles. Try this sample problem:

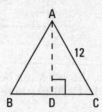

In this equilateral triangle, the length of altitude AD is:

(A) 6

(B) 9

(C) $6\sqrt{2}$

(D) $6\sqrt{3}$

(E) 12

Answer: (D). Look at the 30:60:90 triangle formed by ABD. The hypotenuse is 12, the original side of the equilateral triangle. The base is 6, because it's half the hypotenuse. That makes the altitude $6\sqrt{3}$, according to the formula.

Thanking You 4 Nothing: Quadrilaterals

Still more rules for figures (no, not that whipped cream is bad in bathing suit season):

Any four-sided figure is called a *quadrilateral*.

The interior angles of any quadrilateral sum up to 360 degrees. Any quadrilateral can be cut into two 180-degree triangles.

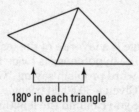

180° in each triangle

A *square* is a quadrilateral with four equal sides and four right angles.

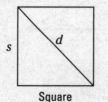

Square

The area of a square is side^2 (also called *base × height*), or ½ *diagonal*^{2}.

A *rhombus* is a quadrilateral with four equal sides and four angles that aren't necessarily right angles.

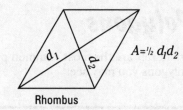

$$A = \tfrac{1}{2}\, d_1 d_2$$

Rhombus

A rhombus often looks like a drunken square, tipsy on its side and wobbly. The area of a rhombus is ½d_1d_2 (½ *diagonal* 1 × *diagonal* 2).

A *rectangle* is a quadrilateral with two opposite and equal pairs of sides.

The top and bottom sides are equal, and the right and left sides are equal. All angles in a rectangle are right angles (rectangle means "right angle"). The area of a rectangle is *length × width* (which is the same as *base × height*).

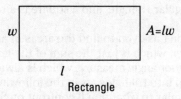

Rectangle

A *parallelogram* is a quadrilateral with two opposite and equal pairs of sides.

The top and bottom sides are equal, and the right and left sides are equal. Opposite angles are equal but not necessarily right (or 90 degrees).

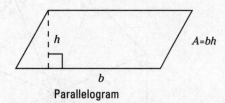

Parallelogram

The area of a parallelogram is *base × height*. Remember that the height always is a perpendicular line from the tallest point of the figure down to the base.

A *trapezoid* is a quadrilateral with two parallel sides and two nonparallel sides.

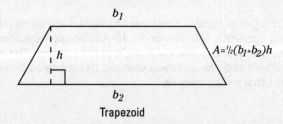

Trapezoid

The area of a trapezoid is ½ (*base* 1 + *base* 2) × *height*. It makes no difference which base you label *base* 1 and which you label *base* 2 because you're adding them together anyway. Just be sure to add them before you multiply by ½.

Playing with Polygons

Triangles and quadrilaterals are the most common polygons tested on the SAT. Table 18-1 notes a few other polygons you may see:

Table 18-1	Some Polygons
Number of Sides	*Name*
5	pentagon
6	hexagon (think of *x* in six and *x* in hex)
8	octagon

A polygon with all equal sides and all equal angles is called *regular*. For example, an equilateral triangle is a regular triangle, and a square is a regular quadrilateral.

The SAT-writers won't ask you to find the areas of any of these polygons. They may ask you to find the *perimeter*, which is just the sum of the lengths of all the sides. They may also ask you to find the *exterior* angle measure, which is always 360. If they ask you about other angles, divide the shape up into triangles, as in the following figure, which is followed by a sample grid-in question similar to what you'll confront on SAT-day:

Find the measure, in degrees, of an internal angle of a regular octagon.

Answer: (135). To solve, draw an octagon and divide it into eight triangles.

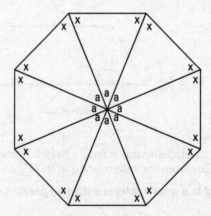

Because the figure is regular, the angles marked *a* are all equal. Because a full circle has 360 degrees, you can write 8*a* = 360, or *a* = 45. All the angles marked *x* are also equal; notice how two of them combine to make each angle of the octagon. But *x* + *x* + *a* must equal 180, because there are two *x*'s and one *a* in each triangle. Because you know *a* = 45, that means *x* + *x* = 135 degrees, and that's your answer.

Unusual shapes

All polygons can be broken down into simpler shapes. As you saw in the preceding section, you can often divide a polygon into a series of triangles. If the shape is *rectilinear* (that is, it contains only right angles), you can break it down into rectangles.

Shaded-area problems

Sometimes you have to use several different shapes to solve a problem, especially when the SAT throws a strange diagram at you and asks you to find the area of a shaded section, a very popular question (popular with the test-makers, not with the test-takers). In the following diagram, a circle of radius 7 is surrounded by a square. How would you find the shaded area?

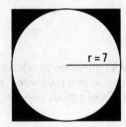

In any problem like this, *the shaded area is equal to the area of the larger shape minus the area of the smaller shape* — in this case, the area of the square minus the area of the circle. Because the circle has a radius of 7, its diameter is 14, which must be the same as the side of the square. The area of the square, then, equals $14 \times 14 = 196$. You can find the circle's area by the formula $\pi r^2 = \pi(7)^2 = 49\pi$. The shaded area, then, equals $196 - 49\pi$ (or 42.06, if you're using decimals).

Running Around in Circles

The SAT loves circles and tosses in enough for a three-ring circus. Circles are easy if you keep these points in mind:

A *radius* goes from the center of a circle to its outer edge.

Radius

A *diameter* connects two points on the outside or edge of the circle, going through the center.

A diameter is equal to two radii.

diameter

The perimeter of a circle is called the *circumference*.

The formula for the length of a circumference is $2\pi r$ or πd (logical because 2 radii = 1 diameter).

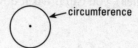

A *chord* connects any two points on a circle.

The longest chord in a circle is the diameter.

You may encounter a wheel question in which you're asked how much distance a wheel covers or how many times a wheel revolves. The key to solving this type of question is knowing that one rotation of a wheel equals one circumference of that wheel. Here's a wheel problem for you:

A child's wagon has a wheel of radius 6 inches. If the wagon wheel travels 100 revolutions, approximately how many feet has the wagon rolled?

(A) 325

(B) 314

(C) 255

(D) 201

(E) 200

Answer: (B). One revolution is equal to one circumference: $C = 2\pi r = 2\pi(6) = 12\pi$ = approximately 37.68 inches. Multiply that by 100 = 3,768 inches, and 3,768 inches ÷ 12 = 314 feet.

The area of a circle is π radius^2.

A central angle has its endpoints on the circumference of the circle and its center at the center of the circle.

The degree measure of a central angle is the same as the degree measure of its intercepted arc.

An inscribed angle has both its endpoints and its center on the circumference of the circle.

The degree measure of an inscribed angle is half the degree measure of its intercepted arc.

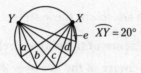

You may see a figure that looks like a string picture you made at summer camp, with all sorts of lines running every which way. Take the time to identify the endpoints of the angles and the center point. You may be surprised at how easy the question suddenly becomes. Still full of math energy? Great. Try this question:

In this figure, find the sum of the degree measures of angles $a + b + c + d + e$.

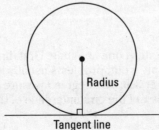

Note: Figure not drawn to scale

(A) 65

(B) 60

(C) 55

(D) 50

(E) 45

Answer: (D). Each angle is an inscribed angle. That means it has half the degree measure of the central angle, or half the degree measure of its intercepted arc. If you look carefully at the endpoints of these angles, they're all the same. They're along arc *XY*, which has a measure of 20°. Therefore, each angle is 10°, for a total of 50.

A *tangent* is a line that touches the circle at exactly one point.

When a tangent line meets a radius of the circle, a 90-degree angle is formed.

Radius

Tangent line

When a central angle and an inscribed angle have the same endpoints, the degree measure of the central angle is twice that of the inscribed angle.

An *arc* is a portion of the circumference of a circle.

The degree measure of an arc is the same as its central angle and twice its inscribed angle.

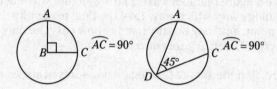

To find the length of an arc, follow these steps:

1. **Find the circumference of the entire circle.**

2. **Put the degree measure of the arc over 360 and reduce the fraction.**

3. **Multiply the circumference by the fraction.**

Now that you know how to calculate arc-length, try this question:

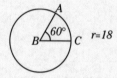

Find the length of arc *AC*.

(A) 36π

(B) 27π

(C) 18π

(D) 60

(E) 6π

Answer: (E). Take the steps one at a time. First, find the circumference of the entire circle: C= 2πr = 36π. Don't multiply π out; problems usually leave it in that form. Next, put the degree measure of the arc over 360. The degree measure of the arc is the same as its central angle, 60° = 60/360 = 1/6. The arc is 1/6 of the circumference of the circle. Multiply the circumference by the fraction: 36π × 1/6 = 6π.

Be very careful not to confuse the *degree measure* of the arc with the *length* of the arc. The length is always a portion of the circumference, always has a π in it, and always is in linear units. If you chose (D) in this example, you found the degree measure of the arc rather than its length.

A *sector* is a portion of the area of a circle.

To find the area of a sector, do the following:

1. **Find the area of the entire circle.**

2. **Put the degree measure of the sector over 360 and reduce the fraction.**

3. **Multiply the area by the fraction.**

Finding the area of a sector is very similar to finding the length of an arc. The only difference is in the first step. Whereas an arc is a part of the circle's *circumference,* a sector is a part of the circle's *area.* How would you find the area of this sector?

First, find the area of the entire circle. $A = \pi r^2 = 64\pi$. Second, put the degree measure of the sector over 360. The sector is 90°, the same as its central angle. $\frac{90}{360} = \frac{1}{4}$. Third, multiply the area by the fraction: $64\pi \times \frac{1}{4} = 16\pi$.

Avoiding Two-Dimensional Thinking: Solid Geometry

From time to time, the SAT-writers like to make an effort to include "real-world math" on the test. Now, if it were *really* about the real world, you'd see questions like "If a student wakes up 20 minutes before school begins, and it takes him 10 minutes to run there at top speed, how many students are going to want to sit near him in class?" But where was I?

Now I remember. The real world is three-dimensional. To reflect that, almost every SAT has a problem or two dealing with a box, a cylinder, or (rarely) some other three-dimensional shape. The key formulas are included in the cheat sheet at the start of each section, but it's worth a quick review.

Volume

The volume of any polygon is *(area of the base)* × *height.* If you remember this formula, you don't have to memorize any of the following more specific formulas.

✔ **Volume of a cube:** e^3

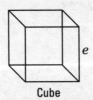

Cube

A *cube* is a three-dimensional square. Think of a die (one of a pair of dice). All of a cube's dimensions are the same; that is, *length* = *width* = *height*. In a cube, these dimensions are called *edges*. The volume of a cube is *edge* × *edge* × *edge* = *edge*^{3} = *e*^{3}.

✔ **Volume of a rectangular solid: *l* × *w* × *h***

Rectangular solid

A rectangular solid is a box. The base of a box is a rectangle, which has an area of *length* × *width*. Multiply that by *height* to fit the original formula: Volume = *(area of base)* × *height*, or V = *l* × *w* × *h*.

✔ **Volume of a cylinder: (π*r*^{2})*height***

Cylinder

Think of a cylinder as a can of soup. The base of a cylinder is a circle. The area of a circle is π*r*^{2}. Multiply that number by the height of the cylinder to get *(area of base)* × *height* = π*r*^{2} × *height*. Note that the top and bottom of a cylinder are identical circles. If you know the radius of either the top base or the bottom base, you can find the area of the circle.

Surface area

On rare occasions, the SAT-devils may ask you to find the surface area of a solid object. The surface area is, sensibly enough, the total area of all the sides (surfaces) of the object. To find the surface area of a box with six sides, you would find the area of each of the rectangles that form a side, and then add them all up.

Chapter 19

Practice Problems in Geometry

In This Chapter

▶ Practicing geometry problems

▶ Focusing on angles, shapes, and distances in sample questions

Even if you'd rather squash a polygon than calculate its measurements, bite the bullet and check out at least some of the practice questions in this chapter. You get two sets. Hit one, check it, read the explanations, and if you've (gasp) stubbed your toe, try the second set. Remember each answer immediately follows its respective question. Don't cheat. Cover the answer with a blank sheet of paper.

Practice Set One

Most of these problems are multiple choice, so even if the correct answer doesn't appear in neon before your eyes, take a stab if you can eliminate two choices. Questions 3 and 6 are grid-ins. (See Chapter 13 for a quick review on grid-ins.)

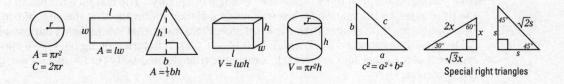

1. In the following square, the length of side *s* is:

(A) 8

(B) $8\sqrt{2}$

(C) $8\sqrt{3}$

(D) 16

(E) $16\sqrt{2}$

When you cut a square in half, you get a 45° – 45° – 90° triangle, with the square's diagonal as the hypotenuse. The freebie information at the beginning of each math section (Nice of them to help you, don't you think?) tells you that in a 45° – 45° – 90° triangle, the length of the hypotenuse equals $\sqrt{2}\,s$, where s is the length of a side of the square. Because the hypotenuse equals $8\sqrt{2}$, the side equals 8. (A) is correct.

2. If the distance between points A and B is 5, and the distance between points B and C is 7, then the distance between points A and C may <u>not</u> equal:

(A) 1

(B) 2

(C) 3

(D) 6

(E) 7

Beware of making assumptions in geometry problems. The first thing to realize is that A, B, and C don't have to make a straight line, though they could. Most people assume that the three points must be on the same line. To answer this question, draw a line connecting A and B, and another one connecting B and C, like so:

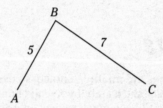

Now you can use a little thing called the "triangle inequality." The distance from A to C forms the third side of a triangle, and a law was made a distant moon ago that the sum of two sides of a triangle must be greater than the third side. Right away, that law makes it impossible for AC to equal 1, because 1 + 5 = 6, which isn't bigger than 7. Before moving on, take a minute to be sure that the other four answers <u>do</u> satisfy the triangle inequality (or I'm in a lot of trouble). (A) is correct.

3. In the following drawing, $\overline{BE} \| \overline{FI}$. Find the measure, in degrees, of the angle marked x.

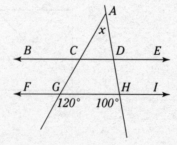

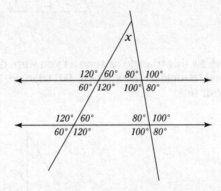

Because this drawing contains parallel lines cut by *transversals* (the two lines meeting at point A), you can fill in a whole lot of angles right off the bat. Each transversal creates eight angles, and these angles come in two groups of four equal angles each. Here they are, filled in:

After you determine the angles, the problem becomes simpler. Because ACD is a triangle, its angles must add to 180°. With a 60° and an 80° angle already accounted for, the missing angle must be **40°** — your correct answer. You don't grid-in the degree symbol, just the number.

4. What is the sum of the angles marked *a, b, c,* and *d* in the following diagram?

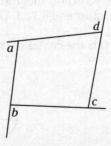

(A) 180°

(B) 360°

(C) 540°

(D) 720°

(E) It cannot be determined from the information given

This one you just have to memorize. The sum of the exterior angles of <u>any</u> shape is always 360°. Remember it. (B) is correct.

5. If an equilateral triangle has sides of length 6, then its altitude has length:

(A) 3

(B) $2\sqrt{3}$

(C) $3\sqrt{2}$

(D) $3\sqrt{3}$

(E) $6\sqrt{3}$

A special triangle problem in disguise. Here's the equilateral triangle with its altitude drawn:

(Of course, you drew this triangle as soon as you were done reading the problem, right?) Each half of the original triangle forms a 30°-60°-90° triangle. Making a second drawing just to be clear is worth your time.

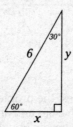

From the formulas, which conveniently are the same formulas the SAT gives you at the beginning of each math section, you know that the side marked x must be half of 6, or 3, which means that y, the altitude, must equal $3\sqrt{3}$. Thus, (D) is correct.

6. In the following diagram, O is the center of the circle. Find, in degrees, the measure of the angle marked x.

The easiest way to think about this problem is to look at the arc marked AB in the following diagram:

Because the central angle at O measures 90°, this arc also measures 90°. Now, angle x is an inscribed angle. Remember the formula that tells you that an inscribed angle equals one-half the measure of its arc? That makes angle x = **45°**.

Practice Set Two

A glutton for punishment, are you? Fine. Try out another set.

1. In this triangle, the measure of angle x is greater than the measure of angle y. Which of the following statements must be *false*?

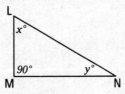

   (A) MN > LM

   (B) $(LN)^2 - (LM)^2 = (MN)^2$

   (C) LN > MN

   (D) LN − LM = MN

   (E) $m\angle y < 45°$

As you often should in these types of problems, go through the answers one by one. (A) is true, because in any triangle the shortest side is opposite the smallest angle. Because y is smaller than x, and both of them must be smaller than 90°, that makes y the smallest angle, and LM the shortest side. (B) is just a fancy way of writing the Pythagorean Theorem. Because LN is the hypotenuse of a right triangle, $(LM)^2 + (MN)^2 = (LN)^2$, so $(LN)^2 - (LM)^2 = (MN)^2$. (C) is true for essentially the same reason as (A): LN must be the longest side of the triangle, because it's across from 90°, the largest angle. (D) wins the "False Award" because of the triangle inequality. In any triangle, the sum of the two short sides must be *greater* than the sum of the longest side. That fact means that LM + MN > LN, so LN – LM can't equal MN. You could stop there, but just to be thorough, check out the last one. (E) is true. Because the sum of the angles of any triangle is 180°, the measures of x and y must add up to 90°. Because x is larger than y, x must be greater than 45°, and y must be less than 45°.

2. A car has wheels with a radius of 1.5 ft. If the car is backed down a driveway that is 95 feet long, about how many complete turns will the wheels make?

    (A) 10

    (B) 13

    (C) 14

    (D) 20

    (E) 32

This one is a classic SAT problem. The key is knowing that one complete rotation equals the circumference of the wheel. Because circumference = $2 \times \pi \times$ radius, you have $C = 2(3.14)(1.5)$ = 9.42 feet. Dividing 95 by 9.42 yields 10.08, so your answer is 10. Give it up for (A).

3. In the following diagram O is the center of the circle, and $\overline{AP}$ and $\overline{CP}$ are tangents. If OA = 8 and BP = 9, find CP.

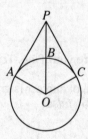

    (A) $\sqrt{17}$

    (B) 9

    (C) $\sqrt{145}$

    (D) 15

    (E) 17

Because $\overline{AP}$ and $\overline{CP}$ are tangents, the angles at A and C must be right angles. (If this fact is a surprise, turn back to Chapter 18. I can almost guarantee that this concept will show up in some form on the test). Triangles OPC and OPA are right triangles, so the Pythagorean Theorem comes into play (and hits the ball out of the park). Because OA = 8, OB and OC are also 8, because all radii are equal. That makes OP = 8 + 9 = 17. OP is the hypotenuse, OC is a leg, and CP is a leg. So $(CP)^2 + (8)^2 = (17)^2$; $(CP)^2 + 64 = 289$; $(CP)^2 = 225$; and CP = 15. (D) is correct.

4. In the next diagram a square is inscribed in a circle. If one side of the square has a length of 10, then the shaded area equals:

    (A) $100\pi - 100$

    (B) $50\pi - 100$

    (C) $100\pi - 50$

    (D) $100 - 25\pi$

    (E) $50\pi - 50$

This one is a shaded-area problem, so your answer must be the circle's area minus the square's area. The square's area is pretty simple to figure out: it's $(10)^2 = 100$. To find the circle's area, you need to know its radius. You can make a diameter by drawing the diagonal of the square, like so:

Look familiar? The diagonal of a square creates a $45° - 45° - 90°$ triangle, so the length of the diagonal is $10\sqrt{2}$. (The SAT-devils *love* special triangles.) The radius is half of the diameter, $10\sqrt{2}$, or $5\sqrt{2}$. Bingo. The area of the circle $\pi\left(5\sqrt{2}\right)^2 = \pi(5)^2\left(\sqrt{2}\right)^2 = \pi(25)(2) = 50\pi$. So your answer is $50\pi - 100$ (B).

5. In the following drawing ACDE is a parallelogram with an area of 36. Find the length of AC.

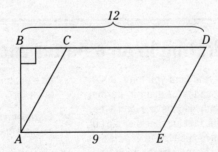

    (A) 3

    (B) $2\sqrt{2}$

    (C) 4

    (D) 5

    (E) $4\sqrt{3}$

The area of a parallelogram uses the same formula as a rectangle: base × height. Because the base, AE, is 9, and the area is 36, the height, AB, must be 4 (Don't be fooled into thinking that AC is the height. The height is always perpendicular to the base, never slanted). So AB = 4. Meanwhile, BC = 12 – 9 = 3. This is yet another right triangle, so you can use the Pythagorean Theorem to get AC = 5. Even better, if you remember the 3-4-5 right triangle, you just know that the answer is 5 without having to do all the work. (D) is your final answer. (Sorry, no million-dollar prizes though!)

6. This cylindrical gas tank, originally empty, has a radius of 2 m and a height of 3 m. At 11 a.m., gas starts being added to the tank at a rate of 10 m³ per hour. The tank will be completely full *closest* to:

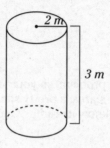

(A) 2 p.m.

(B) 2:30 p.m.

(C) 3 p.m.

(D) 3:30 p.m.

(E) 4 p.m.

The volume of a 3-D figure equals the area of its base times its height. Because the base is a circle, its area is $\pi r^2 = \pi(2)^2 = 4\pi$, or about 12.56 m². Multiplying by 3, the height, gives a volume of 37.68 m³. Dividing 37.68 m³ by 10 m³ per hour gives 3.768 hours to fill the tank. This answer is a little bit closer to four hours than to 3.5 hours (3.75 would be exactly halfway), so you can round up to 4 hours. Four hours after 11 a.m. is 3 p.m. (C) is correct.

Circling in on a better vocabulary

Lots of vocabulary words — the kind you may find in Reading Comprehension passages or even in normal conversation — pop out of math lessons and land in the real world. For example, the line that touches a circle but doesn't pierce it (a *tangent*) gives rise to the expression *going off on a tangent* (moving away from the main topic to something that is only marginally related at best), as in *Fencoop went off on a tangent about eggs when he was supposed to be discussing feather boas.* A related word, *tangential*, shows up in sentences such as *The dry cleaners' association and the United Featherworkers of America criticized Fencoop's tangential remarks.* You probably know how to find the *circumference* of a circle (the distance around the edge). In the same family are the following:

✔ *Circumlocution:* To "talk around" by speaking indirectly and avoiding a clear statement. Politicians in an election year, answering controversial questions, favor *circumlocutions.*

✔ *Circumnavigate:* To sail around, as in *Flesterbub circumnavigated the globe in a leaky washtub.*

✔ *Circumscribe:* To limit. Picture a warden drawing a circle around someone and forbidding him or her to cross the line.

✔ *Circumspect:* Cautious; think of an imaginary circle around yourself that you venture beyond only with extreme care.

✔ *Circumvent:* To go around, as in *Bruckner circumvented the door alarm by breaking through the wall.*

A distant cousin of the *circum* family is *circuitous*, an adjective that may describe the sort of route that taxi drivers take with tourists in the back seat (round and round, just to drive up the fare).

Chapter 20

Playing the Odds: Statistics and Probability

. . . .

In This Chapter
▶ Understanding probability
▶ Solving geometric probability problems
▶ Interpreting scatterplots and other graphs
▶ Thinking logically

. . . .

*I*f you take the SAT 25 times, what are the odds that you'll die of boredom before entering college? Your SAT proctor, even more bored than the 25 test-takers in front of him, launches an ink-filled balloon into the 30-square-foot classroom. What is the probability that it will miss you and land on the mouth-breather in the next row?

These questions — okay, similar but humorless questions — confront you on the SAT Reasoning Test. To increase the odds that you ace the topic of statistics and probability, read this chapter. Also peruse this chapter to get the lowdown on scatterplots and other graphs, as well as logic questions.

Playing the Odds: Probability

The probability of an event is almost always defined as a fraction. So in many probability situations, you have to compute two separate numbers, one for the numerator and one for the denominator of the fraction. What do these numbers stand for? Well, here's the formula:

$$\text{the probability of an event} = \frac{\text{the number of ways for the event to occur}}{\text{the total number of possible outcomes}}$$

Say that you have a jar containing 6 red, 4 yellow, and 8 blue marbles. The probability of picking a blue marble $= \dfrac{8 \text{ blue marbles}}{6 + 4 + 8 = 18 \text{ total marbles}}$, which can be reduced to $\frac{4}{9}$.

Probability can also be written as a percentage. The easiest way to compute the percentage is with your calculator. Suppose the probability that a major label will sign your garage band is $\frac{5}{8}$. (In your dreams, by the way. The real probability is $\frac{5}{89,300,923}$.) Enter 5÷8 on your calculator to get 0.625. Now move the decimal two places to the right. Bingo. The probability of you and your bandmates riding to the MTV studio in a limo (in the imaginary world where channel surfing counts as aerobic exercise) is 62.5%.

When you calculate probability, remember the number 1. All the possible events must have probabilities that add up to 1 (or 100%). That fact leads to a useful rule, which may be stated in three ways:

✔ The probability that an event *won't* happen equals 1 – the probability of the event.

✔ The probability that an event *won't* happen equals 100% – the probability of the event.

✔ The probability that an event *won't* happen equals

$$\frac{\text{total number of possibilities} - \text{number of ways for the event to happen}}{\text{total number of possibilities}}$$

Imagine that you're sitting in class with 19 other students, and your teacher decides to pick one student at random to stay after school for a bout of eraser cleaning. What's the chance that she picks you? It's $\frac{1}{20}$: Out of 20 students, there's only one you (and I'm sure that's a great relief to your teachers).

So what's the chance that she *doesn't* pick you? Figure it out, all three ways:

✔ $1 - \frac{1}{20} = \frac{20}{20} - \frac{1}{20} = \frac{19}{20}$

✔ Because $\frac{1}{20}$ = 5%, 100% – 5% = 95%

✔ Because there are 20 total possibilities (20 students), $\frac{20-1}{20} = \frac{19}{20}$

An event that is *certain* to happen has a probability of one, or 100%. An event that is *impossible* has a probability of zero. Nothing can ever have a probability greater than one or less than zero. Another way to say the second fact: Negative probability doesn't exist.

Psyching Out Multiple Probability Questions

As usual, the SAT-writers have found plenty of ways to make probability problems harder. One of their favorite torture devices is to ask you about a probability involving multiple events. The questions may resemble the following grid-in:

Jenny, recently fired by a real-estate tycoon with a bad comb-over, arranges interviews with a fast-food chain, a television network, and a stockbroker. If each employer has a 50% probability of offering her a job, what's the probability that she gets offered all three?

Answer: 12.5%, which you should grid in as $\frac{1}{8}$ as shown in the following figure. When a problem involves multiple events, the total number of possibilities is the *product* of the number of possibilities for each event. If, for example, you open your closet on laundry day and find two clean shirts and three pairs of pants, the total number of outfits you can make is $2 \times 3 = 6$ (assuming you're not a fashionista and don't care about little things like complementary colors).

This rule is known as the "counting principle," although the "multiplication principle" may be a better name for it. This method works whether you're using whole numbers, percentages, or fractions. Applying it to Jenny's situation, you can say that the probability of her being offered all three jobs is $50\% \times 50\% \times 50\%$, or $\frac{1}{2} \times \frac{1}{2} \times \frac{1}{2} = \frac{1}{8}$.

A little more example music, please:

EXAMPLE

After his Gamblers Anonymous meeting, Oliver rolls two six-sided dice. What are the chances that both dice will show an odd number?

(A) ½

(B) ¼

(C) ⅜

(D) ⅙

(E) 3⁄2

Answer: (B). Before you do anything else, eliminate (E). Why? Because 3⁄2 is bigger than 1, and no probability can ever be greater than 1. Now consider the problem. The first die has six sides, and three of them are odd, so the probability that the first die is odd is $\frac{3}{6} = \frac{1}{2}$. The second die is the same, so it also has a ½ chance of being odd. Now, using the rule, the probability that both are odd is $\frac{1}{2} \times \frac{1}{2} = \frac{1}{4}$, or (B).

Surviving Geometric Probability

Unbelievably, those SAT-writers sometimes expect you to combine your knowledge of two different areas of mathematics: geometry and probability. (Check out Chapter 18 for a geometry review.)

A dart is thrown at this dartboard. If the radius of the circle is 5 inches, then the probability that the dart lands in the square but *not* in the circle is closest to:

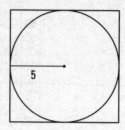

(A) 21%

(B) 22%

(C) 50%

(D) 78%

(E) 79%

Answer: (A). You may recognize this question as a variation of the shaded-area problem. (Check out Chapter 18 for more info on shaded-areas.) Because the problem asks about the four corner regions of the diagram, first you have to figure out the area of these regions. The area of the circle is $\pi r^2 = \pi(5)^2 = 25\pi$ square inches. Because a side of the square equals the circle's diameter, which is 10, the square's area is $10^2 = 100$ square inches. That makes the total area of the corner regions equal to $100 - 25\pi = 100 - 78.54 = 21.46$. Because the square's area is 100, the probability that the dart lands in one of the corners is $^{21.46}\!/_{100} = 21.46\%$.

Reading Graphs

Mark Twain famously cited statistics as a method of lying. But it's not a lie to say that statistics is one of the easier topics covered by the math portion of the SAT. Check out Chapter 14 for the basics of three key concepts: mean, median, and mode. After you master those terms, all that's left (at least in terms of the SAT) is some graph-reading skills.

Some of the math questions on the SAT are called *data interpretation*. That's a pompous name for reading a graph, something you've been doing for years. Don't let graph problems intimidate you. Here are the three most common types of graphs you're likely to see on the SAT.

- ✔ Bar graph
- ✔ Circle or pie graph
- ✔ Two-axes line graph

Sometimes the SAT-writers try to trip you up by asking you to compare statistics in two different graphs.

Bar graphs

A bar graph has vertical or horizontal bars. The bars may represent actual numbers or percentages. If the bar goes all the way from one side of the graph to the other, it represents 100 percent.

Circle or pie graphs

The circle represents 100 percent. The key to this graph is determining the total that the percentages are part of. Below the graph you may be told that in 1994, 5,000 students graduated with PhDs. If a 25-percent segment on the circle graph is labeled "PhDs in history," you know that the number of history PhDs is 25 percent of 5,000, or 1,250.

Two-axes line graphs and scatterplots

A typical line graph has a bottom and a side axis. You plot a point or read a point from the two axes. A special kind of two-axes graph is the *scatterplot*. A *scatterplot* contains a bunch of dots scattered around a two-line graph, like this:

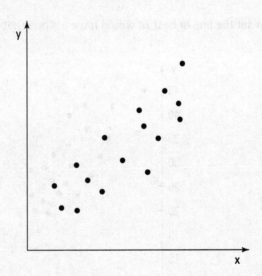

Notice how the points seem to follow a certain trend, getting higher as you move to the right. When a trend is present, you can say that there is a *correlation* between the two things measured by the graph. If both increase together, as in this graph, you have a *positive correlation*. (You also have a positive correlation if they both decrease together.) If one increases while the other decreases, you have a *negative correlation*.

Some scatterplots, like the following one, are just plain scattered. They have *no correlation*. Don't confuse "no correlation" with a negative correlation!

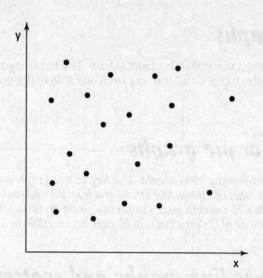

When graphs have a correlation, drawing a line that estimates the behavior of the points is possible. This is known as a "line of best fit." On the test you may have a scatterplot and have to choose the line of best fit from a list of choices, or you may have to estimate the slope of the line of best fit. For example:

For this data set the line of best fit would have a slope that is *closest* to:

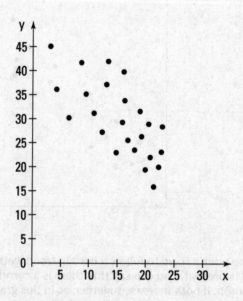

(A) –2

(B) –1

(C) 0

(D) 1

(E) 2

Answer: (A). Because the data moves downwards, it must be (A) or (B). If you look at the top left point, you can estimate its coordinates as (5, 45). The bottom right point is around (20, 15). The slope of the line connecting these points would be $\frac{15-45}{20-5} = \frac{-30}{15} = -2$.

Comparing graphs

Some questions use two graphs in one problem. Run your eyeball over this example.

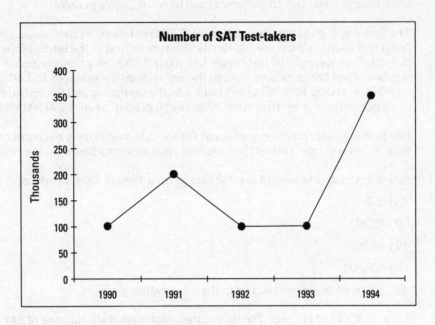

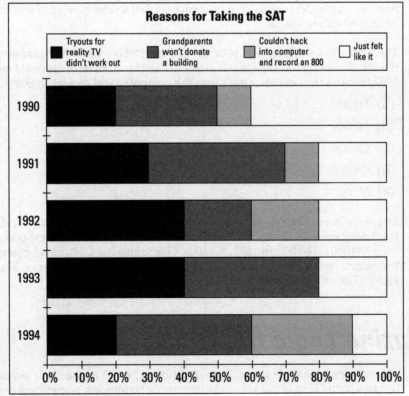

These two graphs must be read together. The second graph is a bar graph going from 0 to 100 percent. Read the graph by *subtracting* to find the appropriate percentage. For example, in 1990, "Grandparents Won't Donate a Building" begins at 20 and goes to 50, a difference of 30 percent. You're falling in a trap if you say that "Grandparents Won't Donate" was 50 percent. In 1993, "Just Felt Like It" goes from 80 to 100, or 20 percent.

The first graph gives you the number of "SAT Test-takers" in thousands. (By the way, I'm not using real statistics from the SAT-devils.) Be sure to look at the labels of the axes. For example, in 1990, there weren't 100 test-takers but 100,000. Use the graphs together to find out the number of test-takers because of a particular reason. For example, in 1991, there were 200,000 test-takers. Also in 1991, "Couldn't Hack into the Computer and Record an 800" (from 70 to 80, or 10 percent) made up 10 percent. Multiply 10 percent or .10 × 200,000 = 20,000 test-takers.

Ready to try some practice questions? On the test, you usually encounter three to five questions below a graph. Answer the following two questions based on the two practice graphs.

How many students were of test-taking age from 1990 to 1994 inclusive?

(A) 850

(B) 8,500

(C) 85,000

(D) 850,000

(E) It cannot be determined from the information given.

Answer: (E). Did I get you? The title of the graph says it all: Number of SAT Test-takers. You have no way to determine what percentage of all students were of test-taking age, or, in fact, what "test-taking age" is.

The number of students who took the SAT in 1994 because their grandparents wouldn't donate a building was how much greater than the number of students who took the SAT in 1992 because they couldn't hack into the computer and record an 800?

(A) 250,000

(B) 140,000

(C) 120,000

(D) 100,000

(E) 20,000

Answer: (C). In 1994, "Grandparents Won't Donate a Building" accounted for 40 percent of test-taking reasons (from 20 to 60). Because there were 350,000 test-takers in 1994, multiply .40 × 350,000 = 140,000. In 1992, "Couldn't Hack into the Computer" counted for 20 percent of test-taking reasons (60 to 80). In 1992, there were 100,000 test-takers. Multiply .20 × 100,000 = 20,000. The correct answer is 140,000 − 20,000 = 120,000, or (C).

Analyzing Logic Questions

The SAT occasionally tosses a logic question at you, disguised as a simple math question. It has two parts. First is the set of statements or conditions, sometimes called the *facts*. These statements describe the relationship between or among people, items, or events. You may, for example, be given statements about students at a school and asked which ones can be assigned to the same classes. You may be told facts about events that can happen on certain days of the week, or what different combinations of items are possible.

A logic question often takes a *long* time. Make the decision whether you have the time — and the patience! — to do it properly. If not, skip the question and come back to it later, if you can. Don't rush yourself.

Before you start doodling and diagramming, be sure you know all the parties involved. Make a "program" of the players by writing down the pool of people or events. For example, if the question talks about five teachers, Mahaffey, Negy, O'Leary, Plotnitz, and Quivera, use initials and jot down M, N, O, P, and Q on the test booklet.

Next, use a diagram to show the relationship between people or events. Here are a few of the most common diagrams.

- **Calendar:** Draw a simple calendar and fill in the events that happen on particular days.

- **Ordering or sequencing:** You may have a relationship problem in which some people are taller or heavier than others. Write a line of people, with A above B if A is taller than B, C at the bottom if she is the shortest, and so on.

- **Grouping or membership:** This problem asks you which items or people could belong to which group. For example, membership in a club may require four out of five characteristics. Often this type of question doesn't require a graph but a lot of "if then" statements, such as "If A is in the group, then B isn't."

- **Personal characteristics:** In this type of problem, you're given information about people and asked what those people can or can't do based on their characteristics. For example, you may be told that Trent has a fear of heights and Lucilla has a fear of horses. If the question asks, "Which of the following could go on a horseback ride along a mountain crest?" eliminate Trent and Lucilla! In other words, look for rules violations.

Check out this example:

Five spices — lemon pepper, marjoram, nutmeg, oregano, and paprika — are aligned next to one another between the left and right sides of a kitchen cabinet. Their arrangement must conform to the following conditions:

The marjoram is to the right of the paprika.

The oregano is first from the left or first from the right.

The lemon pepper is to the left of the nutmeg.

Which of the following conditions would allow a determination of the order of all the spices?

(A) The paprika is first from the left.

(B) The oregano is first from the left.

(C) The paprika is second from the left.

(D) The lemon pepper is second from the left.

(E) The nutmeg is second from the left.

Answer: (E). To help keep track of the information, write out initials for the roster of spices — L, M, N, O, and P — and make five simple dashes to represent the five positions of the spices:

— — — — —

The easiest condition to accommodate is the one that indicates that the oregano must be first from the left or first from the right. Draw these two possibilities:

O — — — —

— — — — O

What not to call the umpire

Mathematicians love baseball — or at least baseball stats. So take a moment to rest from your math labors and watch your favorite team. You can call the ump *disinterested* (fair) but not *uninterested* (bored out of his skull). Unless you want to go down on strikes, avoid *pusillanimous* (cowardly) and *mendacious* (lying). Whatever you think of the pay scale, stay away from *mercenary* (in it only for the money as opposed to love of the game)

and *partial* or *partisan* (taking sides). Nor would an umpire appreciate being labeled *iniquitous* (evil) or *intemperate* (excessive, extreme).

To gain the ump's favor, try *judicious* (showing good judgment) and *discerning* (sharp, perceptive). Describing the umpire's calls as *sonorous* (deep and pleasant in sound) may also get you to first base.

For the other conditions, there are too many possibilities to draw them all, but you can help yourself keep track of your rights and lefts by drawing the spices next to each other.

Quickly think through some of the overall arrangements to get your mind going in the right direction. For example, if O is on the far left, you know from the rules that P must be second, third, or fourth, with M in third, fourth, or fifth. If P is fourth, M has to be fifth, leaving L in second and N in third.

For this question run through the choices, trying each one. (A) isn't the answer, because putting P first would force O to be fifth, but there are still options with M, L, and N. For example, M could be second, with L and N third and fourth, respectively, or M could be third, with L second and N fourth.

(B) is worse than (A) because it fixes only O in place. (C) isn't helpful because P could be second from the left with O either first or fifth. For example, one order could be O, P, M, L, N, and another could be L, P, N, M, O. (D) is very similar to (C). For example, the order could be O, L, N, P, M or P, L, M, N, O. (E) works because N in second forces L, which has to be to the left of N, to be first. Now, you must put O fifth, leaving only third and fourth for P and M. Because M must be to the right of P, P must be third and M fourth.

These problems can take a long time. Take some time to read the problem and see how complicated it looks before diving in. If you're short on time, skip this type of question and concentrate on other, easier ones. Remember, you get the same number of points (1) for a hard question as you do for an easy one.

Chapter 21

Practice Problems in Probability, Statistics, and Logic

. . . .

In This Chapter

▶ Practicing probability, statistics, and logic problems
▶ Poring over sample questions

. . . .

*Y*ou can count on at least a couple of probability, statistics, and logic problems showing up on your particular version of the SAT. Don't freak out! Now is the time to practice with the help of the two sets in this chapter. After you complete the first set in this chapter, check your answers and read the explanations of any problem you answered incorrectly. (The answers immediately follow each question. Use a piece of paper to cover the answers.) Turn back to Chapter 20 for a refresher course in anything that stumped you. Then, if you need more practice, hit set two.

Practice Set One

Most of these problems are multiple-choice questions, but questions 1 and 7 are grid-ins, just to make your life a little more interesting. (See Chapter 13 for tips on answering grid-ins.)

1. A school cafeteria offers two soups, three main dishes, and four desserts. Find the total number of possible meals consisting of one soup, one main dish, and one dessert.

Using the counting principle, $2 \times 3 \times 4 = 24$.

2. The chance of rain tomorrow is ¼. As a percentage, what is the probability that it will not rain tomorrow?

   (A) 4%

   (B) 25%

   (C) 40%

   (D) 75%

   (E) 96%

As a percentage, ¼ = 25%. The probability of an event *not* happening equals 100% minus the probability of it happening, and 100% − 25% = 75%. (D) is correct.

3. In a special deck of 20 cards, 8 cards are red on both sides, 7 cards are blue on both sides, and the other 5 cards are red on one side and blue on the other. If a student picks a card and places it on his desk, what is the probability that the side facing up is blue?

   (A) ¹⁹⁄₄₀

   (B) ¹²⁄₂₀

   (C) ⁷⁄₄₀

   (D) ⁷⁄₂₀

   (E) ¹²⁄₄₀

This one's a little tricky. Even though there are 20 cards, the question asks only about the side of the card facing up, and there are 20 × 2 = 40 possible sides. The 7 cards that are blue on both sides represent 7 × 2 = 14 blue sides, and there are 5 cards with one blue side. 14 + 5 = 19, so the probability is ¹⁹⁄₄₀. (A) is correct.

Problems 4, 5, and 6 use the following graphs:

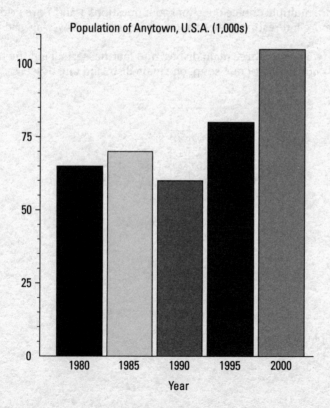

Population of Anytown, U.S.A. (1,000s)

Year

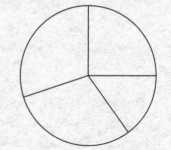

Anytown population by age group, 1995

4. In 1990, what was the approximate number of Anytown residents over the age of 65?

   (A) 55,000

   (B) 50,000

   (C) 25,000

   (D) 14,000

   (E) It cannot be determined from the graphs.

   Don't trip over this one. You can tell from the bar graph that there were approximately 60,000 total residents, but the pie graph tells you only about the ages of the residents in 1995. There's no way to determine anything about the ages in 1990. (E) is correct.

5. During which five-year period did Anytown have the greatest *percent* increase in population?

   (A) 1980–1985

   (B) 1985–1990

   (C) 1990–1995

   (D) 1995–2000

   (E) It cannot be determined from the graphs.

   You can throw out (B) right away, because the population decreased. Don't get fooled by (D); although the population went up by 25,000 people, the *percent* change was $\frac{25,000}{80,000} = 0.3125$, or 31%. But from 1990 to 1995, the population increased by 20,000 from an original population of 60,000. That's $\frac{20,000}{60,000} = 0.3333$, or 33%. Thus, (C) is correct.

6. In 1995, roughly how many Anytown residents were between the ages of 20 and 65?

   (A) 45

   (B) 15,000

   (C) 30,000

   (D) 36,000

   (E) 45,000

   A look at the pie chart tells you that 30 + 15, or 45% of the residents were between 20 and 65 in 1995. Because there were 80,000 residents, change 45% into 0.45, and 0.45 × 80,000 = 36,000. Give it up for (D).

7. A bag contains red, blue, and green marbles. The probability of picking a red marble is $\frac{1}{2}$; the probability of picking a blue marble is $\frac{1}{3}$. If there are seven green marbles in the bag, find the total number of marbles in the bag.

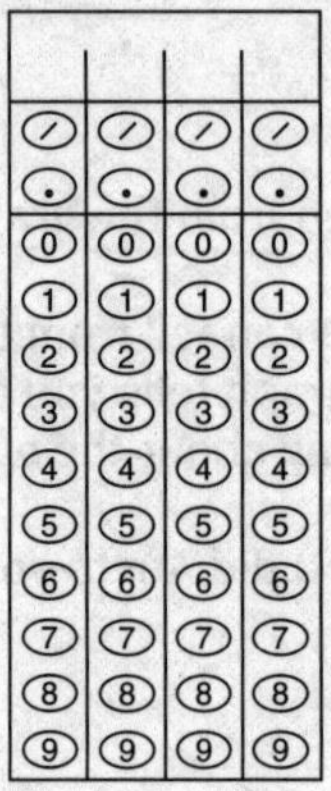

To do this one, you need a little algebra. Because the probability of picking a red marble is $\frac{1}{2}$, half of the marbles are red. Similarly, one-third of the marbles must be blue. So one-half of the marbles, plus one-third of the marbles, plus the seven green marbles, is the number you're looking for. If you let x represent the total number of marbles, you can write $\frac{1}{2}x + \frac{1}{3}x + 7 = x$. Because fractions are annoying, multiply everything by 6 (be careful!) to get $3x + 2x + 42 = 6x$. This equation gives $5x + 42 = 6x$, so $x = 42$. Another way to think about this question: The red and blue marbles represent $\frac{1}{2} + \frac{1}{3} = \frac{5}{6}$ of the marbles. That leaves $1 - \frac{5}{6} = \frac{1}{6}$ of the marbles to be green, and 7 is $\frac{1}{6}$ of 42.

8. If a student picks a square at random on the following grid, what is the probability that he picks a square that is *not* shaded?

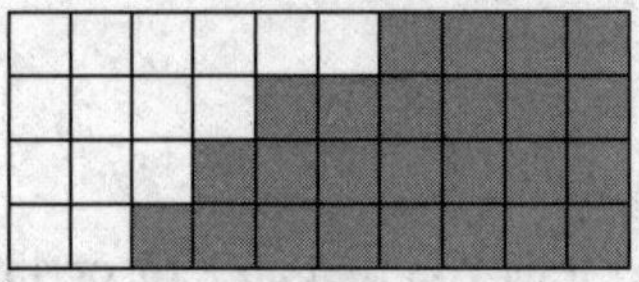

(A) $\frac{3}{5}$

(B) $\frac{3}{8}$

(C) $\frac{2}{5}$

(D) $\frac{5}{8}$

(E) $\frac{3}{10}$

Twenty-five of the 40 squares are shaded, leaving 40 – 25 = 15 unshaded. $\frac{15}{40}$ reduces to $\frac{3}{8}$. (B) is correct.

9. Which graph could represent the line of best fit for this scatterplot?

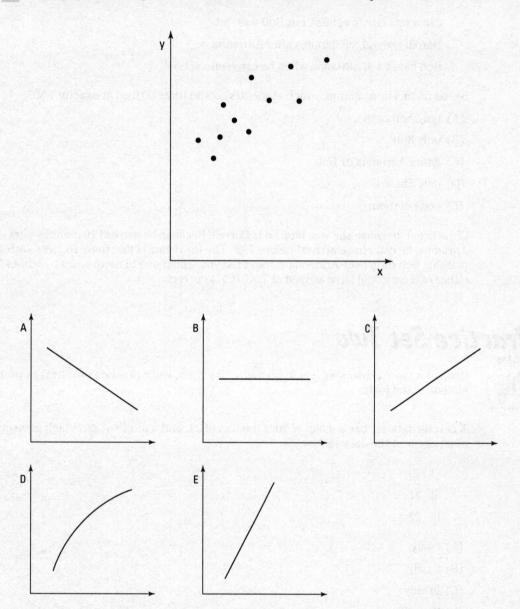

As long as you remember what "the line of best fit" means, this one is easy. (C) is correct.

10. Adrianna, Bob, Chris, and Darrell all arrive at school between 7:30 and 8:00.

> Chris was late to school, but Bob was not.
>
> Darrell arrived ten minutes after Adrianna.
>
> Bob didn't see Adrianna when he came into school.

Based on this information, which student(s) could have arrived at exactly 7:30?

(A) only Adrianna

(B) only Bob

(C) either Adrianna or Bob

(D) only Chris

(E) none of them

Chris is out, because she was late. So is Darrell. Because he arrived 10 minutes after Adrianna, he can't have arrived before 7:40. The third clue is just there to mess with you. The fact that Bob didn't see Adrianna doesn't tell you which one of them came to school first; either of them could have arrived at 7:30. (C) is correct.

Practice Set Two

Ready for more *exhilarating* (exciting) math? Try these eight practice problems in probability, statistics, and logic.

1. A certain data set has a mean of 20, a median of 21, and a mode of 22. Which measurement must occur in the data set?

> I. 20
>
> II. 21
>
> III. 22

(A) I only

(B) II only

(C) III only

(D) II and III

(E) None of the above

If you remember how to compute the "three Ms," you'll realize that the mean and median don't have to be in the data set. (Look in Chapter 14 for more on mean, median, and mode.) But because the mode is the most common measurement, it must be in the set. (C) is correct.

2. A student has a median score of 83 on five tests. If she scores 97 and 62 on her next two tests, her median score will:

(A) Increase to 90

(B) Decrease to 82

(C) Decrease to 79.5

(D) Remain the same

(E) It cannot be determined from the information given

The median is the score in the middle. If 83 is in the middle, adding a 97 on one side and a 62 on the other side doesn't change where the middle is. Three cheers for (D).

3. Alicia picks a number from the set {1, 2, 3, 4, 5, 6}. Michelle picks a number from the set {3, 4, 5, 6, 7, 8}. What is the probability that they select the same number?

   (A) ⅙

   (B) ⁴⁄₃₆

   (C) ⅚

   (D) ¹⁶⁄₃₆

   (E) ⅖

First determine the total number of possibilities. By the counting principle, there are $6 \times 6 = 36$ of them. Because the two sets overlap at 3, 4, 5, and 6, the girls may pick the same number in only four ways. Hence the answer is ⁴⁄₃₆. (Notice that the fraction isn't always reduced in probability questions.) (B) is correct.

4. A magazine did a study of ten cars, comparing the number of miles each car could go on a full tank of gas. Their results are shown below. Of the labeled points, which one represents the car that goes the farthest *per gallon of gas*?

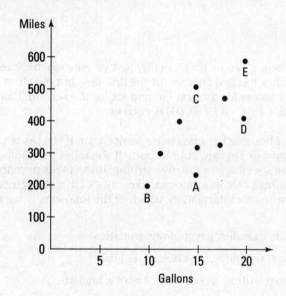

   (A) A

   (B) B

   (C) C

   (D) D

   (E) E

Car (C) travels approximately 500 miles on 15 gallons, for ⁵⁰⁰⁄₁₅ or around 33 miles per gallon. Although car (E) goes almost 600 miles, it needs 20 gallons, for less than 30 miles per gallon. The other cars all travel fewer than 30 miles per gallon. (C) is correct.

5. If a two-digit number is picked at random, what is the probability that the number chosen is a perfect square?

   (A) %₀

   (B) ¹%₀₀

   (C) ⅙₁

   (D) %₉

   (E) %₉

As usual, start by determining the total number of two-digit numbers. The two-digit numbers run from 10 to 99. The formula you can use here is as follows: The total is one more than the difference of the two numbers, or 99 − 10 + 1 = 90. The two-digit numbers that are perfect squares are 16, 25, 36, 49, 64, and 81. Pat yourself on the back if you answered (A).

6. A class contains five boys and seven girls. In how many ways can a teacher line up two boys and two girls, in that order?

   (A) 35

   (B) 140

   (C) 210

   (D) 840

   (E) 1,225

Because cloning people isn't a reality just yet, the teacher can't pick the same person twice. So the teacher has five choices for the first boy, but only four left for the second. Similarly, he has seven choices for the first girl and six for the second. Using the counting principle, the answer is $5 \times 4 \times 7 \times 6 = 840$. (D) is correct.

7. A junior is choosing her classes for senior year. If she takes calculus, she can also take either history or English, but not both. If she takes psychology in the first semester, she cannot take sociology or creative writing. If she takes psychology in the second semester, she cannot take calculus, but can take any elective she wants during the first semester. Based only on this information, which of the following is *not* a possible choice of courses for her?

   (A) English, calculus, psychology, statistics

   (B) History, sociology, psychology, English

   (C) Creative writing, psychology, history, English

   (D) Calculus, psychology, creative writing, history

   (E) Psychology, sociology, English, statistics, creative writing

Start by making a list of things that are impossible:

   calculus, English, history

   first semester psychology, sociology

   first semester psychology, creative writing

   second semester psychology, calculus

Now consider the choices: (A) is fine, if she takes psychology in the first semester. (B) is okay if she takes psychology in the second semester. (C) is fine, if she takes psychology in the second semester. (D) is a problem. If she takes psychology in the first semester, then creative writing is out. But if she takes it in the second semester, then calculus is out. (E) is fine if she takes psychology in the second semester.

8. The following dartboard consists of three circles with the same center. If the circles have radii of 6, 8, and 10 inches, what is the probability that a dart that hits the board lands in the shaded ring?

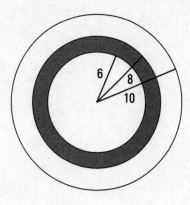

(A) ⅕₅

(B) ⅘

(C) ¾

(D) ⁹⁄₁₆

(E) ¹⁶⁄₂₅

The shaded ring has an outer radius of 8 and an inner radius of 6. So the area is the area of the radius-8 circle minus the area of the radius-6 circle, or $\pi(8)^2 - \pi(6)^2 = 64\pi - 36\pi = 28\pi$. The entire dartboard has a radius of 10, so its area is $\pi(10)^2 = 100\pi$, and the probability equals $^{28\pi}\!/_{100\pi} = ^{28}\!/_{100} = ^{7}\!/_{25}$. (A) is correct.

Part V

Where the Rubber Meets the Road: Practice Tests

The 5th Wave   By Rich Tennant

THEY'RE MOVING ON TO THE READING COMPREHENSION QUESTIONS. THAT SHOULD DAZE AND CONFUSE THEM ENOUGH FOR US TO FINISH CHANGING THE TIRE AND GET THE HECK OUT OF HERE.

SAT TEST BOOK PUBLISHERS

In this part . . .

Time for a reality check. The first time you sit in a silent room facing a SAT test *shouldn't* be on SAT-day. By that morning you should have at least one practice exam under your belt, fortifying you like a hearty breakfast for the rigors of SAT Reasoning. Yes, it does kill a perfectly fine morning (or evening or middle of the night, whenever you prefer to practice), but the investment of time will pay off.

In this part, I thoughtfully (and humbly) provide not just one but two (count 'em) SATs. In the interests of full disclosure (I'm the mother of a lawyer) I must tell you that I wrote them, not the College Board. Your test may differ slightly in number and order of questions. But the tests in this section do prepare you nicely for whatever the SAT-devils throw at you. Try one, score it, review whatever was tough for you (the answers and explanations follow each exam), and then if you have time, try another. You may be bored now, but you'll be smart and prepared for SAT-day.

Answer Sheet

For Section 1, use the following blank pages to write your essay. For Sections 2 through 8, use the ovals and grid-ins to record your answers. Begin with Number 1 for each new section. If any sections have fewer than 35 questions, leave the extra spaces blank.

_____
_____
_____
_____
_____
_____
_____
_____
_____
_____
_____
_____
_____
_____
_____
_____
_____
_____
_____
_____
_____
_____
_____
_____
_____

Section 2

1. Ⓐ Ⓑ Ⓒ Ⓓ Ⓔ	8. Ⓐ Ⓑ Ⓒ Ⓓ Ⓔ	15. Ⓐ Ⓑ Ⓒ Ⓓ Ⓔ	22. Ⓐ Ⓑ Ⓒ Ⓓ Ⓔ	29. Ⓐ Ⓑ Ⓒ Ⓓ Ⓔ
2. Ⓐ Ⓑ Ⓒ Ⓓ Ⓔ	9. Ⓐ Ⓑ Ⓒ Ⓓ Ⓔ	16. Ⓐ Ⓑ Ⓒ Ⓓ Ⓔ	23. Ⓐ Ⓑ Ⓒ Ⓓ Ⓔ	30. Ⓐ Ⓑ Ⓒ Ⓓ Ⓔ
3. Ⓐ Ⓑ Ⓒ Ⓓ Ⓔ	10. Ⓐ Ⓑ Ⓒ Ⓓ Ⓔ	17. Ⓐ Ⓑ Ⓒ Ⓓ Ⓔ	24. Ⓐ Ⓑ Ⓒ Ⓓ Ⓔ	31. Ⓐ Ⓑ Ⓒ Ⓓ Ⓔ
4. Ⓐ Ⓑ Ⓒ Ⓓ Ⓔ	11. Ⓐ Ⓑ Ⓒ Ⓓ Ⓔ	18. Ⓐ Ⓑ Ⓒ Ⓓ Ⓔ	25. Ⓐ Ⓑ Ⓒ Ⓓ Ⓔ	32. Ⓐ Ⓑ Ⓒ Ⓓ Ⓔ
5. Ⓐ Ⓑ Ⓒ Ⓓ Ⓔ	12. Ⓐ Ⓑ Ⓒ Ⓓ Ⓔ	19. Ⓐ Ⓑ Ⓒ Ⓓ Ⓔ	26. Ⓐ Ⓑ Ⓒ Ⓓ Ⓔ	33. Ⓐ Ⓑ Ⓒ Ⓓ Ⓔ
6. Ⓐ Ⓑ Ⓒ Ⓓ Ⓔ	13. Ⓐ Ⓑ Ⓒ Ⓓ Ⓔ	20. Ⓐ Ⓑ Ⓒ Ⓓ Ⓔ	27. Ⓐ Ⓑ Ⓒ Ⓓ Ⓔ	34. Ⓐ Ⓑ Ⓒ Ⓓ Ⓔ
7. Ⓐ Ⓑ Ⓒ Ⓓ Ⓔ	14. Ⓐ Ⓑ Ⓒ Ⓓ Ⓔ	21. Ⓐ Ⓑ Ⓒ Ⓓ Ⓔ	28. Ⓐ Ⓑ Ⓒ Ⓓ Ⓔ	35. Ⓐ Ⓑ Ⓒ Ⓓ Ⓔ

Section 3

1. Ⓐ Ⓑ Ⓒ Ⓓ Ⓔ	8. Ⓐ Ⓑ Ⓒ Ⓓ Ⓔ	15. Ⓐ Ⓑ Ⓒ Ⓓ Ⓔ	22. Ⓐ Ⓑ Ⓒ Ⓓ Ⓔ	29. Ⓐ Ⓑ Ⓒ Ⓓ Ⓔ
2. Ⓐ Ⓑ Ⓒ Ⓓ Ⓔ	9. Ⓐ Ⓑ Ⓒ Ⓓ Ⓔ	16. Ⓐ Ⓑ Ⓒ Ⓓ Ⓔ	23. Ⓐ Ⓑ Ⓒ Ⓓ Ⓔ	30. Ⓐ Ⓑ Ⓒ Ⓓ Ⓔ
3. Ⓐ Ⓑ Ⓒ Ⓓ Ⓔ	10. Ⓐ Ⓑ Ⓒ Ⓓ Ⓔ	17. Ⓐ Ⓑ Ⓒ Ⓓ Ⓔ	24. Ⓐ Ⓑ Ⓒ Ⓓ Ⓔ	31. Ⓐ Ⓑ Ⓒ Ⓓ Ⓔ
4. Ⓐ Ⓑ Ⓒ Ⓓ Ⓔ	11. Ⓐ Ⓑ Ⓒ Ⓓ Ⓔ	18. Ⓐ Ⓑ Ⓒ Ⓓ Ⓔ	25. Ⓐ Ⓑ Ⓒ Ⓓ Ⓔ	32. Ⓐ Ⓑ Ⓒ Ⓓ Ⓔ
5. Ⓐ Ⓑ Ⓒ Ⓓ Ⓔ	12. Ⓐ Ⓑ Ⓒ Ⓓ Ⓔ	19. Ⓐ Ⓑ Ⓒ Ⓓ Ⓔ	26. Ⓐ Ⓑ Ⓒ Ⓓ Ⓔ	33. Ⓐ Ⓑ Ⓒ Ⓓ Ⓔ
6. Ⓐ Ⓑ Ⓒ Ⓓ Ⓔ	13. Ⓐ Ⓑ Ⓒ Ⓓ Ⓔ	20. Ⓐ Ⓑ Ⓒ Ⓓ Ⓔ	27. Ⓐ Ⓑ Ⓒ Ⓓ Ⓔ	34. Ⓐ Ⓑ Ⓒ Ⓓ Ⓔ
7. Ⓐ Ⓑ Ⓒ Ⓓ Ⓔ	14. Ⓐ Ⓑ Ⓒ Ⓓ Ⓔ	21. Ⓐ Ⓑ Ⓒ Ⓓ Ⓔ	28. Ⓐ Ⓑ Ⓒ Ⓓ Ⓔ	35. Ⓐ Ⓑ Ⓒ Ⓓ Ⓔ

Section 4

1. Ⓐ Ⓑ Ⓒ Ⓓ Ⓔ	8. Ⓐ Ⓑ Ⓒ Ⓓ Ⓔ	15. Ⓐ Ⓑ Ⓒ Ⓓ Ⓔ	22. Ⓐ Ⓑ Ⓒ Ⓓ Ⓔ	29. Ⓐ Ⓑ Ⓒ Ⓓ Ⓔ
2. Ⓐ Ⓑ Ⓒ Ⓓ Ⓔ	9. Ⓐ Ⓑ Ⓒ Ⓓ Ⓔ	16. Ⓐ Ⓑ Ⓒ Ⓓ Ⓔ	23. Ⓐ Ⓑ Ⓒ Ⓓ Ⓔ	30. Ⓐ Ⓑ Ⓒ Ⓓ Ⓔ
3. Ⓐ Ⓑ Ⓒ Ⓓ Ⓔ	10. Ⓐ Ⓑ Ⓒ Ⓓ Ⓔ	17. Ⓐ Ⓑ Ⓒ Ⓓ Ⓔ	24. Ⓐ Ⓑ Ⓒ Ⓓ Ⓔ	31. Ⓐ Ⓑ Ⓒ Ⓓ Ⓔ
4. Ⓐ Ⓑ Ⓒ Ⓓ Ⓔ	11. Ⓐ Ⓑ Ⓒ Ⓓ Ⓔ	18. Ⓐ Ⓑ Ⓒ Ⓓ Ⓔ	25. Ⓐ Ⓑ Ⓒ Ⓓ Ⓔ	32. Ⓐ Ⓑ Ⓒ Ⓓ Ⓔ
5. Ⓐ Ⓑ Ⓒ Ⓓ Ⓔ	12. Ⓐ Ⓑ Ⓒ Ⓓ Ⓔ	19. Ⓐ Ⓑ Ⓒ Ⓓ Ⓔ	26. Ⓐ Ⓑ Ⓒ Ⓓ Ⓔ	33. Ⓐ Ⓑ Ⓒ Ⓓ Ⓔ
6. Ⓐ Ⓑ Ⓒ Ⓓ Ⓔ	13. Ⓐ Ⓑ Ⓒ Ⓓ Ⓔ	20. Ⓐ Ⓑ Ⓒ Ⓓ Ⓔ	27. Ⓐ Ⓑ Ⓒ Ⓓ Ⓔ	34. Ⓐ Ⓑ Ⓒ Ⓓ Ⓔ
7. Ⓐ Ⓑ Ⓒ Ⓓ Ⓔ	14. Ⓐ Ⓑ Ⓒ Ⓓ Ⓔ	21. Ⓐ Ⓑ Ⓒ Ⓓ Ⓔ	28. Ⓐ Ⓑ Ⓒ Ⓓ Ⓔ	35. Ⓐ Ⓑ Ⓒ Ⓓ Ⓔ

Section 5

1. Ⓐ Ⓑ Ⓒ Ⓓ Ⓔ	8. Ⓐ Ⓑ Ⓒ Ⓓ Ⓔ	15. Ⓐ Ⓑ Ⓒ Ⓓ Ⓔ	22. Ⓐ Ⓑ Ⓒ Ⓓ Ⓔ	29. Ⓐ Ⓑ Ⓒ Ⓓ Ⓔ
2. Ⓐ Ⓑ Ⓒ Ⓓ Ⓔ	9. Ⓐ Ⓑ Ⓒ Ⓓ Ⓔ	16. Ⓐ Ⓑ Ⓒ Ⓓ Ⓔ	23. Ⓐ Ⓑ Ⓒ Ⓓ Ⓔ	30. Ⓐ Ⓑ Ⓒ Ⓓ Ⓔ
3. Ⓐ Ⓑ Ⓒ Ⓓ Ⓔ	10. Ⓐ Ⓑ Ⓒ Ⓓ Ⓔ	17. Ⓐ Ⓑ Ⓒ Ⓓ Ⓔ	24. Ⓐ Ⓑ Ⓒ Ⓓ Ⓔ	31. Ⓐ Ⓑ Ⓒ Ⓓ Ⓔ
4. Ⓐ Ⓑ Ⓒ Ⓓ Ⓔ	11. Ⓐ Ⓑ Ⓒ Ⓓ Ⓔ	18. Ⓐ Ⓑ Ⓒ Ⓓ Ⓔ	25. Ⓐ Ⓑ Ⓒ Ⓓ Ⓔ	32. Ⓐ Ⓑ Ⓒ Ⓓ Ⓔ
5. Ⓐ Ⓑ Ⓒ Ⓓ Ⓔ	12. Ⓐ Ⓑ Ⓒ Ⓓ Ⓔ	19. Ⓐ Ⓑ Ⓒ Ⓓ Ⓔ	26. Ⓐ Ⓑ Ⓒ Ⓓ Ⓔ	33. Ⓐ Ⓑ Ⓒ Ⓓ Ⓔ
6. Ⓐ Ⓑ Ⓒ Ⓓ Ⓔ	13. Ⓐ Ⓑ Ⓒ Ⓓ Ⓔ	20. Ⓐ Ⓑ Ⓒ Ⓓ Ⓔ	27. Ⓐ Ⓑ Ⓒ Ⓓ Ⓔ	34. Ⓐ Ⓑ Ⓒ Ⓓ Ⓔ
7. Ⓐ Ⓑ Ⓒ Ⓓ Ⓔ	14. Ⓐ Ⓑ Ⓒ Ⓓ Ⓔ	21. Ⓐ Ⓑ Ⓒ Ⓓ Ⓔ	28. Ⓐ Ⓑ Ⓒ Ⓓ Ⓔ	35. Ⓐ Ⓑ Ⓒ Ⓓ Ⓔ

Section 6

1. Ⓐ Ⓑ Ⓒ Ⓓ Ⓔ   3. Ⓐ Ⓑ Ⓒ Ⓓ Ⓔ   5. Ⓐ Ⓑ Ⓒ Ⓓ Ⓔ   7. Ⓐ Ⓑ Ⓒ Ⓓ Ⓔ   9. Ⓐ Ⓑ Ⓒ Ⓓ Ⓔ
2. Ⓐ Ⓑ Ⓒ Ⓓ Ⓔ   4. Ⓐ Ⓑ Ⓒ Ⓓ Ⓔ   6. Ⓐ Ⓑ Ⓒ Ⓓ Ⓔ   8. Ⓐ Ⓑ Ⓒ Ⓓ Ⓔ   10. Ⓐ Ⓑ Ⓒ Ⓓ Ⓔ

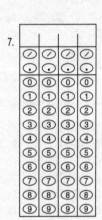

Section 7

1. Ⓐ Ⓑ Ⓒ Ⓓ Ⓔ   8. Ⓐ Ⓑ Ⓒ Ⓓ Ⓔ   15. Ⓐ Ⓑ Ⓒ Ⓓ Ⓔ   22. Ⓐ Ⓑ Ⓒ Ⓓ Ⓔ   29. Ⓐ Ⓑ Ⓒ Ⓓ Ⓔ
2. Ⓐ Ⓑ Ⓒ Ⓓ Ⓔ   9. Ⓐ Ⓑ Ⓒ Ⓓ Ⓔ   16. Ⓐ Ⓑ Ⓒ Ⓓ Ⓔ   23. Ⓐ Ⓑ Ⓒ Ⓓ Ⓔ   30. Ⓐ Ⓑ Ⓒ Ⓓ Ⓔ
3. Ⓐ Ⓑ Ⓒ Ⓓ Ⓔ   10. Ⓐ Ⓑ Ⓒ Ⓓ Ⓔ   17. Ⓐ Ⓑ Ⓒ Ⓓ Ⓔ   24. Ⓐ Ⓑ Ⓒ Ⓓ Ⓔ   31. Ⓐ Ⓑ Ⓒ Ⓓ Ⓔ
4. Ⓐ Ⓑ Ⓒ Ⓓ Ⓔ   11. Ⓐ Ⓑ Ⓒ Ⓓ Ⓔ   18. Ⓐ Ⓑ Ⓒ Ⓓ Ⓔ   25. Ⓐ Ⓑ Ⓒ Ⓓ Ⓔ   32. Ⓐ Ⓑ Ⓒ Ⓓ Ⓔ
5. Ⓐ Ⓑ Ⓒ Ⓓ Ⓔ   12. Ⓐ Ⓑ Ⓒ Ⓓ Ⓔ   19. Ⓐ Ⓑ Ⓒ Ⓓ Ⓔ   26. Ⓐ Ⓑ Ⓒ Ⓓ Ⓔ   33. Ⓐ Ⓑ Ⓒ Ⓓ Ⓔ
6. Ⓐ Ⓑ Ⓒ Ⓓ Ⓔ   13. Ⓐ Ⓑ Ⓒ Ⓓ Ⓔ   20. Ⓐ Ⓑ Ⓒ Ⓓ Ⓔ   27. Ⓐ Ⓑ Ⓒ Ⓓ Ⓔ   34. Ⓐ Ⓑ Ⓒ Ⓓ Ⓔ
7. Ⓐ Ⓑ Ⓒ Ⓓ Ⓔ   14. Ⓐ Ⓑ Ⓒ Ⓓ Ⓔ   21. Ⓐ Ⓑ Ⓒ Ⓓ Ⓔ   28. Ⓐ Ⓑ Ⓒ Ⓓ Ⓔ   35. Ⓐ Ⓑ Ⓒ Ⓓ Ⓔ

Section 8

1. Ⓐ Ⓑ Ⓒ Ⓓ Ⓔ   8. Ⓐ Ⓑ Ⓒ Ⓓ Ⓔ   15. Ⓐ Ⓑ Ⓒ Ⓓ Ⓔ   22. Ⓐ Ⓑ Ⓒ Ⓓ Ⓔ   29. Ⓐ Ⓑ Ⓒ Ⓓ Ⓔ
2. Ⓐ Ⓑ Ⓒ Ⓓ Ⓔ   9. Ⓐ Ⓑ Ⓒ Ⓓ Ⓔ   16. Ⓐ Ⓑ Ⓒ Ⓓ Ⓔ   23. Ⓐ Ⓑ Ⓒ Ⓓ Ⓔ   30. Ⓐ Ⓑ Ⓒ Ⓓ Ⓔ
3. Ⓐ Ⓑ Ⓒ Ⓓ Ⓔ   10. Ⓐ Ⓑ Ⓒ Ⓓ Ⓔ   17. Ⓐ Ⓑ Ⓒ Ⓓ Ⓔ   24. Ⓐ Ⓑ Ⓒ Ⓓ Ⓔ   31. Ⓐ Ⓑ Ⓒ Ⓓ Ⓔ
4. Ⓐ Ⓑ Ⓒ Ⓓ Ⓔ   11. Ⓐ Ⓑ Ⓒ Ⓓ Ⓔ   18. Ⓐ Ⓑ Ⓒ Ⓓ Ⓔ   25. Ⓐ Ⓑ Ⓒ Ⓓ Ⓔ   32. Ⓐ Ⓑ Ⓒ Ⓓ Ⓔ
5. Ⓐ Ⓑ Ⓒ Ⓓ Ⓔ   12. Ⓐ Ⓑ Ⓒ Ⓓ Ⓔ   19. Ⓐ Ⓑ Ⓒ Ⓓ Ⓔ   26. Ⓐ Ⓑ Ⓒ Ⓓ Ⓔ   33. Ⓐ Ⓑ Ⓒ Ⓓ Ⓔ
6. Ⓐ Ⓑ Ⓒ Ⓓ Ⓔ   13. Ⓐ Ⓑ Ⓒ Ⓓ Ⓔ   20. Ⓐ Ⓑ Ⓒ Ⓓ Ⓔ   27. Ⓐ Ⓑ Ⓒ Ⓓ Ⓔ   34. Ⓐ Ⓑ Ⓒ Ⓓ Ⓔ
7. Ⓐ Ⓑ Ⓒ Ⓓ Ⓔ   14. Ⓐ Ⓑ Ⓒ Ⓓ Ⓔ   21. Ⓐ Ⓑ Ⓒ Ⓓ Ⓔ   28. Ⓐ Ⓑ Ⓒ Ⓓ Ⓔ   35. Ⓐ Ⓑ Ⓒ Ⓓ Ⓔ

Chapter 22

Boring You to Tears: Practice Exam 1

In This Chapter
▶ Taking a full-length practice SAT
▶ Adjusting your rate of work to SAT time limits

*T*he first paragraph is usually the spot for my lame jokes (yes, I know, but I inflict them on you anyway), but in this chapter you should be as serious as you can. Clear out your room or find a sheltered spot in the public library. Place a watch in front of you or sit where you can see a wall clock. Tear out the answer sheet that precedes this page and pick up your No. 2 pencil. Allot yourself the official amount of time (at the beginning of each section I tell you how much) and get to work. If you finish a section early, go back and recheck it. Don't even think about looking at other sections — a big no-no on the actual exam and one that will cause the proctor to invalidate your exam. If you run out of time, put your pencil down and move on to the following section. Take two ten-minute breaks between sections 3 and 4 and between sections 6 and 7.

No matter how tempted you are, resist the urge to turn to Chapter 23, where the answers and explanations reside. Save them for later! And good luck.

Section 1

The Essay

Time: 25 minutes

Directions: In response to the following prompts, write an essay in the space provided on the answer sheet. You may use extra space in the question booklet to take notes and to organize your thoughts, but only the answer sheet will be graded.

> Once a person's curiosity, on any subject, is aroused it is surprising just how far it may lead him in pursuit of its object, how readily it overcomes every obstacle.
>
> — Georges Ifrah

> Curiosity is one of the most permanent and certain characteristics of a vigorous intellect.
>
> — Samuel Johnson

Does curiosity help or harm? Discuss the role of curiosity in human life, drawing upon history, literature, current events, or your own experience and observations.

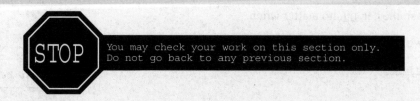

STOP You may check your work on this section only.
Do not go back to any previous section.

Section 2

> Writing: Multiple Choice
>
> Time: 35 minutes
>
> 35 questions

> Directions for questions 1–12: Identify the error in the underlined portion of each sentence. If a sentence contains no errors, choose (E) for "no error." Darken the corresponding oval on your answer sheet.
>
> Example:
>
> Irregardless of the fact that the National
> ___A___
> Weather Service predicted rain, Dexter
> _____B___
> resented the students' request to postpone
> ___C___   ___D___
> the picnic. No error.
> ___E___
>
> The correct answer is (A). ● Ⓑ Ⓒ Ⓓ Ⓔ

1. Annie announced that everyone
   _____A___
   should bring their gym equipment to the
   ___B___   ___C___
   track meet so that she can determine the
   ___D___
   flashiest sports logo. No error.
   _____E___

2. The costliest option of the two plans
   ___A___
   he offered would have cost us more than
   ___B___   ___C___   ___D___
   a million dollars. No error.
   _____E___

3. Because she found the charity's video so
   ___A___   ___B___
   inspiring, Kirsten decided to donate
   ___C___
   three years' salary to the Impoverished Flea
   _____
   Circus Veterans of America. No error.
   _____E___

4. Janine will try and determine the best
   ___A___   ___B___
   time to wash the car, but no matter when
   ___C___
   we start, we must finish before the rain
   ___D___
   begins. No error.
   _____E___

5. Most of his fencing buddies have suffered
   ___A___   ___B___
   from the sport; fortunately the padding
   ___C___
   nearly prevents every serious wound.
   _____D___
   No error.
   ___E___

6. Archie has taught himself to perform
   _____A___
   several difficult gymnastic moves, which
   _____B___   ___C___
   he does better than anyone on his team.
   _____D___
   No error.
   ___E___

7. The janitor generally checked for broken
   _____A___
   windows only when an inspector was
   _____B___
   due, consequently, a surprise visit from
   _____C___
   the superintendent was quite unwelcome.
   _____D___
   No error.
   ___E___

8. One of the students in Albert's comedy
   _____A___
   class, along with three aspiring screen-
   writers, are going to Hollywood to meet
   _____B___   ___C___
   with an agent who may be able to sell the
   _____D___
   script for a great deal of money. No error.
   _____E___

9. Henry can't remember who he should bill
   _____A___
   for the broken window, but he knows that
   _____B___   ___C___
   the responsibility belongs to someone on
   _____D___
   the baseball team. No error.
   _____E___

Go on to next page

10. Marisa told her aunt that she didn't care

A   B

enough about the environment, which

      C

has become more polluted every year.

     D

No error.

  E

11. Agnes was the only one of those historians

   A

who was shocked by the discoveries of

    B

our's that have been published in the

  C   D

university journal. No error.

       E

12. Jenny finds that she has time only for play-

     A   B

ing sports and studying, not to audition for

        C

the school musical as well. No error.

       D   E

Directions for questions 13–26: Each sentence is followed by five choices. Decide which choice best improves the sentence and darken the corresponding oval on the answer sheet. If the underlined portion of the sentence is best left alone, choose (A).

Example: Bert and him went to the store to buy boots in preparation for the approaching storm.

(A) Bert and him went

(B) Bert and he went

(C) Bert and he had gone

(D) Bert and him had gone

(E) Bert and himself went

The correct answer is (B). Ⓐ ● Ⓒ Ⓓ Ⓔ

---

13. Yesterday the weather forecaster noted a sharp fall in barometric pressure, this is an indication that a storm is coming.

    (A) pressure, this is an indication

    (B) pressure; and this is an indication

    (C) pressure, which is an indication

    (D) pressure, which had indicated

    (E) pressure, and indicates

14. The lion had a thorn in it's paw, but the zookeeper was able to take care of the problem.

    (A) in it's paw, but

    (B) in its paw, but

    (C) in it's paw but

    (D) in its paw but

    (E) in its' paw, but

15. The Native American guides objected to him trespassing on sacred ground.

    (A) objected to him trespassing

    (B) has objected to him trespassing

    (C) objected to him having trespassed

    (D) objected that he trespassed

    (E) objected to his trespassing

16. Just between you and I, the school would like to drop grammar questions from the SAT.

    (A) Just between you and I, the school would like

    (B) Just between you and I, the school likes

    (C) Just between you and me, the school would like

    (D) Between just you and I, the school would like

    (E) Between just you and I, the school likes

17. At present, Max's family traveled to California eight years in a row.

    (A) Max's family traveled

    (B) everyone in Max's family traveled

    (C) Max's family has traveled

    (D) Max's family had traveled

    (E) Max's family will have traveled

Go on to next page ➡

18. Impatiently waiting at the curb, the taxi sped past the toddler who was holding his mama's hand.

    (A) Impatiently waiting at the curb, the taxi sped past the toddler who was holding his mama's hand.

    (B) The taxi sped past the toddler who was holding his mama's hand impatiently waiting at the curb.

    (C) Impatiently waiting at the curb, the toddler watched the taxi speed past, holding his mama's hand.

    (D) The toddler impatiently waiting at the curb held his mama's hand and watched the taxi speed past.

    (E) The toddler impatiently waiting at the curb held his mama's hand, and watched the taxi speed past.

19. Duke's rubber bone is one of those adorable dog toys that are sold in every petshop.

    (A) toys that are sold in every petshop.

    (B) toys which are sold in every petshop.

    (C) toys that is sold in every petshop.

    (D) toys, that is sold in every petshop.

    (E) toys, that are sold in every petshop.

20. The reason Helen hates biology is because she doesn't want to dissect a frog.

    (A) Helen hates biology is because

    (B) Helen hates biology is that

    (C) Helen hated biology is because

    (D) Helen has hated biology is because

    (E) Helen had hated biology is that

21. Tina can't understand why Olivia doesn't write as well as him.

    (A) why Olivia doesn't write as well as him

    (B) how Olivia doesn't write as well as him

    (C) the reason why Olivia doesn't write as well as him

    (D) why Olivia doesn't write as well as he

    (E) why Olivia didn't write as well as him

22. Tom prepared the delicious and nutritious casserole, however his wife deserved all the credit for developing the recipe.

    (A) casserole, however his wife deserved

    (B) casserole; however his wife deserved

    (C) casserole, however, his wife deserved

    (D) casserole however his wife deserved

    (E) casserole; however, his wife deserved

23. Deborah gave a piece of birthday cake to whomever she thought would eat it.

    (A) to whomever she thought would eat it

    (B) to whomever she thought would like to eat it

    (C) to whoever she thought would eat it

    (D) to whoever she thought would have eaten it

    (E) to whomever she thought would have eaten it

24. The gas station stood where the supermarket was.

    (A) stood where the supermarket was

    (B) stood where the supermarket has been

    (C) had stood where the supermarket had been

    (D) stood, where the supermarket was

    (E) stood where the supermarket had been

25. Neither the teacher nor the students was willing to forgo the SAT and substitute a road trip to Greece.

    (A) was willing to forgo the SAT and substitute

    (B) were willing to forgo the SAT, and substitute

    (C) was willing to forgo the SAT, and substitute

    (D) were willing to forgo the SAT in order to substitute

    (E) was willing to forgo the SAT, substituting

Go on to next page

26. <u>In the school paper it says that</u> the colleges are considering a ban on exams as a stress reduction measure.

    (A) In the school paper it says that

    (B) In the school paper the article says that

    (C) The school paper reports that

    (D) The school paper, says that

    (E) The school paper it says that

Directions: Questions 27–35 are based on the following essay. Choose the best answer and darken the corresponding oval on the answer sheet.

---

(1) These days it is possible to watch trials on television. (2) Several important trials have been televised for months on end, and a whole TV network shows nothing but this. (3) But you have to wonder whether justice is best served when the camera is rolling. (4) In one big trial a few years ago, the attorneys became television stars and the judge looked at the camera more than at the people in his courtroom. (5) The man on trial got off, perhaps because the jury was influenced by the publicity and glamour surrounding him.

(6) True, the jury cannot see the broadcast. (7) They often must stay in hotels during important trials. (8) However they may still be influenced by the fact that viewers can see the judge and witnesses. (9) Also, attorneys and court employees may play to the camera, acting more dramatic than they should just because the world is watching and they know it.

(10) It is important to have justice open to the public. (11) In a dictatorship, they keep their power partly through secrecy and lies. (12) If you see the judge and understand how the ruling is made, you may be more likely to accept the rule of law. (13) If you hear the verdict and never understand what the witnesses said, you may feel that justice is not really considered.

(14) Every case is different, and the judge ultimately decides whether the television reporters can broadcast live or only comment outside the courtroom. (15) The decision to keep the cameras away, however, should not be taken lightly. (16) The more the public knows about law, the better the law will be served.

27. Which of the following is the best revision of sentence 2?

    (A) Several important trials have been televised for months on end, and a whole TV network shows nothing but this. (No change)

    (B) Several important trials have been televised for months on end, and a whole TV network shows nothing but this sort of thing.

    (C) A number of important trials have been televised for months on end, and an entire network shows nothing but this.

    (D) Several important trials have been televised for months on end, even though a whole TV network shows nothing but this sort of thing.

    (E) Several important trials have been televised for months on end, and an entire television network shows nothing but courtroom proceedings.

28. In the context of this essay, which of the following is the best revision of sentences 1 and 2?

    (A) These days it is possible to watch trials on television. Several important trials have been televised for months on end, and a whole TV network shows nothing but this. (No change)

    (B) These days it is possible to watch trials on television, and several important trials have been televised for months on end, while a whole TV network shows nothing else.

    (C) These days it is possible to watch an actual, live trial on television, sometimes for months. In fact, an entire television network shows nothing but trials.

    (D) The Justice Network broadcasts nothing but trials, some of which last for months. These trials are not fiction. Viewers see live court proceedings with real defendants.

    (E) One television network shows trials, all day, every day. These trials are real, and some last for months.

Go on to next page

29. How should sentences 4 and 5 be improved?

    (A) No change should be made.

    (B) Sentence 4 should be left alone, but sentence 5 should be separated into two parts.

    (C) Sentences 4 and 5 should be combined into one longer sentence.

    (D) Details such as the name of the defendant and the type of criminal charge should be added to the general statements.

    (E) Details such as the name of the defendant and the type of criminal charge should replace the general statements.

30. What is the purpose of paragraph two?

    (A) to show why broadcasting trials is acceptable

    (B) to answer objections to trial broadcasting that may arise

    (C) to argue against broadcasting trials

    (D) to continue the example given in paragraph one

    (E) to prepare the way for paragraph three

31. How may sentences 6 and 7 best be combined?

    (A) True, the jury cannot see the broadcast, they often must stay in hotels during important trials.

    (B) True, the jury, that must often stay in hotels during important trials, cannot see the broadcast.

    (C) True, the jury cannot see the broadcast, due to the fact that they often must stay in hotels during important trials.

    (D) True, the jury cannot see the broadcast because of the fact that they often must stay in hotels during important trials.

    (E) True, the jury, which must often stay in hotels overnight during important trials, cannot see the broadcast.

32. Which of the following is the best revision of sentence 9?

    (A) Also, attorneys and court employees may play to the camera, acting more dramatic than they should just because the world is watching and they know it. (No change)

    (B) Also, attorneys and court employees may behave more dramatically than they should just because they know that the camera allows the world to watch.

    (C) Also, attorneys and court employees may play to the camera, acting more dramatic than they should just because the world is watching and they know they are on television.

    (D) Also, attorneys and court employees may play to the camera, acting more dramatic because the world is watching.

    (E) Also, attorneys and court employees may play to the camera, acting more dramatic than they should just because the world is watching through the camera.

33. How should sentence 10 be changed?

    (A) It is important to have justice open to the public. (No change)

    (B) Most important is the fact that justice should be open to public view.

    (C) On the other hand, justice should be open to the public.

    (D) Despite what you may say, it is important to have justice open to the public.

    (E) It is important if justice is open to the public.

34. How should sentence 11 be improved?

    (A) In a dictatorship, they keep their power partly through secrecy and lies. (No change)

    (B) In a dictatorship, rulers keep their power partly through secrecy and lies.

    (C) In a dictatorship, secrecy and lies give them power.

    (D) Dictators have been able to keep their power partly through secrecy and lies.

    (E) Power has been given to dictators by secrecy and lies.

Go on to next page

35. What is the purpose of the last paragraph?

    (A) to come to a firm conclusion about whether trial broadcasting should be allowed

    (B) to let the reader decide whether trial broadcasting should be allowed

    (C) to emphasize the importance of the issue of judicial fairness

    (D) to emphasize the importance of the decision about broadcasting

    (E) to show why only the judge can decide whether broadcasting is justified

STOP You may check your work on this section only.
Do not go back to any previous section.

Section 3

Critical Reading

Time: 25 minutes

25 questions

Directions for questions 1–9: Select the answer that best fits the meaning of the sentence and darken the corresponding oval on the answer sheet.

Example: After he had broken the dining room window, Hal's mother _____ him.

(A) selected

(B) seranaded

(C) fooled

(D) grounded

(E) rewarded

The answer is (D). Ⓐ Ⓑ Ⓒ ● Ⓔ

---

1. Helen's response to the flood is not simply intellectual, but _____.

   (A) practical

   (B) theoretical

   (C) philosophical

   (D) ethical

   (E) strident

2. _____ research into the origins of Delkong culture indicates that they established a hunter-gatherer society about two thousand years earlier than was previously thought.

   (A) Prior

   (B) Contemporary

   (C) Theoretical

   (D) Antiquated

   (E) Discredited

3. It has been suggested that the _____ references to architectural history _____ the paper's focus on engineering concepts.

   (A) documented . . . affect

   (B) sophisticated . . . enhance

   (C) myriad . . . weaken

   (D) impeccable . . . distort

   (E) obscure . . . sharpen

4. Its presence in all languages has led many to the conclusion that grammar is _____.

   (A) innate

   (B) inevitable

   (C) multifaceted

   (D) extraneous

   (E) coincidental

5. By subsidizing small business, the government hopes to _____ the once prosperous area.

   (A) stagnate

   (B) annex

   (C) enervate

   (D) aggrandize

   (E) reinvigorate

6. Although Deeplock has promised to shorten the agenda, the council is _____ about discussing the topic of global warming and will insist that it be included.

   (A) ambivalent

   (B) adamant

   (C) perplexed

   (D) apathetic

   (E) neutral

Go on to next page

7. Notwithstanding the _____ effort on the part of the entire team, the championship went to the other division for the first time in ten years.

   (A) herculean

   (B) spontaneous

   (C) gratuitous

   (D) pluralistic

   (E) intermittent

8. The revolt against Puritanism in the 18th century was perhaps more intense than the author's _____ conveys.

   (A) dissertation

   (B) historiography

   (C) memoir

   (D) polemic

   (E) diatribe

9. Jazz enthusiasts often make a pilgrimage to that hotel, which in the 1900s was the site of a _____ gathering of writers, painters, sculptors, and musicians who had been stranded by the storm.

   (A) fortuitous

   (B) superfluous

   (C) querulous

   (D) precarious

   (E) omniscient

Directions for questions 10–13: Choose the best answer to each question based on what is stated or implied in the passage or in the introductory material. Darken the corresponding oval on the answer sheet.

Questions 10 and 11 are based on the following passage, excerpted from *The Transformational Leader* by Noel M. Tichy and Mary Anne Devanna (Wiley, 1986, 1990).

Line   Clearly, the ability to decide what the mission and the strategy of the organization will be is a source of significant power. Technically focused textbooks and consulting groups advise organiza-
(05) tions on how to do strategic planning, but they do not shed much light on how to allocate power in the actual strategic decision-making process.

What levels of the organization should be involved in the process? Should technical decisions be made by those with technical expertise (10) or by general managers? Should the chairperson make the decision alone? A set of decisions must be made to determine who will influence the formulation of the mission and strategy.

10. Which statement is implied in the passage?

    (A) There are many different ways to come to a decision in a large organization.

    (B) The same person should not formulate both mission and strategy for an organization.

    (C) Powerful people are the only ones who should make a decision.

    (D) Textbooks that focus on technical matters are not useful.

    (E) All levels of an organization should be involved in decision making.

11. The author believes that power comes from

    (A) technical expertise

    (B) political connections

    (C) the ability to make decisions about goals and methods

    (D) job titles

    (E) recommendations made by consulting groups

Questions 12 and 13 are based on the following passage, excerpted from *Physical Science in the Middle Ages* by Edward Grant (Wiley, 1971).

Line   During the course of the fifth century, the Western half [of the Roman Empire] fell prey to invading Germanic tribes, and by 500 A.D., much of it was in their control. Despite subsequent efforts of the Eastern emperor, Justinian, only the (05) trappings of Empire remained — the substance was dead, and Western Europe evolved new forms of social and governmental activity to cope with conditions drastically different from those of a few centuries earlier. (10)

Go on to next page

12. According to the passage, the Emperor Justinian

    (A) resigned his post as head of the Eastern half of the Roman Empire.

    (B) designed new forms of social and governmental activity.

    (C) attempted to maintain the power and organization of the Roman Empire at its height.

    (D) was in favor of merging the Western and Eastern halves of the Roman Empire.

    (E) fought against the Western half of the Roman Empire.

13. What is the meaning of *trappings* in line 6?

    (A) device to catch enemies

    (B) ornamental factors

    (C) bureaucracy

    (D) spirit

    (E) government

Directions for questions 14–25: Choose the best answer from among those given, based on what the author states or implies in the passage.

Questions 14 to 25 refer to the following passage, an excerpt from *The Knight* by Alan Baker (Wiley, 2003), which discusses feudalism.

Line [M]any attempts . . . have been made to analyze and define it [feudalism], attempts that are far from being closely related to one another. Bearing these caveats in mind, let us attempt a
(05) useful definition of feudalism that will be of some help in our understanding of the society in which the knight lived and operated. The feudal society came into existence in France, Germany, the Kingdom of Burgundy-Aries, and Italy in about the
(10) tenth century. Countries that came under their influence — England, some of the Christian kingdoms of Spain, and the Latin principalities of the Near East — also possessed feudal attributes. Although there are other countries, such as Egypt
(15) and India, that displayed some analogies with feudalism in the distant past, leading some historians to label them (controversially) as feudal, the society that most closely parallels the situation in medieval Europe is Japan.

European feudalism was characterized by (20) obligations of service (especially military service) between the vassal and his lord. In return for the vassal's service, the lord was obliged to offer protection and a livelihood to his vassal, including the land grant. In Japan the daimyos, bushi, (25) or samurai were comparable to the vassals in Europe, and the land that was granted to them was more or less equivalent to that granted to the vassal by his lord in return for his service. In addition, an institution very close to vassalage (30) prevailed in Russia between the thirteenth and sixteenth centuries.

In Europe the lord and the vassal were securely locked into a mutually beneficial arrangement: for the vassal there was protection and (35) land; for the lord, there were days owed in military service, whether in battle or the garrisoning of the castle, plus counsel before embarking on an important course of action. Also among the vassal's obligations to his lord were the fee known (40) as relief, when he received his land; the obligation to contribute to any ransom that might be demanded should his lord be captured; to contribute to his crusading expenses; and to help out when the lord's son was knighted or his daughter (45) married. In addition, permission had to be sought if the vassal wished to marry, or to marry off his own daughter. Upon the vassal's death, his widow and children would be provided for by the lord, who would see to their education and marriage; (50) should he die without a wife or heirs, the land would revert to the lord.

It is easy to see that feudalism was, at its center, defined by the localization of political, military, and economic power in the hands of lords (55) and their vassals, who exercised that power from their castle headquarters, each of which held complete sway over the district in which it was situated. The resulting hierarchy resembled a pyramid, with the lowest vassals at the base and (60) the king, of course, at the summit. This was not the case in every nation, however; in Germany, for instance, the summit of the pyramid did not reach the king, being occupied instead by the great princes. (65)

The results of feudalism were mixed, to say the least. On the negative side, it meant that the state had a relationship with the heads of groups rather than directly with individuals farther down the social scale. Under a weak king, these men (70) claimed sovereignty for themselves, and fought among themselves rather than allowing the state to judge their claims. This resulted in the private wars that scarred the medieval landscape. The

Go on to next page

(75) overlords claimed numerous rights for themselves, including that of issuing private coinage, building private castles, and the power to raise taxes. Each of these manorial groups tried to be self-sufficient and to consolidate its possessions. (80) Skirmishes and all-out wars were frequent and accounted for much of the violence, precariousness, and unpredictability of medieval life. In addition, the powers possessed by the church meant that in times of disputed succession it (85) claimed the right not only to defend itself and maintain order, but also to nominate the ruler. This, of course, made it impossible for the church to remain impartial in matters of state, and the cause of the church frequently became identified (90) with a particular claimant.

This must be balanced against the positive results of feudalism; for instance, the cohesion it supplied to the nations in which it operated. In the absence of any mature concept of nationality (95) in the centuries following the fall of the Roman Empire, feudalism supplied some measure of territorial organization, linking the Germanic and Roman political systems and providing a pyramidal hierarchy that resulted in at least a nominal (100) political and economic stability.

14. In paragraph one, the author implies that
    (A) Feudalism originated in Japan.
    (B) Feudalism spread from England to Spain.
    (C) It is generally agreed that Egypt and India had feudal societies.
    (D) It is impossible to define feudalism.
    (E) No single definition of feudalism will be accepted by all historians.

15. The author mentions Russia (lines 30–32)
    (A) as an additional example of a society with a full-fledged feudal system
    (B) to show that the vassal/lord relationship existed in countries without fully feudal societies
    (C) to contrast Russia's system of vassalage with Japan's
    (D) because Russia had no vassals
    (E) to prove that feudalism existed in the modern era

16. Based on this excerpt, what is the best definition of vassal?
    (A) a lord who commanded knights
    (B) a soldier who fought for his country
    (C) a noble who ruled over a substantial area
    (D) someone who served a lord in return for land and other rights
    (E) a tenant farmer who worked but did not own the land

17. Which idea is implied but not stated in the passage?
    (A) Land was the basis of wealth in feudal society.
    (B) Knights were at war more often than not.
    (C) Japanese daimyos were superior to European vassals.
    (D) Feudalism provided benefits only to the wealthy.
    (E) Marriage was a purely private decision.

18. All of the following are obligations owed to feudal lords by their vassals *except*
    (A) approval of marriage partners
    (B) erection of a castle
    (C) fees in return for land grants
    (D) financial support for important events
    (E) military service

19. According to the passage, feudal lords
    (A) were obliged to accept their vassals' advice
    (B) controlled the peasants
    (C) consulted with other lords before making important decisions
    (D) could seek advice from their vassals
    (E) found marriage partners for the children of their vassals

Go on to next page

20. The author of the passage would most likely agree with which statement?

    (A) Feudalism was directly responsible for the instability of the medieval period.

    (B) Feudalism was weak in Germany because princes had too much power.

    (C) Feudalism worked best when religion played no role.

    (D) The feudal system did not work well in the absence of a strong king.

    (E) Feudalism protected the rights of women.

21. In line 60, the pyramid analogy implies that

    (A) German feudalism was unstable.

    (B) Castles were constructed in the same way as pyramids.

    (C) The king's power equaled that of the ancient Egyptian pharaohs.

    (D) All vassals were equal.

    (E) Vassals had varying degrees of power.

22 The word "this" in line 91 refers to

    (A) Feudalism

    (B) The violence and unpredictability of medieval life

    (C) The impartiality of the church in matters of politics

    (D) The link between the church and a particular claimant of the throne

    (E) All the disadvantages of feudalism described in the preceding paragraph

23. What is the closest meaning of *nominal* (line 99)?

    (A) alleged to be true

    (B) just enough to deserve the name

    (C) justified under the circumstances

    (D) supposed to be true

    (E) purportedly

24. The author's tone may best be described as

    (A) dispassionate

    (B) strident

    (C) didactic

    (D) satirical

    (E) critical

25. The best title for this passage is

    (A) Feudalism in Europe and Japan

    (B) A Definition of Feudalism

    (C) The Rights of Vassals

    (D) The Disadvantages of Feudalism

    (E) The Pyramid of Power

STOP You may check your work on this section only. Do not go back to any previous section.

Section 4

Mathematics

Time: 25 minutes

25 questions

Notes:

✔ You may use a calculator.

✔ All numbers used in this exam are real numbers.

✔ All figures lie in a plane.

✔ All figures may be assumed to be to scale unless the problem specifically indicates otherwise.

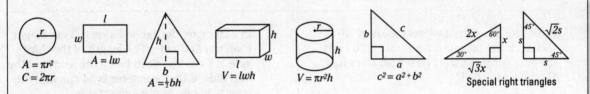

$A = \pi r^2$
$C = 2\pi r$

$A = lw$

$A = \frac{1}{2}bh$

$V = lwh$

$V = \pi r^2 h$

$c^2 = a^2 + b^2$

Special right triangles

There are 360 degrees of arc in a circle.

There are 180 degrees in a straight line.

There are 180 degrees in the sum of the interior angles of a triangle.

Directions: Choose the best answer and darken the corresponding oval on the answer sheet.

1.   In a 28-student class, the ratio of boys to girls is 3:4. How many girls are there in the class?

(A) 4

(B) 9

(C) 12

(D) 16

(E) 25

2.   If $f(x) = 2x^4$, then $f(-2) =$

(A) −256

(B) −32

(C) 0

(D) 32

(E) 256

Go on to next page

3. In a drawer are 7 pairs of white socks, 9 pairs of black socks, and 6 pairs of brown socks. Getting dressed in a hurry, Josh pulls out a pair at a time and tosses them on the floor if they are not the color he wants. Looking for a brown pair, Josh pulls out and discards a white pair, a black pair, a black pair, and a white pair. What is the probability that on his next reach into the drawer he will pull out a brown pair of socks?

   (A) ⅙

   (B) $\frac{3}{11}$

   (C) $\frac{6}{7}$

   (D) $\frac{7}{18}$

   (E) $\frac{9}{22}$

4. A bicycle has a front wheel radius of 18 inches. If the bicycle wheel travels 50 revolutions, approximately how many feet has the bicycle rolled?

   (A) 2,827

   (B) 471

   (C) 353

   (D) 236

   (E) 235

5. Evaluate $(4^0 + 64\frac{1}{2})^{-2}$

   (A) −81

   (B) $\frac{1}{81}$

   (C) ⅙

   (D) 3

   (E) 6

6. The ratio of Dora's money to Lisa's money is 7:5. If Dora has $24 more than Lisa, how much does Dora have?

   (A) $10

   (B) $14

   (C) $60

   (D) $84

   (E) $144

7. In a triangle, the second side is 3 cm longer than the first side. The length of the third side is 5 cm less than twice the length of the first side. If the perimeter is 34 cm, find the length, in cm, of the *longest* side.

   (A) 3

   (B) 8

   (C) 9

   (D) 12

   (E) 13

8. On a number line, point A is at −4, and point B is at 8. What point is ¼ of the way from A to B?

   (A) −2

   (B) −1

   (C) 0

   (D) 1

   (E) 2

Go on to next page ⟹

9. If $2y - c = 3c$, then $y =$

   (A) ⅔

   (B) c

   (C) ⅗

   (D) $2c$

   (E) $3c$

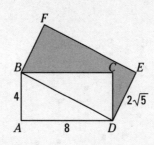

12. Given that ABCD and BDEF are rectangles, find the shaded area in this diagram.

    (A) 24

    (B) $16\sqrt{5}$

    (C) 20

    (D) $8\sqrt{5}$

    (E) 16

10. If $\dfrac{x-1}{x-2} = \dfrac{x+7}{x+2}$, then x equals:

    (A) 1

    (B) 2

    (C) 3

    (D) 4

    (E) 5

13. The volume of a gas, V, in cubic centimeters (cc), is directly proportional to its temperature, T, in Kelvins (K). If a gas has a volume of 31.5 cc at 210 K, then its volume at 300 K would be:

    (A) 121.5 cc

    (B) 49 cc

    (C) 45 cc

    (D) 22.05 cc

    (E) 0.805 cc

11. Let &x be defined as $x + 3$ if x is prime, and as $2x$ if x is composite. Which of the following would produce a result of 18?

    I. &15

    II. &9

    III. &36

    (A) I only

    (B) II only

    (C) III only

    (D) both I and II

    (E) both II and III

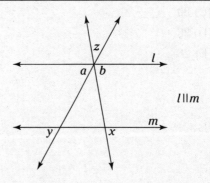

14. In this diagram, $x = 70°$, $y = 30°$. The sum $a + b + z$ equals:

    (A) 40°

    (B) 90°

    (C) 100°

    (D) 120°

    (E) 180°

Go on to next page

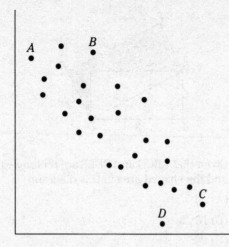

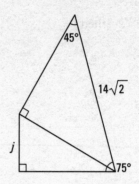

15.   If a line of best fit were drawn for this scatterplot, the line would come *closest* to which pair of points?

(A) A and B

(B) A and C

(C) A and D

(D) B and C

(E) C and D

16.   In a sequence of evenly-spaced numbers, the first term is 7, and the 20th term is 159. The fourth term of the sequence would be:

(A) 32

(B) 31

(C) 30

(D) 29

(E) 28

17.   In this diagram, the measure of side *j* is:

(A) 7

(B) $7\sqrt{2}$

(C) $7\sqrt{3}$

(D) 14

(E) $14\sqrt{2}$

18.   Jan writes down a phone number on a piece of paper. Unfortunately, when she pulls the paper out of her pocket, she discovers that the last two numbers have been smudged. She is certain that at least one of the missing numbers was a "7." How many possibilities are there for the missing two numbers?

(A) 100

(B) 77

(C) 20

(D) 19

(E) 10

Go on to next page

19. In a class of 100 students, 65 take Spanish, 32 take art, and 14 take both Spanish and art. How many students do not take either Spanish or art?

    (A) 3

    (B) 11

    (C) 17

    (D) 18

    (E) 35

20. A square is changed into a rectangle by adding 3 meters to one side and subtracting 2 meters from the other side. The new rectangle has an area of 50 square meters. Find the original length of a side of the square.

    (A) 5 m

    (B) 6 m

    (C) 7 m

    (D) 8 m

    (E) 9 m

21. Max has 3 hours to study for his tests the next day. He decides to spend k percent of this time studying for math. Which of the following represents the number of *minutes* he will spend studying for math?

    (A) $\frac{k}{300}$

    (B) $\frac{3k}{100}$

    (C) $\frac{100k}{180}$

    (D) $\frac{180k}{100}$

    (E) $\frac{18000}{k}$

22. In a set of four positive whole numbers, the mode is 90 and the mean is 80. Which of the following statements is *false*?

    (A) The number 90 must appear two or three times in the set.

    (B) The number 140 cannot appear in the set.

    (C) The number 80 must appear exactly once in the set.

    (D) The four numbers must have a sum of 320.

    (E) The median cannot be greater than 90.

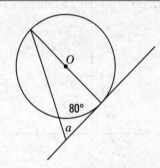

23. In this diagram, where O is the center of the circle, the angle marked a measures:

    (A) 20°

    (B) 40°

    (C) 45°

    (D) 50°

    (E) 80°

24. If $a - b = 8$ and $ab = 10$, then $a^2 + b^2 =$

    (A) 44

    (B) 54

    (C) 64

    (D) 74

    (E) 84

Go on to next page

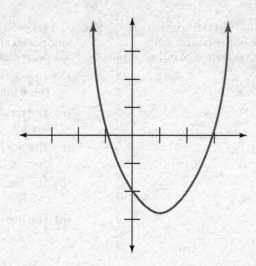

25.   This graph represents a function, *f*(*x*). Which of the following graphs could represent *f*(*x* + 4)?

A

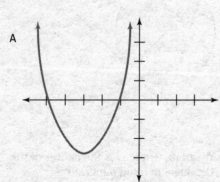

B

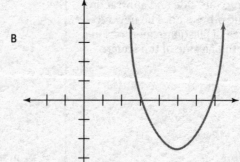

C

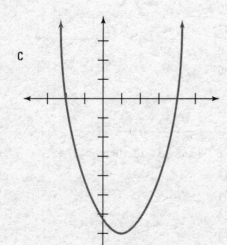

D

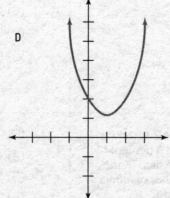

E

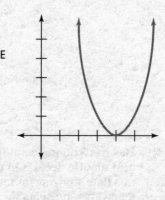

STOP   You may check your work on this section only.
Do not go back to any previous section.

Section 5

Critical Reading

Time: 25 minutes

24 questions

Directions for questions 1–15: Base your answers on information in either or both of these passages. You may also answer questions on what is implied in the passages or about the relationship between the two passages. Darken the appropriate oval on your answer sheet.

Passages I and II are drawn from *Into the House of Ancestors* by Karl Maler (Wiley, 1998).

Passage 1

Line   Joram Mariga never left home without his pocket knife. When he was not working as a government agricultural worker, he could usually be found whittling away on some piece of scrap-

(05) wood that he picked up while riding his motorcycle along the myriad trails that wind through the majestic mountains of eastern Zimbabwe. He was always cutting, chipping, slicing, and shaping wood, something he and his brothers had been

(10) doing since they were teenagers. Enjoyment of crafts, of working with the hands, ran in the family. His mother Edina was particularly gifted at pottery, but it was Mariga's father Sindoga who stirred their interest in carving. "We grew up

(15) loving to carve, and I did it just to please myself," Mariga says. He taught his two best friends, Robert and Titus, to carve too.

    Mariga was a worker for the Ministry of Agriculture in the mid-1950s in Nyanga, a picturesque

(20) region of stunning peaks, forests, lakes, and waterfalls straddling the border with Mozambique, to help small farmers improve their crop production. As he journeyed up and down the hills on his government-issued BSA 350cc motorcycle, it

(25) became apparent that what the area and its farmers needed most were roads. "There were only tracks and only a few big enough to be called roads. It was difficult for the small farmers to bring their produce to the markets." Mariga took

(30) charge of a work gang of forty men and two tractors to clear a road to the district administrator's

office. "The tractors just plowed along, pushing all the stones to one side. I never thought anything about them. They were rocks."

    Then, one cool sunny day in August 1958, at (35) the base of a rocky outcrop known as a *kopje,* the grader blades chipped off a piece of a remarkable stone that caught Mariga's eye. "I admired the color of that small stone. It was greenish, and when you picked it up, you could feel that it was (40) slippery, like soap. I didn't know what it was, and I had never seen anything like it. If you looked through it facing the rays of the sun, it was a little bit translucent." Only later did he learn that he had found a piece of soapstone. Mariga continued (45) with the job of clearing the road that day, but he could not stop fiddling with the stone. As usual, when it was time for a break, out came his knife. "I decided, since it is so slippery, why can't I use my pocket knife on it? And when I did, the knife (50) was able to cut it easily.

    From that moment on, Mariga, at the age of 31, became obsessed with stone carving, a fixation that over the next four decades would spawn one of the most exciting movements in modern (55) African art. It took years and almost a divine amount of luck and coincidence to develop, but when it did, the sculpture from Zimbabwe would be exhibited all over the world and would fetch tens of thousands of dollars apiece on the inter- (60) national market. The sculptors themselves were transformed from largely illiterate farmers and unemployed workers to ambassadors for their country and their continent.

Passage II

    At the end of the twentieth century, educa- (65) tion stands at a crossroads in Africa. While weakening central governments, ever-tightening budgets, and armed conflict have undermined the ambitious plans for training drawn up after independence, everyone agrees that higher edu- (70) cational standards are a prerequisite to economic growth. All the reform programs and much-sought-after foreign investment will make little difference unless Africa's citizens are armed with

Go on to next page

(75) the necessary intellectual firepower to capitalize on them. Building modern economies and establishing democratic political systems without an educated citizenry would be comparable to trying to run a computer without software. Investment (80) in primary education, says the World Bank, is the single biggest factor that sets off the phenomenal growth of the Southeast Asian "tiger" economies from those of the rest of the Third World. John Nkoma, a professor of physics and dean of the (85) Faculty of Science at the University of Botswana, believes homegrown technology must play a role: "Science has been a potent force in driving the technological development of the industrialized countries of Asia. Clearly Africa and the (90) Third World in general cannot be an exception." Unfortunately, right now Africa's drive for knowledge is in reverse gear. Spending on research and development is less than half of 1 percent of the world's total. Roughly half of all grade-school-age (95) children are not enrolled. If attendance continues to fall at the current rate, 59 million African children will be out of school by the year 2000. There is only one region in the world where the percentage of children who do not attend school is (100) rising. It is Africa.

By all accounts, something must be done quickly to reverse the trend. Part of the answer lies in governments allocating more funds to education, spending those resources more efficiently, (105) and placing greater emphasis on educating young girls, who right now are twice as likely to drop out of school as boys. State intervention alone is not enough, especially where governments increasingly lack the economic and political power to (110) effect change.

1. What is the primary purpose of the first paragraph (lines 1–17) of passage I?

(A) to explain the importance of artistic expression

(B) to orient the reader to conditions in Africa

(C) to introduce Joram Mariga and his family and friends

(D) to show the geographical setting for the events in the passage

(E) to explain the basis of Mariga's discovery

2. Mariga's journeys into the mountains (lines 23–29)

(A) was made more difficult by road crews

(B) became impossible because of poor road conditions

(C) enabled him to understand the difficulties farmers faced getting their crops to market

(D) allowed him to carve

(E) was intended to explore local artwork

3. All of the following words may describe the soapstone that Mariga discovered *except*

(A) slick

(B) smooth

(C) green

(D) opaque

(E) soft

4. The passage implies but does not state that Joram Mariga

(A) could not fully appreciate the potential marketing value of soapstone carvings

(B) had no artistic training

(C) gave up his government job in order to concentrate on art

(D) taught many Africans to carve soapstone

(E) was not interested in his job with the Ministry of Agriculture

5. The "largely illiterate farmers and unemployed workers" became "ambassadors for their country and their continent" (lines 62–64) because

(A) the Ministry of Agriculture deals with many foreign countries

(B) the government employed them

(C) their carvings show the creativity and artistry of Africans to all who bought them

(D) they traveled to other countries to sell their artwork

(E) they easily moved their product to market once the roads were improved

Go on to next page ⇨

6. Education in Africa "stands at a crossroads" (lines 65–66) because

   (A) Africans must choose between technology and traditional education.

   (B) The plans for educational advancement have been undermined by political and economic problems.

   (C) Africans must develop strong governments before educational improvements can be made.

   (D) Without changes, education may deteriorate so completely that reform becomes impossible.

   (E) Governments do not want to educate children.

7. The comparison between an uneducated citizenry in a democracy to "a computer without software" (line 79)

   (A) shows that education is necessary for sound political choices

   (B) highlights the importance of technology

   (C) illustrates that education is a political act

   (D) reveals the way in which education is influenced by politics

   (E) emphasizes that citizens must vote in order for democracy to work

8. In passage II the author cites all of the following factors as important to African development *except*

   (A) technology

   (B) foreign investment

   (C) education

   (D) respect for traditional ways

   (E) women's rights

9. In comparison to the economies of Southeast Asia (line 82), Africa

   (A) has more foreign aid

   (B) invests less in technology

   (C) invests more money in university education

   (D) invests more money in primary education

   (E) invests less money in primary education

10. John Nkomas (lines 84–90) is quoted because

    (A) he challenges the importance of education

    (B) "homegrown" technology cannot exist without good education

    (C) he admires the economies of Asia

    (D) he favors economic growth

    (E) physics is a subject taught in schools

11. In the context of passage II, which best describes the meaning of "tiger" (line 82)?

    (A) endangered

    (B) predatory

    (C) powerful

    (D) dangerous

    (E) fierce

12. Which statement would the author be most likely to add to passage II?

    (A) Foreign nations should establish schools in Africa.

    (B) Communities and private individuals must support education.

    (C) Educational reform is dependent upon good government policy.

    (D) Africa should hire teachers from Southeast Asia.

    (E) Taxes to support education must be increased.

13. Between passage I and passage II, the author's attitude toward Africa changes

    (A) from optimism about African development to apathy

    (B) from faith in the power of individuals to calls for government and community action

    (C) from admiration for traditional crafts to skepticism about their market potential

    (D) from respect for government employees to doubts about their dedication

    (E) by becoming more feminist

Go on to next page ⇒

14. Both passages are primarily concerned with
    (A) the hardships of African life
    (B) the future of Africa
    (C) the role of government in Africa
    (D) the link between politics and social welfare
    (E) the development of the African economy

15. Which statement best compares the two passages?
    (A) Passage II is more general than passage I.
    (B) Passage I is less descriptive than passage II.
    (C) Passage I takes a less personal viewpoint than passage II.
    (D) Passage II illustrates the points made in passage I.
    (E) Both passages use narrative to make a point.

Directions for questions 16–24: Select the answer that best fits the meaning of the sentence and darken the corresponding oval on the answer sheet.

Example: Winning the prize, Harold was _____ in praising his competitors.

(A) negligent

(B) obstinate

(C) ridiculous

(D) gracious

(E) foolish

The answer is (D). Ⓐ Ⓑ Ⓒ ● Ⓔ

---

16. Elwood was admired by the citizens of the town who knew him, yet _____ by strangers who had merely read of his exploits in the paper.
    (A) ignored
    (B) revered
    (C) esteemed
    (D) condemned
    (E) adored

17. The ambassadors assumed an early end to hostilities, despite _____ from rebel groups.
    (A) resistance
    (B) surrender
    (C) withdrawal
    (D) compromise
    (E) interrogation

18. The mayor's statement that funds for police and firefighters should be _____ was belied by her insistence that taxes be _____.
    (A) enhanced . . . raised
    (B) decreased . . . lowered
    (C) increased . . . slashed
    (D) cut . . . frozen
    (E) expanded . . . suspended

19. The Supreme Court's decision in *Brown vs. Board of Education* _____ legalized segregation, but more than a half century later, separate schools for black and white children _____.
    (A) sanctioned . . . flourish
    (B) outlawed . . . persist
    (C) permitted . . . lag
    (D) terminated . . . intimidate
    (E) promoted . . . exist

20. Jane Austen wrote many of her novels in a small parlor in the family home in Chawton, relying on a squeaky door to _____ her when visitors approached so that she could hide her manuscript and thus _____ her work.
    (A) entertain . . . publicize
    (B) warn . . . reveal
    (C) surprise . . . disguise
    (D) rationalize . . . preserve
    (E) alert . . . conceal

Go on to next page

21. Although the opposing factions were not able to achieve _____, they left the jury room in _____.

    (A) unity . . . discord

    (B) agreement . . . anger

    (C) leniency . . . silence

    (D) consensus . . . amity

    (E) deliberations . . . disarray

22. After studying cancer for many decades, scientists have come to the conclusion that cancer is not one disease but rather a(n) _____ of conditions with _____ symptoms, ranging from solid tumors to an unchecked proliferation of white blood cells.

    (A) predominance . . . equal

    (B) variety . . . opposing

    (C) array . . . identical

    (D) cluster . . . diverse

    (E) catalog . . . congruent

23. When she won the lottery, her friends expected Eleanor to be _____, but she was surprisingly _____.

    (A) jovial . . . affable

    (B) elated . . . mirthful

    (C) depressed . . . morose

    (D) intimidated . . . confident

    (E) acrimonious . . . cheerful

24. The display of religious artifacts in that store is quite _____, including pieces from many periods and nations.

    (A) ubiquitous

    (B) eclectic

    (C) international

    (D) parochial

    (E) ecclesiastical

STOP You may check your work on this section only.
Do not go back to any previous section.

Section 6

Mathematics

Time: 25 minutes

20 questions

Notes:

☞ You may use a calculator.

☞ All numbers used in this exam are real numbers.

☞ All figures lie in a plane.

☞ All figures may be assumed to be to scale unless the problem specifically indicates otherwise.

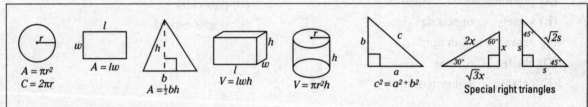

$A = \pi r^2$
$C = 2\pi r$

$A = lw$

$A = \frac{1}{2}bh$

$V = lwh$

$V = \pi r^2 h$

$c^2 = a^2 + b^2$

Special right triangles

There are 360 degrees of arc in a circle.

There are 180 degrees in a straight line.

There are 180 degrees in the sum of the interior angles of a triangle.

Directions for questions 1–10: Choose the best answer and darken the corresponding oval on the answer sheet.

1. If the distance from Springfield to Watertown is 13 miles, and the distance from Watertown to Pleasantville is 24 miles, then the distance from Pleasantville to Springfield in miles could *not* be:

    (A) 10

    (B) 11

    (C) 13

    (D) 24

    (E) 36

2. The number n satisfies the following properties:

    It has three digits.

    Its units digit is the sum of its tens digit and its hundreds digit.

    It is a perfect square.

    Which number could be n?

    (A) 156

    (B) 400

    (C) 484

    (D) 516

    (E) 729

Go on to next page

3. In a certain game, there are only two ways to score points; one way is worth 3 points, and the other is worth 5 points. If Tamsin's total score is 121, which of the following could be the number of 3-point scores that Tamsin had?

 (A) 20

 (B) 21

 (C) 22

 (D) 23

 (E) 24

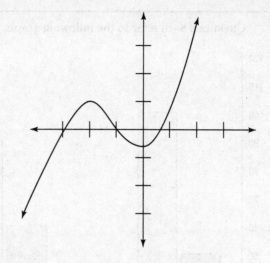

4. If the square of x is twelve less than the product of x and 5, which of the following expressions could be used to solve for x?

 (A) $2x = 12 - 5x$

 (B) $x^2 = 12 - 5x$

 (C) $x^2 = 5x - 12$

 (D) $2x = 5x - 12$

 (E) $x^2 = (x + 5) - 12$

6. If this graph represents $f(x)$, then the number of solutions to the equation $f(x) = 1$ is:

 (A) zero

 (B) one

 (C) two

 (D) three

 (E) It cannot be determined from the information given.

5. A batch of mixed nuts was created by adding 5 pounds of peanuts, costing $5.50 per pound, to 2 pounds of cashews, costing $12.50 per pound. What would be the cost, per pound, of the resulting mixture?

 (A) $7.35

 (B) $7.50

 (C) $9.00

 (D) $10.50

 (E) $12.00

7. The solution set to the equation $|3x - 1| = 7$ is:

 (A) {2}

 (B) {2⅔}

 (C) {-2}

 (D) {-2,2⅔}

 (E) {-2,2}

Go on to next page

Questions 8–10 refer to the following graph:

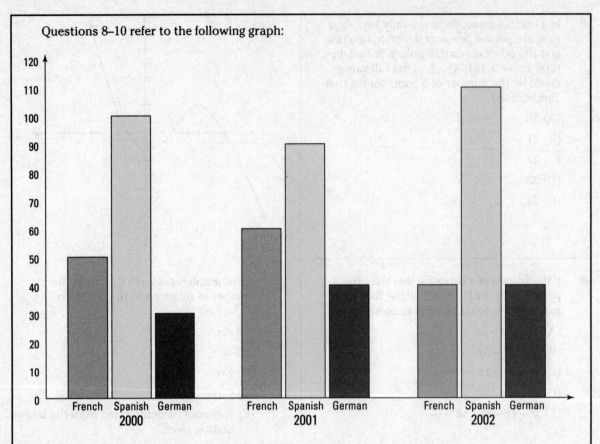

Each ninth grader at Springfied High School must study one foreign language: French, Spanish, or German. This graph represents the number of ninth graders enrolled in each language over a three-year period.

8. In which year or years was the ninth grade class the largest?

(A) 2000 only

(B) 2001 only

(C) 2002 only

(D) 2000 and 2001

(E) 2001 and 2002

9. In 2001, roughly what percent of students took French?

(A) 32%

(B) 40%

(C) 48%

(D) 60%

(E) 67%

10. What was the median number of students enrolled in German over the three-year period?

(A) 40

(B) 36⅔

(C) 35

(D) 33⅓

(E) 30

Go on to next page

Directions for student-produced responses: Questions 11–20 require you to solve the problem and then blacken the oval corresponding to the answer, as shown in the following example. Note the fraction line and the decimal points.

Answer: $7/2$ Answer: 3.25   Answer: 853

Write your answer in the box. You may start your answer in any column.

Although you do not have to write the solutions in the boxes, you do have to blacken the corresponding ovals. You should fill in the boxes to avoid confusion. Only the blackened ovals will be scored. The numbers in the boxes will not be read.

There are no negative answers.

Mixed numbers, such as 3½, may be gridded in as a decimal (3.5) or as a fraction (⅞). Do not grid in 3½; it will be read as ³¹⁄₂.

Grid in a decimal as far as possible. Do not round it.

A question may have more than one answer. Grid in one answer only.

---

11. Lauren took seven exams. Her scores on the first six are 91, 89, 85, 92, 90, and 87. If her average (arithmetic mean) on all *seven* exams is 90, what did she get on the seventh exam?

13. In a school survey, 40% of all students chose history as their favorite subject; 25% chose English; and 14 chose some other subject as their favorite. How many students were surveyed?

12. The number *n* is greater than one. When *n* is divided by 2, 3, 4, 5, or 6, it leaves a remainder of one. What is the smallest possible value for *n*?

14. The ratio of a rectangle's length to its width is 2:5. If its perimeter is 84 feet, find its length, in feet.

Go on to next page

15. Darren receives $9 an hour for his after-school job, but gets paid 1½ times this salary for each hour he works on a weekend. If he worked 18 hours one week and received $189, how many of these hours did he work on weekends?

18. Renting a private party room in a restaurant can be modeled as a linear function. If the cost of a party of 8 is $270, and the cost of a party of 10 is $320, find the cost, in dollars, of a party of 18.

16. Find the value of x that satisfies
$\sqrt{4x-8} + 1 = 7$

19. If $p > 0$, and the distance between the points $(4, -1)$ and $(-2, p)$ is 10, find p.

17. For all numbers p and q, where $p \neq 4$, let $p\backslash\backslash q$ be defined as $\dfrac{pq}{p-4}$. For what value of p does $p\backslash\backslash 7 = 21$?

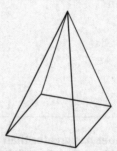

20. The pyramid above has a square base of length 10 cm and a height of 12 cm. Determine the total surface area of all five faces, in square cm.

STOP   You may check your work on this section only. Do not go back to any previous section.

Section 7

Critical Reading

Time: 20 minutes

15 questions

Directions for questions 1–4: Choose the best answer from information supplied or implied by the passages and darken the corresponding oval on the answer sheet.

Passage I is drawn from Mary Shelley's famous novel, *Frankenstein*. In this excerpt the narrator describes his scientific studies. Passage II comes from *Basic Statistics* by Olive Jean Dunn (Wiley, 1964, 1977) and discusses the role of statistics in medical research.

Passage I

Line (01)   Two years passed in this manner, during which I paid no visit to Geneva, but was engaged, heart and soul, in the pursuit of some discoveries which I hoped to make. None but those who

(05) have experienced them can conceive of the enticements of science. In other studies you go as far as others have gone before you, and there is nothing more to know; but in a scientific pursuit there is continual food for discovery and

(10) wonder. A mind of moderate capacity which closely pursues one study must infallibly arrive at great proficiency in that study; and I, who continually sought the attainment of one object of pursuit and was solely wrapped up in this,

(15) improved so rapidly that at the end of two years I made some discoveries in the improvement of some chemical instruments, which procured me great esteem and admiration at the university.

Passage II

(19)   The use of numerical methods in the field

(20) of medical research creates a problem for the research worker, whose training and interests are often quite nonmathematical. Some look back with longing to the good old days of medical research, when biostatistics was unheard of

(25) and when statistics seemed to have no role to play. The number of research workers who use numerical methods is increasing, however, as is the number of articles in medical journals that involve statistics. Thus the research worker must make some kind of adjustment to the (30) newer ways in research.

1. In passage I, "food" (line 9) can best be defined as

   (A) thirst
   (B) hunger
   (C) recipe
   (D) fuel
   (E) nutrition

2. In passage II, the author's attitude toward biostatistics may be characterized as

   (A) critical
   (B) nostalgic
   (C) fearful
   (D) favorable
   (E) adverse

3. The author of passage II would agree with which of the following statements?

   (A) Medicine in times past was more technological than statistical.
   (B) Medical researchers should take a course in statistics.
   (C) Mathematics has no place in medical training.
   (D) The inclusion of statistics makes publication of medical research less likely.
   (E) Old-fashioned doctors were better equipped to treat patients.

Go on to next page

4. In contrast to the author of passage II, the narrator in passage I

   (A) gives credit to the role of passion in science

   (B) places more emphasis on literature

   (C) is uninterested in mathematics

   (D) publishes in many medical journals

   (E) does not mention research in the context of education

Directions for questions 5–16: Read the following passage. Answer these questions based on the passage and darken the appropriate oval on your answer sheet.

This passage is excerpted from Jane Austen's novel, *Northanger Abbey*. **Note:** A "living" is an appointment to the post of minister in a particular area. A "living" carries a salary.

Line   No one who had ever seen Catherine Morland in her infancy would have supposed her born to be a heroine. Her situation in life, the character of her father and mother, her own person and dispo-
(05) sition, were all equally against her. Her father was a clergyman, without being neglected, or poor, and a very respectable man, though his name was Richard — and he had never been handsome. He had a considerable independence besides
(10) two good livings — and he was not in the least addicted to locking up his daughters. Her mother was a woman of useful plain sense, with a good temper, and, what is more remarkable, with a good constitution. She had three sons before
(15) Catherine was born; and instead of dying in bringing the latter into the world, as anybody might expect, she still lived on — lived to have six children more — to see them growing up around her, and to enjoy excellent health herself. A family of
(20) ten children will be always called a fine family, where there are heads and arms and legs enough for the number; but the Morlands had little other right to the word, for they were in general very plain, and Catherine, for many years of her life,
(25) as plain as any. She had a thin awkward figure, a sallow skin without colour, dark lank hair, and strong features — so much for her person; and not less unpropitious for heroism seemed her mind. She was fond of all boy's plays, and greatly
(30) preferred cricket not merely to dolls, but to the more heroic enjoyments of infancy, nursing a dormouse, feeding a canary-bird, or watering a

rose-bush. Indeed she had no taste for a garden; and if she gathered flowers at all, it was chiefly for the pleasure of mischief — at least so it was (35) conjectured from her always preferring those which she was forbidden to take. Such were her propensities — her abilities were quite as extraordinary.
    She never could learn or understand any- (40) thing before she was taught; and sometimes not even then, for she was often inattentive, and occasionally stupid. Her mother was three months in teaching her only to repeat the "Beggar's Petition"; and after all, her next sister, (45) Sally, could say it better than she did. Not that Catherine was always stupid — by no means; she learnt the fable of "The Hare and Many Friends" as quickly as any girl in England. Her mother wished her to learn music; and Catherine was (50) sure she should like it, for she was very fond of tinkling the keys of the old forlorn spinner; so, at eight years old she began. She learnt a year, and could not bear it; and Mrs. Morland, who did not insist on her daughters being accomplished (55) in spite of incapacity or distaste, allowed her to leave off. The day which dismissed the music-master was one of the happiest of Catherine's life. Her taste for drawing was not superior; though whenever she could obtain the outside of a letter (60) from her mother or seize upon any other odd piece of paper, she did what she could in that way, by drawing houses and trees, hens and chickens, all very much like one another. Writing and accounts she was taught by her father; (65) French by her mother: her proficiency in either was not remarkable, and she shirked her lessons in both whenever she could. What a strange, unaccountable character! — for with all these symptoms of profligacy at ten years old, she had (70) neither a bad heart nor a bad temper, was seldom stubborn, scarcely ever quarrelsome, and very kind to the little ones, with few interruptions of tyranny; she was moreover noisy and wild, hated confinement and cleanliness, and loved nothing (75) so well in the world as rolling down the green slope at the back of the house.
    Such was Catherine Morland at ten. At fifteen, appearances were mending; she began to curl her hair and long for balls; her complexion (80) improved, her features were softened by plumpness and colour, her eyes gained more animation, and her figure more consequence. Her love of dirt gave way to an inclination for finery, and she grew clean as she grew smart; she had now the (85) pleasure of sometimes hearing her father and mother remark on her personal improvement.

Go on to next page ⮕

5   According to paragraph 1 (lines 1–39) a heroine ordinarily

(A) takes part in normal family life

(B) comes from a troubled family

(C) is wealthy

(D) has two surviving parents

(E) must not suffer

6. What does the author imply about men named Richard (line 8)?

(A) they are usually not respectable

(B) they are inclined to spiritual pursuits

(C) they are seldom rich

(D) they suffer from neglect

(E) they can be trusted completely

7. What, according to the passage, is the most surprising fact about Mrs. Morland?

(A) she loves her daughter

(B) she is not particularly good looking

(C) her lack of sense

(D) her tendency to nervousness

(E) her good health

8. What phrase best defines "good constitution" (line 14)?

(A) intelligence

(B) sensible nature

(C) sturdy body

(D) respect for the law

(E) robust health

9. All of the following describe the young Catherine Morland *except*

(A) mischievous

(B) thin

(C) athletic

(D) plain

(E) studious

10. Based on the passage, it is likely that "The Hare and Many Friends," compared to the "Beggar's Petition," (lines 45–49)

(A) contains more difficult language

(B) was required by Mrs. Morland

(C) is longer

(D) is easier to memorize

(E) holds less interest for Catherine

11. What best defines "bear" (line 54) in the context of this passage?

(A) stand

(B) learn

(C) continue

(D) excel

(E) remove

12. Catherine's reaction to the dismissal of the music master (line 58) is probably

(A) the opposite of what her mother expected

(B) literally true

(C) exaggerated by the author for comic effect

(D) typical of a girl of her time

(E) unexpected by all

13. One can infer from the passage that which of the following subjects were part of the normal instruction of a young girl of Catherine's time?

(A) sports

(B) languages

(C) geography

(D) dancing

(E) sculpture

14. A good title for this selection might be

(A) English Families

(B) Girls' Education

(C) The Morland Family

(D) A Surprising Heroine

(E) Catherine Morland

Go on to next page

15. The tone of the passage is best described as

    (A) critical
    (B) approving
    (C) dispassionate
    (D) mocking
    (E) descriptive

STOP You may check your work on this section only. Do not go back to any previous section.

Section 8

Mathematics

Time: 15 minutes

15 questions

Notes:

✔ You may use a calculator.

✔ All numbers used in this exam are real numbers.

✔ All figures lie in a plane.

✔ All figures may be assumed to be to scale unless the problem specifically indicates otherwise.

$A = \pi r^2$
$C = 2\pi r$

$A = lw$

$A = \frac{1}{2}bh$

$V = lwh$

$V = \pi r^2 h$

$c^2 = a^2 + b^2$

Special right triangles

There are 360 degrees of arc in a circle.

There are 180 degrees in a straight line.

There are 180 degrees in the sum of the interior angles of a triangle.

Directions: Choose the best answer and darken the corresponding oval on the answer sheet.

1. If an eight-slice pizza has a diameter of 12 inches, what is the area of one slice, in square inches?

    (A) 2.25π

    (B) 4.5π

    (C) 9π

    (D) 18π

    (E) 36π

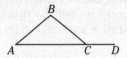

2. In this drawing, where B is an obtuse angle, which statement is *not* true?

    (A) AB + BC < AC

    (B) AC > BC

    (C) m∠BCD + m∠BCA = 180

    (D) m∠A + m∠B = m∠BCD

    (E) m∠A + m∠BCA < 90

Go on to next page

3. A certain radioactive element has a half-life of 20 years. Thus, a sample of 100 grams deposited in 1980 would have decayed to 50 grams by 2000 and to 25 grams by 2020. How much of this sample would remain in 2100?

   (A) 0 grams

   (B) 1¹⁵/₁₆ grams

   (C) 2½ grams

   (D) 3⅛ grams

   (E) 5 grams

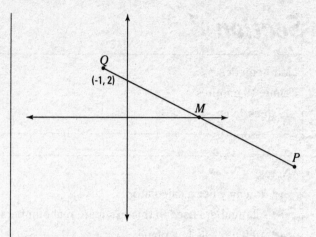

6. In this figure, the slope of line *m* is -⅓, and M is the midpoint of the line PQ. What are the coordinates of point P?

   (A) (8, –1)

   (B) (9, –1)

   (C) (10, –2)

   (D) (11, –2)

   (E) (12, –2)

4. Set *S* contains the numbers 20 to 50, inclusive. If a number is chosen at random from *S*, what is the probability that this number's second digit is greater than its first digit?

   (A) ¹⁵/₃₀

   (B) ¹⁸/₃₀

   (C) ¹⁸/₃₁

   (D) ¹⁹/₃₁

   (E) ²²/₃₁

5. If *a* > 0, which of the following statements must be true?

   (A) $a^2 > a$

   (B) $a > \frac{1}{a}$

   (C) $\sqrt{a} < a$

   (D) $2a > a$

   (E) $\frac{1}{a} < 1$

7. If *p* and *q* are positive integers, then $(5^{-p})(5^{q+1})^p$ is equivalent to:

   (A) 5

   (B) 5^{pq+p}

   (C) 5^{pq}

   (D) 5^{pq-p}

   (E) 5^{q+1}

8. The number *g* is divisible by 3, but not by 9. Which of the following is a possible remainder when 7g is divided by 9?

   (A) 0

   (B) 2

   (C) 4

   (D) 6

   (E) 8

Go on to next page

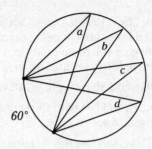

9. In this "magic square", each number from 1 to 9 will appear once, with the result that each row, column, and diagonal has the same sum. What number must appear in the space marked *n*?

    (A) 3

    (B) 4

    (C) 5

    (D) 6

    (E) 7

12. In this figure, find the sum of the degree measures of angles $a + b + c + d$.

    (A) 60

    (B) 90

    (C) 120

    (D) 180

    (E) 240

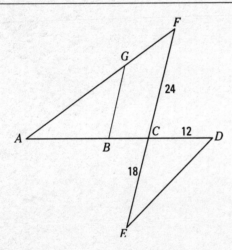

13. A number *n* is defined as a "tweener" if both $n - 1$ and $n + 1$ are prime. Which of the following numbers is a tweener?

    (A) 2

    (B) 8

    (C) 30

    (D) 36

    (E) 48

10. In this diagram, $AF \parallel ED, GB \parallel EF$, and AG = GF. The length of AB is (figure is not drawn to scale):

    (A) 24

    (B) 18

    (C) 16

    (D) 12

    (E) 8

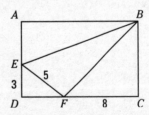

14. Given that ABCD is a rectangle, and triangle BCF is isosceles, find the length of the line segment BE in this diagram.

    (A) $\sqrt{89}$

    (B) $8\sqrt{2}$

    (C) 12

    (D) $\sqrt{153}$

    (E) 13

11. If $2a + 3b = 17$ and $2a + b = 3$, then $a + b =$

    (A) 1

    (B) 5

    (C) 7

    (D) 7.5

    (E) 10

Go on to next page ➡

15. Melvin, Chris, Enoch, Dave, Carey, Mike, Dan, and Peter are choosing dorm rooms for college. Each room holds four people. They have the following wishes:

    (i) Mike and Melvin refuse to live together.

    (ii) Enoch will live with Chris or Carey (or possibly both).

    (iii) If Dave and Dan live together, Peter will live with them.

    When rooms are chosen, Melvin and Carey live together. Which of the following pieces of information would *not* be sufficient to allow you to determine everyone's location?

    (A) Dave and Dan live together.

    (B) Chris lives with Melvin.

    (C) Peter lives with Carey, but Dan does not.

    (D) Enoch lives with Mike.

    (E) Dan lives with Chris, but Peter does not.

STOP

You may check your work on this section only.
Do not go back to any previous section.

Answer Key for Practice Exam 1

Section 1, the essay, may be scored according to the scoring guidelines in Chapter 25.

Answers for Sections 2 – 8 of Practice Test One						
Section 2	*Section 3*	*Section 4*	*Section 5*	*Section 6*	*Section 7*	*Section 8*
1. C	1. A	1. D	1. E	1. A	1. D	1. B
2. A	2. B	2. D	2. C	2. E	2. D	2. A
3. E	3. C	3. A	3. D	3. C	3. B	3. B
4. B	4. A	4. B	4. D	4. C	4. A	4. C
5. D	5. E	5. B	5. C	5. B	5. B	5. D
6. D	6. B	6. D	6. D	6. C	6. A	6. D
7. C	7. A	7. E	7. A	7. D	7. E	7. C
8. B	8. A	8. B	8. D	8. E	8. E	8. D
9. A	9. A	9. D	9. E	9. A	9. E	9. D
10. B	10. A	10. C	10. B	10. A	10. D	10. E
11. C	11. C	11. B	11. C	11. 96	11. A	11. B
12. C	12. C	12. A	12. B	12. 61	12. C	12. C
13. C	13. B	13. C	13. B	13. 40	13. B	13. C
14. B	14. E	14. E	14. E	14. 12	14. D	14. C
15. E	15. B	15. B	15. A	15. 6	15. D	15. D
16. C	16. D	16. B	16. D	16. 11		
17. C	17. A	17. A	17. A	17. 6		
18. D	18. B	18. D	18. C	18. 520		
19. A	19. D	19. C	19. B	19. 7		
20. B	20. D	20. C	20. E	20. 360		
21. D	21. E	21. D	21. D			
22. E	22. E	22. C	22. D			
23. C	23. B	23. D	23. D			
24. E	24. A	24. E	24. B			
25. D	25. B	25. A				
26. C						
27. E						
28. D						
29. E						
30. B						
31. E						
32. B						
33. C						
34. B						
35. D						

Scoring Your Exam

Check Chapter 23 for instructions on how to score the essay. For the multiple-choice answers, mark skipped questions with an O, correct answers with a check, and wrong answers (gasp! You had some!) with an X. Then calculate your raw scores as follows.

Scoring the Writing multiple-choice section

You probably tore out your answer sheet before taking the practice test; resist the urge to shred it before figuring out your raw score, which you can do by following these steps:

1. **Count the number of correct answers in Section 2 and place the number on line 1.**

2. **Multiply the number of wrong answers by ¼ and round to the nearest whole number. Place your answer on line 2.**

3. **Subtract line 2 from line 1 to get the raw score.**

4. **Convert the raw Writing score by using the chart in the following "Converting the raw multiple choice Writing score" section.**

Line 1 _____
Line 2 _____
Raw Writing Score _____

Converting the raw multiple-choice Writing score

The colleges will receive two writing scores for you: the essay score (2–12) and a multiple-choice score (20–80). After you figure out the raw score on the multiple-choice writing, find the converted score with the following table.

Multiple-Choice Writing Conversion Table					
Raw	**Converted**	**Raw**	**Converted**	**Raw**	**Converted**
36	80	22	54	9	35
35	80	21	52	8	34
34	78	20	50	7	33
33	76	19	47	6	32
32	74	18	45	5	30
31	72	17	44	4	28
30	70	16	43	3	27
29	68	15	42	2	25
28	66	14	40	1	24
27	64	13	39	0	23
26	62	12	38	–1	20
25	60	11	37	–2	20
24	58	10	36	below –2	20
23	56				

Scoring the Critical Reading sections

Of course you got everything right on the Critical Reading, didn't you? No? Okay then, join the human race, or at least the vast majority that makes errors on SAT reading questions. Then take a pencil and figure out your raw score, using the following method.

1. **Count the number of correct answers in Sections 3, 5, and 7 and place the number on line 1.**

2. **Multiply the number of wrong answers by ¼ and round to the nearest whole number. Place your answer on line 2.**

3. **Subtract line 2 from line 1 to get the raw score.**

4. **Convert the raw Critical Reading score by using the chart in the following "Converting the raw Critical Reading score" section.**

Line 1 _____
Line 2 _____
Raw Critical Reading Score _____

Converting the raw Critical Reading score

The raw score of the Critical Reading sections must be converted to the standard 200–800 SAT "converted" score, according to the following chart.

Critical Reading Conversion Table

Raw	Converted	Raw	Converted	Raw	Converted
64	800	41	590	18	420
63	800	40	580	17	420
62	800	39	580	16	410
61	800	38	570	15	400
60	790	37	560	14	390
59	780	36	550	13	390
58	770	35	550	12	380
57	760	34	540	11	370
56	750	33	530	10	360
55	740	32	520	9	350
54	720	31	520	8	340
53	710	30	510	7	330
52	680	29	500	6	320
51	670	28	490	5	310
50	670	27	480	4	300
49	660	26	480	3	280
48	650	25	480	2	270
47	640	24	470	1	240
46	630	23	460	0	230
45	620	22	450	–1	210
44	620	21	450	–2	200
43	610	20	440	below –2	200
42	600	19	430		

Scoring the Math sections

After the exam is over, you may be tired of numbers, but muster up the energy to tackle just a few more — the raw score and the converted math scores. First, figure out your raw score.

1. **Count the number of correct answers in Sections 4, 6, and 8 and place the number on line 1. Count both multiple choice and grid-ins for this step.**

2. **Ignore the grid-ins for this step. Multiply the number of wrong answers to everything except the grid-ins by ¼ and round to the nearest whole number. Place your answer on line 2.**

3. **Subtract line 2 from line 1 to get the raw math score.**

4. **Convert the raw score by using the chart in the following "Converting the raw Math score" section.**

Line 1 _____
Line 2 _____
Raw Math Score _____

Converting the raw Math score

One last math problem: Locate your raw math score in the following table and match it with the equivalent "converted" (standard SAT) score.

Mathematics Conversion Table

Raw	Converted	Raw	Converted	Raw	Converted
60	800	38	570	16	420
59	800	37	570	15	410
58	790	36	560	14	410
57	770	35	550	13	400
56	750	34	540	12	390
55	740	33	540	11	380
54	720	32	530	10	380
53	710	31	520	9	370
52	700	30	510	8	360
51	690	29	510	7	350
50	680	28	500	6	340
49	670	27	490	5	330
48	660	26	490	4	320
47	650	25	480	3	310
46	640	24	470	2	290
45	630	23	470	1	280
44	620	22	460	0	260
43	620	21	450	−1	250
42	610	20	450	−2	230
41	600	19	440	−3	200
40	590	18	430	below −3	200
39	580	17	430		

Chapter 23

Facing the Music: Checking Your Answers to Practice Exam 1

In This Chapter

▶ Assessing your skills

▶ Checking your work on practice exam 1

*N*o shortcuts here: Even if you answered a question correctly, still read these explanations because I tuck in some additional information that will be useful on the real SAT.

Section 1: The Essay

In 25 minutes you can't write a masterpiece about curiosity. But you should be able to make a couple of points on the subject, introducing your thoughts with a brief paragraph and coming to at least some sort of a conclusion. Here's one possible outline:

Paragraph one: State your thesis. *(Curiosity killed the cat, but it is a quality worth dying for because life without curiosity is not worth living.)* Mention the supporting points. *(Curiosity impels the great explorers. Without curiosity there would be no scientific discoveries.)*

Paragraphs two and three: Explore the supporting points, one in each paragraph. Mention a couple of explorers and their discoveries, which would be lost to humanity if not for curiosity. Then go on to talk about research scientists who are driven by the need to know. Again, use some specifics.

Paragraph four: State your conclusion. *(Curiosity drives the human race forward, but this quality is not without drawbacks. Nuclear arms, for example, would not have been developed if humans were content to stay with what was already known. Still, the rich knowledge of the universe and the benefits of modern medicine may be attributed to curiosity, so overall humanity benefits from this trait.)*

Scoring your own essay is difficult but not impossible. Give it a try. After you finish with the practice SAT and you're calm, go back over your work. Start with a perfect score of six and then measure your essay against this scoring guide:

Mechanics: If you have only a couple of grammar, spelling, and punctuation errors, give yourself full credit for this category. If you have three or four mistakes in each paragraph, deduct one point. If you find even more than three or four mistakes per paragraph, deduct two points.

Organization: I describe one logical outline earlier in this section, but many other patterns will work. Check your essay's structure. Does it proceed logically from idea, to evidence, to conclusion? If so, you're fine. If the logical thread breaks anywhere or if you skipped a step — the conclusion, perhaps — deduct one point for each deficiency.

Evidence: You need to have at least three or four details in each body paragraph or one piece of evidence that is described at length. Your body paragraphs should be heavy on specifics and light on general statements. If you find several general statements in the body of the essay, deduct a point. If you have good detail, give yourself full marks for this quality.

By the way, the SAT-devils don't care where your evidence comes from, so long as you provide support for your thesis. Essay graders are under orders not to give more credit to writers who cite history or literature instead of personal experience. So if you want to discuss, say, the time you peeked out the window and broke your nose, go for it.

Fluency: This quality is hard to describe but easy to discern. Read the essay aloud. Does the language flow freely, easily, and naturally? Could you imagine reading it in a book? Or is it choppy and disjointed? Fluid language = no deduction. Choppy or awkward = deduct a point.

After you get a score, double it. That's your essay grade. Twelve means you can go dancing; two indicates that you have some work to do. Turn to Chapter 10 for additional practice.

Section 2: Multiple-Choice Writing

1. **(C).** The key here is "everyone," a singular word that must be paired with another singular word such as "his or her" but definitely not "their," which is plural.

2. **(A).** *Costliest* compares one thing to everything else. *Costlier* compares two things.

   In general use *-er* comparisons between two things and *-est* for larger groups.

3. **(E).** No error. Did I trip you up on (D)? Perhaps the apostrophe surprised you, because apostrophes are usually associated with missing letters or with possession. But whenever you're talking about time and money, you may find an apostrophe, as in *an hour's homework* or *two weeks' pay*.

4. **(B).** Janine isn't doing two separate things — *trying* and *determining*. She will try *to determine*.

5. **(D).** If the padding *nearly prevents*, it doesn't prevent at all. If it *prevents nearly every* wound, then one or two stabs slip through. The *nearly* has to be moved.

6. **(D).** If it's *his* team, then Archie is on it, so he should do better than *anyone else* on his team.

7. **(C).** *Consequently* looks like the kind of strong word that is capable of joining two sentences, but it's actually a weakling. To join the sentences, add a semicolon before *consequently*.

8. **(B).** The *along with* is just camouflage; the real subject is *one*. The verb must match the subject, so *are* should change to *is*.

9. **(A).** *Who* is for subjects and *whom* is for objects. In this sentence, *whom* is the object of *should bill*. Think of the sentence as *he should bill whom* and the answer becomes obvious.

10. **(B).** Who didn't care — Marisa or her aunt? The word *she* must be clarified.

11. **(C).** No possessive pronoun — including *ours* — ever has an apostrophe.

12. **(C).** Playing, studying, and to audition don't match. Change to audition to *for auditioning*.

13. **(C).** (A) is no good because you have two sentences joined by a comma — a big no-no. (B) is overkill: You don't need a semicolon and a joining word *(and)*. (D) drops out because the verb tense is wrong, and (E) makes no sense.

14. **(B).** The SAT-writers are testing two different punctuation marks in this question, the apostrophe and the comma. You don't need an apostrophe because a possessive pronoun *(its)* never has one. You do need a comma because when you glue two sentences together with a joining word (in this sentence, *but*) you must place a comma before the joining word.

15. **(E).** The guides aren't objecting to *him,* just to the *trespassing.* To place the emphasis on *trespassing,* change the *him* to *his.*

16. **(C).** *Between* is a preposition and takes an object, not a subject pronoun. In nongrammar-speak, say *between you and me,* not *between you and I.*

17. **(C).** This sentence connects the present to the past. The verb *has traveled* (present perfect tense for you grammar buffs who just have to know) connects those two time periods.

18. **(D).** The rule for introductory verb forms: The next person in the sentence has to be doing the action of the verb. In this sentence, the taxi can't speed and wait at the same time, so the toddler has to be waiting. So you can rule out (A) immediately. Other choices drop away because of misplaced descriptions. (B) is out because the *hand* is waiting. (C) hits the mat because the taxi is holding hands. (E) has an unnecessary comma.

Whenever you see a sentence on the SAT beginning with a verb form, watch out! The SAT-makers love to mix up who's doing what in the sentence.

19. **(A).** The rubber bone isn't the only toy sold; it is one of a group of toys. The group of toys *are* sold, so you can rule out (C) and (D). *Which* usually comes after a comma, and *that* is used without a comma. So (B) and (E) drop away.

20. **(B).** The *reason is that* is correct, never *the reason is because.* (E) has the wrong verb tense.

21. **(D).** The missing words in this sentence are *as well as he can.* You wouldn't say *as well as him can* unless you're playing caveman (or cavewoman).

22. **(E).** *However* can't join sentences, so you need a semicolon. The comma after the *however* isn't the most important piece of punctuation you'll ever meet, but given a choice between (B) and (E), (E) is better.

23. **(C).** The subjects and verbs pair up this way: *she thought, whoever/whomever would eat.* The pronoun *whoever* is for subjects and *whomever* is for objects. In this sentence, therefore, you need *whoever.* (C) beats out (D) because of verb tense.

24. **(E).** Don't you hate verb tense? But the rule on *had* is simple: The helping verb *had* places an action further in the past than the straight, unadorned past tense. So you have a supermarket being torn down and replaced by a gas station. The supermarket is further in the past, so it gets the *had,* or more specifically, the *had been.*

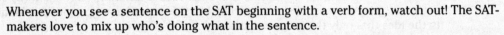

Be sure you understand the sequence of events when checking verb tense.

25. **(D).** With *neither/nor* sentences (and also *either/or*), match the verb to the closest subject. *Students* takes a plural verb, so you need *were.* The comma in (B) isn't needed, so (D) is best.

26. **(C).** The *it* of choices (A) and (E) is unnecessary, as is *the article* in (B). (Also, articles don't *say* because they can't speak.) (D) has an extra comma.

27. **(E).** All pronouns must have clear *antecedents* (an antecedent is the word the pronoun replaces), preferably in the sentence but at minimum in the immediate neighborhood. The pronoun has to replace one word, not a whole bunch of words. The problem with sentence 2 is that the pronoun *this* has no clear antecedent. (E) fixes the problem more elegantly than "this sort of thing" (as in choices [B] and [D]).

28. **(D).** The more detail the better. (D) provides the name of the network and delivers the remaining facts concisely and clearly.

29. **(E).** The specifics persuade the reader to pay attention. The reader can reason from specific to general, so providing both general statements along with specific details isn't necessary. In this essay if the writer had mentioned, say, a major murder trial of a former football star, the reader could then easily envision the circus-like atmosphere and the writer's point would be clearly understood.

30. **(B).** A useful technique in essay writing — one you may use when you write your own SAT essay — is called *concession and reply.* With this technique you anticipate the reader's objections to your argument and answer those objections in advance. The second paragraph presents some of the arguments in favor of broadcasting trials and responds to those arguments.

31. **(E).** Tucking the information about hotel stays into the first sentence is effective. Clauses beginning with *that* are seldom set off by commas.

32. **(B).** Sentence 9 in its original version is wordy and contains two grammar errors — *dramatic* instead of *dramatically* and a vague pronoun (*it*). (B) is clearer and shorter.

33. **(C).** When starting a new paragraph, look for a transition — a word or phrase that shows the reader the logical connection between the two paragraphs. (C) and (D) are the only two with transitions, but (D) introduces a completely irrelevant *you*.

34. **(B).** The pronoun *they* must be clarified because it's too vague in the original sentence (A) and in (C). (D) introduces a new tense without justification, and (E) is passive (*has been given by*), nearly always a poor construction.

35. **(D).** The writer takes pain to explain that each case is different, so (A) and (B) are non-starters. (C) is too broad. (E) is tempting, but the writer hasn't provided evidence to back up the idea that only the judge can decide.

Section 3: Critical Reading

1. **(A).** The clues are *not* and *but,* which set up a contrast. The best contrast to *intellectual* is *practical. Theoretical* and *philosophical* are in the land of ideas, as is *intellectual,* so no contrast there. *Ethical* (moral) and *strident* (loud and unpleasant, like the guy who sits next to me at Yankee games) aren't opposites of *intellectual.*

TIP

   Look for negative words that signal a change of direction for the sentence.

2. **(B).** The clue in the sentence is "than was previously thought." If you were to place your own word in the blank, you may choose "new" or "current." *Contemporary* (occurring now) is the only answer that reflects the right time. *Prior* (earlier, happening before) and *antiquated* (old-fashioned) don't make sense. *Theoretical* (not concrete, existing only in thought) just doesn't fit the context.

3. **(C).** Crack this sentence by considering the contrasting nature of the two elements — *architectural history* and *engineering.* A paper on engineering shouldn't have architectural history in it, so those references would blur or weaken the focus. This concept takes you to (C), where you find *myriad* (countless). Bingo. You're home. Were you tempted by (D)? *Impeccable* is often used with *references,* especially when I'm applying for a job, but *impeccable* means "faultless" and thus doesn't fit the meaning of the sentence.

4. **(A).** (B) may tempt you, because if grammar is everywhere, its presence — and your days of fun with nouns and verbs — may seem *inevitable* (unavoidable). But *innate* means "inborn," or "natural." If every language has grammar, it probably comes from within. The sentence makes it clear that grammar can't be *extraneous* (extra, unnecessary) or *coincidental* (just happens to be there). *Multifaceted* (many-sided, versatile) could apply to grammar, but the sentence has no hook to attach that meaning.

5. **(E).** The clue is *once prosperous.* The government is adding money to the economy (*subsidize* = pay part of the costs). Why? So the politicians can get re-elected. Oops. That's the answer in the real world. On the SAT, the answer is to *reinvigorate* (add life to) the area. Two bad but appealing choices are (C) and (D). *Enervate* resembles "energy," so you may have thought the word meant "energize." Nope. *Enervate* means "weaken." *Aggrandize* means "to add power," so it isn't an impossible selection, but (E) is still better. *Stagnate* (to grow stale, to remain without change) and *annex* (to make part of) aren't even close.

6. **(B).** The council is clearly insisting that global warming be the subject of Deeplock's meeting. *Adamant* means "uncompromising, insistent." *Ambivalent* (having mixed feelings), *apathetic* (not caring), and *neutral* (not taking a position) don't fit. *Perplexed* could be a choice, because if the council is confused, they may want to discuss the issue. However, (B) is best because it matches the "won't take no for an answer" tone of the sentence.

7. **(A).** Zero in on *notwithstanding,* a nice mouthful that means "despite" or "in spite of." Okay, so the sentence tells you that despite some kind of effort, the team lost. The best choice has to have something to do with "a great effort" or "a really strong effort." *Herculean* — a word that is derived from the name of the Greek hero Hercules — fits the bill. Hercules was famous for being "great and strong," and that's what his name now means.

   Spontaneous (spur of the moment, unplanned), *gratuitous* (needless, uncalled for), *pluralistic* (reflecting many viewpoints), and *intermittent* (stopping and starting at irregular intervals) don't do the job.

8. **(A).** Did (B) fool you? The sentence has to do with history, so you may have been tempted by its resemblance to that word. But *historiography* is the study of how history is written, not history itself. Because the sentence is referring to history, *dissertation* (a scholarly paper), is appropriate. *Memoir* is made up of personal reminiscences. *Polemic* (a bitter argument, especially about religion) and *diatribe* (a verbal attack) are intense, and the sentence seeks the opposite.

9. **(A).** *Fortuitous* means "happening by chance," with a happy tinge. Think "fortunate but unexpected." So (A) beats out *superfluous* (unnecessary), *querulous* (complaining — though if I were stranded, you'd certainly hear my bellyaching!), and *precarious* (uncertain). *Omniscient* (all-knowing) doesn't fit because if they'd known about the storm, they would have stayed home.

10. **(A).** In my ideal world, (E) would be the answer, because then even my lowly level (teacher) would have a role in decision-making. But the questions in the middle of the paragraph provide the key to the correct answer. If you're asking about who should make a decision, you're implying that more than one possible path to a decision exists when deciding whether to buy gourmet coffee for the faculty lounge or to go with the no-name brand. Hence (A) is a good idea. (B) is out because nothing in the passage separates mission and strategy. (C) hits the mat because it's the opposite of (A), as the questions make clear. Strategic planning is useful, as are some (unbelievably boring) texts that teach this discipline, so (D) is out of the running.

11. **(C).** Sentence one, which deals with the source of "significant power," is the crucial part here. "Goals" = "mission" and "methods" = "strategy," so (C) is just sentence one, reworded.

12. **(C).** Justinian made "efforts" but could salvage only the appearance, not the "substance" of the Empire. So what kind of efforts did he make? That's the crucial question. Check out the last sentence: Western Europe evolved new forms of social and governmental activity. Thus Justinian must have been trying to keep the old forms, without success. (C) wins the prize.

13. **(B).** Speaking of traps, this question illustrates one of the SAT-devils' favorites. In the normal, I-speak-like-a-human world, *trap* is something that catches you, so you may have zeroed in on (A). Bad idea. In the context of the paragraph, *trappings* refers to appearance, especially ornamental details, not substance.

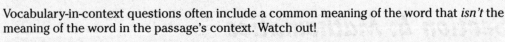

   Vocabulary-in-context questions often include a common meaning of the word that *isn't* the meaning of the word in the passage's context. Watch out!

14. **(E).** The first sentence states that attempts to define feudalism are "far from being closely related to one another," so disagreement exists. You can rule out (A) because the paragraph states that feudalism "came into existence" in France. The paragraph contains no information about feudalism's spreading from England to Spain (B). The labeling of Egypt and India as feudal (C) is described as controversial, not generally agreed upon. (D) is a dud because the author does define feudalism (ruling out "impossible to define").

15. **(B).** The author provides only one detail about Russia, that it had a system "very close" to vassalage. So you can dump (A) and (D). (E) bites the dust because the 16th century is pretty far from modern, as Shakespeare's sometimes impossible vocabulary shows. Both (B) and (C) are possible answers, but you need more information to contrast Russia and Japan, so (B) is the best choice.

16. **(D).** The easy definition — a knight — isn't a choice, but the passage makes clear that vassals traded military service and other obligations for land and other rights such as protection of widows and children.

17. **(A).** The passage details how land is transferred (lines 25–29, 51) but mentions no other economy, so inferring that land was the basis of wealth is safe. Little evidence in the passage supports (B) and (C), and the passage directly contradicts (D) and (E).

18. **(B).** The castle had to be *garrisoned* (line 37), that is, equipped with soldiers. The passage says nothing about the poor slobs who had to carve and carry all those stones.

19. **(D).** (B) is out because the peasants don't play a role in this passage, though in real life they did all the work, as peasants always do. (Trust me, teachers are the peasants of the modern era, so I know.) (E) is a nonstarter because the lord gives permission but doesn't do matchmaking duty. The other three choices concern advice, and the crucial sentence appears in lines 38–39. "Counsel" is listed as one of the lord's advantages, a service given to him by vassals. Forced advice (A) is *not* an advantage (imagine your mom *advising* you to do your homework), and the passage says nothing about lords seeking advice from their peers.

20. **(D).** (A) is appealing at first glance because lines 80–82 talk about instability. However, (D) is better because the instability is linked to the absence of a strong ruler (sort of like a game of dodgeball when the ref ducks out for a cup of coffee). The passage doesn't support (B), (C), and (E).

21. **(E).** A pyramid is narrow at the top and gradually widens as you move toward the base. In the analogy, the king is the top of the pyramid, but those under him (the vassals) are ranked from highest (just under the king) to the lowest (the base).

22. **(E).** This question, dear to an English teacher's heart (mine), forces you to figure out which word or idea the pronoun *this* replaces. Your clue is the end of the sentence, which mentions "the positive results of feudalism" which balance *this.* Okay, the balance of something positive is something negative. Because *this* follows a whole list of negatives, you can safely conclude that the whole list is tucked into that one word.

23. **(B).** *Nominal* comes from the root word for *name.* As the passage makes clear, plenty of infighting disturbed the political and economic order. But the passage also states that feudalism supported "some measure of territorial organization." Bingo, (B) is your answer.

24. **(A).** No, *dispassionate* has nothing to do with the reason men take Viagra. It means "without emotion, logical, calm." The author isn't yelling at you; he's simply discussing feudalism and evaluating it reasonably.

25. **(B).** Okay, I confess that I like (E), but the pyramid is just one analogy, not enough to carry the whole piece. (A), (C), and (D) are good for *parts* of the passage, but the more general (B) is best.

Section 4: Mathematics

1. **(D).** If you add the numbers in the ratio, you get 7. There are 28 total students, which is 7×4. Therefore, multiply the original ratio numbers by 4, to get 12 boys and 16 girls. Double-checking, $12 + 16 = 28$.

2. **(D).** Plugging in gives you $2(-2)^4$. Remembering PEMDAS (See Chapter 14 if you *don't* remember), do the exponent first: $(-2)^4 = (-2)(-2)(-2)(-2) = +16$, and $2(16) = 32$.

3. **(A).** The drawer had 22 pairs of socks originally. However, Josh has thrown four pairs on the floor (and you can bet his mom's going to have something to say about that). So there are now 18 pairs to choose from, of which 6 are brown. His probability of success is therefore $\frac{6}{18} = \frac{1}{3}$.

4. **(B).** Ah, yes, an SAT classic. (They should have their own cable channel.) Every time a wheel rotates, it covers the equivalent of one circumference of distance. The circumference equals $2\pi r$, but you have to be careful about units. The wheel has a radius of 18 inches, but your answer needs to be in feet. So the circumference is $2 \times 18 \times \pi$ inches = 36π inches = 3π feet = about 9.4248 feet. Therefore, 50 revolutions covers $50 \times 9.4248 = 471$ feet.

5. **(B).** You did fine on this one if you remembered your exponent rules. $4^0 = 1$ by definition. $64^{1/2}$ is the square root of 64, which is 8. So the expression in parentheses equals $1 + 8 = 9$. 9^{-2} means the reciprocal of 9^2, which is 81, so the answer is $\frac{1}{81}$.

6. **(D).** Don't be fooled by this one. Thinking that the girls have $24 combined is tempting, but that's not what the problem says. You need to find two numbers in the ratio 7:5 that have a *difference* of 24. There are a couple of ways to work this problem. One is to use algebra: You can call Dora's money $7x$ and Lisa's money $5x$. Then you can say that $7x = 5x + 24$, or $7x - 5x = 24$. Thus, $2x = 24$, and $x = 12$. Plugging back in (always an important step) tells you that Lisa's money is $5(12) = \$60$, and Dora's is $7(12) = \$84$. You also could subtract the numbers in the ratio, instead of adding them. Because $7 - 5 = 2$, and 2 goes in to 24 12 times, you can multiply the original ratio numbers by 12.

7. **(E).** Quick quiz: What's the first thing you need to do when you read this problem? If you answered, "Draw the triangle," you win a prize. (The prize, of course, is improved SAT scores.) Drawing the triangle is only half the battle; you also have to label the triangle properly. Here you can use a guideline developed by a former colleague of mine: Let your variable stand for the *second* thing mentioned in the problem. In this case, the second thing mentioned is the first side, so let x = the first side. The second side is then $x + 3$, and the third side is $2x - 5$. Don't fall into the trap of thinking it's $5 - 2x$. The finished triangle looks like this:

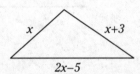

The perimeter, 34, is the sum of all the sides, so $(x) + (x + 3) + (2x - 5) = 34$. Combining the like terms on the left side gives $4x - 2 = 34$. Adding two to each side gives $4x = 36$, and $x = 9$. Now you need to plug in: the first side is 9 cm, the second is $(9) + 3 = 12$ cm, and the third is $2(9) - 5 = 13$ cm. Because this side is the longest, it's also the answer.

8. **(B).** You can draw the line and count spaces to determine that the points are 12 units apart, or you can simply subtract: $8 - (-4) = 12$ (*distance* always involves a *difference*). ¼ of 12 is 3, so you're looking for the point 3 units to the right of -4, and $-4 + 3 = -1$.

9. **(D).** To solve for y, isolate y on one side of the equation:

$$2y - c = 3c$$
$$ +c \quad +c$$
$$\frac{2y}{2} = \frac{4c}{2}$$
$$y = 2c$$

10. **(C).** On the real SAT, try all the numbers by plugging them in. I'm going to do it the long way, though, just so you can practice your algebra skills. Cross-multiplying gives $(x - 1)(x + 2) = (x + 7)(x - 2)$. Now you can use FOIL to get $x^2 + 2x - 1x - 2 = x^2 - 2x + 7x - 14$. Simplifying each side, you have $x^2 + x - 2 = x^2 + 5x - 14$. A neat thing happens when you start to combine the like terms on different sides. You can subtract x^2 from both sides, which means that both x^2 terms just disappear, leaving the simple linear equation $x - 2 = 5x - 14$. Subtracting x from both sides yields $-2 = 4x - 14$. Now you add 14 to each side to get $12 = 4x$, and $x = 3$.

11. **(B).** Because 15 is composite (it's 3×5), $\&15 = 2(15) = 30$. 9 is also composite, so $\&9 = 2(9)$ $= 18$. 36 is composite, too, so $\&36 = 2(36) = 72$. Only II works.

12. **(A).** ABD is a right triangle, so you can find BD with the Pythagorean theorem: $(4)^2 + (8)^2 = c^2$; $16 + 64 = c^2$; $80 = c^2$; so $c = \sqrt{80}$. Because DE $= 2\sqrt{5}$, the area of BDEF is $\sqrt{80} \times 2\sqrt{5} = 2\sqrt{400} = 2(20) = 40$. Now, the shaded region's area is the area of the rectangle BDEF minus the area of the triangle CBD, and the area of CBD equals $\frac{1}{2} \times base \times height = \frac{1}{2} \times 8 \times 4 = 16$. Thus, the area of the shaded region is $40 - 16 = 24$.

13. **(C).** Direct variation problems require a ratio — in this case, the ratio of volume to temperature. Thus, you can write $\frac{cc}{K} = \frac{cc}{K}$, $\frac{31.5}{210} = \frac{x}{300}$. Cross-multiply to get $210x = 9450$, and divide by 210 to get $x = 45$.

14. **(E).** To be honest, you don't even need to be told what x and y equal in this problem. Look at the angle marked c in the diagram below. c and z are vertical angles, which means that their measures are equal. Also, a, c, and b form a straight line, so $a + c + b = 180°$. Therefore, $a + b + z = 180°$. By the way, there's nothing wrong with actually figuring out the angles: $a = 30°$, $b = 70°$, and $z = 80°$.

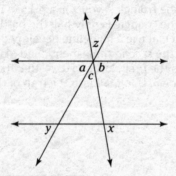

15. **(B).** This scatterplot shows a negative trend, so the line of best fit would go roughly from the top left to the bottom right. However, point D is significantly lower than the rest of the points. If you try drawing a line between A and D, or B and D, you'll see that it's really not that close to a lot of the points. However, the line from A to C is a good approximation of the scatterplot as a whole, as you can see in this diagram.

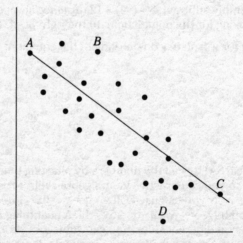

16. **(B).** There are 19 terms between 7 and 159. Because 159 – 7 = 152, and 152 ÷ 19 = 8, each term must be 8 units greater than the one before it. So the sequence begins 7, 15, 23, 31, and there's your answer.

17. **(A).** Do you remember your special triangle ratios? If not, don't panic. They're at the top of each Math section of the SAT. First, you had to realize that the triangles in this problem were special, by breaking up the 75° angle at the bottom right into a 45° and a 30° angle. The top right triangle is a 45°-45°-90° triangle, which makes both of its legs equal to 14. The bottom leg is also the hypotenuse of the 30°-60°-90° triangle at the bottom. In a 30°-60°-90° triangle, the hypotenuse must be twice the shortest leg, which is j. Therefore, j equals 7.

18. **(D).** Honestly, the easiest way to do this problem is to list all the possibilities: 70, 71, 72, 73, 74, 75, 76, 77, 78, 79; 07, 17, 27, 37, 47, 57, 67, 87, 97. Notice the trap: 77 was already in the first part of the list, so I didn't list it again in the second. There are 19 total pairs of digits.

19. **(C).** If you know how to solve this problem with a Venn diagram, feel free to do so, but I'm going to do it with simple arithmetic. If you add up the 65 Spanish students and the 32 art students, you get 97 total students. However, the 14 students who take both would have been counted twice, so you need to subtract 14, giving 83 students in either Spanish or art. (This method always works to find the total number of things in two groups combined: Add up the number in each group, and then subtract the overlap.) If 83 students are in Spanish and/or art, you're left with 100 – 83 = 17 who don't take either subject.

20. **(C).** As is so often the case, trial and error works great here. Or you could call the original side of the square x, making the rectangle's sides $x + 3$ and $x - 2$. Because the area is 50, you write $(x + 3)(x - 2) = 50$. FOIL gives you $x^2 - 2x + 3x - 6 = 50$, or $x^2 + x - 56 = 0$. (Remember, to solve a quadratic equation, you must make one side equal zero.) You can factor this equation into $(x + 8)(x - 7) = 0$. This equation is true when x equals –8 or 7, but it wouldn't make any sense for a square to have a side of –8. So 7 is your answer.

21. **(D).** Because the answer is supposed to be in minutes, start by turning 3 hours into 180 minutes. You know that k percent of these 180 minutes is going to be used for math. What does k percent mean? Why, it means $k/100$. Taking a percent of a number involves multiplication, so your answer is $180 \times k/100$, or $180k/100$.

22. **(C).** Take them one at a time. (A) is true. The mode appears most often, so there will be two or three 90s. (B) requires you to remember the formula $total = number \times mean$. In this case, the four numbers must add up to $4 \times 80 = 320$. Because you know there are at least two 90s, which add up to 180, the other two numbers must add up to 140. But, because the numbers are both positive, there would be no room for a fourth number if 140 were in the set. (C) is false. Making a list whose average is 80 without including any 80s in the list is easy. Try it yourself and see. (D) is definitely true.

In (E), the median is usually the middle number. However, because you have four numbers here, the median would be the average of the two numbers closest to the middle. So, if the median were greater than 90, at least two of the four numbers would have to be greater than 90. But you already know from (A) that there must be at least two 90s in the list. And there's no way that you could have a list with two 90s and two numbers greater than 90, and still have the average be 80. Thus, the median can't be greater than 90.

23. **(D).** To solve this problem, remember that a diameter makes a 90-degree angle when it meets a line tangent to a circle. Also, recall that an inscribed angle, like the one at the top of the circle, is one-half its arc. In this case, it's 40°. Now you have two angles of a triangle, which means that you can figure out the third. Because 90° + 40° = 130°, your answer is 180° – 130° = 50°.

24. **(E).** You could try to figure out what a and b equal, but doing so isn't worth the energy. The key to getting this question right is remembering the formulas discussed in Chapter 16 — specifically, the one that says that $(a - b)^2 = a^2 - 2ab + b^2$. Do you see how this helps? You know that $(a - b) = 8$, so $(a - b)^2 = a^2 - 2ab + b^2 = 64$. You're being asked for $a^2 + b^2$, which is $(a^2 - 2ab + b^2) + 2ab$, or $64 + 2(10) = 84$. Pat yourself on the back if you got this one right; I think it's the hardest problem in this section.

25. **(A).** This question is straight-up memorization: $f(x + 4)$ moves the graph 4 units to the left.

Section 5: Critical Reading

1. **(E).** Paragraph one makes it clear that Mariga carves all the time, and because of his family background and talents, he's open to artistic possibilities. By explaining these background facts, the author paves the way (Get it? The passage is about stone!) for the discovery of soapstone as a carving material.

2. **(C).** You can rule out (A), (B), and (E) because they contradict information in the passage. Mariga's trips were easier after the road crew did their work, and the journey was clearly not impossible, because he made it. Nor did Mariga travel for artistic purposes; he was sent by the Ministry of Agriculture. (D) is a good (but wrong) answer, because he did carve. But paragraph one tells you that he would be carving no matter where he was, because carving was his passion. So the best answer is (C), because the paragraph clearly sets up a cause-and-effect relationship. Mariga bumps along and sympathizes with the farmers who have to get their crops over the nonexistent roads.

3. **(D).** The passage states that if you hold the stone up to the light, it is *translucent.* The opposite of translucent, which means "to let light pass through," is *opaque.*

4. **(D).** The last paragraph of passage one skips from Mariga's obsession with soapstone to a small industry based on the creation of soapstone carvings. The author doesn't explain how those two are related, but the passage strongly implies that Mariga was at least partly responsible. Also, the first paragraph of passage one presents Mariga as a teacher who couldn't resist showing his friends, Titus and Robert, how to carve. The only other *enticing* (tempting) choices are (C) and (E), because Mariga probably had more fun carving than agriculturing. (Give me a break! I know it isn't a word. I just wanted to see if you were still awake.) Nonetheless, the passage more strongly supports (D).

5. **(C).** Line 59 explains that the soapstone carvings were "exhibited all over the world." The author clearly admires the artwork, and the SAT-makers are deathly afraid of offending any group, so (C) is your best bet.

6. **(D).** The passage describes the crisis in Africa that has limited educational growth (war, funding, and so on) and also states that "something must be done quickly to reverse the trend" (lines 101–102). The implication is that if the situation isn't changed now, it may never be.

7. **(A).** You can't run a computer without software because the software is the "brain" telling the computer what to do. Ditto voters. If the voters aren't educated, you end up with politicians like (here fill in the name of the politician you hate the most).

8. **(D).** The author doesn't say anything about traditional ways, but each of the other choices pops up somewhere in passage II.

9. **(E).** "Investment in primary education" differentiates Southeast Asia from Africa. The whole passage describes the problems of African education, so you can safely bet that Africa invests less, not more, in primary education.

10. **(B).** John Nkoma doesn't want Africa to be "the exception" to the rule of technological development stemming from basic science. Basic science is a short hop (just a skip, really) from good education.

11. **(C).** The SAT-writers describe the economies of Southeast Asia in a positive way, so go with (C).

12. **(B).** The passage ends with the idea that governments can't do it all, especially the weak governments that exist in some parts of Africa. So (B) is the next logical statement.

13. **(B).** The first passage deals with the discovery and marketing of soapstone carvings, concentrating on the role of one man. The second discusses the need for government investment in education, which is described as only part of the solution, with community action essential as well. (B) fills the bill.

14. **(E).** A couple of these choices lose by a nose (I grew up next to a racetrack) because they fit *most* of the material in these two passages, but not all. The key is to look for the best answer. Hardships (A) occur in the hilly country of passage I and are implied by the lack of education in passage II, but neither passage focuses on that aspect of African life. (B) and (C) are fine for passage II, but not passage I. (D) is a poor fit. Winner: (E), because the development of the art market dominates passage I, and passage II links education to African economic development.

15. **(A).** Passage I tells a story of one specific individual and his experience. Passage II contains broader, more general statements about education, the economy, and technology.

16. **(D).** The word *yet* signals a change in direction for the sentence — a contrast between *admired* and something else. (D) is the only choice that opposes *admired*. (B), (C), and (E) are synonyms of *admired,* and if they're reading about Elwood, the strangers haven't *ignored* him.

17. **(A).** The whole sentence revolves around the word *despite*. The ambassadors have made an assumption that is challenged, but not overturned, by the word in the blank. *Resistance* fills the bill here. (B), (C) (*withdrawal* = pulling out), and (D) (*compromise* = giving in a bit) don't challenge the ambassadors' views. *Interrogation* (questioning) is in another universe entirely.

18. **(C).** The choices all contain relatively easy words, but the tricky part of this question is *belied,* or "proved false." After you get that, you know you're looking for an impossible pair. *Increase* services and *slash* taxes? What every politician promises and none can deliver.

19. **(B).** SAT questions don't rely on historical knowledge. But if you know anything about segregation and the courts, you have a leg up with this question. Segregation isn't legal, so you can immediately drop answers (A), (C), and (E), which allow the practice. When you check out (B) and (D), you see that *persist* (continue) easily beats out *intimidate* (threaten).

20. **(E).** The most important clue here is *hide*. If she's hiding her manuscript, *publicize* and *reveal* are out, as are (A) and (B). Check out the three remaining possibilities: *alert* and *conceal* go together nicely.

Don't stop when you find a word that fits the first blank in the sentence. Always check both blanks.

21. **(D).** *Although* is the word to watch. Check out the first half of the sentence. What are juries trying to achieve? A 12 to 0 vote on a verdict. So the first blank may be filled by (A), (B), or (D) because all imply agreement. The *although* signals that the second blank is a bit of a surprise, so *amity* (friendship) is better than *discord* (disagreement, which you already know) and *anger* (which you may expect when people have differing views).

22. **(D).** Focus on two important spots in the sentence: *not . . . but*. This pair tells you that you're looking for the opposite of *one disease.* Still in the running at this point is (B), (C), (D), and (E). Now send your eyeball to the end of the sentence, which gives you two very different details — *solid tumors* and *proliferation* (rapid growth) *of white blood cells.* The best choice here is *diverse,* so (D) scores the point.

23. **(D).** This one is a devil. Filling in the blanks with your own words may lead you to "happy" and "sad," given that the word *but* signals a contrast. (A) and (B) start you off with happy words and then let you down. (*Affable* = friendly and *mirthful* = full of laughter.) (C) and (E) bite the dust because no one expects a lottery winner to be *depressed* or *acrimonious* (bitter). But you may think a shy person would be *intimidated* (threatened) by wealth and surprised to see her *confident.*

24. **(B).** The second half of the sentence holds the key: The items are of various ages and from lots of countries. *Eclectic* (from different sources) plops into the sentence nicely. The question-writer (okay, me, but I'm just doing what those tricksters at the SAT will do to you) tucked in (D) and (E), two church references, to distract you. Ditto (C), which makes sense with the *many . . . nations* part of the sentence but ignores *periods. Ubiquitous* (appearing everywhere, sort of like Cameron and Justin or Brad and Jen) doesn't work at all.

Section 6: Mathematics

1. **(A).** Make a quick drawing of the situation. (Remember, the towns don't have to be in a straight line.)

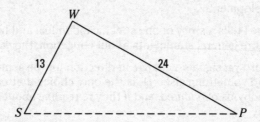

The distance you're interested in is the dotted line. Hey, wait a minute: This is a triangle! So you can use the triangle inequality, which tells you that the sum of any two sides of a triangle must be greater than the third side. The number 10 doesn't satisfy the inequality, because $10 + 13 = 23$, which is less than 24.

2. **(E).** All the numbers have three digits. Only (A), (D), and (E) have a units (ones) digit that equals the sum of the other two digits. And a calculator can tell you that the square roots of 156 and 516 are decimals, while the square root of 729 is 27.

3. **(C).** If you multiply each of the choices by 3 points, you get 60, 63, 66, 69, and 72. Because all the other scores are worth 5 points, you must be able to add a multiple of 5 to one of these numbers to get 121. The only one that works is 66, because $66 + 55 = 121$.

4. **(C).** Don't fall for the old "less than" trick. Twelve less than something is the thing minus 12, not the other way around. So you want an expression that says "x squared is 5 times x minus 12," and (C) is the winner.

5. **(B).** Five pounds of peanuts times $5.50 is $27.50, and two pounds of cashews times $12.50 is $25.00, so the total cost is $52.50 for seven pounds. $52.50 divided by 7 is $7.50.

6. **(C).** The number of solutions to the equation $f(x) = 1$ is just the number of times that the graph has a height of 1, as shown here.

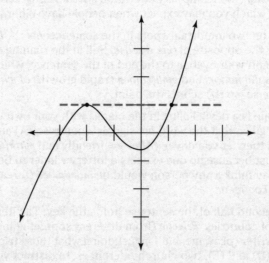

7. **(D).** In general, absolute-value equations have two solutions. So, if you were just guessing, guess either (B) or (D). Solving it the long way:

$$|3x - 1| = 7$$
$$3x - 1 = 7 \quad \text{or} \quad 3x - 1 = -7$$
$$\underline{+1 \quad +1} \qquad\qquad \underline{+1 \quad +1}$$
$$\frac{3x}{3} = \frac{8}{3} \qquad\qquad \frac{3x}{3} = \frac{-6}{3}$$
$$x = 2\frac{2}{3} \quad \text{or} \qquad x = -2$$

8. **(E).** Adding up all three columns for each year gives you 180 ninth graders in 2000, 190 in 2001, and 190 in 2002.

9. **(A).** Sixty of the 190 students took French in 2001, and 60 divided by 190 is 0.3158 = 31.58% = about 32%.

10. **(A).** Don't over-think this one. The median is the middle number in a list. Because the number of German students was 30, 40, or 40, the middle number is 40.

11. **96.** This problem is easy if you remember the trick *total = number × average*. In this case, the total must equal $7 \times 90 = 630$. Adding up Lauren's first six scores gives 534, and $630 - 534 = 96$. Another good way to do this problem is to play the "over/under" game. For each score, figure out how much it is over or under the average. In this case, you would get +1, –1, –5, +2, 0, and –3. Adding up these numbers gives –6, so Lauren is 6 points under average before her last exam. She needs 6 over average, or 96, on the last exam.

12. **61.** Unfortunately, you can't just multiply all the numbers and add one. What you need to do is find the Least Common Multiple of 2, 3, 4, 5, and 6, and then add one. Although there is a formula for this problem, just thinking about the factors and doing a trial and error is easier. Because the LCM has to be divisible by 2, 3, and 5 (which are prime), it must be divisible by $2 \times 3 \times 5 = 30$. But 30 isn't divisible by 4. So try doubling 30 to get 60, and now you're happy: 60 is divisible by 2, 3, 4, 5, and 6. Remember, though, that you wanted a remainder of one, so your answer is $60 + 1 = 61$.

13. **40.** Sixty-five percent chose history or English, leaving 35 percent for other subjects. This 35 percent represents 14 students, so you're basically being asked, "35% of what number is 14?" You can use the "is/of" method: $\frac{14}{x} = \frac{35}{100}$, $35x = 1400$, $x = 40$.

14. **12.** When you're told the ratio of unknown quantities, you can just tack an x on the end of each number. Thus, the length is $2x$ and the width is $5x$. Now it can't hurt to draw and label a rectangle:

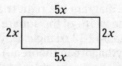

Don't fall into the trap of writing $2x + 5x = 84$; a rectangle has four sides, not two. Write either $2x + 5x + 2x + 5x = 84$ or $2(2x + 5x) = 84$. Either way, the left side is $14x$, so $14x = 84$, and $x = 6$. Another trap lurks here: 6 *isn't* the answer. You represented the length with $2x$, so the length is $2(6) = 12$ feet.

15. **6.** Trial and error can be your guide here, but I'm going to use algebra, because you'll see a lot of good review stuff in this one. Darren makes $9 an hour on weekdays, and $1\frac{1}{2} \times \$9 = \$13.50$ on weekends. If you let d equal his weekday hours and e equal his weekend hours, you know that $\$9(d) + \$13.50(e) = \$189.00$. You also know that $d + e = 18$ (his total hours), so you can solve this by substitution: $d = 18 - e$, which you can plug into the other equation. This gives $\$9(18-e) + \$13.50e = \$189$. Distributing: $\$162-\$9e + \$13.50e = \$189$. Combining like terms, $\$162 + \$4.50e = \$189$. Now just subtract 162 from both sides and divide by 4.50, to give $e = 6$. Simple, right?

16. **11.** In a radical or absolute-value problem, you first need to isolate the radical or absolute value. That means that you have to subtract 1 from both sides before doing anything else, giving $\sqrt{4x - 8} = 6$. Now you can square both sides to eliminate the radical: $4x - 8 = 36$. Adding 8 and dividing by 4 gives $x = 11$.

17. **6.** Using the definition, $p \backslash\backslash 7 = \dfrac{p(7)}{p - 4}$ or just $\dfrac{7p}{p - 4}$. Because this equals 21, write $\dfrac{7p}{p - 4} = 21$. Cross-multiplying as usual (you can put 21 over 1 if it helps), you get $7p = 21(p - 4)$ or $7p = 21p - 84$. Subtracting $21p$ from both sides gives $-14p = -84$, and dividing by -14 yields $p = 6$. Double-checking: $6 \backslash\backslash 7 = {}^{(6)(7)}\!/_{6 - 4} = {}^{42}\!/_{2} = 21$.

18. **520.** A linear function has the form $y = mx + b$. In this problem, x is the number of people, while y is the cost. There are several ways to work this out, but I focus on the slope, which is the change in y divided by the change in x. When the number of people increased by 2, the cost increased by \$50. Therefore, the slope $m = {}^{50}\!/_{2} = 25$. Now, because a party for 10 costs \$320, a party of 18 adds 8 people, for $8 \times \$25 = \$200$ more. So a party of 18 costs \$520.

19. **7.** Remember the distance formula? It tells you that the distance between two points, (x_1, y_1) and (x_2, y_2) is $\sqrt{(x_2 - x_1)^2 + (y_2 - y_1)^2}$. Substituting your numbers gives $10 = \sqrt{((-2) - (4))^2 + (p - (-1))^2} = \sqrt{(-6)^2 + (p + 1)^2} = \sqrt{36 + (p + 1)^2}$. Because this is a radical equation, square both sides, so $100 = 36 + (p + 1)^2$. Subtracting 36 gives $64 = (p + 1)^2$. There's more than one way to solve this, but the easiest is to think about squares. If a quantity (in this case, $p + 1$) squared is 64, then the quantity must equal 8 or -8. But the problem told you that p was positive. So, $p + 1 = 8$, and $p = 7$.

20. **360.** The total surface area is the sum of the area of the square and the area of the four triangles. The square is easy: it's $10 \times 10 = 100$. The triangles are tougher. They *don't* have a height of 12. 12 is the height of the pyramid, but the triangles are slanted. However, if you look at the following diagram, you'll see that you can find the height of the slanted triangles by using the Pythagorean theorem.

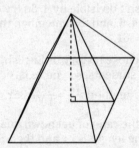

That little triangle in the diagram is a right triangle. One leg is 12, the height of the pyramid. The second leg is half the width of the square, or 5. This is actually the world's second-most famous right triangle, the 5-12-13 triangle. (If you didn't remember this one, you could have figured it out with the Pythagorean theorem.) The hypotenuse, 13, is the altitude of each of the tilted triangles that make up the sides of the pyramid. Because the triangle's area is $\frac{1}{2} \times$ *base* $\times$ *height*, each triangle's area is $\frac{1}{2} \times 10 \times 13 = 65$. The four triangles together have an area of $4 \times 65 = 260$. Adding in the 100 from the base gives 360.

Section 7: Critical Reading

1. **(D).** This one is tricky. (A), (B), (C), and (E) all deal with aspects of the stuff-your-face experience, but the author is talking about motivation. Fuel comes closest, in the sense that you *fuel* or *power* "discovery and wonder."

2. **(D).** If the researcher "must make" an adjustment to biostatistics, then they are the wave of the future. The researcher may be *critical, nostalgic, fearful,* or *adverse* (all wrong answers) but the author is *favorable.*

3. **(B).** No matter how much they tear their hair out, medical researchers have to know statistics, as the last two sentences of the passage make clear.

4. **(A).** Passage two doesn't mention passion at all, but passage I's narrator (the mad scientist who creates the "monster," by the way) says that he is into his work "heart and soul." (B) is a trap. The first passage is from a novel but isn't about literature at all. (C) and (D) fall because the first passage doesn't give any evidence either way. Both passages mention education, so (E) is a nonstarter.

5. **(B).** The passage begins with Austen's trademark irony. No one would think that Catherine was a heroine because her parents are alive, they have enough money, and they're sensible people. To answer the question, then, you need to figure out how Catherine differs from a heroine, which points the way to (B).

6. **(A).** Her father was "a very respectable man, though his name was Richard," so you can infer that men named Richard aren't generally respectable.

7. **(E).** The passage states that Mrs. Morland, "instead of dying in bringing the latter [Catherine] into the world, as anybody might expect . . . still lived." The passage also mentions her "good constitution" — a reference to good health.

8. **(E).** The passage elaborates on Mrs. Morland's survival and the fact that she bore ten children and still enjoyed good health. Those details clue you in to the fact that a "good constitution" is *robust,* or strong, health.

9. **(E).** A girl after my own heart (and yours, as you study for the SATs), Catherine will do anything rather than study.

10. **(D).** The passage makes clear that Catherine isn't a student and her mother doesn't make a big deal out of her daughter's education. So if Catherine can learn a piece, it is probably a no-brainer. (D) is the only one that fits this criteria.

11. **(A).** She can't take it any more and gives up her lessons. Thus, she couldn't "stand" it.

12. **(C).** This passage's tone is humorous exaggeration, and this line is no exception. However much you hate a teacher, you probably won't see his/her dismissal as one of the happiest days of your life.

13. **(B).** French is mentioned, as well as "account" (math), drawing, writing, and music. The other activities aren't part of Catherine's official education.

14. **(D).** (A) and (E) are too general; the passage focuses on one family only and describes only Catherine's childhood. (B) and (C) are too narrow. You can figure out a lot about girls' education, but that title doesn't take into account the material about heroines. Similarly, the information about the family is only part of the passage. (D) covers all bases, because the definition of heroine seems, according to the passage, to take in education, temperament, and family background.

15. **(D).** Austen is clearly mocking the conventional idea of a heroine using irony and exaggeration.

Section 8: Mathematics

1. **(B).** The area of the pizza is πr^2. Because the diameter is 12, the radius is 6, and the area is 36π. Dividing by eight slices gives 4.5π.

2. **(A).** If you remembered the triangle inequality, you'd realize immediately that (A) was wrong because it's the exact opposite of the triangle inequality. Check out the others, just to be sure. (B) is true, because the longest side of a triangle is always across from the largest angle.

Because B is obtuse, it's the largest angle, and AC must be longer that the other sides. (C) is true, because the two angles given make a straight line. (D) is closely related to (C). Because the three angles of the triangles add up to 180°, you can write m∠A + m∠B + m∠BCA = 180°. But you know from (C) that m∠BCD + m∠BCA = 180°. If you look at these two equations, you realize that they have the exact same endings, but different beginnings. Logically, then, m∠A + m∠B = m∠BCD. (E) is true because B is obtuse, which leaves less than 90° for the other two angles.

3. **(B).** Just make a table for this one, dividing by 2 every 20 years:

2000	2020	2040	2060	2080	2100
50	25	12.5	6.25	3.125	1.5625

The final answer, 1.5625, is the same as 1⅑₆.

4. **(C).** First off, you must realize that there are 31 numbers, not 30, to choose from. Remember that to find the size of a list of numbers, you subtract the first and last numbers, and then add one. (Count them if you don't believe me.) Now you just have to find the numbers whose second digit is greater than the first. In the 20s, that's 23 through 29, or 7 numbers. In the 30s, it's 34 through 39, or six numbers. And in the 40s, it's 45 through 49, or five numbers. Put 'em all together, and you get 18 out of 31.

5. **(D).** A lot of these answers look true. However, if you let *a* equal 1, or a number less than 1, you realize that most of them become false. This question is an old SAT trap; numbers between zero and one (such as fractions) behave in funny ways. The only statement that is true for all positive numbers is (D): Twice any positive number must be bigger than the original number.

6. **(D).** A slope of -⅓ means that the line goes down 1 space every time it moves 3 spaces to the right. Because M is on the *x*-axis, the line has gone down 2 spaces by the time it reaches M, so it must have moved 6 spaces to the right. That means that M is at (5,0). M is the midpoint, which means that it's halfway to P. So, to get to P, you need to move another 2 spaces down and 6 spaces right, which puts you at (11, –2).

7. **(C).** Exponent laws at work: When you take a power of a power, such as $(5^{q+1})^p$, you multiply the powers. So this expression equals $(5^{p(q+1)}) = 5^{pq+p}$. Also, when you multiply exponents, you add the powers, so $(5^{-p})(5^{q+1})^p = (5^{-p})5^{pq+p} = 5^{(-p+pq+p)} = 5^{pq}$.

8. **(D).** Possible numbers for *g* are numbers like 3, 6, 12, 15, 21, and so on. If you try multiplying these numbers by 7, and then dividing by 9, you discover that the remainder is always 3 or 6. Because 3 isn't on your list, 6 is it.

9. **(D).** You may have to play around with the square before making an important discovery — the middle number has to be 5. This makes a lot of sense, because 5 is the median of the numbers 1 through 9. So put the 5 in the center, and now look at the spaces marked *x*, *y*, and *z* in my diagram:

n		2
x	5	9
y		*z*

The only numbers you could possibly fit that would complete the row, column, and diagonal you're looking for are *x* = 1, *y* = 8, and *z* = 4. These numbers would give all three of the lines in question a sum of 15. Then, because *z* = 4, and 5 is in the center, *n* must be 6, in order to have its diagonal add to 15.

10. **(E).** Because there are parallel lines in this problem, you need to look for angles that are congruent. You can find them by looking for lines that make a "Z" or a backwards "Z". Looking first at the bigger triangles, you can mark the diagram as follows:

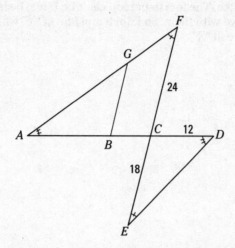

Notice that the two angles in the middle are vertical, so they're also equal. This is a picture of similar triangles: F matches E, A matches D, and C matches itself. Therefore, you can use a ratio to figure out the length of AC: $\frac{AC}{CD} = \frac{CF}{CE}$, $\frac{AC}{12} = \frac{24}{18}$. Be very careful that you match up the right parts when writing a ratio. If you matched AC with CE by accident, you'd get the wrong answer. Cross-multiplying your ratio tells you that 18(AC) = 288, and AC = 16. Now, because $GB \parallel EF$, triangle ABG is similar to ACF, as well. And, because AG = GF, the line GB cuts triangle ACF in half. That means that AB is half of AC, or 8.

11. **(B).** If you add the two expressions you're given, you discover that $4a + 4b = 20$, so $a + b = 5$. You could also have solved for the variables to get $a = -2$ and $b = 7$.

12. **(C).** Each of the four angles is inscribed, which means that each angle is one-half of 60°, or 30°. So, the total is 120°.

13. **(C).** Don't fall into the trap of thinking that 1 is prime; for reasons that no one's really ever explained to me, it's "special." So 2 isn't a tweener, because 2–1 = 1 isn't prime. 8 isn't a tweener, because 8 + 1 = 9 isn't prime (it's 3 × 3). But 30 works, because 30 – 1 = 29 is prime, and so is 30 + 1 = 31. As always, check that 36 and 48 don't work.

14. **(E).** Because BCF is isosceles, BC = CF = 8. Because angle D is a right angle, triangle DEF is the world-famous 3-4-5 right triangle, and DF = 4. Because DC = 4 + 8 = 12, AB is also 12. And, because AD = BC = 8, AE = 8 – 3 = 5. Now you're ready to find EB, the hypotenuse of the right triangle ABE. That means that you're face to face again with a 5-12-13 right triangle, and BE = 13.

15. **(D).** Okay, this problem is a long one. Call the room shared by Melvin and Carey room "X," and the other room "Y." Because Mike and Melvin won't live together, Mike must be in "Y." Go through the choices: (A) If Dave and Dan live together, Peter lives with them. The only room with three empty spaces is "Y." So they must be in "Y" with Mike, which puts everyone else in "X." (B) If Chris lives with Melvin, they are in "X" with Carey. Then Enoch must be in "X" with them, placing everyone else in "Y." (C) This puts Peter, Carey, and Melvin in "X," while Dan and Mike are in "Y." But condition (iii) tells you that, if Dave lives with Dan, Peter must live with them. So Dave can't live with Dan, and he must be in "X," filling that room. (D) If Enoch lives with Mike in "Y," Chris must live there, too, by condition (ii). That leaves Dave, Dan, and Peter. All three of them can't fit in one room, so Dave and Dan can't

live together by condition (iii). But there are two ways to do this: Dave and Peter could live in "X" with Melvin and Carey, or Dan and Peter could live in "X." This looks like the answer. (E) If Dan and Chris live together, they can't live in "X," because then Chris and Carey would both be in "X," but there wouldn't be room for Enoch. So Dan and Chris must live in "Y" with Mike. The fourth person can't be Dave, because if Dave and Dan live together, Peter must live with them. So Enoch must be in "Y" with Dan, Chris, and Mike, while the other four live in "X."

Answer Sheet

For Section 1, use the following blank pages to write your essay. For Sections 2 through 8, use the ovals and grid-ins to record your answers. Begin with Number 1 for each new section. If any sections have fewer than 35 questions, leave the extra spaces blank.

Section 2

1. Ⓐ Ⓑ Ⓒ Ⓓ Ⓔ	8. Ⓐ Ⓑ Ⓒ Ⓓ Ⓔ	15. Ⓐ Ⓑ Ⓒ Ⓓ Ⓔ	22. Ⓐ Ⓑ Ⓒ Ⓓ Ⓔ	29. Ⓐ Ⓑ Ⓒ Ⓓ Ⓔ
2. Ⓐ Ⓑ Ⓒ Ⓓ Ⓔ	9. Ⓐ Ⓑ Ⓒ Ⓓ Ⓔ	16. Ⓐ Ⓑ Ⓒ Ⓓ Ⓔ	23. Ⓐ Ⓑ Ⓒ Ⓓ Ⓔ	30. Ⓐ Ⓑ Ⓒ Ⓓ Ⓔ
3. Ⓐ Ⓑ Ⓒ Ⓓ Ⓔ	10. Ⓐ Ⓑ Ⓒ Ⓓ Ⓔ	17. Ⓐ Ⓑ Ⓒ Ⓓ Ⓔ	24. Ⓐ Ⓑ Ⓒ Ⓓ Ⓔ	31. Ⓐ Ⓑ Ⓒ Ⓓ Ⓔ
4. Ⓐ Ⓑ Ⓒ Ⓓ Ⓔ	11. Ⓐ Ⓑ Ⓒ Ⓓ Ⓔ	18. Ⓐ Ⓑ Ⓒ Ⓓ Ⓔ	25. Ⓐ Ⓑ Ⓒ Ⓓ Ⓔ	32. Ⓐ Ⓑ Ⓒ Ⓓ Ⓔ
5. Ⓐ Ⓑ Ⓒ Ⓓ Ⓔ	12. Ⓐ Ⓑ Ⓒ Ⓓ Ⓔ	19. Ⓐ Ⓑ Ⓒ Ⓓ Ⓔ	26. Ⓐ Ⓑ Ⓒ Ⓓ Ⓔ	33. Ⓐ Ⓑ Ⓒ Ⓓ Ⓔ
6. Ⓐ Ⓑ Ⓒ Ⓓ Ⓔ	13. Ⓐ Ⓑ Ⓒ Ⓓ Ⓔ	20. Ⓐ Ⓑ Ⓒ Ⓓ Ⓔ	27. Ⓐ Ⓑ Ⓒ Ⓓ Ⓔ	34. Ⓐ Ⓑ Ⓒ Ⓓ Ⓔ
7. Ⓐ Ⓑ Ⓒ Ⓓ Ⓔ	14. Ⓐ Ⓑ Ⓒ Ⓓ Ⓔ	21. Ⓐ Ⓑ Ⓒ Ⓓ Ⓔ	28. Ⓐ Ⓑ Ⓒ Ⓓ Ⓔ	35. Ⓐ Ⓑ Ⓒ Ⓓ Ⓔ

Section 3

1. Ⓐ Ⓑ Ⓒ Ⓓ Ⓔ	8. Ⓐ Ⓑ Ⓒ Ⓓ Ⓔ	15. Ⓐ Ⓑ Ⓒ Ⓓ Ⓔ	22. Ⓐ Ⓑ Ⓒ Ⓓ Ⓔ	29. Ⓐ Ⓑ Ⓒ Ⓓ Ⓔ
2. Ⓐ Ⓑ Ⓒ Ⓓ Ⓔ	9. Ⓐ Ⓑ Ⓒ Ⓓ Ⓔ	16. Ⓐ Ⓑ Ⓒ Ⓓ Ⓔ	23. Ⓐ Ⓑ Ⓒ Ⓓ Ⓔ	30. Ⓐ Ⓑ Ⓒ Ⓓ Ⓔ
3. Ⓐ Ⓑ Ⓒ Ⓓ Ⓔ	10. Ⓐ Ⓑ Ⓒ Ⓓ Ⓔ	17. Ⓐ Ⓑ Ⓒ Ⓓ Ⓔ	24. Ⓐ Ⓑ Ⓒ Ⓓ Ⓔ	31. Ⓐ Ⓑ Ⓒ Ⓓ Ⓔ
4. Ⓐ Ⓑ Ⓒ Ⓓ Ⓔ	11. Ⓐ Ⓑ Ⓒ Ⓓ Ⓔ	18. Ⓐ Ⓑ Ⓒ Ⓓ Ⓔ	25. Ⓐ Ⓑ Ⓒ Ⓓ Ⓔ	32. Ⓐ Ⓑ Ⓒ Ⓓ Ⓔ
5. Ⓐ Ⓑ Ⓒ Ⓓ Ⓔ	12. Ⓐ Ⓑ Ⓒ Ⓓ Ⓔ	19. Ⓐ Ⓑ Ⓒ Ⓓ Ⓔ	26. Ⓐ Ⓑ Ⓒ Ⓓ Ⓔ	33. Ⓐ Ⓑ Ⓒ Ⓓ Ⓔ
6. Ⓐ Ⓑ Ⓒ Ⓓ Ⓔ	13. Ⓐ Ⓑ Ⓒ Ⓓ Ⓔ	20. Ⓐ Ⓑ Ⓒ Ⓓ Ⓔ	27. Ⓐ Ⓑ Ⓒ Ⓓ Ⓔ	34. Ⓐ Ⓑ Ⓒ Ⓓ Ⓔ
7. Ⓐ Ⓑ Ⓒ Ⓓ Ⓔ	14. Ⓐ Ⓑ Ⓒ Ⓓ Ⓔ	21. Ⓐ Ⓑ Ⓒ Ⓓ Ⓔ	28. Ⓐ Ⓑ Ⓒ Ⓓ Ⓔ	35. Ⓐ Ⓑ Ⓒ Ⓓ Ⓔ

Section 4

1. Ⓐ Ⓑ Ⓒ Ⓓ Ⓔ	8. Ⓐ Ⓑ Ⓒ Ⓓ Ⓔ	15. Ⓐ Ⓑ Ⓒ Ⓓ Ⓔ	22. Ⓐ Ⓑ Ⓒ Ⓓ Ⓔ	29. Ⓐ Ⓑ Ⓒ Ⓓ Ⓔ
2. Ⓐ Ⓑ Ⓒ Ⓓ Ⓔ	9. Ⓐ Ⓑ Ⓒ Ⓓ Ⓔ	16. Ⓐ Ⓑ Ⓒ Ⓓ Ⓔ	23. Ⓐ Ⓑ Ⓒ Ⓓ Ⓔ	30. Ⓐ Ⓑ Ⓒ Ⓓ Ⓔ
3. Ⓐ Ⓑ Ⓒ Ⓓ Ⓔ	10. Ⓐ Ⓑ Ⓒ Ⓓ Ⓔ	17. Ⓐ Ⓑ Ⓒ Ⓓ Ⓔ	24. Ⓐ Ⓑ Ⓒ Ⓓ Ⓔ	31. Ⓐ Ⓑ Ⓒ Ⓓ Ⓔ
4. Ⓐ Ⓑ Ⓒ Ⓓ Ⓔ	11. Ⓐ Ⓑ Ⓒ Ⓓ Ⓔ	18. Ⓐ Ⓑ Ⓒ Ⓓ Ⓔ	25. Ⓐ Ⓑ Ⓒ Ⓓ Ⓔ	32. Ⓐ Ⓑ Ⓒ Ⓓ Ⓔ
5. Ⓐ Ⓑ Ⓒ Ⓓ Ⓔ	12. Ⓐ Ⓑ Ⓒ Ⓓ Ⓔ	19. Ⓐ Ⓑ Ⓒ Ⓓ Ⓔ	26. Ⓐ Ⓑ Ⓒ Ⓓ Ⓔ	33. Ⓐ Ⓑ Ⓒ Ⓓ Ⓔ
6. Ⓐ Ⓑ Ⓒ Ⓓ Ⓔ	13. Ⓐ Ⓑ Ⓒ Ⓓ Ⓔ	20. Ⓐ Ⓑ Ⓒ Ⓓ Ⓔ	27. Ⓐ Ⓑ Ⓒ Ⓓ Ⓔ	34. Ⓐ Ⓑ Ⓒ Ⓓ Ⓔ
7. Ⓐ Ⓑ Ⓒ Ⓓ Ⓔ	14. Ⓐ Ⓑ Ⓒ Ⓓ Ⓔ	21. Ⓐ Ⓑ Ⓒ Ⓓ Ⓔ	28. Ⓐ Ⓑ Ⓒ Ⓓ Ⓔ	35. Ⓐ Ⓑ Ⓒ Ⓓ Ⓔ

Section 5

1. Ⓐ Ⓑ Ⓒ Ⓓ Ⓔ	8. Ⓐ Ⓑ Ⓒ Ⓓ Ⓔ	15. Ⓐ Ⓑ Ⓒ Ⓓ Ⓔ	22. Ⓐ Ⓑ Ⓒ Ⓓ Ⓔ	29. Ⓐ Ⓑ Ⓒ Ⓓ Ⓔ
2. Ⓐ Ⓑ Ⓒ Ⓓ Ⓔ	9. Ⓐ Ⓑ Ⓒ Ⓓ Ⓔ	16. Ⓐ Ⓑ Ⓒ Ⓓ Ⓔ	23. Ⓐ Ⓑ Ⓒ Ⓓ Ⓔ	30. Ⓐ Ⓑ Ⓒ Ⓓ Ⓔ
3. Ⓐ Ⓑ Ⓒ Ⓓ Ⓔ	10. Ⓐ Ⓑ Ⓒ Ⓓ Ⓔ	17. Ⓐ Ⓑ Ⓒ Ⓓ Ⓔ	24. Ⓐ Ⓑ Ⓒ Ⓓ Ⓔ	31. Ⓐ Ⓑ Ⓒ Ⓓ Ⓔ
4. Ⓐ Ⓑ Ⓒ Ⓓ Ⓔ	11. Ⓐ Ⓑ Ⓒ Ⓓ Ⓔ	18. Ⓐ Ⓑ Ⓒ Ⓓ Ⓔ	25. Ⓐ Ⓑ Ⓒ Ⓓ Ⓔ	32. Ⓐ Ⓑ Ⓒ Ⓓ Ⓔ
5. Ⓐ Ⓑ Ⓒ Ⓓ Ⓔ	12. Ⓐ Ⓑ Ⓒ Ⓓ Ⓔ	19. Ⓐ Ⓑ Ⓒ Ⓓ Ⓔ	26. Ⓐ Ⓑ Ⓒ Ⓓ Ⓔ	33. Ⓐ Ⓑ Ⓒ Ⓓ Ⓔ
6. Ⓐ Ⓑ Ⓒ Ⓓ Ⓔ	13. Ⓐ Ⓑ Ⓒ Ⓓ Ⓔ	20. Ⓐ Ⓑ Ⓒ Ⓓ Ⓔ	27. Ⓐ Ⓑ Ⓒ Ⓓ Ⓔ	34. Ⓐ Ⓑ Ⓒ Ⓓ Ⓔ
7. Ⓐ Ⓑ Ⓒ Ⓓ Ⓔ	14. Ⓐ Ⓑ Ⓒ Ⓓ Ⓔ	21. Ⓐ Ⓑ Ⓒ Ⓓ Ⓔ	28. Ⓐ Ⓑ Ⓒ Ⓓ Ⓔ	35. Ⓐ Ⓑ Ⓒ Ⓓ Ⓔ

Section 6

1. Ⓐ Ⓑ Ⓒ Ⓓ Ⓔ   3. Ⓐ Ⓑ Ⓒ Ⓓ Ⓔ   5. Ⓐ Ⓑ Ⓒ Ⓓ Ⓔ   7. Ⓐ Ⓑ Ⓒ Ⓓ Ⓔ   9. Ⓐ Ⓑ Ⓒ Ⓓ Ⓔ
2. Ⓐ Ⓑ Ⓒ Ⓓ Ⓔ   4. Ⓐ Ⓑ Ⓒ Ⓓ Ⓔ   6. Ⓐ Ⓑ Ⓒ Ⓓ Ⓔ   8. Ⓐ Ⓑ Ⓒ Ⓓ Ⓔ   10. Ⓐ Ⓑ Ⓒ Ⓓ Ⓔ

Section 7

1. Ⓐ Ⓑ Ⓒ Ⓓ Ⓔ   8. Ⓐ Ⓑ Ⓒ Ⓓ Ⓔ   15. Ⓐ Ⓑ Ⓒ Ⓓ Ⓔ   22. Ⓐ Ⓑ Ⓒ Ⓓ Ⓔ   29. Ⓐ Ⓑ Ⓒ Ⓓ Ⓔ
2. Ⓐ Ⓑ Ⓒ Ⓓ Ⓔ   9. Ⓐ Ⓑ Ⓒ Ⓓ Ⓔ   16. Ⓐ Ⓑ Ⓒ Ⓓ Ⓔ   23. Ⓐ Ⓑ Ⓒ Ⓓ Ⓔ   30. Ⓐ Ⓑ Ⓒ Ⓓ Ⓔ
3. Ⓐ Ⓑ Ⓒ Ⓓ Ⓔ   10. Ⓐ Ⓑ Ⓒ Ⓓ Ⓔ   17. Ⓐ Ⓑ Ⓒ Ⓓ Ⓔ   24. Ⓐ Ⓑ Ⓒ Ⓓ Ⓔ   31. Ⓐ Ⓑ Ⓒ Ⓓ Ⓔ
4. Ⓐ Ⓑ Ⓒ Ⓓ Ⓔ   11. Ⓐ Ⓑ Ⓒ Ⓓ Ⓔ   18. Ⓐ Ⓑ Ⓒ Ⓓ Ⓔ   25. Ⓐ Ⓑ Ⓒ Ⓓ Ⓔ   32. Ⓐ Ⓑ Ⓒ Ⓓ Ⓔ
5. Ⓐ Ⓑ Ⓒ Ⓓ Ⓔ   12. Ⓐ Ⓑ Ⓒ Ⓓ Ⓔ   19. Ⓐ Ⓑ Ⓒ Ⓓ Ⓔ   26. Ⓐ Ⓑ Ⓒ Ⓓ Ⓔ   33. Ⓐ Ⓑ Ⓒ Ⓓ Ⓔ
6. Ⓐ Ⓑ Ⓒ Ⓓ Ⓔ   13. Ⓐ Ⓑ Ⓒ Ⓓ Ⓔ   20. Ⓐ Ⓑ Ⓒ Ⓓ Ⓔ   27. Ⓐ Ⓑ Ⓒ Ⓓ Ⓔ   34. Ⓐ Ⓑ Ⓒ Ⓓ Ⓔ
7. Ⓐ Ⓑ Ⓒ Ⓓ Ⓔ   14. Ⓐ Ⓑ Ⓒ Ⓓ Ⓔ   21. Ⓐ Ⓑ Ⓒ Ⓓ Ⓔ   28. Ⓐ Ⓑ Ⓒ Ⓓ Ⓔ   35. Ⓐ Ⓑ Ⓒ Ⓓ Ⓔ

Section 8

1. Ⓐ Ⓑ Ⓒ Ⓓ Ⓔ   8. Ⓐ Ⓑ Ⓒ Ⓓ Ⓔ   15. Ⓐ Ⓑ Ⓒ Ⓓ Ⓔ   22. Ⓐ Ⓑ Ⓒ Ⓓ Ⓔ   29. Ⓐ Ⓑ Ⓒ Ⓓ Ⓔ
2. Ⓐ Ⓑ Ⓒ Ⓓ Ⓔ   9. Ⓐ Ⓑ Ⓒ Ⓓ Ⓔ   16. Ⓐ Ⓑ Ⓒ Ⓓ Ⓔ   23. Ⓐ Ⓑ Ⓒ Ⓓ Ⓔ   30. Ⓐ Ⓑ Ⓒ Ⓓ Ⓔ
3. Ⓐ Ⓑ Ⓒ Ⓓ Ⓔ   10. Ⓐ Ⓑ Ⓒ Ⓓ Ⓔ   17. Ⓐ Ⓑ Ⓒ Ⓓ Ⓔ   24. Ⓐ Ⓑ Ⓒ Ⓓ Ⓔ   31. Ⓐ Ⓑ Ⓒ Ⓓ Ⓔ
4. Ⓐ Ⓑ Ⓒ Ⓓ Ⓔ   11. Ⓐ Ⓑ Ⓒ Ⓓ Ⓔ   18. Ⓐ Ⓑ Ⓒ Ⓓ Ⓔ   25. Ⓐ Ⓑ Ⓒ Ⓓ Ⓔ   32. Ⓐ Ⓑ Ⓒ Ⓓ Ⓔ
5. Ⓐ Ⓑ Ⓒ Ⓓ Ⓔ   12. Ⓐ Ⓑ Ⓒ Ⓓ Ⓔ   19. Ⓐ Ⓑ Ⓒ Ⓓ Ⓔ   26. Ⓐ Ⓑ Ⓒ Ⓓ Ⓔ   33. Ⓐ Ⓑ Ⓒ Ⓓ Ⓔ
6. Ⓐ Ⓑ Ⓒ Ⓓ Ⓔ   13. Ⓐ Ⓑ Ⓒ Ⓓ Ⓔ   20. Ⓐ Ⓑ Ⓒ Ⓓ Ⓔ   27. Ⓐ Ⓑ Ⓒ Ⓓ Ⓔ   34. Ⓐ Ⓑ Ⓒ Ⓓ Ⓔ
7. Ⓐ Ⓑ Ⓒ Ⓓ Ⓔ   14. Ⓐ Ⓑ Ⓒ Ⓓ Ⓔ   21. Ⓐ Ⓑ Ⓒ Ⓓ Ⓔ   28. Ⓐ Ⓑ Ⓒ Ⓓ Ⓔ   35. Ⓐ Ⓑ Ⓒ Ⓓ Ⓔ

Chapter 24

Slightly More Fun Than a Root Canal: Practice Exam 2

In This Chapter

▶ Focusing on the SAT (Satan's Attitude Test) once more

▶ Taking a full-length practice SAT exam

*I*f you survived Practice Exam 1, you should be at the movies right now, throwing popcorn at the latest Hollywood shoot-em-up. Still here? Okay, I guess that means you want to try again. Follow the same procedures: Sit in a quiet room, turn off the phone, and place a timer (an ordinary watch or clock works fine) right in front of your face. Spend no more than the allotted time on each part (I tell you how much at the beginning of the section) and resist the temptation to (a) fold the answer sheet into a paper airplane and fly it out the window (b) peek at Chapter 25, which contains the answers and explanations, or (c) call a friend to set up your weekend party schedule.

Section 1

> The Essay
>
> Time: 25 minutes
>
> Directions: In response to the following prompts, write an essay in the space provided on the answer sheet. You may use extra space in the question booklet to take notes and to organize your thoughts, but only the answer sheet will be graded.
>
> > Both the man of science and the man of art live always at the edge of mystery, surrounded by it.
> >
> > —J. Robert Oppenheimer, scientist who worked on the atomic bomb
>
> > But the creative person is subject to a different, higher law than mere national law. Whoever has to create a work, whoever has to bring about a discovery or deed which will further the cause of all of humanity, no longer has his home in his native land but rather in his work.
> >
> > —Stephan Zweig, Austrian writer
>
> To what extent should a scientist, an explorer, or a creative artist consider the consequences of his or her work? Drawing upon your own observations and experience or your knowledge of history, current events, and literature, comment on the obligation of an artist, explorer, or scientist to the public good.

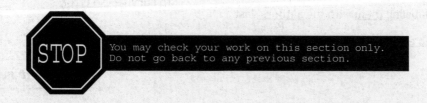

STOP   You may check your work on this section only. Do not go back to any previous section.

Section 2

> Writing: Multiple Choice
>
> Time: 35 minutes
>
> 35 questions

Directions for questions 1–12: Identify the error in the underlined portion of each sentence below. If a sentence contains no errors, choose (E) for "no error." Darken the corresponding oval on your answer sheet.

Example:

Irregardless of the fact that the National
<u>A</u>
Weather Service predicted rain, Dexter
<u>B</u>
resented the students' request to postpone
<u>C</u>   <u>D</u>
the picnic. No error.
<u>E</u>

The correct answer is (A). ● Ⓑ Ⓒ Ⓓ Ⓔ

1. One glance at the curator's notes
<u>A</u>
reveals that the ceramic pot, which is a
<u>B</u>   <u>C</u>
valuable antique, should of been repaired
<u>D</u>
during the night. No error.
<u>E</u>

2. Gazing up at the stars, the telescope was
<u>A</u>   <u>B</u>
not strong enough to please my uncle, who
<u>C</u>
is an ardent amateur astronomer. No error.
<u>D</u>   <u>E</u>

3. For Mortimer's plan to be successful, several
<u>A</u>   <u>B</u>
factors must fall into place immediately, and
<u>C</u>
I don't believe they will. No error.
<u>D</u>   <u>E</u>

4. With efficiency and accuracy, Agatha and
<u>A</u>
Erle placed the mystery novels on the
<u>B</u>
shelves, labeling them with the authors' last
<u>C</u>   <u>D</u>
names. No error.
<u>E</u>

5. The mayor, who we all know is a great
<u>A</u>   <u>B</u>
champion of the poor, has asked the city
<u>C</u>
council to repeal the tax on food and
<u>D</u>
shelter. No error.
<u>E</u>

6. If the bird would have flown a little faster,
<u>A</u>
he would have gone farther and arrived at
<u>B</u>   <u>C</u>   <u>D</u>
the nest before the cat. No error.
<u>E</u>

7. The class trip to the museum was a great
<u>A</u>
success, however, the students missed a
<u>B</u>   <u>C</u>
great deal of normal class work because of
<u>D</u>
their outing. No error.
<u>E</u>

8. His work in advanced mathematics
<u>A</u>
is equally as important as her work
<u>B</u>
in physics, but he is paid less because his
<u>C</u>   <u>D</u>
employer is nearly bankrupt. No error.
<u>E</u>

9. Cinderella's jealous stepsisters objected to
<u>A</u>
Cinderella marrying the prince and stealing
<u>B</u>   <u>C</u>
the attention from themselves. No error.
<u>D</u>   <u>E</u>

10. The affect of the newest forms of technology
<u>A</u>   <u>B</u>
cannot be exaggerated; the recording indus-
<u>C</u>
try must undergo a radical change in order
<u>D</u>
to survive. No error.
<u>E</u>

Go on to next page

11. With ten seconds to go, the students in
    A
    the packed stadium are clapping in the
    B
    belief that either Marshall or his teammates
    C
    has the ability to save the game. No error.
    D   E

12. When Bob read Homer's famous
    A
    epic, *The Odyssey,* he returned the book
    B   C
    to the library and took out still another
    D
    work by the great Greek poet. No error.
    E

Directions for questions 13–26: Each sentence is followed by five choices. Decide which choice best improves the sentence and darken the corresponding oval on the answer sheet. If the underlined portion of the sentence is best left alone, choose (A).

Example: Bert and him went to the store to buy boots in preparation for the approaching storm.

(A) Bert and him went

(B) Bert and he went

(C) Bert and he had gone

(D) Bert and him had gone

(E) Bert and himself went

The correct answer is (B). Ⓐ Ⓒ Ⓓ Ⓔ

---

13. Watching the whale slide effortlessly through the water, the passengers who had all paid high prices for the voyage applauded.

    (A) the passengers who had all paid high prices for the voyage applauded.

    (B) the passengers that had all paid high prices for the voyage applauded.

    (C) the passengers, who had all paid high prices for the voyage, applauded.

    (D) the passengers, that had all paid high prices for the voyage, applauded.

    (E) the passengers all paid high prices for the voyage and applauded.

14. The star shortstop was more skillful at scooping up ground balls than anyone on her team.

    (A) more skillful at scooping up ground balls than anyone

    (B) more skillful at scooping up ground balls than anyone else

    (C) the most skilled at scooping up ground balls than anyone

    (D) skillful at scooping up ground balls more than anyone

    (E) more skilled at scooping up ground balls, than anyone

15. Not only sipping extremely hot coffee but also if you pick up a heated plate without an oven mitt can be dangerous.

    (A) but also if you pick up a heated plate

    (B) but also, if you pick up a heated plate

    (C) but also to pick up a heated plate

    (D) but also picking up a heated plate

    (E) but also if you were picking up a heated plate

16. When the supermarket chain added a prepared foods section, it was clearly a wise move.

    (A) When the supermarket chain added a prepared foods section, it

    (B) The supermarket chain added a prepared foods section, and it

    (C) The supermarket chain having added a prepared foods section, it

    (D) The supermarket chain's adding a prepared foods section

    (E) The supermarket chain adding a prepared foods section

17. Everyone in the chorus, except Tomas and I, is going to wear black robes for tonight's concert.

    (A) the chorus, except Tomas and I, is going

    (B) the chorus except Tomas and I is going

    (C) the chorus, except Tomas and I, are going

    (D) the chorus, except Tomas and me, is going

    (E) the chorus, accept Tomas and I, is going

Go on to next page

18. The photograph that everyone is searching for, which <u>was taken last July, has been sitting</u> in my album for three weeks and is still there.

    (A) was taken last July, has been sitting

    (B) had been taken last July, has been sitting

    (C) has taken last July, has been sitting

    (D) was taken last July, have been sitting

    (E) was taken last July, will have been sitting

19. The huge slate of candidates means that the voters may select <u>whoever they like the best</u> for the post of vice-president.

    (A) whoever they like the best

    (B) whoever they like best

    (C) whoever they like better

    (D) who they like the best

    (E) whomever they like the best

20. Doris's grandmother traveled around the world and <u>only mailed three postcards, not the ninety that she had bought.</u>

    (A) only mailed three postcards, not the ninety that she had bought.

    (B) mailed only three postcards, not the ninety that she had bought.

    (C) only mailed three postcards, not the ninety that she bought.

    (D) mailed three postcards, not the ninety that she only bought.

    (E) only mailed three postcards, not the ninety she had bought.

21. By the time she graduates from college, <u>Marisa will have taken courses</u> in every major subject.

    (A) Marisa will have taken courses

    (B) Marisa has taken courses

    (C) Marisa took courses

    (D) Marisa would have taken courses

    (E) courses will be taken by Marisa

22. <u>To write a good essay, a dictionary and a word processing program are helpful.</u>

    (A) To write a good essay, a dictionary and a word processing program are helpful.

    (B) A dictionary and a word processing program are helpful to write a good essay.

    (C) To write a good essay, a dictionary and a word processing program is helpful.

    (D) Writing a good essay, a dictionary and a word processing program are helpful.

    (E) To write a good essay, you may find that a dictionary and a word processing program are helpful.

23. <u>She feels very bad about having forgotten</u> the little boy's name, but she plans to apologize for the lapse.

    (A) She feels very bad about having forgotten

    (B) She feels very badly about having forgotten

    (C) She feels very badly about forgetting

    (D) She feels very badly that she forgot

    (E) Having forgotten, she feels bad about

24. <u>There's three pencils and a stack of paper</u> on the editor's desk, supplies for the busy reporters of a major newspaper.

    (A) There's three pencils and a stack of paper

    (B) There are three pencils and a stack of paper

    (C) There is three pencils and a stack of paper

    (D) They're three pencils and a stack of paper

    (E) There is a stack of paper and three pencils

Go on to next page

25. <u>Children in kindergarten love paints and markers; this often</u> results in messy hands and clothing.

    (A) Children in kindergarten love paints and markers; this often

    (B) Children in kindergarten love paints and markers, and this often

    (C) Children in kindergarten love paints and markers, this often

    (D) Kindergarten children's love of paints and markers often

    (E) Kindergarten childrens' love of paints and markers often

26. <u>Interested in family history, Lucy is searching for information about her father's mother, her grandmother,</u> in order to construct a complete family tree.

    (A) Interested in family history, Lucy is searching for information about her father's mother, her grandmother,

    (B) Having become interested in family history, Lucy is searching for information about her father's mother, her grandmother,

    (C) Interested in family history, Lucy is searching for information about her grandmother,

    (D) Interested in family history Lucy is searching for information about her grandmother,

    (E) Interested, Lucy is searching for information about her grandmother,

> Directions: Questions 27–35 are based on the essay below. Choose the best answer and darken the corresponding oval on the answer sheet.

(1) In choosing a college the possibility of studying in a foreign country should be considered. (2) Whether saying *guten tag* or *buenos dias* or *bon jour,* the chance to learn about another culture cannot be duplicated. (3) Personally, in my opinion I think that no true education is complete without at least one semester abroad.

(4) I studied in Spain. (5) I learned about Spanish history from people who lived it. (6) My art lessons in the United States were only taught from slides and reproductions, but in Spain I studied in the Prado, the most famous art museum in the country. (7) This is a great advantage to students because the paintings are very vivid when seen personally. (8) I attended a bullfight twice, consequently I understood that this ancient ritual is not just about the animal being killed but rather about a struggle against death that must be lost by everyone some day.

(9) Students go to many countries for this sort of education, and they return better than when they went. (10) Their language skills are not the only improvement. (11) In a recent study by psychologists it says that students who have lived in more than one country show more tolerance of the different customs they may encounter in their daily life. (12) This reason, along with many others, justifies the time and expense of foreign study. (13) In conclusion, I think that everyone should study outside of their own country at least once in their lives.

27. The best revision for sentence 1 is

    (A) In choosing a college the possibility of studying in a foreign country should be considered. (no change)

    (B) Everyone should consider the possibility of studying in a foreign country when they are choosing a college.

    (C) To choose a college, consider the possibility that you may study abroad.

    (D) In choosing a college, consider the possibility of foreign study.

    (E) Everyone, in choosing a college, should consider whether they can study abroad.

Go on to next page

28. A good revision for sentence 2 is

    (A) Whether saying *guten tag* or *buenos dias* or *bon jour,* the chance to learn about another culture cannot be duplicated. (no change)

    (B) Whether you say *guten tag* or *buenos dias* or *bon jour,* the chance to learn about another culture is unique and can't be duplicated.

    (C) Whether you say *guten tag* or *buenos dias* or *bon jour,* the chance to learn about another culture is unique.

    (D) The chance to learn about another culture can't be duplicated according to whether one says *guten tag* or *buenos dias* or *bon jour.*

    (E) It doesn't matter whether you say *guten tag* or *buenos dias* or *bon jour,* the chance to learn about another culture can't be duplicated.

29. Sentence 3 needs

    (A) its repetitive material deleted

    (B) a more general viewpoint

    (C) more detail, including examples

    (D) a more emphatic statement of opinion

    (E) to be broken into two sentences

30. The best way to combine sentences 4 and 5 is

    (A) I studied in Spain, I learned about Spanish history from people who lived it.

    (B) Studied in Spain, I learned about Spanish history from people who lived it.

    (C) I studied in Spain, and I learned about Spanish history from people who lived it.

    (D) When I studied in Spain, I learned about Spanish history from people who lived it.

    (E) Given that I studied in Spain, I learned about Spanish history from people who lived it.

31. The main purpose of paragraph two is to

    (A) amplify the author's statement that all foreign sites may be educational

    (B) argue with the reader who sees disadvantages to foreign study

    (C) support the idea that studying abroad gives insight into culture

    (D) give the reader an impression of life in Spain

    (E) to introduce the narrator of the piece on a personal level

32. What is the best revision of sentence 7?

    (A) This is a great advantage to students because the paintings are very vivid when seen personally. (no change)

    (B) A student who views the paintings and not reproductions has a great advantage.

    (C) This great advantage makes the paintings vivid.

    (D) To view the paintings vividly is a great advantage.

    (E) When seen personally, a student has a great advantage in terms of paintings.

33. What is the best revision of sentence 8?

    (A) I attended a bullfight twice, consequently I understood that this ancient ritual is not just about the animal being killed but rather about a struggle against death that must be lost by everyone some day. (No change)

    (B) Attending two bullfights, I understood that this ancient ritual presents a no-win struggle against death.

    (C) After two bullfights, I saw that the ancient ritual presents a struggle against death that is doomed to failure, not simply the killing of an animal.

    (D) I couldn't understand the real meaning of the bullfight until I saw two. It is about the struggle against death that we lose.

    (E) Attending two bullfights, consequently I understand the meaning of the ancient ritual, which is that everyone dies.

Go on to next page

34. How should sentences 9 and 10 be combined?

   (A) Students go to many countries for this sort of education, and they return better than when they went because not only are their language skills improved.

   (B) Students return better than when they went from many countries, in more than language skills.

   (C) Language skills are not the only improvement for students studying in foreign countries.

   (D) Students' language skills are not the only improvement.

   (E) Students better their language skills and other things.

35. What is the best revision of sentence 11?

   (A) In a recent study by psychologists it says that students who have lived in more than one country show more tolerance of the different customs they may encounter in their daily life. (no change)

   (B) A recent psychological study reported that students who have lived in more than one country show more tolerance of different customs encountered in daily life.

   (C) A recent study by psychologists says that students who have lived in more than one country show more tolerance of the different customs they may encounter in their daily life.

   (D) In a recent study by psychologists it says that students who have lived in more than one country are more tolerant of different customs in their daily life.

   (E) More tolerance of different customs they may encounter in daily life is the result of living abroad, according to a recent psychology study.

STOP You may check your work on this section only. Do not go back to any previous section.

Section 3

> Critical Reading
>
> Time: 25 minutes
>
> 25 questions

> Directions for questions 1–12: Choose the best answer to each question based on what is stated or implied in the passage or in the introductory material. Darken the corresponding oval on the answer sheet.

This passage from *Freud: Darkness in the Midst of Vision* by Louis Breger (Wiley, 2000) discusses the work of Jean-Marie Charcot, a 19th century pioneer of psychology who studied hysteria.

Line

By the late 1880s, Charcot had turned his attention to hysteria, and it was here that his need for power and control most interfered with his scientific aims. Hysteria — from the Greek
(05) word for "womb" — was a little understood condition, sometimes believed to be no more than malingering. It was stigmatized by the medical establishment and associated with witchcraft and medieval states of possession. Hysterical patients
(10) displayed a variety of symptoms including amnesias, paralyses, spasms, involuntary movements, and anesthesias. Closely related were cases of so-called neurasthenia, characterized by weakness and lassitude. Unlike the neurological con-
(15) ditions that Charcot had previously studied, no anatomical basis could be found for these syndromes. Looking back from today's vantage point, it is doubtful if there ever was a single entity that could be described as hysteria. The diagnosis
(20) was, rather, a grab bag for a variety of conditions whose common feature was that they were "psychological," that no discernable physical causes could be found for them. From a modern standpoint, the so-called hysterics comprised a diverse
(25) group: some probably had medical conditions that were undiagnosable at the time, others psychotic and borderline disorders, and many — it seems clear from the descriptions — suffered from severe anxiety, depression, the effects of a
(30) variety of traumas, and dissociated states.

Charcot made crucial contributions to the understanding of hysteria, clarifying the psychological-traumatic nature of symptoms and conducting convincing hypnotic demonstrations. In addition to the so-called hysterical women on (35) the wards of the [hospital], there were a number of persons of both sexes who had been involved in accidents — for example, train wrecks — who displayed symptoms such as paralyses after the accident. Some of them were classified as cases of (40) "railway spine" and "railway brain" because their symptoms mimicked those found after spinal cord or brain injuries. Physicians debated, with much fervor, whether these conditions had a physical basis. Charcot studied several such patients and (45) was able to demonstrate the absence of damage to the nervous system, hence proving the psychological nature of the symptoms. His most convincing demonstration relied on the use of hypnosis, a procedure which he had rehabilitated and made (50) scientifically respectable. He was able to hypnotize subjects and suggest that when they awoke from their trances their limbs would be paralyzed. These hypnotically induced symptoms were exactly the same as those of both hysterical (55) patients and the victims of accidents. He was also able to remove such symptoms with hypnotic suggestion. In a related demonstration, he was able to distinguish between hysterical and organic amnesia, using hypnosis to help (60) patients recover lost memories, which was not possible, of course, when the amnesia was based on the destruction of brain tissue. While these demonstrations established the psychological nature of hysterical symptoms, it was a psychol- (65) ogy without awareness. The patients were not conscious, either of the origin and nature of their symptoms — they were not malingering or deliberately faking — or of their reactions to the hypnotic suggestions. Charcot spoke of a post- (70) traumatic "hypnoid state" — what today would be called dissociation — the blotting out of consciousness of events and emotions associated with traumatic events.

Charcot's genuine contributions were several. (75) He made hysteria a respectable subject of scientific study, described and classified syndromes on the basis of symptoms, and differentiated the condition from known neurological diseases. By

Go on to next page

(80) documenting a number of cases of male hysteria, he disproved the old link between the condition and the organs of female sexuality. He reestablished hypnotism as a research tool and showed how it could be employed to induce and remove (85) hysterical and post-traumatic symptoms. Finally, and perhaps most significant in terms of its long-range importance for Freud, all these findings and demonstrations gave evidence of an unconscious mind.

1. According to the passage, hysteria was once considered

   (A) cause for lifelong hospitalization

   (B) treatable only with powerful drugs

   (C) fully understood

   (D) incurable

   (E) possession by an evil spirit

2. The author cites all of the following conditions as hysterical *except*

   (A) lack of feeling

   (B) inability to move

   (C) uncontrolled bodily activity

   (D) wild laughter

   (E) memory loss

3. The meaning of "psychological" (lines 21–22) in this context may best be described as

   (A) mentally ill

   (B) requiring psychotherapy

   (C) not arising from a physical condition

   (D) the result of childhood events

   (E) unconscious

4. According to the passage, Charcot

   (A) linked hysteria to disturbing events in the patient's life

   (B) cured hysteria

   (C) understood that hysteria was actually a group of illnesses, not one condition

   (D) relied primarily on drug therapy for his patients

   (E) could not prove the effectiveness of this treatment

5. The author probably mentions patients "of both sexes" (line 37)

   (A) to counter the idea that only females become hysterical

   (B) to be fair to both male and female patients

   (C) even though Charcot treated only women

   (D) to show that Charcot treated everyone who asked

   (E) because Charcot believed that hysteria was linked to female anatomy

6. "Railway spine" and "railway brain" (line 41) are

   (A) injuries resulting from train accidents

   (B) terms once used for conditions resembling paralysis and head injuries

   (C) imaginary ailments intended to deceive insurance companies

   (D) physical injuries that take a psychological toll

   (E) states displayed only under hypnosis

7. Charcot used hypnosis for all of the following except

   (A) to distinguish between physical and psychological symptoms

   (B) to enable a patient to move body parts that were previously immobile

   (C) to restore memories to some patients

   (D) to paralyze a patient

   (E) to retrieve memories from brain-damaged patients

8. "Dissociation" (line 72) results from

   (A) a blow to the head

   (B) an unconscious process

   (C) physical trauma

   (D) a desire to deceive the doctor

   (E) a deliberate forgetting of disturbing experiences

Go on to next page

9. By inserting the word "genuine" into line 75, the author implies that

    (A) some of Charot's work did not advance science

    (B) Charcot was sincere in his belief that hysteria was a real illness

    (C) Charcot should not be overly praised

    (D) Charcot was more important than Freud

    (E) Charcot's work can be duplicated by other scientists

10. Based on information in the passage, the author would probably agree with which of the following statements?

    (A) Hysteria is best treated with hypnosis.

    (B) Hysterics should not be treated medically.

    (C) Hysteria is always linked to severe physical danger, such as a train wreck.

    (D) To scientists today, *hysteria* is a meaningless term.

    (E) Hysteria is a condition of female patients.

11. The author's tone may best be described as

    (A) nostalgic

    (B) admiring

    (C) biased

    (D) informative

    (E) critical

12. A good title for this passage is

    (A) Charcot's Work on Hysteria

    (B) Charcot and Psychology

    (C) Charcot's Influence on Freud

    (D) The Life of Jean-Marie Charcot

    (E) Hysteria from Ancient through Modern Times

Directions for questions 13–16: Choose the best answer to each question based on what is stated or implied in the passage or in the introductory material. Darken the corresponding oval on the answer sheet.

Questions 13 and 14 are based on the following passage, excerpted from *The Hidden Universe* by Roger J. Tayler (Wiley, 1994).

Some direct study of the past is in fact possible because light from distant objects such as galaxies has taken a very long time to reach the Earth. Although light travels 300,000 kilometers in a second, it is possible to observe galaxies (05) which are so distant that light has taken much more than a thousand million years to reach us. We are therefore seeing these galaxies as they were a very long time ago, whereas we are seeing nearby galaxies as they were only a few million (10) years ago and the Sun as it was eight minutes ago.

13. According to the passage

    (A) Nearby galaxies give off light that is older than light from distant galaxies.

    (B) It is possible to see a current view of distant galaxies.

    (C) Light from the sun shows that the sun is farther from the Earth than other stars.

    (D) Light that reaches our eyes may have originated during different time periods.

    (E) Light travels at different speeds depending upon which galaxy it originates from.

14. A good title for this passage would be

    (A) Time Travel

    (B) The Speed of Light

    (C) Direct Study of the Past

    (D) Characteristics of Light

    (E) The Relationship between Light, Time, and Distance

Go on to next page

Questions 15 and 16 are based on the following passage, excerpted from *Rogue Asteroids and Doomsday Comets* by Duncan Steel (Wiley, 1995).

Line   If one asks another casual visitor to that megalithic monument [Stonehenge] to define its purpose, the answer will generally be along the lines of, "I think it has something to do with
(05) astronomy and observing the Sun." What I am going to argue is that the first part of that answer is correct — that it does have something to do with astronomy — but that the original construction at Stonehenge was for observing an astro-
(10) nomical phenomenon that as yet has not been recognized. The conundrum of the original motivation of Stonehenge is abstruse and recondite, even profound, and has occupied archaeologists and astronomers alike for decades.

15. According to the passage, Stonehenge

(A) was built to study the position of the sun

(B) was intended to study another aspect of astronomy

(C) can be understood by archaeologists

(D) has not been studied well

(E) should be considered an unsolvable mystery

16. The words inside the dashes (lines 7–8) are intended to

(A) give an example of a mistake often made about Stonehenge

(B) explain the author's view of archaeology

(C) show people's misconceptions about Stonehenge

(D) illustrate the "first part of the answer" that the author refers to

(E) specify the monument's purpose

Directions for questions 17–25: Select the answer that best fits the meaning of the sentence and darken the corresponding oval on the answer sheet.

Example: After he had broken the dining room window, Hal's mother _____ him.

(A) selected

(B) serenaded

(C) fooled

(D) grounded

(E) rewarded

The answer is (D). Ⓐ Ⓑ Ⓒ ● Ⓔ

17. The vice president was _____ by the behavior of the president, who did not even glance at his second-in-command during the inauguration ceremony.

(A) buoyed

(B) reassured

(C) intimidated

(D) inspired

(E) affected

18. The _____ of various city states into one nation triggered a period of extraordinary artistic and social growth.

(A) segregation

(B) integration

(C) polarization

(D) proclamation

(E) division

19. Angered by the loss of _____ evidence, the detective _____ his subordinates.

(A) crucial . . . upbraided

(B) insignificant . . . scolded

(C) outdated . . . demoted

(D) compelling . . . promoted

(E) adverse . . . affronted

Go on to next page

20. The _____ corporation took pains to safeguard its _____ production methods.

    (A) deregulated . . . multifaceted

    (B) moribund . . . innovative

    (C) affluent . . . lucrative

    (D) secretive . . . well-publicized

    (E) scrupulous . . . unethical

21. The pragmatic teacher's goal was not to create a test that was particularly easy or hard for her pupils but rather one that _____ their studies.

    (A) discouraged

    (B) heightened

    (C) repressed

    (D) daunted

    (E) motivated

22. The variety of characters Shakespeare created makes his plays unique, and actors from every age strive to interpret the _____ roles he created.

    (A) myriad

    (B) convoluted

    (C) versatile

    (D) intuitive

    (E) nebulous

23. Lucy continued her crusade to save the rainforest; furthermore, she strove to _____ the local animal population.

    (A) annihilate

    (B) decimate

    (C) eradicate

    (D) preserve

    (E) proliferate

24. Dagmar was always _____ in her approach to homework, never completing today what she could postpone until the last possible minute.

    (A) doleful

    (B) doctrinaire

    (C) diffident

    (D) diligent

    (E) dilatory

25. The _____ performance by that actor garnered few _____ from the audience.

    (A) conventional . . . critiques

    (B) effective . . . ovations

    (C) convincing . . . plaudits

    (D) affected . . . kudos

    (E) explicit . . . explanations

STOP You may check your work on this section only. Do not go back to any previous section.

Section 4

Mathematics

Time: 25 minutes

25 questions

Notes:

✔ You may use a calculator.

✔ All numbers used in this exam are real numbers.

✔ All figures lie in a plane.

✔ All figures may be assumed to be to scale unless the problem specifically indicates otherwise.

$A = \pi r^2$
$C = 2\pi r$

$A = lw$

$A = \frac{1}{2}bh$

$V = lwh$

$V = \pi r^2 h$

$c^2 = a^2 + b^2$

Special right triangles

There are 360 degrees of arc in a circle.

There are 180 degrees in a straight line.

There are 180 degrees in the sum of the interior angles of a triangle.

Directions: Choose the best answer and darken the corresponding oval on the answer sheet.

1. Including one and itself, which of the following numbers has the greatest number of factors?

   (A) 16

   (B) 20

   (C) 24

   (D) 28

   (E) 32

2. If $p = -5$ and $q = -4$, then $p(p - q) =$

   (A) −45

   (B) −5

   (C) 4

   (D) 5

   (E) 45

Go on to next page

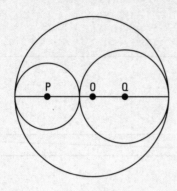

3. In this circle, point O is the center of the large circle, and points P and Q are the centers of the two smaller circles. If the distance PQ = 6, then the area of the large circle is

(A) 144π

(B) 72π

(C) 36π

(D) 12π

(E) 6π

4. If the ratio of k to m is the same as the ratio of m to n, then which of the following must be true?

(A) $kn = m^2$

(B) $k + m = m + n$

(C) $kn = 2m$

(D) $km = mn$

(E) $k - m = m - n$

5. Two circles lie in a plane and share the same center. A line is drawn such that the line never enters the smaller circle. What is the maximum number of total points at which the line could touch the circles?

(A) 0

(B) 1

(C) 2

(D) 3

(E) 4

6. A coat was on sale for 50% off. Katie bought the coat, using a "25% off the current price" coupon. If she paid $36 for the coat, what was its original price?

(A) $40

(B) $72

(C) $90

(D) $96

(E) $144

Go on to next page

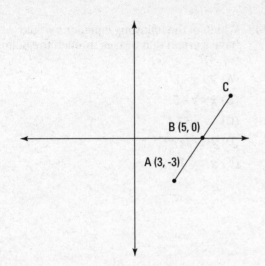

9. Let >*n* be defined as the smallest perfect square greater than *n*. For example, >3 = 4 and >4 = 9. Which of the following is equal to >5 + >9?

  (A) >10

  (B) >14

  (C) >20

  (D) >25

  (E) >45

7. Given that B is the midpoint of line segment AC, which of the following is *not* true?

  (A) The distance from A to C is 5 units.

  (B) Point C has coordinates (7, 3).

  (C) The distance from A to B is equal to the distance from B to C.

  (D) The line segment connecting A to B has the same slope as the line segment connecting B to C.

  (E) The slope of AC is positive.

8. Given that *o* is odd and that *e* is even, which of the following must be odd?

  (A) *oe*

  (B) $(o - e)(o + e)$

  (C) $o(o + 1)$

  (D) $(e + 1)(o - 1)$

  (E) $e(o - e)$

10. A train leaves the station at 10:45 p.m., and arrives at its destination at 2 a.m. the next day (without changing time zones). The train was stopped for ½ hour while it had engine trouble; the rest of the time, it averaged 80 miles per hour. What total distance did it travel?

  (A) 120 miles

  (B) 140 miles

  (C) 220 miles

  (D) 240 miles

  (E) 260 miles

11. How many hours are in *w* weeks and *d* days?

  (A) $7w + d$

  (B) $168w + 24d$

  (C) $24w + 168d$

  (D) $168w + d$

  (E) $7w + 24d$

Go on to next page

12. A list of three integers has an average (arithmetic mean) of 6. If the median of the numbers is –1, what is the smallest positive number that could appear in the list?

(A) 1

(B) 6

(C) 18

(D) 20

(E) 21

14. Which of the following equations would have a graph that passes through the point (–1, 4)?

(A) $y = x - 5$

(B) $x + y = 5$

(C) $-x + 3 = y$

(D) $2y - 3x = 5$

(E) $y = x^2 + 5$

13. Getting ready for a party, Nandan expected to set up ⅓ of the tables needed. Unfortunately, one of the people helping him did not show up. As a result, he now had to set up ½ of the tables. If he had to set up 4 more tables than he expected, what was the total number of tables set up for the party?

(A) 8

(B) 12

(C) 20

(D) 24

(E) 30

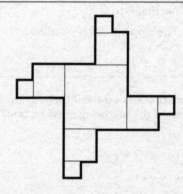

15. In this figure, each side of the large center square is twice as long as each side of the four medium-sized squares. Each side of the medium-sized squares is twice as long as each side of the four small squares. If the small squares have sides of length 1 cm, find the perimeter of the entire figure.

(A) 40 cm

(B) 52 cm

(C) 60 cm

(D) 64 cm

(E) 80 cm

Go on to next page

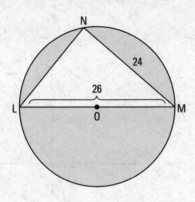

16. Find the shaded area in this figure, where O is the center of the circle.

    (A) $676\pi - 240$

    (B) $676\pi - 120$

    (C) $576\pi - 120$

    (D) $169\pi - 240$

    (E) $169\pi - 120$

17. The three-digit number ABC has the following properties:

    The middle digit is the sum of the first and last digits.

    None of the digits repeat.

    ABC is divisible by 5.

    Which of the following could equal B?

    (A) 6

    (B) 5

    (C) 4

    (D) 3

    (E) 2

Questions 18–20 deal with the following graph of $f(x)$:

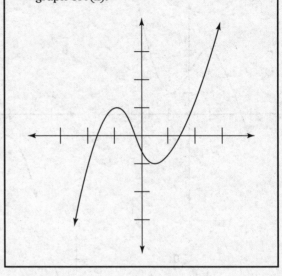

18. The number of solutions to $f(x) = 0$ is:

    (A) 0

    (B) 1

    (C) 2

    (D) 3

    (E) It cannot be determined from the graph alone.

Go on to next page

19.   Which of the following graphs represents $f(x) - 2$?

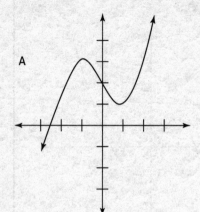

A

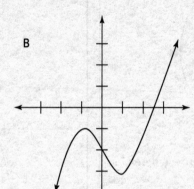

B

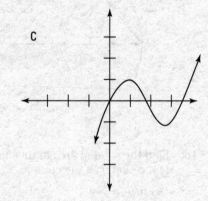

C

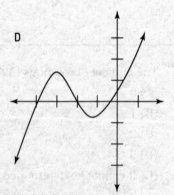

D

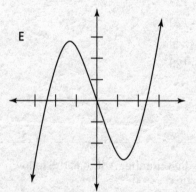

E

20.   If a line were drawn connecting $f(3)$ and $f(-2)$, the slope of this line would be:

(A) positive

(B) negative

(C) zero

(D) not a real number

(E) It cannot be determined from the graph alone.

21.   If $|a - b| < 4$ and $|a| < 3$, then b could be:

(A) –8

(B) –7

(C) –6

(D) 7

(E) 8

Go on to next page

22. At 1 p.m., a 5-foot tall boy casts a shadow that is 1 foot 3 inches long. How tall is a tree that casts a shadow that is 7 feet long at the same time?

    (A) 35 feet

    (B) 28 feet

    (C) 26 feet, 9 inches

    (D) 10 feet, 9 inches

    (E) 1 foot, 8 inches

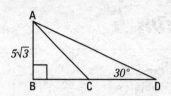

24. In this triangle, AC bisects angle BAD. Find AC. (Figure is not drawn to scale.)

    (A) $5\sqrt{2}$

    (B) $5\sqrt{3}$

    (C) $10\sqrt{3}$

    (D) 5

    (E) 10

23. If $vw = x$, $wx = y$, and $xy = z$, which of the following would be equal to yz?

    (A) v^2w^2

    (B) v^3w^5

    (C) v^4w^4

    (D) v^4w^6

    (E) v^5w^8

25. Rick and Jacob play a game in which each one rolls two six-sided dice [each die is numbered from one to six]. Rick's score is the sum of his two rolls. Jacob's score is three times the lowest number that he rolls; for example, if he rolls a 2 and a 5, his score is 6. On his first roll, Rick rolls a 4 and a 5. Find the probability that Jacob's rolls will result in his having exactly the same score as Rick.

    (A) $\frac{1}{12}$

    (B) $\frac{1}{12}$

    (C) $\frac{2}{36}$

    (D) $\frac{1}{36}$

    (E) $\frac{3}{36}$

STOP You may check your work on this section only. Do not go back to any previous section.

Section 5

Critical Reading

Time: 25 minutes

24 questions

Directions for questions 1–15: Base your answers on information in either or both of these passages. You may also answer questions on what is implied in the passages or about the relationship between the two passages. After choosing the best answer, darken the corresponding oval on your answer sheet.

Passage I is an excerpt from *The Big Splat, or How Our Moon Came to Be* by Dana Mackenzie (Wiley, 2003). It discusses problems involved in creating an accurate measure of longitude. Passage II, which is taken from *A Brief History of Flight* by T.A. Heppenheimer (Wiley, 2000), describes ways in which early aircraft pilots navigated.

Passage 1

Line   In the 1700s and 1800s, as the world economy became increasingly dependent on long-distance sea voyages and exploration of unknown lands, navigation on the open seas became one of the
(05) greatest scientific problems of the day. Even in charted waters, a ship could run aground if its course had been plotted incorrectly. And in uncharted waters, what would be the use of discovering a new island or harbor if you might
(10) never find it again?

    The position of a ship can be described by its latitude and longitude. Finding the latitude — the ship's distance north or south of the equator, measured in degrees — was a fairly routine
(15) matter. In the northern hemisphere, it is especially simple. The higher in the sky the North Star is, the farther you are from the equator; for example, if it is fifty degrees above the horizon, you are at fifty degrees north latitude. If it is just
(20) on the horizon, you are on the equator.

    Longitude was a whole different matter. Nowadays, longitude is measured in terms of the number of degrees east or west of the prime meridian, which passes through the Royal Obser-
(25) vatory in Greenwich, England. However, that has

been the custom only since 1884; before then, a captain would measure his position with respect to a port in his home country.

    The lack of a standard "starting place" for
(30) longitudes was only a minor part of the main problem, which was that no one had a good way of measuring east-to-west distances. Because of Earth's rotation, the longitude difference corresponds to the difference between local time and
(35) the time at your port of departure, with each hour of time corresponding to fifteen degrees of longitude. The local time is easy to determine, because the sun is highest in the sky at noon. But it is not so easy to keep track of the time in your
(40) port of origin. Until 1761, there were no clocks capable of keeping steady time on board a rocking ship. Even as late as the early 1800s, naval chronometers were still too expensive to be standard equipment. Thus sailors had to look for
(45) other ways to keep track of the time back home.

Passage II

    Pilots navigated by following railroad tracks, swooping down to read a town's name from a water tower. When the weather closed in, they came down to low altitudes and continued
(50) onward, still following the tracks. This practice developed such nuances as keeping to the right, to avoid collisions with low-flying oncoming planes. Hazards of the business included running into a locomotive, or hitting a hill pierced
(55) by a tunnel.

    In 1923 Paul Henderson began lighting airways across the nation. The effort featured lighthouses, 50-foot steel towers supporting revolving beacons of 500,000 candlepower that were fitted
(60) with 6-inch reflectors. These marked the main airfields and could be seen a hundred miles away. Smaller beacons, visible for sixty miles, marked the emergency fields. Flashing acetylene lamps, spaced every three miles, defined the route.

    The first such airway ran between Chicago
(65) and Cheyenne, Wyoming, in flat country where construction was easy. It covered the central one-third of the country. Flights could then take off

Go on to next page

from either coast at dawn, reach the airway by (70) dusk, then fly through the night along its length and continue onward the next day. In initial tests, Henderson showed that his aircraft could beat the trains by two or even three days. He spanned the nation by extending his lighted airways across (75) the Appalachians and the Rockies, and launched a scheduled coast-to-coast service. It began in mid 1924 and soon settled down to definite times of less than thirty hours eastbound and under thirty-six hours westbound.

(80) The Commerce Department extended these lighted airways during the subsequent decade; its lines of beacons formed an eighteen-thousand-mile network by 1933. Again, though, pilots could see and follow these lights only when visibility (85) was adequate. When this was not the case, they continued to rely on the time-honored procedure of following the railroad tracks. They even did this at night, turning on landing lights. The steel rails, brightly illuminated, looked like ribbons of (90) silver as they rolled past.

Radio also became useful for navigation, creating beamlike transmissions that fliers could follow from one transmitter to the next. It was not possible to produce a true beam like that from a (95) searchlight; that would have demanded the use of microwave frequencies, which were beyond the state of the art. Instead the emphasis was on the clever use of low-frequency methods, with which it proved possible to offer a valuable (100) service.

The key was the loop antenna, a rectangular circuit of wires rising vertically from the ground. It gave the strongest signal when facing the loop edge-on, as well as for some distance to the left (105) or right. But there was little or no signal at right angles to this direction. German investigators had learned of this as early as 1908, and the firm Telefunken had introduced a radio navigation system for the wartime dirigibles. It did not work (110) well, particularly at long distances, and after the war the U.S. Army's Signal corps asked the National Bureau of Standards to come up with something better.

1. Both Passage I and Passage II primarily concern

   (A) human ingenuity in the face of difficulty

   (B) difficulties in navigation

   (C) the importance of determining where you are located

   (D) flight navigation

   (E) ship navigation

2. The tone of both passages may best be described as

   (A) inspirational

   (B) critical

   (C) entertaining

   (D) informational

   (E) sentimental

3. In contrast to Passage I, Passage II

   (A) concerns a more modern era

   (B) is more scientific

   (C) gives more detail about navigation

   (D) focuses more on the problems of navigation

   (E) has a more historical view

4. Passage I implies that "charted waters" (line 6)

   (A) are more shallow than uncharted waters

   (B) are not safe if the chart is followed incorrectly

   (C) are close to land, not on the open sea

   (D) may be charted inaccurately

   (E) are more dangerous than open water

5. The words "Longitude was a whole different matter" (line 21)

   (A) emphasize the ease of determining latitude

   (B) alert the reader to the fact that different methods were used to calculate longitude

   (C) refer to the difficulty in calculating latitude

   (D) explain why longitude was easier to calculate than latitude

   (E) set up a contrast with latitude

Go on to next page

6. Passage I relates time to distance because

    (A) neither can be measured with complete accuracy

    (B) distance is relative to the time of day

    (C) the distance between two points may be measured by the difference in local time at each point

    (D) time is relative when you are traveling

    (E) it takes time to travel

7. Passage I implies that accurate time-pieces

    (A) were invented by the Royal Navy

    (B) were destroyed by the movement of a ship

    (C) were invented in order to facilitate navigation

    (D) did not always work at sea before 1761

    (E) did not exist until 1761

8. According to Passage I, naval chronometers (lines 42–43) are probably

    (A) clocks especially adapted to tell time at sea

    (B) devices that have been in existence since ancient times

    (C) useful only at sea

    (D) part of the Royal Navy's battle equipment

    (E) difficult to use

9. According to Passage II, early pilots

    (A) could navigate without visual cues

    (B) could not fly too high

    (C) faced danger on the ground

    (D) were required to fly at night

    (E) gained experience on railroads

10. Pilots descended in bad weather (lines 48–50) in order to

    (A) avoid lightning

    (B) see landmarks more clearly

    (C) be ready for emergency landings

    (D) alert a train conductor to their routes

    (E) save fuel

11. In the context of Passage II, which of the following descriptions do not refer to "Lighthouses" (lines 57–58)?

    (A) navigational aids for planes

    (B) moving displays of lights

    (C) markers at prominent airfields

    (D) towers with reflectors and high-power lamps

    (E) navigational aids for ships

12. Passage II implies that lighted airways

    (A) were bad for the environment

    (B) made air travel competitive with train travel

    (C) crisscrossed hilly areas before they were built on flat surfaces

    (D) made air travel less expensive

    (E) helped train travel compete with air travel

13. The "landing lights" (line 88) probably

    (A) were better than lightways in clear weather

    (B) could be turned on only when the plane was on land

    (C) could be used only during landing

    (D) illuminated the earth under the plane

    (E) alerted the airport that the plane was about to land

14. The invention of radio (lines 91–102)

    (A) perfected long distance navigation

    (B) had no effect on aviation

    (C) made air travel easier

    (D) depended upon a loop antenna

    (E) was achieved by a German company

Go on to next page

Directions for questions 15–24: Select the answer that best fits the meaning of the sentence and darken the corresponding oval on the answer sheet.

Example: Fearful of _____ insulting his host, Mike read a book about the etiquette of the country he was visiting.

(A) purposely

(B) politely

(C) happily

(D) accidentally

(E) unconsciously

The answer is (D). Ⓐ Ⓑ Ⓒ ● Ⓔ

15. According to animal behaviorists, all breeds share _____ characteristics, though each dog exhibits _____ traits.

(A) exceptional . . . extreme

(B) ordinary . . . everyday

(C) genetic . . . significant

(D) common . . . unique

(E) adverse . . . shared

16. After hours of intense study and with the help of a powerful computer, the detective was able to decipher the meaning of the victim's _____ note.

(A) cryptic

(B) unintelligible

(C) legible

(D) noxious

(E) restrained

17. The malfunction of even one connection _____ the entire system.

(A) surmounts

(B) nullifies

(C) consolidates

(D) jeopardizes

(E) champions

18. The assortment of dolls in the heir's room was quite _____, ranging from heroic soldiers to delicate infants to exotic fashion figures.

(A) eclectic

(B) uniform

(C) universal

(D) mundane

(E) expensive

19. Curiosity about the _____ of life on Mars has resulted in a(n) _____ examination of the Red Planet.

(A) pestilence . . . cursory

(B) possibility . . . sustained

(C) existence . . . advantageous

(D) eradication . . . scientific

(E) withdrawal . . . intrusive

20. The establishment of a new broadcast network must be the work of _____ who are _____ as well as businesslike.

(A) visionaries . . . prosaic

(B) artists . . . culpable

(C) innovators . . . creative

(D) opportunists . . . conservative

(E) despots . . . collegial

21. Even more exciting than the final score can be the _____ plays of the tournament.

(A) generic

(B) integral

(C) intemperate

(D) ubiquitous

(E) critical

22. After so many years of experience, the interviewer couldn't be _____ by any questions the potential employee asked.

(A) jaded

(B) bored

(C) nonplussed

(D) exhausted

(E) inspired

Go on to next page

23. Their _____ relationship was characterized by _____ arguments.

    (A) affable . . . jocular

    (B) vivacious . . . sententious

    (C) amicable . . . continual

    (D) adversarial . . . infrequent

    (E) malevolent . . . innocuous

24. No one who is _____ will travel abroad _____.

    (A) conscientious . . . extensively

    (B) prescient . . . neutrally

    (C) organized . . . listlessly

    (D) xenophobic . . . willingly

    (E) fatuous . . . foolishly

STOP You may check your work on this section only. Do not go back to any previous section.

Section 6

Mathematics

Time: 25 minutes

20 questions

Notes:

✔ You may use a calculator.

✔ All numbers used in this exam are real numbers.

✔ All figures lie in a plane.

✔ All figures may be assumed to be to scale unless the problem specifically indicates otherwise.

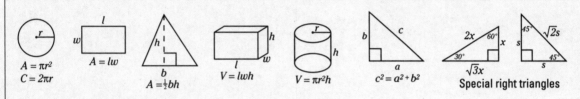

$A = \pi r^2$
$C = 2\pi r$

$A = lw$

$A = \frac{1}{2}bh$

$V = lwh$

$V = \pi r^2 h$

$c^2 = a^2 + b^2$

Special right triangles

There are 360 degrees of arc in a circle.

There are 180 degrees in a straight line.

There are 180 degrees in the sum of the interior angles of a triangle.

Directions for questions 1–10: Choose the best answer and darken the corresponding oval on the answer sheet.

1. What is the result when –8 is subtracted from 10?

   (A) 18

   (B) 2

   (C) –2

   (D) –18

   (E) –80

2. A certain shipping company charges $3.99 per pound for packages of 15 pounds or less, and $3.49 per pound for packages weighing more than 15 pounds. If Lyle sends two ten-pound packages, and Gretchen sends one twenty-pound package, what is the difference between their total costs?

   (A) $0

   (B) $0.50

   (C) $7.50

   (D) $10

   (E) $69.80

Go on to next page

3. How many degrees of arc does the minute hand of a clock cover in 20 minutes?

    (A) 180

    (B) 120

    (C) 60

    (D) 30

    (E) 20

5. Which of the following numbers is the smallest?

    (A) π

    (B) $3\frac{1}{7}$

    (C) 3.14

    (D) $3.1\overline{4}$

    (E) $\sqrt{10}$

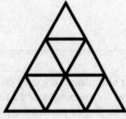

4. How many total triangles (of any size) are in this drawing?

    (A) 9

    (B) 10

    (C) 11

    (D) 12

    (E) 13

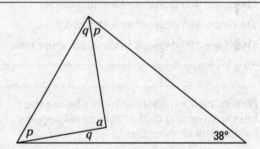

6. What is the value in degrees of a in this diagram?

    (A) 38

    (B) 76

    (C) 90

    (D) 109

    (E) 142

Go on to next page

Questions 7 and 8 both deal with the equation $\frac{ax}{x+2} = b$, where $a \neq b$.

7. For what value of x does this equation have no solution?

(A) −2

(B) −1

(C) 0

(D) 1

(E) 2

8. When the equation has a solution, $x =$

(A) $\dfrac{2}{a-b}$

(B) $\dfrac{2b}{a-b}$

(C) $\dfrac{2b}{a}$

(D) $b + 2$

(E) $a - 2b$

9. The shortest side of triangle T is 10 cm long, and triangle T's area is 84 cm². Triangle U is similar to triangle T, and the shortest side of triangle U is 15 cm long. What is the area of triangle U?

(A) 89 cm²

(B) 126 cm²

(C) 168 cm²

(D) 189 cm²

(E) 336 cm²

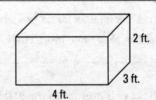

10. Gasoline is being poured into a cylindrical container with a radius of 5 feet and a height of 6 feet. Originally, the gasoline was stored in the box-shaped containers shown here. Roughly how many of these containers would be needed to fill the tank completely?

(A) 8

(B) 10

(C) 15

(D) 20

(E) 100

Go on to next page

Directions for student-produced responses: Questions 11–20 require you to solve the problem and then blacken the oval corresponding to the answer, as shown in the following example. Note the fraction line and the decimal points.

Answer: $^7/_2$

Answer: 3.25

Answer: 853

Write your answer in the box. You may start your answer in any column.

✔ Although you do not have to write the solutions in the boxes, you do have to blacken the corresponding ovals. You should fill in the boxes to avoid confusion. Only the blackened ovals will be scored. The numbers in the boxes will not be read.

✔ There are no negative answers.

✔ Mixed numbers, such as 3½, may be gridded in as a decimal (3.5) or as a fraction (⁷/₂). Do not grid in 3½; it will be read as ³¹/₂.

✔ Grid in a decimal as far as possible. Do not round it.

✔ A question may have more than one answer. Grid in one answer only.

11. If 2½ sticks of butter measure 20 tablespoons, how many tablespoons are in 4 sticks of butter?

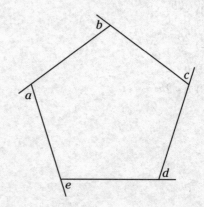

13. In this regular pentagon, find the sum, in degrees, of the angles *a*, *b*, *c*, *d*, and *e*.

12. Find the smallest *even* number that is divisible by 3, 5, and 7.

14. A certain fraction is equivalent to ⅔. If the fraction's denominator is 12 less than twice its numerator, find the denominator of the fraction.

Go on to next page

15. Find a solution to the equation $p^2 = 3p + 40$.

18. If all of the integers from 1 to 2004 inclusive were written down, how many total digits would appear?

16. A sequence of numbers begins 1, 5, 4, 8, 7, 11, 10. What would be the 21st term of this sequence?

19. If $xy = 120$, and $\frac{1}{x} + \frac{1}{y} = \frac{1}{4}$, find $x + y$.

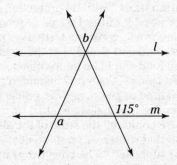

20. At a family reunion, 6 men have a grandson present, 35 have a son present, and 62 have a father present. What is the minimum number of men that could be at the reunion?

17. In this diagram, lines l and m are parallel. Find $a - b$, in degrees.

STOP You may check your work on this section only. Do not go back to any previous section.

Section 7

Critical Reading

Time: 20 minutes

15 questions

Directions for questions 1–12: Choose the best answer from information supplied or implied by the passages and darken the corresponding oval on the answer sheet.

This passage from *Ice Blink* by Scott Cookman (Wiley, 2000) discusses early 19th century explorer John Franklin's search for a northwest passage, a shorter, safer, Arctic route to the Far East.

Line   [John Franklin's] plan was to ascend today's Snare River, cross over to the headwaters of the Coppermine River, descend to its mouth on the shores of the Arctic Ocean, follow the coastline
(05) eastward in search of the Northwest Passage, and return. The fact that this involved paddling and portaging over 1,200 miles through some of the most unforgiving wilderness in the world did not seem to trouble him much. He had been given his
(10) chance.

Governor Sir George Simpson, head of the Hudson's Bay Company, who had agreed to support the expedition, didn't think much of it. No light judge of character, he was blunt in his esti-
(15) mation of Franklin: "Lieut Franklin, the Officer who commands the party, has not the physical powers required for the labor of moderate Voyaging in this country; he must have three meals per diem, Tea is indispensible, and with
(20) the utmost exertion he cannot walk Eight miles on one day."

Indeed, Franklin set out like an unprepared summer camper. By his own admission, he embarked with only "...two casks of flour, 200
(25) dried reindeer [caribou] tongues, some dried moosemeat, portable [dried] soup and arrowroot, sufficient in the whole for ten days' consumption [for his entire party]." He naively presumed that a band of Chippewyan natives hired at Fort
(30) Providence (a chief named Akaitcho, two guides, and seven hunters) could feed them all. Ten days later, the hunters having found no game, the food was gone. Franklin's fishing nets produced only

"4 carp." The hungry voyageurs "broke into open discontent" and refused to continue unless they
(35) were fed.

Franklin threatened to "...inflict the heaviest punishment on any who should persist in their refusal to go on." He was saved making good on this completely hollow threat (his Englishmen
(40) were out-numbered five to one, after all, and couldn't go anywhere without the voyageurs) only when the Chippewyan hunters providentially arrived with the flesh of two caribou. Hunger, which was to stalk the expedition all of its days,
(45) was momentarily kept at bay. But it was, to say the least, an inauspicious beginning.

Less than three weeks out of Fort Providence, at a lake above the headwaters of the Snare River, even this shaky beginning came to
(50) an end. By Franklin's calendar it was only August 19th and, in his mind, the height of the summer voyaging season. Despite the scarcity of food, he was determined to press ahead, straight across the height of land and down the Coppermine to
(55) the frozen ocean. Akaitcho, the Chippewyan chief, was operating on an entirely different calendar. He pointed out the falling leaves and told Franklin winter was near and it was too late in the season to proceed. He said that eleven days'
(60) travel would put them north of the tree line, out in the "barren lands," with no protection from the weather or wood for fires. He said descending the Coppermine would consume forty days more, that the caribou had already left the river for the
(65) winter, and food would be impossible to find in the "barren lands." Akaitcho concluded that if Franklin wanted to go on, he was a dead man. Franklin replied the Englishmen had "instruments by which we could tell the state of the air and
(70) water" and that winter was not "so near as he [Akaitcho] supposed." The chief threw up his hands and said that "as his advice was neglected, his presence was useless, and he would therefore return to Fort Providence with his hunters."
(75) Franklin, as completely dependent upon the Chippewyans for food as he was upon the voyageurs for transport, had no choice but to "reluctantly" halt for the winter. He had not

Go on to next page

(80) reached the Coppermine, much less descended it. In fact, he had traveled only seventeen days from Fort Providence and had already exhausted all his provisions and experienced two near mutinies.

Eleven days later, true to Akaitcho's predic-
(85) tion, the temperatures turned freezing. Franklin put his voyageurs to work building a "dwelling house" for the Englishmen. By December (about the time he would have been returning from the Arctic Ocean, if Akaitcho hadn't stopped him
(90) from going) the outside temperature plummeted to 57 degrees below zero.

1. The first paragraph (lines 1–10) implies that Franklin's plan

   (A) relied on established routes

   (B) would be difficult if not impossible

   (C) depended upon chance

   (D) was well thought out

   (E) could be accomplished easily by anyone brave enough to try

2. In the context of this passage, *light* (line 14) may best be defined as

   (A) illuminating

   (B) insignificant

   (C) spiritual

   (D) all-knowing

   (E) perceptive

3. Governor Simpson's comment (line 19) that "Tea is indispensable" shows

   (A) the need for hot beverages in a cold climate

   (B) the universal appeal of tea

   (C) that Simpson judged Franklin fit to lead the expedition

   (D) that Franklin intended to maintain high standards during his trip

   (E) Simpson's poor opinion of Franklin's ability to adapt to the wilderness

4. The author's comment that "Franklin set out like an unprepared summer camper" (lines 22–23) is intended to

   (A) contrast with Governor Simpson's point of view

   (B) relate Franklin's journey to the reader's personal experience

   (C) stress that the voyage took place during warm weather

   (D) emphasize how greatly Franklin underestimated the difficulty of the expedition

   (E) elicit sympathy for Franklin

5. The material in quotation marks in paragraph three (lines 24–28) is most likely drawn from

   (A) a biography of Franklin

   (B) a diary kept by Franklin during the expedition

   (C) an account by the Native American guides

   (D) Governor Simpson's records

   (E) a scholarly book on the Franklin expedition

6. Franklin's leadership, according to the passage,

   (A) relied on threats

   (B) took into account the needs of the expedition members

   (C) did not take into account the abilities of the Native Americans

   (D) was based on meticulous planning

   (E) changed in a wilderness setting

7. August 19th (lines 51–52) is cited because

   (A) the author had good records of the events of that date

   (B) Franklin made a crucial mistake on that date

   (C) the Native Americans saw that date as the midpoint of summer

   (D) it was a turning point of the expedition

   (E) it was a rare point of agreement between the Native Americans and Franklin

Go on to next page

8. The argument about weather between Franklin and Akaitcho

   (A) emphasizes Franklin's incompetence

   (B) shows that Franklin's confidence is justified

   (C) is never resolved

   (D) reveals the prejudices of both Franklin and Akaitcho

   (E) illustrates the superiority of scientific instruments

9. The mutinies are described as "near" (line 83) because

   (A) they rose above the level of threats

   (B) they did not break out into open fighting

   (C) they were led by people close to Franklin

   (D) they occurred close together in time

   (E) they took place within the expedition itself

10. The author would most likely disagree with which statement?

   (A) Franklin's travel plan was too ambitious.

   (B) Governor Simpson should not have approved Franklin's expedition.

   (C) Native American ability to predict the weather is overrated.

   (D) Arctic travel should not be attempted without adequate preparation.

   (E) Franklin's arrogance was a factor in the failure of his expedition.

11. By mentioning the temperature in December (line 91) the author implies that

   (A) Franklin was correct in his estimation of the weather

   (B) Akaitcho was wrong

   (C) the temperature was severe but not life-threatening

   (D) Franklin's expedition could not have survived such a temperature

   (E) the cold weather was far off

12. A good title for this passage is

   (A) Foolish Expeditions

   (B) Early Explorers

   (C) The Franklin Expedition

   (D) Akaitcho and Franklin: A Cultural Clash

   (E) The Northwest Passage

Directions for questions 13–16: Choose the best answer and darken the corresponding oval on the answer sheet.

Passage I is an excerpt from *The House of Science* by Philip R. Holzinger (Wiley, 1990). It discusses the origins of the earth. Passage II is an excerpt from *The Big Splat, or How Our Moon Came to Be* by Dana Mackenzie (Wiley, 2003). In Passage II the author discusses Immanuel Kant's theories on the origin and nature of the solar system.

Passage 1

The story of our earth begins about 4.6 billion years ago — a time when the rest of the planets in our solar system were also forming. Early in its history, our planet was made up of a hodgepodge of materials, some of which were radioactive. (05) These radioactive materials generated great quantities of heat, as did the large number of meteors that struck the earth at this time. The heat generated was sufficient to melt most of the planet, making our early earth a forbidding (10) molten world!

Passage 11

Kant's model of the solar system began with an initial, formless cloud of gas or smoke, which contracts under the force of gravity. One might expect the cloud to simply collapse to a point, (15) end of story. But Kant assumed that the "fine particles" in the cloud would also repel each other. (He made an incorrect analogy to the diffusion of smoke, which he thought was due to a repulsive force.) This repulsion would give them (20) a sideways motion and allow them to take up circular orbits around the growing Sun. After many collisions between these orbiting particles [Kant thought], an overall direction of rotation would be established. (25)

Go on to next page

13. The exclamation point at the end of Passage I
    (A) emphasizes the great contrast between the earth we know today and the earth when it was formed
    (B) reveals that the molten earth was hotter than the earth today
    (C) shows that the author disapproves of this theory of the earth's formation
    (D) stresses the dangers of radioactive material
    (E) underlines the danger of molten minerals

14. In the context of Passage I, "forbidding" (line 10) means
    (A) hindering
    (B) denying
    (C) not allowing
    (D) possessing difficult characteristics
    (E) hot

15. In Passage II, the best interpretation of "end of story" (line 16) is that
    (A) the solar system would end after a complete collapse
    (B) there is no more to say about Kant's theory
    (C) Kant's theory is completely incorrect
    (D) Kant could not reason further than this point
    (E) a point, like a period, ends a story

16. Both passages primarily concern
    (A) astronomy
    (B) astrology
    (C) theories later proved wrong
    (D) the beginnings of planets and other heavenly bodies
    (E) science

STOP You may check your work on this section only. Do not go back to any previous section.

Section 8

Mathematics
Time: 15 minutes
15 questions

Notes:

✔ You may use a calculator.

✔ All numbers used in this exam are real numbers.

✔ All figures lie in a plane.

✔ All figures may be assumed to be to scale unless the problem specifically indicates otherwise.

$A = \pi r^2$
$C = 2\pi r$

$A = lw$

$A = \frac{1}{2}bh$

$V = lwh$

$V = \pi r^2 h$

$c^2 = a^2 + b^2$

Special right triangles

There are 360 degrees of arc in a circle.

There are 180 degrees in a straight line.

There are 180 degrees in the sum of the interior angles of a triangle.

Directions: Choose the best answer and darken the corresponding oval on the answer sheet.

1. In football, a touchdown is worth 6 points, a field goal is worth 3 points, and an extra point is worth 1 point. Which formula represents the total number of points scored by a team if they scored *t* touchdowns, *f* field goals, and *e* extra points?

    (A) $6t + 3f + e$

    (B) $t^6 + f^3 + e$

    (C) $6(t + 3f + e)$

    (D) $3t + 6f + e$

    (E) $(6 + t) + (3 + f) + (1 + e)$

2. Sean claims that every number is either prime or the product of two primes. Which number could Vickie use to disprove Sean's statement?

    (A) 2

    (B) 10

    (C) 15

    (D) 18

    (E) 57

Go on to next page

3. On a number line, four evenly spaced marks are placed between –2 and 13. What is the coordinate of the second such mark?

   (A) 1

   (B) 4

   (C) 5.5

   (D) 7

   (E) 7.5

4. Which of the following is true for the data set 3, 4, 7, 5, 2, 5, 9, 1 ?

   (A) median > mode

   (B) median > mean

   (C) median = mode

   (D) mean = mode

   (E) median = mean

5. What is the width of a rectangle whose perimeter is 40 inches and whose length is 8 inches?

   (A) 2½ inches

   (B) 5 inches

   (C) 12 inches

   (D) 16 inches

   (E) 32 inches

6. Owen needs to travel 400 miles in 8 hours. If he averages m miles per hour for the first three hours, what does his average speed need to be for the remaining 5 hours?

   (A) $\dfrac{400 - 3m}{5}$

   (B) $\dfrac{400 - 3m}{8}$

   (C) $\dfrac{400 - m}{5}$

   (D) $50 - \frac{3m}{5}$

   (E) $80 - 3m$

7. Which point is *not* 5 units from the origin?

   (A) (–5, 0)

   (B) (5, 5)

   (C) (3, –4)

   (D) (0, 5)

   (E) (0, –5)

8. Find the perimeter of a square whose diagonal has length $6\sqrt{2}$ m.

   (A) 6 m

   (B) $12\sqrt{2}$ m

   (C) 24 m

   (D) $24\sqrt{2}$ m

   (E) 48 m

9. How many two-digit numbers contain one even digit and one odd digit?

   (A) 20

   (B) 25

   (C) 45

   (D) 50

   (E) 55

Go on to next page

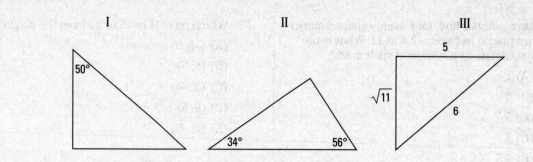

10. Which of these three triangles must be a right triangle? (Figures are not drawn to scale.)

    (A) I only

    (B) II only

    (C) I and III

    (D) II and III

    (E) I, II, and III

11. If $d^{1/2} + 5 = 9$, then $d^{-1} =$

    (A) −16

    (B) −4

    (C) −2

    (D) ½

    (E) ⅟₁₆

Go on to next page

Questions 12 and 13 use the following graphs:

Majors at State University

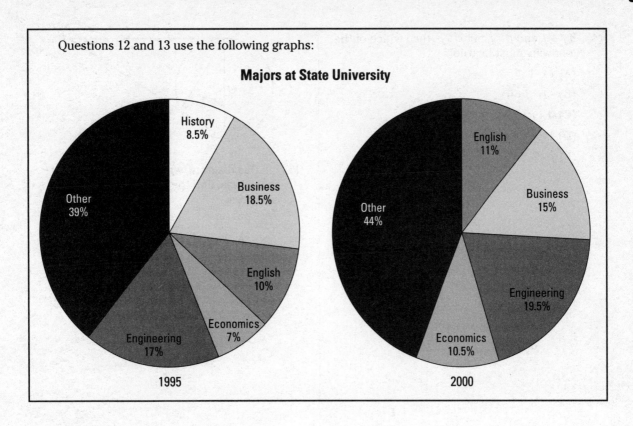

1995

2000

12. If 5,000 students attended State U. in 1995, how many majored in history or English?

    (A) 185

    (B) 425

    (C) 500

    (D) 925

    (E) 1,850

13. Which is a valid conclusion, based on the graphs alone?

    (A) English was more popular in 2000 than in 1995.

    (B) More students majored in business in 1995 than in 2000.

    (C) History was the most popular major in 1995

    (D) Fewer students majored in economics in 1995 than in 2000.

    (E) In 2000, more students majored in Engineering than in English.

Go on to next page

14. If $j^2 > j$, and $j^3 > j$, but $j^2 > j^3$, then which of the following must be true?

    (A) $j < -1$

    (B) $-1 < j < 0$

    (C) $0 < j < 1$

    (D) $1 < j < 2$

    (E) $j > 2$

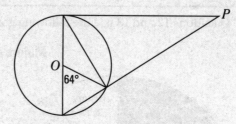

15. In this diagram, where O is the center of the circle, find the measure of angle P, in degrees.

    (A) 32

    (B) 36

    (C) 45

    (D) 58

    (E) 64

STOP   You may check your work on this section only.
Do not go back to any previous section.

Answer Key for Practice Exam 2

Section 1, the essay, may be scored according to the scoring guidelines in Chapter 25.

Answers for Sections 2 – 8 of Practice Test Two

Section 2	Section 3	Section 4	Section 5	Section 6	Section 7	Section 8
1. D	1. E	1. C	1. B	1. A	1. B	1. A
2. A	2. D	2. D	2. D	2. D	2. B	2. D
3. E	3. C	3. C	3. A	3. B	3. E	3. B
4. C	4. A	4. A	4. B	4. E	4. D	4. E
5. E	5. A	5. D	5. E	5. C	5. B	5. C
6. A	6. B	6. D	6. C	6. D	6. A	6. A
7. B	7. E	7. A	7. D	7. A	7. D	7. B
8. B	8. B	8. B	8. A	8. B	8. A	8. C
9. B	9. A	9. C	9. C	9. D	9. B	9. C
10. A	10. D	10. C	10. B	10. D	10. C	10. D
11. D	11. D	11. B	11. E	11. 32	11. D	11. E
12. A	12. A	12. D	12. B	12. 210	12. C	12. D
13. C	13. D	13. D	13. D	13. 360	13. A	13. E
14. B	14. E	14. C	14. C	14. 36	14. D	14. B
15. D	15. B	15. A	15. D	15. 8	15. A	15. A
16. D	16. D	16. E	16. A	16. 31	16. D	
17. D	17. C	17. A	17. D	17. 65		
18. A	18. B	18. D	18. A	18. 6909		
19. E	19. A	19. B	19. B	19. 30		
20. B	20. C	20. A	20. C	20. 68		
21. A	21. E	21. C	21. E			
22. E	22. A	22. B	22. C			
23. A	23. D	23. B	23. A			
24. B	24. E	24. E	24. D			
25. D	25. D	25. D				
26. C						
27. D						
28. C						
29. A						
30. D						
31. C						
32. B						
33. C						
34. C						
35. B						

Scoring Your Exam

Check Chapter 25 for instructions on how to score the essay. For the multiple-choice answers, mark skipped questions with an O, correct answers with a check, and wrong answers (gasp! You had some!) with an X. Then calculate your raw scores as follows.

Scoring the Writing multiple-choice section

Time to act like a teacher and score your writing exam. Follow these steps:

1. **Count the number of correct answers in Section 2 and place the number on line 1.**

2. **Multiply the number of wrong answers by ¼ and round to the nearest whole number. Place your answer on line 2.**

3. **Subtract line 2 from line 1 to get the raw score.**

4. **Convert the raw Writing score by using the chart in the following "Converting the raw multiple-choice Writing score" section.**

Line 1 _____

Line 2 _____

Raw Writing Score _____

Converting the raw multiple-choice Writing score

The colleges receive two writing scores for you: the essay score (2–12) and a multiple-choice score (20–80). After you figure out the raw score on the multiple-choice writing, find the converted score with the following table.

Multiple Choice Writing Conversion Table

Raw	Converted	Raw	Converted	Raw	Converted
36	80	22	54	9	35
35	80	21	52	8	34
34	78	20	50	7	33
33	76	19	47	6	32
32	74	18	45	5	30
31	72	17	44	4	28
30	70	16	43	3	27
29	68	15	42	2	25
28	66	14	40	1	24
27	64	13	39	0	23
26	62	12	38	−1	20
25	60	11	37	−2	20
24	58	10	36	below −2	20
23	56				

Scoring the Critical Reading sections

Sharpen your red pencil and prepare to score. (Not *that* kind of scoring. I'm talking Critical Reading here.)

1. **Count the number of correct answers in Sections 3, 5, and 7 and place the number on line 1.**

2. **Multiply the number of wrong answers by ¼ and round to the nearest whole number. Place your answer on line 2.**

3. **Subtract line 2 from line 1 to get the raw score.**

4. **Convert the raw Critical Reading score by using the chart in the following "Converting the raw Critical Reading score" section.**

Line 1 _____

Line 2 _____

Raw Critical Reading Score _____

Converting the raw Critical Reading score

The raw score of the Critical Reading sections must be converted to the standard 200–800 SAT "converted" score, according to the following table.

	Critical Reading Conversion Table				
Raw	**Converted**	**Raw**	**Converted**	**Raw**	**Converted**
64	800	41	590	18	420
63	800	40	580	17	420
62	800	39	580	16	410
61	800	38	570	15	400
60	790	37	560	14	390
59	780	36	550	13	390
58	770	35	550	12	380
57	760	34	540	11	370
56	750	33	530	10	360
55	740	32	520	9	350
54	720	31	520	8	340
53	710	30	510	7	330
52	680	29	500	6	320
51	670	28	490	5	310
50	670	27	480	4	300
49	660	26	480	3	280
48	650	25	480	2	270
47	640	24	470	1	240
46	630	23	460	0	230
45	620	22	450	−1	210
44	620	21	450	−2	200
43	610	20	440	below −2	200
42	600	19	430		

Scoring the Math sections

Just when you thought it was safe to throw your calculator in the ocean (just kidding — you need it for the test), it's time to score the math section. Follow these steps:

1. **Count the number of correct answers in Sections 4, 6, and 8 and place the number on line 1. Count both multiple choice and grid-ins for this step.**

2. **Ignore the grid-ins for this step. Multiply the number of wrong answers to everything except the grid-ins by ¼ and round to the nearest whole number. Place your answer on line 2.**

3. **Subtract line 2 from line 1 to get the raw math score.**

4. **Convert the raw score by using the chart in the following "Converting the raw Math score" section.**

Line 1 _____
Line 2 _____
Raw Math Score _____

Converting the raw Math score

Locate your raw Math score in the following table and match it with the equivalent "converted" (standard SAT) score.

Mathematics Conversion Table

Raw	Converted	Raw	Converted	Raw	Converted
60	800	38	570	16	420
59	800	37	570	15	410
58	790	36	560	14	410
57	770	35	550	13	400
56	750	34	540	12	390
55	740	33	540	11	380
54	720	32	530	10	380
53	710	31	520	9	370
52	700	30	510	8	360
51	690	29	510	7	350
50	680	28	500	6	340
49	670	27	490	5	330
48	660	26	490	4	320
47	650	25	480	3	310
46	640	24	470	2	290
45	630	23	470	1	280
44	620	22	460	0	260
43	620	21	450	−1	250
42	610	20	450	−2	230
41	600	19	440	−3	200
40	590	18	430	below −3	200
39	580	17	430		

Chapter 25

Arriving at the Moment of Truth: Checking Your Answers to Practice Exam 2

. . . .

In This Chapter

▶ Looking at your strengths and weaknesses

▶ Checking your work on practice exam 2

. . . .

This chapter contains plenty of good stuff, even for people — and of course you're one — who answered every question correctly. I sneak some tips and warnings into the explanations to be sure you're ready-set-go for the actual SAT.

Section 1: The Essay

The SAT sends English teachers to long, caffeine-fueled workshops on how to score the essay, but here I provide the "short story" version of what the SAT-devils consider "mini-series" material. You can handle this question in a couple of ways, but the first quotation gives you a huge hint about their expectations. As you know, the atomic bomb exists, and not everyone is happy about it. J. Robert Oppenheimer, the author of the first quotation, helped create the bomb. He later had second thoughts about his work, but you don't have to know that fact. What you do have to know — and reflect in your essay — is the complexity of the situation. Because the SAT-writers aren't quoting the inventor of, say, cancer-fighting drugs, they're expecting you to say something about the drawbacks of the human urge to discover and invent (such as the fact that we can now blow up the entire planet). On the other hand, they're unlikely to smile upon an essay that declares that the human race should be content with couch-potatohood.

Your best bet is to come up with one or two examples of human discoveries or creations and then talk about the pros (one paragraph) and the cons (one paragraph). Introduce the essay with something about consequences and your view on how well an inventor/artist/scientist can foresee them and how much the inventor/artist/scientist should worry about them. Then add two body paragraphs (the pro and con) and a conclusion (your final opinion on responsibility). Here are two possible outlines, one for a scientist and one for an artist:

Science introduction: Human beings need to stretch the body of knowledge. Without our restlessness, we'd still be living in caves eating uncooked twigs. But scientists must consider the probable uses of their discoveries.

Science pro paragraph: Description of some of the wonders created by science, including advances in medicine and technology.

Avoid the essay trap of example overkill. This topic could be illustrated by literally millions of examples. Don't turn the essay into a giant list. Choose one or two examples and explain them.

Science con paragraph: Drawbacks of the examples from the preceding paragraph. Modern medicine, for example, can prolong life way past the point where it is worth living. Technology has not saved us from pollution and has taken away some of the personal interactions that raise the quality of life.

Science conclusion: No one can foresee everything, but scientists should take reasonable precautions to control the results of their work because they have the power to affect millions of people for good or evil.

Now for the artistic view:

Art introduction: Artists debate whether their duty is to their own personal need for expression or to the betterment of society.

Art paragraph one: This paragraph goes with the personal view. An artist creates only to express herself; an artist must work in complete freedom, regardless of audience reaction. Each new artistic movement — cubism, for example — has shocked audiences when it was first conceived. If fear of the audience's reaction inhibits artists, they become mere copyists.

Art paragraph two: Artists don't work in a vacuum. If their work supports stereotypes or hateful ideas, they can harm real people with their creations. The art of the Nazi era or the racial stereotypes in early 20th century American films, for example, fueled and justified prejudice and discrimination.

Art conclusion: Here's the spot for your personal idea of the artist's responsibility in the freedom/responsibility debate.

Reread your essay and score it in this way, starting from a basis of six points, the SAT perfect score from one reader:

Mechanics: If you have only a couple of grammar, spelling, and punctuation errors, give yourself full credit for this category. If you have three or four mistakes in each paragraph, deduct one point. If you find even more than three or four mistakes per paragraph, deduct two points.

Organization: I describe two logical outlines earlier in this section, but many other patterns will work. Check your essay's structure. Does it proceed logically from idea, to evidence, to conclusion? If so, you're fine. If the logical thread breaks anywhere or if you skipped a step — the conclusion, perhaps — deduct one point for each deficiency.

Evidence: You need to have at least three or four details in each body paragraph or one piece of evidence that is described at length. Your body paragraphs should be heavy on specifics and light on general statements. If you find several general statements in the body of the essay, deduct a point. If you have good detail, give yourself full marks for this quality.

Fluency: Read the essay aloud. Does the language flow freely, easily, and naturally? Could you imagine reading it in a book? Or is it choppy and disjointed? Fluid language = no deduction. Choppy or awkward = deduct a point.

After you get a score, double it, because two readers will read your essay and both scores count. The doubled score is your essay grade. Twelve means you can go dancing; two indicates that you have some work to do. Turn to Chapter 10 for additional practice.

Section 2: Multiple-Choice Writing

1. **(D).** These expressions don't exist in proper English: *must of, should of, could of, would of.* The *of* should be changed to *have.* The confusion arises from the shortening of the expressions, as in *should've,* which sounds like *should of.*

2. **(A).** When a sentence begins with a verb form, the subject should be performing that action. In this sentence, *the telescope* is gazing. Nope. Because *telescope* isn't underlined, go for the introductory verb form, *gazing up at the stars.*

3. **(E).** Sometimes the hardest questions are the ones that have no errors because after a couple of SAT sentences, you tend to find mistakes *everywhere.* This one, however, is fine.

4. **(C).** What does *them* refer to? As the sentence reads now, *them* could refer to either *novels* or *shelves.* Grammar sometimes has rules just for the sake of making you miserable, but one important rule actually makes sense: Your sentences have to communicate meaning clearly. To put it another way, all pronouns must refer to one and only one noun.

5. **(E).** Did you stub your toe on (A)? Somehow, *whom* sounds right. However, you need a subject for *is,* and *who* is a subject pronoun. *Whom* is for objects. Here's another way to think about this sentence: *we all know* is a distraction. Cover those words with your thumb and read the sentence. Now *who* sounds better.

6. **(A).** This sentence states a "condition contrary to fact," as grammarians (yes, we have no life whatsoever) say because the bird did *not* fly farther. The "if" portion of this kind of sentence never has *would* in it. The sentence should read, "If the bird had flown . . ."

7. **(B).** *However* isn't allowed to join two sentences. You need to insert a semicolon before *however.*

8. **(B).** Dump *equally.* The expression *equally as* is improper, according to the grammar police.

9. **(B).** The big-footed stepsisters object to the marriage and the attention theft, not to Cinderella herself. The sentence should read, *to Cinderella's marrying . . . and stealing.*

10. **(A).** In almost every sentence (and in every sentence on the SAT), *affect* is a verb, as in *ten days without sleep can affect your SAT score.* The word you need in sentence 10 is *effect,* which in SAT-land is usually a noun but sometimes a verb, as in *to effect* (bring about) a change.

11. **(D).** With *either . . . or* and *neither . . . nor* sentences, the verb must match the closest subject. In sentence 11, *teammates* is closest and should match with *have.*

12. **(A).** You can't *read* and *return* at the same time, so the sentence should say, *When Bob had read.* The *had* places the action of reading before the action of returning.

13. **(C).** The expression *who had all paid high prices for the voyage* is extra, not essential or identifying information. Set off extra information with commas. (D) isn't acceptable because *that* usually signals essential or identifying information, *which* is inserted in the sentence without commas.

14. **(B).** The sentence indicates that the shortstop is on the team, so *else* must be inserted into the sentence.

15. **(D).** The pair *not only . . . but also* should link two similar grammatical structures. To put it another way, the pair should link expressions that match. *Sipping* doesn't match *if you pick,* but *sipping* is a good mate for *picking.*

16. **(D).** The pronoun *it* should be deleted from the sentence because according to the grammar gods, a pronoun may replace one and only one word (a noun). (D) is better than (E) because the *adding* was the wise move, not the chain.

17. **(D).** *Except* is a preposition, so the expression is *except Tomas and me.* The pronoun *I* is only for subjects and subject complements.

18. **(A).** When you read this sentence, think *tense* (but don't be nervous). The first verb, *was,* is okay because you're just expressing an action in the past. The second verb, *has been sitting,* connects past (*the last three weeks*) and present (*still there*). *Has* added to a verb connects present and past.

19. **(E).** *Who and whoever* are for subjects and *whom and whomever* are for objects. In sentence 19, all the verbs have subjects: *slate means, voters may select, they like.* Because you don't need a subject, you must need an object, or *whomever* (which is, in fact, the object of *like*).

20. **(B).** The word *only* sets up a comparison between the stack of cards she bought and the three she sent. *Only* belongs in front of *three,* because that's where the comparison is.

21. **(A).** *Will have taken* implies a deadline, and the first part of the sentence supplies one: Marisa's college graduation, which is far in the future and which will cost her parents a fortune in tuition, given that Marisa changes her major as frequently as other people change their underwear.

22. **(E).** Who's writing that essay? In (A) through (D), no one. (E) is the only one to insert a writer — *you* — into the sentence.

23. **(A).** Surprised? If you *feel badly,* your sense of touch is damaged or maybe you're wearing mittens. If your mood is sad, you *feel bad.*

24. **(B).** The pencils and paper, added together, make a plural subject. (They also make great missiles when the editor is angry.) A plural subject needs a plural verb, so (A) (implied verb = *is*), (C) and (E) don't make the cut. (D) is out because *they're* = *they are,* not *there are.*

25. **(D).** The pronoun *this* is a problem in the original sentence because it replaces not one word but a whole bunch (*Children in kindergarten love paints and markers*). The best solution is to rewrite the sentence so that no pronoun is needed, as in (D) and (E). (E), however, has a misplaced apostrophe, so (D) is best.

26. **(C).** The original sentence has an unnecessary repetition, the definition of grandmother. No need to change tense, commas, or anything else.

27. **(D).** Short but sweet, gets the job done. That's the characteristic of (D). The original is wordy and relies on passive voice (*should be considered*) — never a good choice. Also, *everyone* can't be paired with *they* because *everyone* is singular and *they* is plural.

28. **(C).** The original is missing a subject, and choices (B) through (E) supply one. (B) is repetitive (*unique* = *can't be duplicated*) and (D) is wordy. (C) is concise, so it's the best.

29. **(A).** The sentence indulges in overkill: *in my opinion* and *I think* say the same thing, and both may be deleted, along with *personally,* because why say it if you don't think it?

30. **(D).** Choice (A) is a run-on sentence, and (B) has a tense problem. (C) would be okay, but *and* is the most basic joiner and could in this case be improved on. (E) is wordy.

31. **(C).** Each detail shows why foreign study adds to one's education.

32. **(B).** (A) (the unchanged sentence) has a vague pronoun (*this*). (C) and (D) change the meaning of the sentence, and (E) has a grammatical error (no logical subject for *seen*).

33. **(C).** The original sentence is a run-on (*consequently* can't join sentences). The choice that conveys all the main ideas of the original without wordiness is (C).

34. **(C).** The first two choices — (A) and (B) — are too wordy, and the last two — (D) and (E) — are too minimal. (C) hits it right on the nose — concise but complete.

35. **(B).** The pronoun *it* is flapping around unnecessarily in (A) and (D). (C) is wordy, and (E) provides no clear meaning for *they.*

Section 3: Critical Reading

1. **(E).** Check out lines 8–9, which tells you that hysteria used to be "associated with witchcraft and medieval states of possession."

Because question 1 comes up right away, the odds are that the answer will be in the first few lines of the passage. As you've probably guessed, questions toward the end may refer to the end of the passage. However, this rule goes out the window for questions that take into account the entire reading selection.

2. **(D).** Did the SAT-devils trip you up on this one? When you think of hysteria, you probably picture out-of-control laughter that brings forth a slap ("for his own good"). But lines 10–12 mention "amnesias" (E), "paralyses" (B), "spasms, involuntary movements" (C), and "anesthesias" (A). Only laughter is missing.

Real-world knowledge helps on the SAT, but the final answer must always be true in the context of the reading provided.

3. **(C).** The passage defines "psychological" as a state with "no discernable physical causes." (C) is the closest to this definition.

4. **(A).** Paragraph two says that Charcot clarified the "psychological-traumatic nature of symptoms" and mentions survivors of train wrecks.

(C) is a favorite SAT trap: It contains a statement that actually appears in the passage but doesn't fit the question.

5. **(A).** The term *hysteria* comes from the Greek word for "womb," and the passage thus implies that it was once thought to be only a female disease. Hence "of both sexes" counters that idea. Also, line 81 mentions "the old link" between hysteria and women.

6. **(B).** According to lines 41–42, Charcot the "railways" were cases in which "symptoms mimicked those found after spinal cord or brain injuries." This question is chock-full of little traps. (A) tempts because it mentions trains, and (E) may have grabbed your attention because Charcot did use hypnosis. But (B) fits best.

7. **(E).** Lines 61–63 tells you that memories blotted out by physical injuries to the brain couldn't be retrieved by hypnosis.

8. **(B).** Charcot's "hypnoid state" is linked to the term "dissociation," which is clearly defined as a "blotting out" of certain memories. Line 66 says that patients aren't aware of what they are doing, so choices (D) and (E) aren't acceptable.

9. **(A).** The last paragraph lists several of Charcot's accomplishments, but the word "genuine" immediately sets up a comparison. If these are the genuine accomplishments, Charcot must have made some unsupported claims or performed some doubtful research.

10. **(D).** The runner-up is (A), because Charcot did treat hysteria with hypnosis. But Charcot worked in the late 19th century, and (A) contains a present-tense verb *(is)*. Medicine has certainly changed in the last hundred years or so, and for this reason (A) doesn't measure up. (D), on the other hand, is supported by line 24, which refers to "so-called hysterics."

11. **(D).** The author's "just the facts" presentation may best be described as "informative."

12. **(A).** (B) and (E) are too broad, and (C) is too narrow. (D) doesn't make the grade because the passage doesn't tell you anything about Charcot's life.

13. **(D).** The light isn't new or old, according to the passage. It just travels different distances. So depending upon what you're looking at, you're seeing different times.

14. **(E).** The first four choices are too general. "Direct Study of the Past," (C), may be what I do when I clean out my pockets after a night out with friends or watch the videotape we made of . . . well, don't expect me to tell.

15. **(B).** The passage states that the monument wasn't built to study the sun because only "the first part of the answer is correct." The author also explains that no one yet knows what "astronomical phenomenon" Stonehenge was built to observe.

16. **(D).** (E) is the runner-up, because the author is attempting to explain Stonehenge's purpose. However, the comment inside the dashes is simply clarifying the meaning of "the first part of the answer," not giving a theory all by itself. Therefore (D) wins the prize.

17. **(C).** Process of elimination gets you through this one, as well as some life experience in being ignored by a boss or teacher. How do you feel? Not *buoyed* (spirits lifted), *reassured* (calmed, given confidence), or *inspired* (stimulated, stirred by ideas). But *intimidated* (threatened) is a good match, far better than the too general *affected* (influenced).

18. **(B).** The word that probably popped into your head (no, I don't mean "lunchtime"!) is *unification.* But that's not a choice. The closest is *integration,* which is more or less the opposite of choices (A), (C), and (E). (D) is on Mars somewhere, because you can't make a *proclamation into* something. (A *proclamation* is an official declaration.)

19. **(A).** Okay, you can dump (D) immediately because real-world knowledge tells you that angry people don't hand out promotions. (B) and (C) fail because losing *insignificant* or *outdated* material won't send any detective for ulcer medicine. (E) isn't bad because *affront* means "to insult," but (A) is better. *Crucial* = essential and *upbraid* = the kind of yelling you hear from drill sergeants during basic training.

20. **(C).** If the corporation is *affluent,* it's making lots of money, and *lucrative* means "profitable." (A) doesn't make much sense, though the SAT-writers want you to relate *deregulated* (rules removes) with *multifaceted* (lots of variety). Choices (B), (D), and (E) are nonstarters because the pairs are opposites and the sentence calls for similar words.

Mor- or mort- relates to death. (Think *mortuary, morbid, mortal.*) *Moribund* = dying, or in this context, so stale that the corporation may as well be dead. *Innovative* contains the root *nov,* or new. *Scrupulous* applies to the kind of person who follows every rule and considers every aspect of morality, no matter how tiny — not a good pair for *unethical,* which means disregarding *ethics* (principles of right and wrong).

21. **(E).** If the teacher is *pragmatic,* she's practical. She wants to get the job done. So *motivated* (giving reason to act) fits best. A close second is (B), but *heighten* intensifies feelings, so it's a poor fit for *studies.* Choices (A), (C), and (D) are the opposite of what you want.

22. **(A).** Notice the *and?* That word tells you to look for a continuation of meaning, not a change in direction. The first half of the sentence talks about variety, and *myriad* means "various, diverse." *Convoluted* (complicated or elaborate) and *versatile* (multitalented, adaptable) are there to lead you astray because both contain an element of *variety. Intuitive* (relying on instinct or gut feeling) and *nebulous* (cloudy, vague) aren't in the running.

23. **(D).** The clue here is *furthermore,* which tells you that the two halves of the sentence more or less match. If she's "saving" the rainforest, she's not trying to wipe out (*annihilate, decimate,* and *eradicate*) Bambi and friends. *Proliferate* sounds good, but you can't *proliferate* something else. The animals can *proliferate* all by themselves, but Lucy has to *preserve* them.

24. **(E).** Crack the sentence by filling in your own word. *Irresponsible* comes to mind, at least to those of us who are teachers. Normal people may say *slow* or *reluctant.* All those D's contain only one that fits with the why-should-I-do-it-now-when-it-isn't-due-for-two-whole-hours attitude: *dilatory,* which means "tending to delay."

Diligent (responsible, hard-working) travels in the opposite direction. *Doleful* (sad), *doctrinaire* (rigid in belief), and *diffident* (shy) can't get the job done.

25. **(D).** An audience doesn't give *kudos* (praise) to an *affected* performance, which is "unreal" or "phony." (At least not in theory; boy bands continue to earn lots of cash.)

The key to sentence 25 is to think of the real world — what does the audience give to a good or bad performance? After you answer that question, look for pairs that fit. A *conventional* performance is stale and boring, so it will gather a lot of *critiques,* (detailed criticism) not a few. An *effective* (one that does the job — that is, entertains the audience) performance will receive many, not few *ovations* (round of applause) because both are good. So is the pair of words in choice (D).

Section 4: Mathematics

1. **(C).** Just straightforward list-making here. Listing factors in pairs is easier so I do that in this explanation:

   (A) 16 equals 16×1, or 8×2, or 4×4. Five factors (don't count 4 twice).

   (B) 20 equals 20×1, 10×2, or 5×4. Six factors.

   (C) 24 equals 24×1, 12×2, 8×3, or 6×4. Eight factors.

   (D) 28 equals 28×1, 14×2, or 7×4. Six factors.

   (E) 32 equals 32×1, 16×2, or 8×4. Six factors, and (C) is the winner.

2. **(D).** Plugging in -5 and -4 to $p(p - q)$ gives $(-5)((-5) - (-4)) = (-5)(-5 + 4) = (-5)(-1) = 5$.

3. **(C).** The key thing to notice is that the line containing O, P, and Q is a diameter of the large circle, and that it also contains the diameters of the two smaller circles. So the diameter of circle O equals the sum of the diameters of circles P and Q. Meanwhile, the line segment PQ is composed of the radii of the two small circles. Because these two radii add up to 6, the diameters of the small circles add up to 12. The diameter of circle O is 12 and its radius is 6. Finally, because the circle's area is πr^2, the large circle's area is $\pi(6)^2 = 36\pi$.

4. **(A).** "Ratio" is just a fancy name for a fraction, so this problem says that $\frac{x}{m} = \frac{y}{n}$. Cross-multiplying gives you (A).

5. **(D).** Drawing time! Here are the circles:

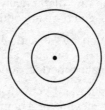

By the way, circles sharing the same center are called *concentric.* The problem says that the line can't enter the small circle, but it doesn't say that it can't *touch* it. This is the kind of subtle thing that the SAT-folks do to mess with you. You can draw your line like this:

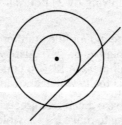

The line touches the circles at three points.

6. **(D).** First, what *not* to do: Don't add the percents and decide that Katie got 75% off the original price. Percents are based on multiplication, not addition. So how should you do this problem? Here's one way: The coat was already 50% off, so 50% was left. Katie got to subtract 25% from that 50%. Because $0.25 \times 0.50 = 0.125 = 12.5\%$, Katie got to take an extra 12.5% off, leaving her with $50\% - 12.5\% = 37.5\%$ of the original price left. Okay now, 37.5% of the original price equals $36. Using the percent proportion (yes, ratios again), you can write $\frac{36}{x} = \frac{37.5}{100}$; notice that x is in the denominator, because you're looking for the original price. Cross-multiplying, as always, gives $37.5x = 3600$, and dividing tells you that $x = \$96$.

7. **(A).** As always, do these one at a time. (A) requires the distance formula, but first you need to find the coordinates of point C. You could use a formula, but common sense works best. To get from A to B, move 2 spaces to the right and 3 spaces up. Because (B) is the midpoint of AC, do the same thing to get from B to C. Starting from (5, 0), moving 2 spaces to the right and 3 spaces up puts you at (7, 3). To find the distance from A to C, use the formula: distance = $\sqrt{(x_2-x_1)^2+(y_2-y_1)^2}$ and plug in $\sqrt{((7)-(3))^2+((3)-(-3))^2} = \sqrt{(4)^2+(6)^2} = \sqrt{16+36} = \sqrt{52}$, which doesn't equal 5.

When you take the real SAT, you don't have to check every possibility if you're pretty sure about your answer. If you get done early, you can always go back and double-check.

(B) is true, as you already discovered. (C) could send you back to the distance formula again, but this is really just the definition of the midpoint; if B is the midpoint of AC, this statement must be true. If you really want to do the math, both distances are $\sqrt{13}$. (D) sure looks like it should be true, but this is a good excuse to haul the slope formula out of storage. Slope = $\frac{y_2-y_1}{x_2-x_1}$. Using A and B gives $m = \frac{(0)-(-3)}{(5)-(3)} = \frac{3}{2}$; using B and C gives $m = \frac{(3)-(0)}{(7)-(5)} = \frac{3}{2}$, and they're equal. (E) follows logically from your answers to (D). If both pieces have a slope of ⅔, then so does the whole line AC. Notice, by the way, that you don't add slopes as you would distances.

8. **(B).** All these problems involve multiplication, and the only way to get an odd number as the answer to a multiplication problem is to multiply two odd numbers. Thus you can throw out (A) and (E) right away, because you're multiplying by e in both of them. (C) and (D) are also no good: If o is odd, $o - 1$ and $o + 1$ are both even. These calculations leave you with (B). As always, check to make sure that it really does work. An odd, plus or minus an even, is always odd, so both $o - e$ and $o + e$ are odd, and the product must also be odd.

9. **(C).** Following the definition, >5 = 9, and >9 = 16, and 9 + 16 = 25. Now don't go for the "obvious" answer, choice (D), because >25 must be *greater* than 25. The correct choice is (C), because 25 is the smallest perfect square greater than 20.

10. **(C).** From 10:45 to midnight was 1 hour 15 minutes, and from midnight to 2 a.m. was another 2 hours. So the train was moving for 3 hours 15 minutes, minus the 30 minutes (½ hour) it was stopped, which is 2 hours 45 minutes. Two hours times 80 miles per hour is 160 miles. Because 45 minutes is ¾ of an hour, you need to add another ¾ × 80 = 60 miles, for a total of 220 miles.

11. **(B).** You know that there are 24 hours in a day, so to find the number of hours in a week, do 24 hours × 7 days = 168 hours. Another approach: in w weeks and d days, there are $7w + d$ total days. Multiplying by 24 hours in a day gives $24(7w + d)$, and distributing gives $168w + 24d$.

12. **(D).** The median must be the middle number when the three numbers are listed in order. So you could list the numbers as a, –1, b. Also, you know that the mean is 6, which means that the total of the three numbers is 18. (Do you remember why? *The total = average × number of things.* This formula is really worth knowing.)

Now comes the tricky part: a can't be greater than –1, but there's nothing preventing it from *equaling* –1. It's tempting to make $a = -2$, which would make $b = 21$. But if you let $a = -1$, then b can equal 20. If you play around with other possible values for a, you see that b can never be less than 20.

13. **(D).** You could write an algebra equation for this problem, but reasoning it out works fine, too. The fraction of the tables that Nandan had to set up changed from ⅓ to ½. In math, "change" is always a cue to subtract, and ½ – ⅓ = ⅙ (solve this without a calculator just for the practice). So Nandan had to set up ⅙ more tables than he expected — 4 tables, according to the problem. If 4 is ⅙ of the total, then the total number of tables was $4 \times 6 = 24$.

14. **(C).** Don't waste your time trying to draw graphs. If the graph of an equation passes through a point, then the coordinates of the point are a solution to the equation. So you should plug in –1 for x and 4 for y in each of the equations. Make sure you don't mix up the numbers — for example, if you carelessly put –1 in for y and 4 for x in (A), you'd think that (A) was correct. Do the work for the remaining choices. In (C), the key is to realize that $-(-1) = 1$, so the equation becomes $1 + 3 = 4$.

15. **(A).** Because the small squares have sides of length 1 cm, the medium squares' sides are 2 cm each, and the big square's sides are 4 cm each. Labeling the diagram:

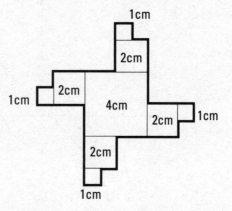

The key now is to count only the sides on the *outside* of the figure, which I conveniently darken in the previous drawing. Because the figure is symmetrical, focus on just one side. Here's the right side of the previous drawing:

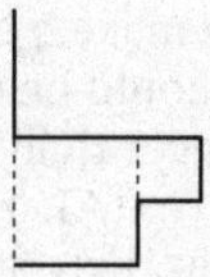

Three little sides makes 3 cm. The medium square has two full sides and one half-side contributing to the perimeter, for $2 \times 2 + 1 = 4 + 1 = 5$ cm more. And the big square also gives a half-side to the perimeter, for another 2 cm. 3 cm + 5 cm + 2 cm = 10 cm. Because there are four sides just like this one, the answer is 10 cm × 4 = 40 cm.

16. **(E).** LM is a diameter, which means that it divides the circle into two 180° arcs. Because N is an inscribed angle (it's on the edge of the circle), its measure is half of the lower 180° arc, or 90°. A right triangle! And, because you know two sides, you can find the third. Remember that 26 is the hypotenuse, so your equation should say $x^2 + (24)^2 = (26)^2$, which gives $x^2 + 576 = 676$, $x^2 = 100$, and $x = 10$. On to the *real* problem, finding the shaded area, which equals the area of the circle minus the area of the triangle. The circle's diameter is 26, so its radius is 13, and area $= \pi r^2 = \pi(13)^2 = 169\pi$. The triangle's area is ½bh, but you need to be careful. Twenty-six *isn't* the base, because you don't have a height to go with it. Instead, use the two legs of the right triangle as the base and height. (It may help to rotate the book if you have trouble visualizing.) So the triangle's area is ½(10)(24) = 120, and the answer is $169\pi - 120$.

17. **(A).** Start with the last fact, that ABC is divisible by 5. Every number that's divisible by 5 ends in either 0 or 5, so C must be one of those. But the first and second facts make it impossible for C to be zero, because that would make A and B equal to each other, which is illegal. Therefore C must be 5. Because B = A + C, and A must be at least 1, B must be at least 6.

18. **(D).** When $f(x) = 0$, the graph has a height of 0; in other words, it crosses the x-axis. As you can see from the graph, this happens in three places. Notice that you don't actually need to know *where* this happens. You just need to count the number of times it happens.

19. **(B).** Here you just need to move the graph down 2 spaces.

20. **(A).** To figure out what kind of slope a line has, imagine an ant walking on the line from left to right. If it's going uphill, the slope is positive. Downhill is a negative slope, while a horizontal (flat) line has a slope of zero. If the line's vertical, the ant could be going either up or down, so officially there's no slope ([D] in this case). Here's the line in question:

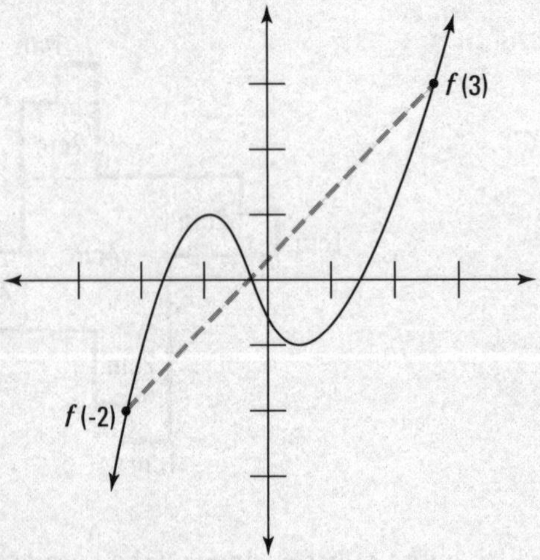

Looks like your friend's going uphill. As an SAT-taker, I'm sure you sympathize!

21. **(C).** This one is tough. If a problem looks complicated, start with the simplest thing you can see. In this case, $|a| < 3$. If you make a positive, the result must be less than 3. So a could be a number like 1, 2, 2.3, $\frac{1}{8}$, or it could be the negative versions of any of these numbers. What *can't* a be? It can't be 3, or bigger than 3, or –3, or less than –3. Okay, time to tackle $|a - b| < 4$. See what happens when you try (A), $b = -8$. Then $|a - b| = |a - (-8)| = |a + 8|$. If you try some possible a values, you see that there's no way to make this less than 4. The same thing happens when you try (B), (D), or (E). But if you try (C), you get $|a - b| = |a - (-6)| = |a + 6|$. Now, if you let $a = -2.5$, or any number between –2 and –3, the answer is less than 4.

TIP

Problem 21 is a lot of work. On the real SAT, you should probably skip a problem if it looks time-consuming. Save your energy for easier problems.

22. **(B).** This is a classic ratio problem, made more complicated by the presence of both feet and inches. You could change everything into inches, but because I like fractions (sad, but true), I'm going to make 1 foot 3 inches into $1\frac{1}{4}$ feet. So the ratio says that $\frac{1\frac{1}{4}}{5} = \frac{7}{x}$. Notice that the top numbers both stand for the shadows, while the bottom ones stand for the height of the objects in question. Doing that crazy cross-multiplication thing gives $(1\frac{1}{4})(x) = (5)(7)$ or $1\frac{1}{4}x = 35$. Now don't be scared: You have to divide both sides by $1\frac{1}{4}$, or $\frac{5}{4}$. To divide 35 by $\frac{5}{4}$, multiply by the reciprocal, or $\frac{4}{5}$. $35 \times \frac{4}{5} = \frac{140}{5} = 28$.

23. **(B).** The answer choices have only *v* and *w* in them, so you should turn everything into those letters. You already know that $x = vw$, so $y = wx = w(vw) = vw^2$. Two things to remember: First, that the *w*s both have an "invisible one" as their exponents, and second, that you need to add exponents when you multiply powers of the same bases. Because $z = xy$, $z = (vw)(vw^2) = v^2w^3$. Almost there: You're looking for *yz*, which your work tells you equals $(vw^2)(v^2w^3) = v^3w^5$.

24. **(E).** You knew there'd be a special right triangle in here somewhere, right? ABD is a 30-60-90 right triangle, with ∠*BAD* measuring 60 degrees. Because AC bisects ∠*BAD*, both ∠*CAD* and ∠*BAC* measure 30 degrees. Hey! That makes ABC a 30-60-90 triangle, too! In this triangle, $\overline{AB}$ is opposite the 60° angle, which means that it equals the shortest side times $\sqrt{3}$. The shortest side, $\overline{BC}$, is therefore 5. And the longest side is always twice as long as the shortest side, so $\overline{AC} = 10$.

25. **(D).** Rick's score was 9. For Jacob to have the same score, three times his lowest roll must also be 9, so his lowest roll must be 3. So he could roll a 3 and a 3, a 3 and a 4, a 3 and a 5, or a 3 and a 6. Ah, but be careful. To roll a 3 and a 4, for example, he could roll 3, then 4, or 4, then 3. There are really 7 possibilities: (3, 3); (3, 4); (4, 3); (3, 5); (5, 3); (3, 6); or (6, 3). What about the denominator, which counts the total number of possibilities? Well, if you remember the counting principle, you know that you always multiply the number of possibilities for each action. In this case, there are six possibilities for each die, so there are $6 \times 6 = 36$ total possibilities, and your answer is $\frac{7}{36}$.

Section 5: Critical Reading

1. **(B).** (A) is too general, and (D) and (E) are too limited because each applies to only one passage. The runner-up is (C), but the passages say much less about *why* you want to know where you are and much more about how hard it was for early seafarers and pilots to navigate.

2. **(D).** These two passages do in fact contain some inspirational material (A), the ability of human's to rise to a challenge. But overall they sound like a competent, somewhat interesting science or social studies teacher, instructing you about longitude and navigation.

3. **(A).** Passage I discusses the 18th century problem of determining longitude, while Passage II deals with the early part of the 20th century.

4. **(B).** This one contains a few sandbars that can run your SAT ship aground if you're not careful. (A) and (C) make sense in terms of real-life experience, because it stands to reason that the water nearest land will be mapped, or charted, first. But the passage doesn't give you much to go on, and the SAT doesn't rely on real life. (D) doesn't jibe with the passage, which refers to a course being plotted incorrectly. (E) has no basis in the passage at all.

5. **(E).** The paragraph preceding this sentence (lines 11–20) discusses how easy figuring out latitude is. The lines after this sentence (lines 29–45) explain why longitude was tough to calculate. This sentence, therefore, sets up the comparison.

6. **(C).** Check out paragraph four of Passage I, which goes into detail about 15° equaling one hour and the problem of keeping time after you've left your home port. These details point to (C).

7. **(D).** Lines 40–42 explain that until 1761, "there were no clocks capable of keeping steady time on board a rocking ship." On land — at least in non-earthquake zones — time pieces may have been great before 1761.

8. **(A).** The sentence about naval chronometers follows one that discusses telling time on board a rocking ship, strongly implying that these two are the same.

9. **(C).** Crashing into locomotives and hills certainly fits my definition of "danger on the ground" (lines 53–55).

10. **(B).** They descended, according to line 50, to continue "following the tracks." In this context, *tracks* = landmarks.

11. **(E).** In the real world (*not* on MTV and *not* on the SAT), lighthouses are those cute little towers on seacoasts. In Passage II they light the way for planes, not ships.

A typical SAT ploy is to lead you to the wrong answer by providing a logical (but wrong) real-world answer. Always choose your answer according to the information in the passage.

12. **(B).** Much is made in the third paragraph of Passage II (lines 65–79) about the aircraft that "could beat the trains by two or even three days" (line 73) after lightways were constructed. So assuming that lightways made planes an acceptable alternative to trains is reasonable . . . unlike the present day, when you're in the security line for three hours, only to find that your flight was cancelled.

13. **(D).** When the lightways weren't visible, the pilots followed the tracks, which they illuminated with the landing lights at night, according to lines 85–89.

14. **(C).** Radio assisted, but didn't perfect navigation and thus made air travel easier, until someone invented those annoying background music systems that play in grounded airplanes (not to mention elevators).

15. **(D).** The signal word here, the one that should light up in neon in your head, is *though*. *Though* (like its cousin, *although*) tells you that the sentence is changing direction. So right away you can rule out (A) and (B), which are synonyms. Your next task is to decode the sentence. The first blank is about sharing — think *common* — and the second about what isn't shared — think *unique*.

16. **(A).** The sentence contains the vital clue. If the note is clear, hours of intense study and a computer aren't needed to figure it out. So you need the opposite of *clear* for this sentence. (A) and (B) are both possible, but (A) is better because the note was deciphered eventually, making *unintelligible* too strong. *Cryptic* = puzzling.

17. **(D).** Placing your own word in the sentence may lead you to *crashes* especially if you're thinking about computer systems. The closest choice is (D), because *to jeopardize* means "to place in danger."

Surmount means "overcome," and *to nullify* is "to counteract" or "to undo the effect of," as in this sentence: *One burp was enough to nullify the impression of courtesy that Flink had been laboring to create.*

18. **(A).** The sentence emphasizes variety, listing three separate types of dolls. So (B) bites the dust instantly. (C) is tempting, but *universal* (true throughout the universe) has to come in second to *eclectic*, which means (you'll never guess) "from varied sources or origins."

Don't be swayed by one word in a sentence. In question 18, *heir* may make you consider (E) *(expensive)* because you associate inheriting with money. But the rest of the sentence doesn't support that choice.

19. **(B).** Before you looked at the choices, you probably thought of *possibility* or *existence* for the first blank because in the real, not the SAT, world people are always wondering about whether little green guys are wandering around the Red Planet. (B) triumphs over (C) because *sustained* (constant, unceasing) is better than *advantageous* (giving an advantage).

20. **(C).** Who makes a new network? Checking only the first blank, you can rule out only (E), because *despots* are tyrants. Okay, maybe you've read about some of the media moguls and kept (E). No matter. You still need to narrow the field, and the second blank is where all the action is. The sentence tells you that the people who establish a new network must be *businesslike* and have one other quality. Chances are that quality will contrast to *businesslike* or at least complement the term. What's a good pair for *businesslike? Creative* — which, by the way, is the opposite of *prosaic*.

21. **(E).** This question relies on your vocabulary more than anything else. If a play is *generic*, it's common, not special in any way. *Integral* (essential) is a possibility, but *intemperate* (lacking self control) and *ubiquitous* (appearing everywhere) aren't. The best choice is *critical*, which describes the kind of play (homerun, double play, spectacular catch) that the Yankees always make when I duck into the kitchen for a snack.

22. **(C).** The interviewer has probably seen it all, and then some, so *nonplussed* (rattled, shaken up) isn't going to happen.

23. **(A).** This question is a no-go for anyone who hasn't swallowed a dictionary. For the normal people out there: *affable* and *amicable* = friendly, *vivacious* = lively, and *malevolent* = evil. If you crack the vocabulary code for the first blank, you're still stuck for the second, which should match the first in tone. (A) fits because *jocular* is a fancy way to say *joking*. If you're friendly, you can still have mock arguments (during which you throw hilarious frying pans at each other). Just to finish the word-building exercise: *sententious* refers to arguments with a moral tone and *innocuous* = innocent.

24. **(D).** Another vocab special. *Xenophobia* is the Greek word for "fear of foreigners," and if you're afraid of foreigners, you don't go abroad, or out of the country. If you answered this one correctly, you're definitely Ivy League material, whether the admissions officers realize it or not.

Section 6: Mathematics

1. **(A).** The killer here is the phrase "subtracted from." "Two subtracted from five," for example, means 5 – 2, not 2 – 5. Take care not to write –8 – 10. Instead, do 10 – –8 = 10 + 8 = 18.

   A bunch of phrases signal subtraction — "subtracted from," "less than," and "fewer than" are the most common — and they all require you to switch the order of the things being subtracted.

2. **(D).** Lyle's cost is 2 packages × 10 pounds × $3.99 = $79.80. Gretchen's cost is 20 pounds × $3.49 = $69.80, and $79.80 – $69.80 = $10.

3. **(B).** Twenty minutes is one-third of an hour, so the minute hand covers one-third of a circle. Because a full circle has 360°, one-third of a circle is ⅓ × 360° = 120°.

4. **(E).** Seeing that there are 9 little triangles is fairly easy. Adding the big triangle gives you 10, but there are also some "mama bear" triangles, as you can see here:

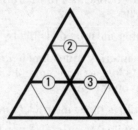

   Adding in these three gives you 13 total triangles.

5. **(C).** First do a little estimating: π is about 3.1415. 3⅐ = 3.142857. 3.14 is just 3.14. $3.1\overline{4}$ = 3.14444..., and $\sqrt{10}$ is around 3.16. Thus 3.14 is the smallest.

6. **(D).** Look first at the large triangle. You know one angle, 38°, and the other two angles are both equal to $p + q$. Thus you can write $(p + q) + (p + q) + 38 = 180$, which gives $2p + 2q + 38 = 180$, $2p + 2q = 142$. At this point, some people frustrate themselves by trying to figure out what p and q equal. Unfortunately, you don't have enough information to do that calculation; however, if $2p + 2q = 142$, you can divide both sides by 2 to get $p + q = 71$. If you look at the little triangle, you realize that this is all the information you need. Because the angles of the little triangle are a, p, and q, you can write $a + p + q = 180$; because $p + q = 71$, $a + 71 = 180$; and $a = 109$.

7. **(A).** Two big things are illegal in algebra: You can't take the square root of a negative number, and you can't divide by zero. The denominator here is $x + 2$, which would equal zero when $x = –2$, so that's your forbidden value.

8. **(B).** When solving an equation like this, some people are more comfortable making both sides into fractions. So you could write $\frac{ax}{x+2} = \frac{b}{1}$, and then cross-multiply to get $ax = b(x + 2)$, or $ax = bx + 2b$. To solve for x, you need all the xs on one side, so subtract bx from both sides, to get $ax - bx = 2b$. Now, because x is in both terms on the left side, you can factor it out: $x(a - b) = 2b$. And, finally, dividing by $a - b$ gives $\frac{2b}{a - b}$, which is (B).

9. **(D).** You don't really need a diagram to solve this one, but draw one out of habit, anyway:

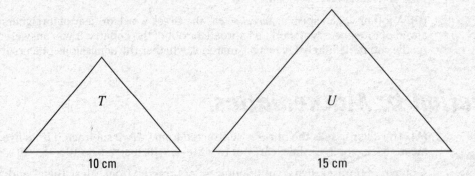

10 cm   15 cm

The sides of triangle U are 1½ times bigger than the sides of triangle T (because $15 \div 10 = 1½$). Now you need to remember an obscure fact: The ratio of the areas of similar figures is the *square* of the ratio of their sides because the area of a triangle is ½ × *base* × *height,* and both the base and the height are 1½ times bigger. So the area is 1½ × 1½ = 2¼ times bigger. Okay: $84 \text{ cm}^2 \times 2¼ = 189 \text{ cm}^2$.

10. **(D).** The original containers have a volume of $2 \times 3 \times 4 = 24$ cubic feet. If you forget the volume of a cylinder, it's in the reference table at the top of the test: $V = \pi r^2 h = \pi(5)^2(6) = 150\pi =$ about 471. Next, $471 \div 24 = 19.6$, or roughly 20.

11. **32.** This question is best done as a ratio problem: $\frac{2\frac{1}{2}}{20} = \frac{4}{x}$, so $2½x = 80$. Dividing by 2½ gives $x = 80 \div 2½ = 80 \div 5⁄2 = 80 \times 2⁄5 = {}^{160}⁄_5 = 32$.

12. **210.** Every even number must be divisible by 2, so $2 \times 3 \times 5 \times 7 = 210$.

13. **360.** This is an old "semi-trick" question: In *any* shape, the sum of the exterior angles is always 360 degrees. As long as you remember what an exterior angle looks like, you should ace this if it shows up on the SAT.

14. **36.** This problem employs the same trick I mention in question 1: If you let the numerator equal n, then the denominator is $2n - 12$, not $12 - 2n$. Thus $\frac{2}{3} = \frac{n}{2n - 12}$. So, $2(2n - 12) = 3n$, or $4n - 24 = 3n$. Subtracting $4n$ from both sides gives $-24 = -n$, and dividing by -1 gives $n = 24$. But wait! That's not the answer: n is the numerator, but the problem wanted the denominator. So plug 24 in to $2n - 12$: $2(24) - 12 = 36$. If you have time, take a minute to check that ${}^{24}⁄_{36}$ really does equal ⅔.

15. **8.** Although you may get the answer by trial and error, this problem is really begging to be factored. To factor a quadratic equation (that is, an equation with a "squared" in it), you must first make the answer equal zero. Making the squared term negative is never a good idea, so you should solve as follows:

$$p^2 = 3p + 40$$
$$-3p \quad -3p$$

$$p^2 - 3p = 40$$
$$-40 \quad -40$$

$$p^2 - 3p - 40 = 0$$

This factors out to $(p - 8)(p + 5) = 0$. This has two solutions: $p = 8$ and $p = -5$. Because you can't grid a negative answer, your choice should be 8.

16. **31.** This problem is an example of an alternating sequence; it alternates adding 4 and subtracting 1 from each term. You could just follow the pattern out to the 21st term, but there's a better way. Look at all the odd terms: 1, 4, 7, 10. Each term is 3 more than the previous term. So, the 21st term must follow this pattern. You could solve by making a list of only the odd terms, like this:

1st	3rd	5th	7th	9th	11th	13th	15th	17th	19th	21st
1	4	7	10	13	16	19	22	25	28	31

17. **65.** This is another one of those problems where you can't actually figure out a and b. Because the problem asks for $a - b$, one good way to start is to look for an angle that would be equal to $a - b$. First off, look at the angle marked p in the diagram below, in which p and b are vertical angles. Hence $p = b$. Now check out the (unnamed) angle where I've drawn a curve. Because this drawing contains parallel lines, this angle is equal to a; these angles are called "corresponding."

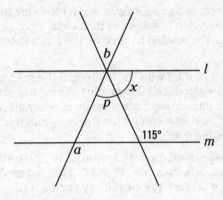

The angle marked x is equal to $a - b$. Again, you can use the properties of parallel lines: x corresponds to the (unmarked) angle right below 115°. Because this angle and 115° make a straight line, it must equal 180° – 115° = 65°. So $x = 65$, and $a - b = 65$.

18. **6909.** Wow, that's a lot of numbers. They would come in four groups:

One-digit numbers: 1 to 9, for $9 \times 1 = 9$ digits.

Two-digit numbers: 10 to 99, for $90 \times 2 = 180$ digits. Did you remember the formula to count the numbers? It's $99 - 10 + 1 = 90$.

Three-digit numbers: 100 to 999, for $900 \times 3 = 2{,}700$ digits.

Four-digit numbers: 1000 to 2004, for $1005 \times 4 = 4{,}020$ digits.

Your total is $9 + 180 + 2700 + 4020 = 6{,}909$.

19. **30.** This one's all about working with fractions. Consider $\frac{1}{x} + \frac{1}{y} = \frac{1}{4}$. When you're working with fractions, getting a common denominator on each side is a good idea. You could do that as follows:

$$\left(\frac{y}{y}\right)\frac{1}{x} + \left(\frac{1}{y}\right)\frac{x}{x} = \frac{1}{4}$$

$$\frac{y}{xy} + \frac{x}{xy} = \frac{1}{4}$$

$$\frac{x+y}{xy} = \frac{1}{4}$$

Notice how I always put the letters in alphabetical order; that's standard practice in algebra. Does anything about the left-side fraction look familiar? It should: The numerator is $x + y$, which is what you're looking for; the denominator is xy, which equals 120. Now you can write $\frac{x+y}{120} = \frac{1}{4}$, so $4(x + y) = 120$, and $x + y = 30$.

20. **68.** Six grandfathers are at the reunion. Because every one of them is also a father, include them in the 35 men who have a son present. That makes 6 grandfathers and 35 – 6 = 29 fathers. If these fathers are all sons of the 6 grandfathers, then they can be included in the 62 men who have a father present. That leaves 62 – 29 = 33 men left. So there must be at least 6 grandfathers, 29 fathers, and 33 sons, for a total of 68 men.

Section 7: Critical Reading

1. **(B).** Line 8 mentions the "most unforgiving wilderness in the world." As the rest of the passage makes clear, the fact that the difficulty "did not seem to trouble him much" says more about Franklin's ego than the possibility of success.

2. **(B).** The negative may have tripped you up here. Simpson is "no light judge" of character and reads Franklin accurately. So he's a good judge, not an insignificant one.

3. **(E).** Franklin, according to Simpson, wasn't the sort to rough it. Though he was set to travel 1,200 miles, he couldn't walk more than eight miles on a good day. The tea example shows how much Franklin needed to survive, the equivalent of requiring a whirlpool bathtub on a camping trip.

4. **(D).** (A) and (C) conflict with the content of the passage; Simpson thought Franklin was extremely unprepared, and the weather during the planned trip would be far from summery. (B) and (E) are interesting but not really appropriate. How many SAT-takers can relate to an Arctic voyage? And why should the reader sympathize with someone who set off without supplies? (D)'s the one!

5. **(B).** The language is appropriate for the early 19th century, but the passage begins by stating that it is Franklin's "admission" (line 23). This fact probably rules out (C) and (D). Because no other author is cited, the most likely source is (B).

6. **(A).** Franklin "threatened to ' . . . inflict the heaviest punishment on any who should persist in their refusal to go on'" (lines 37–39) but his threat was "completely hollow" (line 40) because he was outnumbered. Because his men were hungry, you can rule out (B) and (D). (E) isn't supported by any evidence. (D) is tempting because Franklin *didn't* take into account the Native Americans' ability to predict the weather. However, he did consider their hunting skills, so (A) is best overall.

7. **(D).** That date is when the expedition came to an end (line 79).

8. **(A).** Franklin thinks, just like those guys on the radio (not to mention the Internet), that he can predict the weather with scientific instruments. Ha! Franklin ignores the experienced traveler (Akaitcho), who is proved correct by the cold temperatures.

9. **(B).** The mutinies of the expedition were averted by the killing of a caribou (providing food) and Franklin's decision to halt. Open fighting never took place.

10. **(C).** The passage makes clear that Akaitcho was correct in his weather forecast.

   Anxious not to offend anyone, the SAT-writers are extremely unlikely to place a negative comment about an ethnic group in the test unless that comment is proved wrong.

11. **(D).** This one's easy, unless you know something about weather-proofing that has escaped the rest of the human race (in which case you should drop the SAT prep and apply for a patent). If it's 57 below, you're in trouble. Big trouble.

12. **(C).** (A), (B), and (E) are too general. (D) is too narrow. (C) is, in the immortal words of Goldilocks, "just right."

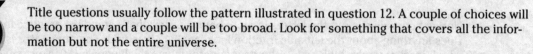

   Title questions usually follow the pattern illustrated in question 12. A couple of choices will be too narrow and a couple will be too broad. Look for something that covers all the information but not the entire universe.

13. **(A).** Walked over any liquid rocks, lately? The world in Passage I resembles that of a sci-fi special. The exclamation point is supposed to underline the contrast between the real (non-molten) earth and the image of a melting planet presented in the passage.

14. **(D).** Okay, melted rock is certainly hot, but (E) doesn't cut it because the word "forbidding" describes the world, which certainly sounds as if it possessed "difficult characteristics."

15. **(A).** Kant's view is that the "formless cloud" would draw in on itself more and more until it would "collapse to a point," which would end the solar system before it even began, certainly signaling the "end of story" for everyone and everything else.

16. **(D).** A couple of the other choices are close, but (D) fits best. Passage I talks about the early (*very* early) earth. Passage II hits the solar system at its beginning.

Section 8: Mathematics

1. **(A).** I hope that this one didn't take too much effort.

2. **(D).** Two is prime. Ten = 2×5, $15 = 3 \times 5$, and $57 = 3 \times 19$. Each of these is the product of two primes. But $18 = 2 \times 9$ or 3×6, and neither 9 nor 6 is prime.

3. **(B).** Here's the number line for you:

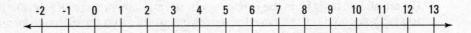

Notice that you have four marks but *five* spaces. The distance between the endpoints is $13 - -2 = 15$. Thus each of the five spaces is three units wide. So from left to right, the four marks are at 1, 4, 7, and 10.

4. **(E).** The numbers add up to 36, so the mean is $36 \div 8 = 4.5$. The mode is 5, because it shows up twice. To find the median, rewrite the list as 1, 2, 3, 4, 5, 5, 7, 9. There's no middle number, but 4 and 5 are the closest, so the median is $(4 + 5)/2 = 4.5$. The median is the same as the mean.

5. **(C).** As always, a drawing can't hurt:

8 in.   8 in.

Notice that I put 8 inches on two sides. Don't write something like $x + 8 = 40$; a rectangle has four sides, not two. If you call the two missing sides in the diagram x, you would write $x + x + 8 + 8 = 40$, or $2x + 16 = 40$. Then $2x = 24$, and $x = 12$.

6. **(A).** You know that *distance = speed × time,* so Owen has traveled $3m$ miles so far. That journey leaves him with $400 - 3m$ miles still to go in 5 hours. Because *distance = speed × time,* speed = $\frac{distance}{time}$, (A) is your answer.

7. **(B).** Don't pick (C) just because it doesn't have any 5s in it. If you do a quick drawing of (C), you'll realize that it's your old friend, the 3/4/5 triangle:

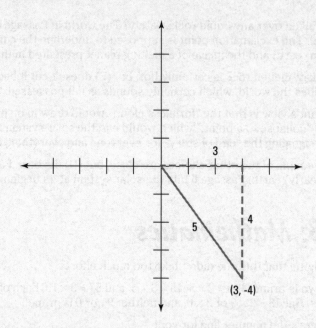

You could also use the distance formula to find that the distance is 5. (A), (D), and (E) are all five units from the origin — left, up, and down, respectively. But (B) is too far. You could see it by making a drawing, or by using the distance formula:
$\sqrt{((5)-(0))^2+((5)-(0))^2} = \sqrt{(5)^2+(5)^2} = \sqrt{25+25} = \sqrt{50}$, which is not 5.

8. **(C).** Here's the square with the diagonal drawn:

Hopefully, you recognized that the triangles in this drawing are both 45-45-90 triangles. So the hypotenuse — which is also the diagonal of the square — equals a leg times $\sqrt{2}$. Because the legs are just the sides of the square, each leg equals 6 m, and the perimeter is 4×6 m = 24 m.

9. **(C).** First, realize that there are two possibilities for this problem: an even number followed by an odd, or an odd followed by an even. If the first number is even, it's either 2, 4, 6, or 8: four possibilities. The second number must then be 1, 3, 5, 7, or 9: five possibilities. Using the counting principle, $4 \times 5 = 20$ possible numbers. If the first number is odd, it could be 1, 3, 5, 7, or 9. Then the second number could be 0, 2, 4, 6, or 8; don't forget about zero! So you have $5 \times 5 = 25$ more possibilities, for a total of $20 + 25 = 45$ possible two-digit numbers.

10. **(D).** Triangle I looks like a right triangle, but there's no actual evidence that it is. Triangle II, on the other hand, has two angles that add up to 90°, so the third angle must be 90°. Triangle III has sides of 5, $\sqrt{11}$, and 6. You can test whether a triangle is right by using the Pythagorean theorem: $(5)^2 + (\sqrt{11})^2 = 25 + 11 = 36$, which is 6^2, so this is a right triangle, too.

11. **(E).** $d^{1/2}$ is the same as $\sqrt{d}$, so $\sqrt{d} + 5 = 9$, and $\sqrt{d} = 4$. This fact doesn't mean that $d = \sqrt{4} = 2$, but that $d = 4^2 = 16$. So $d^{-1} = (16)^{-1} = \frac{1}{16}$.

12. **(D).** For history and English combined, 8.5% + 10% = 18.5%. Next, 18.5% of 5000 = 0.185 × 5000 = 925.

13. **(E).** Well, (C) is obviously false, judging by the first graph. (A), (B), and (D) all suffer from the same problem — you have no idea how many students attended State U. in 2000. Comparing the number of people in each major in the two different years is impossible. The second graph shows that (E) is true.

14. **(B).** The first two statements aren't unusual, but the third is a little weird. If you try a "normal" number, like 4, for j, then $4^2 = 16$ and $4^3 = 64$, and j^2 wouldn't be greater than j^3. What about a fraction, like ½? Then $(½)^2 = ¼$, and $(½)^3 = ⅛$, and $j^2 > j^3$. But wait a minute: Now j^2 and j^3 are both smaller than j, which contradicts the first two statements. So how about a negative number, like –2? Well, $(-2)^2 = 4$, which is greater than –2, but $(-2)^3 = -8$, which isn't. So you're left with a negative fraction. Try -½. $(-½)^2 = ¼$, which is greater than -½. $(-½)^3 = -⅛$, which is also greater than -½, because it's farther to the right on a number line. And $¼ > -⅛$, so the third condition is satisfied. This works for any number between 0 and –1.

15. **(A).** I take the liberty of naming the three unnamed points in my diagram:

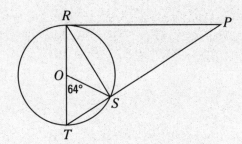

The one angle that you know, 64°, is a central angle. Arc ST must also be 64°. Because arc RST is a semicircle, arc RS must measure 180° – 64° = 116. Now you can look at some angles. ∠PRT is the meeting of a tangent line and a diameter, so it must be 90° (this fact is worth memorizing). ∠T is inscribed, so it must be half of its arc, 116°, and ½ × 116° = 58°. And, because triangle PRT must contain 180°, that leaves 180° – (90° + 58°) = 180° – 148° = 32° for ∠P.

Part VI
The Part of Tens

The 5th Wave — By Rich Tennant

"My SAT scores? Why would you want to know my SAT scores?"

In this part . . .

The Big Day is a staple of television series. Sitcom writers think it's hilarious when the bride gets lost on the way to her wedding or the expectant father drives to the hospital without his pregnant wife. But on your own personal Big Day, situations like these aren't funny. In this part you find out how to make SAT-day as smooth, relaxed, and productive as possible.

Chapter 26

Ten Things to Double-Check

● ●

In This Chapter

▶ Making SAT-day as smooth as possible

▶ Eliminating mistakes that sink your SAT score

● ●

You may have made a list and checked it twice at some point in your life, and I'm sure that the list reader appreciated your *assiduousness* (diligence, carefulness). Yes, even here, in the Part of Tens, you can cram a few extra words into your vocabulary. *Meticulous* (also means careful) and *judicious* (wise) rechecks really boost your SAT (*Somnolent Austere* Torture) score. (By the way, *somnolent* = tending to put you to sleep and *austere* = undecorated, plain.) In this chapter I describe ten ways to make SAT-morning less painful, so you can arrive at the test center in the proper mood to ace the test.

Stashing Your Admission Ticket

Before you go to sleep — at a reasonable hour, not after an all-night SAT Stinks Party — place your admission ticket, car keys or carfare, pencils, calculator, watch, and everything else you need in plain sight.

Firing Blanks

You may skip a question here and there. No problem. Just be sure that the answers you *do* fill in end up in the correct row. As you bubble, consciously match the question number and the number on the answer sheet. At the end of a section, recheck that you've finished at the right number.

Keeping It Legal

When the proctor says, "Turn to Section 3," triple-check that you've actually opened the booklet to Section 3. You'd be surprised what sweaty hands can do.

Gridding Your Teeth

When you face a *grid-in* (the math torture chamber that makes you come up with an actual answer without supplying five handy choices), remember that you can't grid in a mixed number (2½, for example). The computer will read it as "21 divided by 2," or 10.5. (Instead, grid-in ⁵⁄₂.) Also, don't leave any blank grid-ins. You don't lose points for a wrong answer, so give every grid-in your best shot.

Ordering the Operations

In the heat of battle, you may forget to attack a math problem in the proper order. When you start a math section, take a moment to write PEMDAS at the top of the page. (For an explanation of PEMDAS, turn to Chapter 14.) Then recheck the order of operations.

Giving Them What They Want

No matter how much you understand about a topic, if you don't give the SAT-writers what they ask for, you're wrong. For example, they may want to know the number of people with orange ties in a problem chock-full of information about people with purple, tied-dyed, spaghetti-stained, and other ties. One of the answers will be the number of people with tie-dyed ties. Always double-check that it's what they've asked for.

Staying in Context

Once upon a time, before you started preparing for the SAT, you may have had a real life. And that life gave you some experience and knowledge that may help you on the SAT (Synchronized Awesome Tawdriness). (For vocab fans: *synchronized* = occurring at the same time, *tawdriness* = cheap gaudiness.) But be sure to answer Reading Comprehension questions in the passage's context. Real life can help, but don't let it distract you from the material provided.

Scrapping Meaningless Paper

The SAT scoring brigade (mostly a machine, with minimal human help) doesn't read the scrap paper. Be sure that all your answers actually make it to the answer sheet.

Erasing the Errors

You may (shocking as it may seem) make a mistake from time to time. Before you sign off on a changed answer, take care that the wrong answer has truly disappeared. If the scoring machine detects two answers for one question, it marks you wrong.

Writing Legibly

I've taught ninth grade on and off for 30 years, so I know bad handwriting. And the 21st-century's increasing reliance on computers means that penmanship is a lost art. Okay, your essay doesn't have to look great in the Writing Sample, but it does have to be readable. If it resembles the flight of a drunken chicken, the scorer won't be happy. And you definitely want a happy scorer. Recheck your essay and neatly rewrite any illegible words.

Chapter 27

Ten Ways to Calm Down

. . . .

In This Chapter
▶ Soothing the SAT-age nerves
▶ Pacifying your angst

. . . .

What's that grinding noise? Oh, it's your teeth. The SAT (Superlative Auspicious Talisman) can ratchet up the anxiety level of even the most zenned-out test-taker. But a few techniques can help you de-stress — ten, to be exact. (By the way, *superlative* = highest quality, *auspicious* = favorable, *talisman* = thing with magic powers.)

Preparing Well

Well before SAT-day, make sure that you've gone over this book carefully and shored up your weak spots. Try a practice test or two in Part V. Now rest because you're ready for the big time.

Sleeping It Off

Don't party the night before SAT-day, though I certainly understand your need to celebrate when the whole thing's over. Fight SAT nerves with restful sleep. Also, don't study on the last night before the exam. Watch television, build an anthill, or do whatever you find relaxing. Then hit the sheets at a decent hour.

Starting Early

On SAT morning, set your alarm for a little earlier than you think you need to be up and about. Don't go overboard! You don't want too much extra time to obsess about all the things you haven't mastered yet. With a safety margin of, say, arrival at the testing center a half an hour before the test begins, you can ready yourself for the exam with minimal pressure. Plus you have time to find the room, get a good seat, admire the view, and run to the restroom.

Making a List

SAT morning jitters are no fun. To *alleviate* (ease) them, on exam eve make a list of everything you need to do before leaving the house and everything you need to take to the exam. Then go through the tasks one by one, and leave the house secure in the knowledge that you are *ready*. (See Chapter 2 with a list of items you don't want to forget.)

Stretching Your Muscles

Before you start a SAT section, stretch your arms above your head as high as they'll go. Slide your legs straight out in front of you and wriggle your ankles. Feel better?

Rolling Your Head

Not the type of rolling that occurs after a session with the guillotine, but a yoga-inspired exercise that *induces* (brings about) calmness. Close your eyes whenever you feel yourself tensing up. Let your head drop all the way forward, roll it in a circle, open your eyes, and hit the test again.

Breathing Deeply

Breathing is always a good idea, and deep breathing is a better one. When the SAT overwhelms, pull in a slow bucketful of air and then exhale even more slowly.

Isolating the Problem

On SAT-day, friends are a pain in the neck. Why? Because your friends will say things like "What's the meaning of *supercilious*?" "How do you solve for three variables?" And you'll think *I don't know what* supercilious *means! I have no idea what a variable is? I'm going to fail and no college will take me and my life will be ruined.* Make a pact with your friends to stay silent about SAT questions or SAT-related information or sit by yourself in the corner.

Becoming Fatalistic

A *fatalist* (one who accepts that much of life is out of control and that whatever happens, happens) does best on the SAT. Stop obsessing. Just sit down and do the test. You can worry about how you did after you've handed in the paper.

Focusing on the Future

No matter how bad it is, when you're taking the SAT, you're getting ever closer to a truly wonderful time: The moment when you realize that the SAT is over, done, history. Focus on the future — that moment — when you feel yourself clench.

Index

Notes

Notes

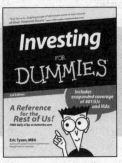
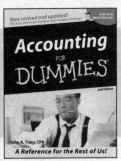

FOR DUMMIES®

A world of resources to help you grow

HOME, GARDEN & HOBBIES

Feng Shui FOR DUMMIES
A Reference for the Rest of Us!
0-7645-5295-3

Gardening FOR DUMMIES
A Reference for the Rest of Us!
0-7645-5130-2

Guitar FOR DUMMIES
A Reference for the Rest of Us!
0-7645-5106-X

Also available:

Auto Repair For Dummies
(0-7645-5089-6)

Chess For Dummies
(0-7645-5003-9)

Home Maintenance For Dummies
(0-7645-5215-5)

Organizing For Dummies
(0-7645-5300-3)

Piano For Dummies
(0-7645-5105-1)

Poker For Dummies
(0-7645-5232-5)

Quilting For Dummies
(0-7645-5118-3)

Rock Guitar For Dummies
(0-7645-5356-9)

Roses For Dummies
(0-7645-5202-3)

Sewing For Dummies
(0-7645-5137-X)

FOOD & WINE

Cooking FOR DUMMIES
A Reference for the Rest of Us!
0-7645-5250-3

Cookies FOR DUMMIES
A Reference for the Rest of Us!
0-7645-5390-9

Wine FOR DUMMIES
A Reference for the Rest of Us!
0-7645-5114-0

Also available:

Bartending For Dummies
(0-7645-5051-9)

Chinese Cooking For Dummies
(0-7645-5247-3)

Christmas Cooking For Dummies
(0-7645-5407-7)

Diabetes Cookbook For Dummies
(0-7645-5230-9)

Grilling For Dummies
(0-7645-5076-4)

Low-Fat Cooking For Dummies
(0-7645-5035-7)

Slow Cookers For Dummies
(0-7645-5240-6)

TRAVEL

Italy FOR DUMMIES
A Travel Guide for the Rest of Us!
0-7645-5453-0

Hawaii FOR DUMMIES
A Travel Guide for the Rest of Us!
0-7645-5438-7

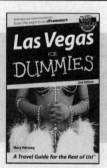

Las Vegas FOR DUMMIES
A Travel Guide for the Rest of Us!
0-7645-5448-4

Also available:

America's National Parks For Dummies
(0-7645-6204-5)

Caribbean For Dummies
(0-7645-5445-X)

Cruise Vacations For Dummies 2003
(0-7645-5459-X)

Europe For Dummies
(0-7645-5456-5)

Ireland For Dummies
(0-7645-6199-5)

France For Dummies
(0-7645-6292-4)

London For Dummies
(0-7645-5416-6)

Mexico's Beach Resorts For Dummies
(0-7645-6262-2)

Paris For Dummies
(0-7645-5494-8)

RV Vacations For Dummies
(0-7645-5443-3)

Walt Disney World & Orlando For Dummies
(0-7645-5444-1)

FOR DUMMIES®

Plain-English solutions for everyday challenges

COMPUTER BASICS

0-7645-0838-5

0-7645-1663-9

0-7645-1548-9

Also available:

PCs All-in-One Desk Reference For Dummies (0-7645-0791-5)

Pocket PC For Dummies (0-7645-1640-X)

Treo and Visor For Dummies (0-7645-1673-6)

Troubleshooting Your PC For Dummies (0-7645-1669-8)

Upgrading & Fixing PCs For Dummies (0-7645-1665-5)

Windows XP For Dummies (0-7645-0893-8)

Windows XP For Dummies Quick Reference (0-7645-0897-0)

BUSINESS SOFTWARE

0-7645-0822-9

0-7645-0839-3

0-7645-0819-9

Also available:

Excel Data Analysis For Dummies (0-7645-1661-2)

Excel 2002 All-in-One Desk Reference For Dummies (0-7645-1794-5)

Excel 2002 For Dummies Quick Reference (0-7645-0829-6)

GoldMine "X" For Dummies (0-7645-0845-8)

Microsoft CRM For Dummies (0-7645-1698-1)

Microsoft Project 2002 For Dummies (0-7645-1628-0)

Office XP For Dummies (0-7645-0830-X)

Outlook 2002 For Dummies (0-7645-0828-8)

Get smart! Visit www.dummies.com

- **Find listings of even more *For Dummies* titles**

- **Browse online articles**

- **Sign up for Dummies eTips™**

- **Check out *For Dummies* fitness videos and other products**

- **Order from our online bookstore**

Available wherever books are sold. Go to www.dummies.com or call 1-877-762-2974 to order direct.

FOR DUMMIES®

Helping you expand your horizons and realize your potential

INTERNET

0-7645-0894-6

0-7645-1659-0

0-7645-1642-6

Also available:

America Online 7.0 For Dummies
(0-7645-1624-8)

Genealogy Online For Dummies
(0-7645-0807-5)

The Internet All-in-One Desk Reference For Dummies
(0-7645-1659-0)

Internet Explorer 6 For Dummies
(0-7645-1344-3)

The Internet For Dummies Quick Reference
(0-7645-1645-0)

Internet Privacy For Dummies
(0-7645-0846-6)

Researching Online For Dummies
(0-7645-0546-7)

Starting an Online Business For Dummies
(0-7645-1655-8)

DIGITAL MEDIA

0-7645-1664-7

0-7645-1675-2

0-7645-0806-7

Also available:

CD and DVD Recording For Dummies
(0-7645-1627-2)

Digital Photography All-in-One Desk Reference For Dummies
(0-7645-1800-3)

Digital Photography For Dummies Quick Reference
(0-7645-0750-8)

Home Recording for Musicians For Dummies
(0-7645-1634-5)

MP3 For Dummies
(0-7645-0858-X)

Paint Shop Pro "X" For Dummies
(0-7645-2440-2)

Photo Retouching & Restoration For Dummies
(0-7645-1662-0)

Scanners For Dummies
(0-7645-0783-4)

GRAPHICS

0-7645-0817-2

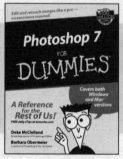

0-7645-1651-5

0-7645-0895-4

Also available:

Adobe Acrobat 5 PDF For Dummies
(0-7645-1652-3)

Fireworks 4 For Dummies
(0-7645-0804-0)

Illustrator 10 For Dummies
(0-7645-3636-2)

QuarkXPress 5 For Dummies
(0-7645-0643-9)

Visio 2000 For Dummies
(0-7645-0635-8)

Available wherever books are sold. Go to www.dummies.com or call 1-877-762-2974 to order direct.

FOR DUMMIES®

The advice and explanations you need to succeed

SELF-HELP, SPIRITUALITY & RELIGION

0-7645-5302-X

0-7645-5418-2

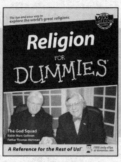
0-7645-5264-3

Also available:

The Bible For Dummies
(0-7645-5296-1)

Buddhism For Dummies
(0-7645-5359-3)

Christian Prayer For Dummies
(0-7645-5500-6)

Dating For Dummies
(0-7645-5072-1)

Judaism For Dummies
(0-7645-5299-6)

Potty Training For Dummies
(0-7645-5417-4)

Pregnancy For Dummies
(0-7645-5074-8)

Rekindling Romance For Dummies
(0-7645-5303-8)

Spirituality For Dummies
(0-7645-5298-8)

Weddings For Dummies
(0-7645-5055-1)

PETS

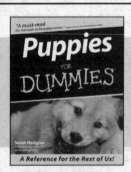
0-7645-5255-4

0-7645-5286-4

0-7645-5275-9

Also available:

Labrador Retrievers For Dummies
(0-7645-5281-3)

Aquariums For Dummies
(0-7645-5156-6)

Birds For Dummies
(0-7645-5139-6)

Dogs For Dummies
(0-7645-5274-0)

Ferrets For Dummies
(0-7645-5259-7)

German Shepherds For Dummies
(0-7645-5280-5)

Golden Retrievers For Dummies
(0-7645-5267-8)

Horses For Dummies
(0-7645-5138-8)

Jack Russell Terriers For Dummies
(0-7645-5268-6)

Puppies Raising & Training Diary For Dummies
(0-7645-0876-8)

EDUCATION & TEST PREPARATION

0-7645-5194-9

0-7645-5325-9

0-7645-5210-4

Also available:

Chemistry For Dummies
(0-7645-5430-1)

English Grammar For Dummies
(0-7645-5322-4)

French For Dummies
(0-7645-5193-0)

The GMAT For Dummies
(0-7645-5251-1)

Inglés Para Dummies
(0-7645-5427-1)

Italian For Dummies
(0-7645-5196-5)

Research Papers For Dummies
(0-7645-5426-3)

The SAT I For Dummies
(0-7645-5472-7)

U.S. History For Dummies
(0-7645-5249-X)

World History For Dummies
(0-7645-5242-2)

Available wherever books are sold. Go to www.dummies.com or call 1-877-762-2974 to order direct.

FOR DUMMIES®

We take the mystery out of complicated subjects